along the way

Along the Way: A One-Year Journey of Grace, Truth, and Light
Copyright © 2022 Mark DuPré

All rights reserved.

No part of this publication may be reproduced in a retrieval system, or transmitted in any form or by any means—electronic, mechanical, photocopying, recording, or otherwise—without the prior written permission of the publisher.

This manuscript has undergone viable editorial work and proofreading, yet human limitations may have resulted in minor grammatical or syntax-related errors remaining in the finished book. The understanding of the reader is requested in these cases. While precaution has been taken in the preparation of this book, the publisher and author assume no responsibility for errors or omissions, or for damages resulting from the use of the information contained herein.

This book is set in the typeface Athelas designed by Veronika Burian and Jose Scaglione.

Paperback ISBN: 9781955546195

A Publication of Tall Pine Books
119 E Center Street, Suite B4A | Warsaw, Indiana 46580
www.tallpinebooks.com

| 1 22 22 20 16 02 |

Published in the United States of America

along the way

a ONE-YEAR JOURNEY *of* GRACE, TRUTH, *and* LIGHT

mark dupré

"I have a select few classic devotionals I read every day: *My Utmost for His Highest* and *Living the Message*. *Along the Way* is right there with Oswald and Eugene. Mark DuPré is relentless in bringing you face to face with God and yourself, your faith, and your doubt.

He walks you through truth like a friend who has traveled this way before, knowingly guiding your heart through the terrain of questions and the obstacles of discouragement. It's worth the journey...daily. Mark's promptings reveal the eternal Father you want to know and love while awakening the eternity in your heart in that has been there all along."

–John Leach
Executive Pastor, *Life Center Ministries*,
Harrisburg, PA

"When my pastor friend Rev. Mark DuPré released this daily devotional, I was eager to use it as my own personal daily devotion for two years. Because of Mark's pastoral, teaching, and creative background, he has been able to expound scripture in a fresh way for everyday Christians.

My wife and I have been personally challenged and blessed, and I've found a number of topics I've preached on. Daily reading will "set your mind on things above. Read and Grow in Grace."

–Rev. Paul Johansson
President, *Emeritus of Elim Bible Institute and College*
M.A., Brockport College

"Okay, yes, we have the same last name because he's my brother. There, it's been said. But that aside, Mark DuPré's devotional, *Along the Way*, is an absolutely wonderful addition to your daily reading. Each page, each day is a delight. A relevant scripture followed by a spot on and meaningful contemplation.

Like many, I grew up on *My Utmost for His Highest*, which has been the standard devotional for a long time. Mark's book doesn't replace it, but it certainly comes alongside it to aid us in our daily understanding of God's heart and nature and walking out His life within us."

–Chris DuPré
Author of *The Wild Love of God*

"This is the most transformative devotional we've ever used. In a culture that revolves around the current trend and the "hottest new thing," it is empowering to be presented afresh every day with the transforming Word of God in the form of this Devotional.

Mark DuPré has meticulously depicted the Word of God in a framework that is not fluff or full of catchy phrases, but a treasure of clear biblical principles and practical wisdom shared from a wealth of knowledge and experience.

I am excited to endorse *Along the Way* as a devotional like none other. Mark's insights will challenge you, encourage you, equip you, and empower you for the journey ahead while unveiling the Glory, the Grace, and the Goodness of God. *Enjoy!*"

—BISHOP HENRY AND CAROLYN JOYNER
Overseers, *Impact DMV Church,*
Washington, DC

"There is a river whose streams make glad the city of God" (Ps. 46:4). Mark DuPré's devotional, *Along the Way,* is a neat skiff to slip you right into the currents of that delightful river. Perhaps the Holy Spirit would even be your oarsman.

—MICHAEL COTTEN,
Antioch International Ministries

The Lord indeed loves us just the way we are. He also loves us enough not to leave us as He found us. His love is transformative, working to change us more and more into the image of Jesus Christ. To that end, He reveals His Father's heart to us. He affirms us, challenges us, teaches us, and pours His Spirit upon us. He brings us through trials, calls us to repentance, heals our wounds, and draws us ever closer to Himself.

He also draws us into His Word, which renews our minds and reveals to us His wondrous thoughts and ways, which are so marvelously different from ours. His Word is a lamp to our feet, making the pathway clear on our road to transformation.

May these devotional readings bring light to your spiritual eyes and encouragement to your soul. As you read and meditate, open your heart to the working of God's Spirit within you. God has a specific and personal plan for you to become more like Jesus. Remember, God never changes, so in our ever-growing relationship with Him, we must do the changing. Thankfully, He knows just how to do that, and knows exactly what we need and how to help us.

JANUARY 1
KNOW WHO WE ARE

"Jesus, knowing that the Father had given all things into His hands, and that He had come from God and was going to God, rose from supper and laid aside His garments, took a towel and girded Himself. After that, He poured water into a basin and began to wash the disciples' feet, and to wipe them with the towel with which He was girded." (John 13:3–5)

This is one of the most profound passages in Scripture in terms of knowing who we are and how self-identity affects serving. Here is Jesus at His highest moment of self-awareness: He knows where He's come from (heaven); He knows what is going on in His life (His imminent suffering and death); He knows where He is going (heaven, again); and He knows His future position of glory and what He will ultimately possess. No identity crisis here. The self-awareness He possessed at age twelve and demonstrated at the temple in Jerusalem has now reached a peak. He is fully mindful of who He is and what He has.

What does He do with this self-knowledge? Start a business? Fight a great battle? Get revenge on those who oppose Him? No, He serves. He takes the job of the most menial servant in a house—washing feet. And He washes the feet not of earthly kings and rulers, but of those under His authority—in effect, those who should be washing His feet.

What is the result of your knowing who you are? Is it feeling better about yourself? Or is it greater love for others? Does greater self-awareness bring you closer to others or does it make you pull back and focus more on yourself?

Jesus shows us how true self-awareness expresses itself. It serves. If Jesus is led to serve at the height of His own self-understanding, how much more should we?

Lord, deliver me from a self-awareness that causes me to become more self-centered. Let me find myself in You and hear the call to serve others.

JANUARY 2
BEING IN CHRIST

"You call Me Teacher and Lord, and you say well, for so I am. If I then, your Lord and Teacher, have washed your feet, you also ought to wash one another's feet. For I have given you an example, that you should do as I have done to you." (John 13:13–15)

If we're born again, we are "in Christ." That's a truth beyond our comprehension, but it's filled with realities, gifts, and a new identity. If we're in Christ, then we have the same Spirit working in us who led Jesus to serve at the Last Supper, who also leads us to serve others because we know who we are.

If we're in Christ, God is leading us to the same understandings Jesus had in John 13: We know where we've come from (we're all fallen creatures in desperate need of forgiveness). We know where we're going (here and now, into the image of Christ; later, into His presence). We also know that there are as-yet-unknowable joys awaiting us (1 Corinthians 2:9).

If we have a hard time doing the most menial thing for others, perhaps we have an identity issue. Maybe we find it hard to serve because we don't really know who we are. Perhaps we've forgotten where we've come from spiritually or what incredible mercies we've received or who we really are in Him and the glories and joys that await us. Or perhaps we know all that but have spun it into either serving ourselves or simply failing to serve others. In either case, it's worth meditating on the fact that the central person of the universe, at His highest moment of earthly self-awareness, bent as low as possible to serve.

Lord, help me see the connection between knowing who I am in You and serving others— and then direct my actions accordingly. As I continue to discover who I am in You, help me to become more focused on others.

MARK DUPRÉ

JANUARY 3

QUESTIONS WITH STRANGE ANSWERS: ACTS 1

"Therefore, when they had come together, they asked Him, saying, "Lord, will You at this time restore the kingdom to Israel?" And He said to them, "It is not for you to know times or seasons which the Father has put in His own authority. But you shall receive power when the Holy Spirit has come upon you; and you shall be witnesses to Me in Jerusalem, and in all Judea and Samaria, and to the end of the earth." (Acts 1:6–8)

Just as Jesus did with His disciples, God doesn't always answer us according to how we pose our questions. Yet His answers are His answers, and we must pay attention to them. We often accuse God of not answering our prayers when He has answered—it's just that He's not answered us along the lines of how we phrased the question.

Here, Jesus first pushed away the blatant error: "It is not for you to know." Then He addressed the question at the heart of the disciples' inquiries. They asked: "What do You wish us to do to extend Your kingdom?" His answer: "You shall receive power when the Holy Spirit has come upon you ...".

The disciples were unable to understand life on the other side of Pentecost until it happened. Jesus knew that and didn't bother trying to explain it to them; they were going to have to experience it themselves. Then they would know what to do.

The Lord is still answering us that way. His response to our prayers is often: "It's not for you to know. It's for you to do." When we want to know, we need to listen closely to His answer. It may well be direction or instruction instead of knowledge. But as with the disciples, when they obeyed, they also came to understand.

Father, help me to hear what You're saying as I bring things to You in prayer. Change my heart and my mind so that I can more easily receive what You're saying to me, no matter what it may be. Thank You that You hear me and that You know what is best for me to do.

JANUARY 4

FANNING THE FLAME

"Therefore I remind you to stir up the gift of God which is in you through the laying on of my hands." (2 Timothy 1:6)

From Paul's perspective, Timothy had spiritual gifts that weren't maturing or being used as well as they could be used. In the ESV translation of this verse, Paul urges Timothy to "fan into flame the gift of God, which is in you."

What gifts are in you? Are you using them? Are they going through a testing and growth phase? Can you see progress? If not, maybe you've fallen into the same trap as Timothy. Another reading of this letter might be helpful. You may need some of the same encouragement as Timothy.

Sometimes, everyday life distracts us from using our unique giftings. While we're called to be faithful in what we call the mundane aspects of life, we're also called to faithfully use those individual spiritual gifts God's given us. Is yours evangelism? Helps? Administration? Faith, knowledge, wisdom? What about healings, miracles, or prophecies?

Many believers fall into a common trap of our culture: they want to be stirred up by the new. But what God is saying is what's important, whether it feels new or not. Our hope for what's new may not be something that feels fresh but may simply be the next expression of an old gift.

We'll never know what "fanning the flame" or "stirring up the gift" looks like until we do it; only the enemy would try to slow us down by suggesting that tomorrow will be like yesterday. Let's ask God to shine His light on a gift that needs our attention. Let's fan and stir. What happens next will be newer and more exciting than we can know.

> *Father, please help me see what needs stirring up in me. Show me how to do that. I receive Your vision and Your encouragement for me to fan the flames of what You've already given me.*

MARK DUPRÉ

JANUARY 5

ANSWER ME THIS

"And they heard the sound of the Lord God walking in the garden in the cool of the day, and Adam and his wife hid themselves from the presence of the Lord God among the trees of the garden. Then the Lord God called to Adam and said to him, "Where are you?" (Genesis 3:8–9)

There are two questions—one from the Old Testament and one from the New—that encapsulate all God's done for us and the basis of our relationship with Him. When Adam and Eve sinned, God asked the ironic question, "Where are you?" Of course God knew where they were, but the question shows He began seeking man immediately after man's rebellion. That's never stopped. Even now, God is asking, "Where are you?" to all the unsaved. He's seeking men and women everywhere—in alleyways, in boardrooms, on the streets, in their homes. He's asking a question to which He knows the answer. But as with Adam, He asks seeking a response.

Set against that heartfelt cry is another question—one that arises for all mankind now that the Messiah has come. In Mark 8:29, Jesus asked His disciples, "Who do you say that I am?" It's the second question of the ages, one He asks each of us—the saved and the unsaved. It's the one we answer by coming to Him and the one we ask others as God continues His ministry of reconciliation through us.

God's second question focuses us on Jesus Christ, the only name by which we can be saved. This question goes deep into our hearts, forcing us to make the eternal life-or-death decision about who Jesus is. Is He just a man, a great teacher, or the Messiah, Savior, and God-in-flesh? That's the most important question we'll ever be asked.

Father, thank You for pursuing us when we turned away. Thank You for still pursuing me when I turn away from You. Help me to know the answer to Your second question more deeply and personally every year.

JANUARY 6
REAL… FROM THE INSIDE OUT

"Woe to you, scribes and Pharisees, hypocrites! For you are like whitewashed tombs which indeed appear beautiful outwardly, but inside are full of dead men's bones and all uncleanness. Even so you also outwardly appear righteous to men, but inside you are full of hypocrisy and lawlessness." (Matthew 23:27–28)

It's God's desire that we're integrated, authentic, and for lack of a better word, real. We read the Scripture above and are slightly taken aback at how hard Jesus came down on the hypocritical Pharisees. Yet we're more like them than we care to admit.

Many Christians are genuinely kind, pleasant, easy to be with, and outwardly gracious. Yet underneath we can be judgmental, suspicious, and rebellious—and almost completely unaware of it. Most believers don't want to be unkind, rude, or divisive. Yet deep down there can sometimes be another "us" that's locked away and rarely let out to play.

Perhaps we'd never rob a bank, commit adultery, or cheat on our taxes. But there's a gap between who we are on the outside and what's going on underneath. God's plan for all of us is to bring whatever is underneath up to the surface. What is good needs to be expressed in greater measure and what is not needs to be brought to the light for repentance, healing, and change.

God wants us to be real from the inside, where His Spirit dwells, to the outside, where people see and hear us. It takes a lifetime, but we can never stop the process and divide ourselves into two.

We're called to be gracious, kind, and loving to others. At the same time, we must let God continue to renew our inward parts until our hearts are cleansed and what is expressed externally reflects the grace, wisdom, and love He's put within us.

Father, I want to be a completely integrated believer, having Your truth in the deepest parts of my mind and heart. Forgive my efforts to resist Your Spirit's working. "Create in me a clean heart, O God, and renew a right spirit within me" (Psalm 51:10 ESV).

MARK DUPRÉ

JANUARY 7
THE MASTER'S HAND

"Unto You I lift up my eyes, O You who dwell in the heavens. Behold, as the eyes of servants look to the hand of their masters, as the eyes of a maid to the hand of her mistress, so our eyes look to the Lord our God, until He has mercy on us." (Psalm 123:1–2)

This psalm paints a picture of a servant looking to the hand of his master or a maid to the hand of her mistress. Consider how focused their attention had to be! The servant's highest purpose was meeting his master's needs. The master's goal was to give the servant the smallest signal that he or she could understand. The servant's goal was to never miss that signal and respond immediately.

But the master's hand did more than communicate his wishes. It also represented supply, as the servant's wages and other blessings would come from that hand. Commentators point to other associations original readers would have understood; they would have seen the master's hand as protection, correction, and even reward.

For all these reasons, we need to embrace this metaphor and its implications for us. The Lord wants us to know Him well enough—and His will well enough—that the slightest blowing of the wind of the Holy Spirit will be enough to prompt us to respond.

This perspective—literal and figurative—is the opposite of the ways of the carnal Christian. Do we tend to look to God when we need something from Him, then listen for His will as it relates to our specific request? This isn't wrong, but it's just the beginning. We should always be looking to Him, seeking His will and His face, asking in our hearts, "What do you want me to do, Lord?" This is what the servant of the Lord does. Let's learn to look to our Master's hand.

Father, turn me around from "accessing" You when I'm looking for something, and help me to be like the servant that constantly has his eye on his master. Switch me from a focus on self to a focus on You.

JANUARY 8
SEEING THE KINGDOM

"Jesus answered and said to him, "Most assuredly, I say to you, unless one is born again, he cannot see the kingdom of God." (John 3:3)

In John 3:5, Jesus says, "unless one is born of water and the Spirit, he cannot enter the kingdom of God." But two verses earlier, He makes a distinction that's often missed. He says that if we're not born again, we cannot *see* the kingdom of God.

Both are true, of course. But we can sometimes be in the kingdom and never really have the eyes to see it. Paul said, "But the natural man does not receive the things of the Spirit of God, for they are foolishness to him; nor can he know them, because they are spiritually discerned" (1 Corinthians 2:14).

This is why those who don't know the Lord misunderstand so much of our lives and why most media representations of Christianity miss the mark by a country mile. They're like descriptions made by the blind of actions they can hear but can't see.

As believers, we need to continually grow in spiritual sight. We're given eyes to see at our spiritual birth, but we must press in, become disciples, and walk in faith day after day, month after month, and year after year to grow in our ability to discern the kingdom. We also need to ask God—even cry out to Him—to help us see His kingdom more clearly.

Satan has been defeated. Jesus is Lord. His kingdom is growing and is ever increasing. Do you see that? The world can't. Too many Christians can't. Be one who can.

Father, open my eyes that I may see Your kingdom. Help me to be humble enough to allow my perspectives to be changed. Help me to be obedient so that I can continue to grow in spiritual sight.

MARK DUPRÉ

JANUARY 9
GREAT EXPECTATIONS

"For I know that this will turn out for my deliverance through your prayer and the supply of the Spirit of Jesus Christ, according to my earnest expectation and hope that in nothing I shall be ashamed, but with all boldness, as always, so now also Christ will be magnified in my body, whether by life or by death." (Philippians 1:19–20)

When we hear, "What did you expect?" it's normally a mildly cynical response to our hope or expectation that something positive would happen and it didn't. But the present-tense version—"What do you expect?"—is a powerful question we should wrestle with from time to time.

We can claim to believe; we can claim to have faith. We believe Jesus' sacrifice paid for our sin. We have faith that Jesus is the only way to heaven. We believe He lived a sinless life, rose from the dead, and is coming again.

Yet these are past and future events. How about now—today? What do you really believe as you face trials or as life moves you into a new season? What we really believe is what we expect down in the bottom of our hearts.

We shouldn't expect that God will do things the way we want all the time. But there are things we can work to expect if we don't yet believe them: We can expect God to be faithful. We can expect He'll hear, and answer, our prayers. We can expect He'll work everything together for our good as we love Him and walk in His ways.

Check your heart. What do you really expect from God through the ups and downs of life? What we really believe at any moment is what we really expect. The good news is that as we press into God, the expectations of our hearts will align more and more with the faith of our minds and lips.

Lord, help me to be real with my faith. Show me what my expectations are, as opposed to what I say I believe but might not believe deep down. Touch my heart to expect in truth and in trust.

JANUARY 10
NOT SEEING CAN STILL BE BELIEVING

"Jesus said to him, "Thomas, because you have seen Me, you have believed. Blessed are those who have not seen and yet have believed." (John 20:29) These [Abraham, Noah, Moses, Jacob, etc.] all died in faith, not having received the promises, but having seen them afar off were assured of them." (Hebrews 11:13)

In John 20, Jesus spoke to Thomas about those who wouldn't get the opportunity to put their hands into Jesus' side, those who'd believe solely because of the power of the gospel. Every Christian since the time of Christ is in that camp. But the second half of this verse offers "those who have not seen and yet have believed" a blessing and challenge in every area of faith.

This applies to many aspects of our Christian walk, but perhaps it applies most greatly to prayer. It doesn't take long to discover that answers to prayers don't come quickly or in the form we anticipate. Eventually we realize our prayers are part of something much larger than us. They're being joined with those of others— including our family around the world—to bring about something of greater scope than we realize.

Yet there comes that moment when we decide whether or not we believe what Jesus says. We either believe God hears our prayers and that our fervent prayers "avail much," or we quietly decide that, since we aren't seeing what we'd hoped to see in response to our prayers, prayer really isn't worth the time or effort.

We're not going to see every answer to our prayers. The faithful ones described in Hebrews 11 didn't; neither will we. But we are in good—nay, great—company here. The question is, will we continue to pray, believing? According to Jesus, there is a blessing there for us and for those for whom we pray.

> *Lord, stir my heart to greater faith on the issue of prayer. Help me see with Your eyes the great power released in prayer. Show me where the enemy has sown doubt in my heart, so that I may repent and believe.*

MARK DUPRÉ

JANUARY 11
WEEP AND REJOICE

"Rejoice with those who rejoice, and weep with those who weep." (Romans 12:15)

Most of us aren't averse to sharing in some of the sadness of those who grieve or expressing joy with those who rejoice. But this Scripture calls us to something much deeper—something only possible with God's grace.

We often don't like to go near the two strong emotions called for here, except superficially. Sharing someone's sorrow can trigger all sorts of emotional reactions we'd rather not deal with. Perhaps there are losses we haven't come to terms with yet. Perhaps we're not ready to open our hearts that much to another person's loss.

There's also the sin of *schadenfreude*, a German word that describes the ugliest and pettiest of reactions to someone's pain: taking pleasure in it. What resides in the heart is known to God, and it's a more common response than we want to admit.

The success or great blessing of another can also set off emotional triggers in us. Perhaps another's success reminds you of what you (think you) don't have. Are your own frustrations stirred when others' goals are met or they receive a wind-fall? God's call is for us to blast past those demonic attempts at emotional bondage and genuinely rejoice along with others who are rejoicing.

We've all experienced the tender loveliness of sorrow shared. Let's allow our own emotional healing to continue by genuinely sharing the emotional burdens of others in a healthy way. And let's remember that the rejoicing of others is meant to be shared as part of God's provision of joy for us.

Father, thank You for the love and unity You have put in Your body. Help me to experience it more fully as I learn to weep and rejoice with others. Continue to open and heal my heart that I may be more like You in responding to the ups and downs of those around me.

JANUARY 12

WE HAVE ALL WE NEED

"His divine power has given to us all things that pertain to life and godliness." (2 Peter 1:3)

The "all things" of 2 Peter 1 means ... all things. We don't need any new revelation. We don't need *The Book of Mormon*, the *Qur'an*, *Dianetics*, *The Secret*, *The Rules*, or the latest secret book on belief or conduct.

What we need is to grow in understanding and walk in faith. We'll always need more illumination, but Peter says there's no more *revelation* available beyond what we've received in Christ. All we need is what God's done through Jesus' life, death, and resurrection, what He's revealed in His Word, and a humble heart and mind willing to be led into all truth by God's Spirit.

Christianity is truth, not *a* truth or one legitimate belief system among many. Now there's more to Jesus, the Scriptures, and the whole Christian life than we'll ever get to experience this side of the grave. But anything that claims to be a new revelation outside of Jesus and the Word is simply wrong. If it has a strong allure, there's probably something in us that needs to be healed, or filled, by the Lord. But if Jesus isn't at the center of it, it's a poison pill. Not only will it be harmful—it will prevent the healing we need from reaching what hurts.

Along with seeking the Lord for more understanding of Him and His ways, we need to keep taking steps of faith. That's how we first come into the kingdom of God, and it's the way we move forward. This year, let's determine to keep our minds and hearts centered in Christ.

Lord, You've given us all we need to move forward in life and in understanding Your kingdom. Thank You for that provision. Help me to keep recognizing the treasures inside Your Word and the treasures of understanding given by Your Spirit. Help me not to look outside of Your kingdom for truth and life, but to keep seeking it until I find it in You.

MARK DUPRÉ

JANUARY 13
THE GREAT WAR

"For we do not wrestle against flesh and blood, but against principalities, against powers, against the rulers of the darkness of this age, against spiritual hosts of wickedness in the heavenly places." (Ephesians 6:12)

There have been innumerable conflicts throughout the ages. But in reality, there's one great battle behind all other battles: it's between God and Satan. Simply put, God is raising up an (ultimately) unblemished bride and extending His rule throughout creation. Meanwhile, Satan is holding on to the remnants of his kingdom in a desperate attempt to hold back his eternal punishment. We're in the middle.

God loves us and wants our best. Satan hates us with cold indifference. He wants to hurt us because that hurts God and can temporarily slow down the advance of God's kingdom and judgment. Ultimately, this battle is really not about us at all.

One of Satan's greatest victories is obscuring this truth. He wants us to see ourselves in other battles, with people (particularly our Christian family) as the enemy. In actuality, it's us—with Jesus—on one side. Satan is on the other, opposing us and all that God is doing in and through us. It's not you on one side of a fence and your troublesome friend, spouse, or relative on the other. It's you and whoever on one side and Satan on the other, trying to make it look like he's not there trying to pull strings.

Yes, people can do terrible things. But they're not our enemy. We have a real enemy, and he's more terrible than we're currently allowed to see. If we start to view things this way and ask God for eyes to see this more clearly, it will change our lives.

Father, help me see things from Your perspective, especially regarding this great battle. I thank You that You've won this battle on the cross and that You're spreading Your victory even now. Thank You that because of Your grace, those who know You are on the side of victory.

JANUARY 14
TAKING GOD'S SIDE

"He who is not with Me is against Me, and he who does not gather with Me scatters abroad." (Matthew 12:30)

In Matthew 12, Jesus draws the great line of delineation. We're either with Him or against Him. This is the human side of the Great War between God and Satan.

As believers, we take God's side in this battle by following Christ—and continuing to follow Him. This is a separate issue from salvation. John 10:27–28 says, "My sheep hear My voice, and I know them, and they follow Me. And I give them eternal life, and they shall never perish; neither shall anyone snatch them out of My hand." This isn't about whether we know Him or not; it's about whether we're following Him.

We can know Christ and by not following Him actually be working against His purposes. This is hard to hear. But it's the reality of the war we're in; there is no neutral position. But what warm grace the Lord shows us in this! First, He showed His love by dying for us while we were still sinners (Romans 5:8). Now, He's ever patient and steadfast in His love as we occasionally lose focus, drift away, get distracted, and even deliberately sin.

We've been born again to do the good works He's prepared for us (Ephesians 2:10). In doing so, we take His side in the great war. Even when we stray and find ourselves working against Him, He's faithful to forgive us, cleanse us from all unrighteousness (1 John 1:9), and draw us back to Himself. What an infinitely patient and merciful God we have!

Lord, help me to stay close to You that I may follow You. Thank You for the mercy and steadfast love You show me at all times. Thank You that You still seek me during those times when I'm not seeking You.

MARK DUPRÉ

JANUARY 15

FROM BAD TO WORSE TO GREAT

"Now therefore, if it seems good to the king, let a search be made in the king's treasure house, which is there in Babylon, whether it is so that a decree was issued by King Cyrus to build this house of God at Jerusalem, and let the king send us his pleasure concerning this matter." (Ezra 5:17)

After their Babylonian captivity ended around 557 BC, the Jews returned home and began rebuilding the temple. Opposition arose, so the governor composed a letter to the Babylonian king asking for verification that the work was legitimate. Ezra tells us that years earlier, a note from the king had stopped the rebuilding efforts. This set a fearful precedent for God's people.

Things didn't look good. The governor was involved, the Samaritans were always on their back, and who knew if a one-hundred-plus-year-old document could even be found? It looked like the Jews were going to be told to stop work once more.

Nothing was found in the capitol. But a copy of the letter was discovered in another province three hundred miles away. Not only was the original decree affirmed but an accompanying decree told the opposition to keep their hands off and released funds from the royal coffers to support the work. What looked like the end turned out to be not just okay, but better than before.

How about you and your situation? Has your own history made you afraid of what's to come? Has opposition worsened in your life, with the "possibility" of even worse things ahead? Remember what the Lord did for His people here. Were it not for the opposition against them, the request for the search for the original decree would never have been made, and the new blessings would never have been released. The Jews' identity as God's people was reestablished, and the work of their hands was greatly blessed.

Father, help me remember what You did here when I only see opposition and dark skies. Thank You that You can turn opposition into blessing. Help me to stand strong in faith and watch for Your salvation.

| ALONG THE WAY

JANUARY 16
ROOT-BOUND?

"I press on, that I may lay hold of that for which Christ Jesus has also laid hold of me. Brethren, I do not count myself to have apprehended; but one thing I do, forgetting those things which are behind and reaching forward to those things which are ahead, I press toward the goal for the prize of the upward call of God in Christ Jesus." (Philippians 3:12–14)

Plants grow when they're healthy. If plants aren't growing well, they may have become rootbound. This occurs when plants outgrow the container they're currently in. We too can become root-bound—spiritually—for a variety of reasons.

We might be doing the same things we've always done to keep ourselves spiritually healthy, but we keep bumping into the same "walls" of unforgiveness, bitterness, or anger. Perhaps there's a step of faith we need to take, but we keep backing away from it, building up a kind of resistance to God's Spirit. Maybe we've just gotten a little lazy or too busy. Our pursuit of money or success may be choking out the life of God in our hearts.

When we get root-bound, our ability to receive nourishment is compromised. Even watering and fertilizing can have little impact.

How to change the situation? Let God trim your roots. Let Him cut away the rot and any part that's no longer receiving life. Are there activities that prevent you from receiving spiritual life— things that compete with your time with God or time in His Word or with His people? Let Him prune these so you can start growing again.

Are there worries, fears, "sensitive areas," or strivings in your soul that are robbing your peace and your connection with Him? Let Him—perhaps finally—touch those places and heal you. The process, like trimming, may hurt a bit. But your new ability to receive sustenance will be well worth the effort.

Father, show me where I might be root-bound. Where I'm not receiving Your consolation or grace or power or encouragement, please trim me. Open up my connections with You that have grown dry or blocked. I want to be open to Your workings and to everything You have to give me.

JANUARY 17

GETTING REPLANTED

"Grow in the grace and knowledge of our Lord and Savior Jesus Christ." (2 Peter 3:18)

Yesterday we looked at becoming spiritually root-bound. We saw how God's pruning can help revive us when we aren't really growing. Aside from the barriers we discussed yesterday, there's another reason we might be root-bound: perhaps we've gotten too big for our container and need to be replanted.

This isn't a situation where we think more highly of ourselves than we should (Romans 12:3). It's where we're made for other things than what we've been doing. Perhaps our ministries have grown too small in comparison to other parts of our lives, or we've stayed in the shadows when God wants us to serve in a greater capacity. God might be calling you out of your comfort zone, out of life as you know it—even to another church or city.

In the natural world, soaking a root-bound plant with water allows it to be more easily removed from its container. This helps prevent any roots stuck to the sides from breaking and compromising its nourishment system.

To prepare for a move of God, we need to soak ourselves as well—in His presence, in His Word, in worship, and in prayer. Make some sacrifices and spend more time with Him. When you go to church, fully open your heart, like a hungry baby bird looking to be fed by its mother.

Do you want God to move in your life? Soak yourself in all He has for you. If you've grown too large for your current container, you can trust God will find a new, more appropriate one for you!

Lord, I never want to get "stuck" where You have planted me. Help me to soak myself in You to the point where You can move me anywhere, at any time. Thank You for the many ways You do that.

JANUARY 18
SECRET TO THE GOOD LIFE

"Therefore do not worry, saying, 'What shall we eat?' or 'What shall we drink?' or 'What shall we wear?' For after all these things the Gentiles seek. For your heavenly Father knows that you need all these things. But seek first the kingdom of God and His righteousness, and all these things shall be added to you." (Matthew 6:31–33)

What's the secret to happiness? Success? The good life? The world is desperately seeking "the secret" to everything from successful job interviews to the perfect cup of coffee. God has a secret for us too. It's only a secret because it isn't as well known or understood as it could be: "Seek first the kingdom of God. Is it really that simple?" Yes, it is!

Let's break it down: Seeking the kingdom is advancing God's formation and extension of His invisible kingdom. It's as distinct from this world as Oz is from Kansas. It's the mind of Christ and heart of God put into action on earth. "His righteousness" refers to our character being "conformed to the image of His Son" (Romans 8:29).

As Christians, the key difference between thriving and simply surviving is seeking these things first. Many Christians want to guarantee the houses, clothes, cars, and retirement packages of this life. With what time, money, and energy they have left, they'll serve the Lord. God is gracious and will reward all our service to Him. But the secret to great joy, peace, and "spiritual success" is seeking His kingdom and righteousness first.

This is a major step of faith. It isn't easy. It will call for changes in every area of our life. But the Lord will guide us through this process if we're willing to let Him lead. There's no other path than putting these things first.

There are two kinds of Christians: those who put God's kingdom and righteousness first and those who don't. What's really first in your life?

Father, help me to put Your kingdom and righteousness first. Show me the path by Your Spirit, and help me move past my fears, stubbornness, and love of the things of this world. Thank You for the grace that leads me.

JANUARY 19
GOD OUR DELIVERER

"The children of Israel groaned because of the bondage, and they cried out; and their cry came up to God because of the bondage. So God heard their groaning, and God remembered His covenant."(Exodus 2:23–24); "But you are a chosen generation, a royal priesthood, a holy nation, His own special people, that you may proclaim the praises of Him who called you out of darkness into His marvelous light; who once were not a people but are now the people of God." (1 Peter 2:9–10)

In these two passages, one from the Old Testament and one from the New, there's a pattern. God created His nation in the Old Testament by freeing an enslaved people using His chosen servant. He delivered them, then He made a covenant with them. After four hundred years of slavery, God brought them out of Egypt, and then spent the next few thousand years working to get Egypt out of them.

Two thousand years ago, God brought another servant out of their midst. He also delivered His people and made a covenant with them, putting His law in their hearts and minds (Hebrews 10:16). This same God is still at work in His people, freeing them from bondage and working to bring forth Christ in their lives.

In both instances, God wanted to be known as the One who delivers. Many passages in the Old Testament refer to God as the One who brought His people out of Egypt. Yes, He was their Creator, but He put more emphasis on Himself as deliverer.

For the ancient Hebrews, who emphasized movement and action rather than concept in their speech and their writing, this act of deliverance was central to how they viewed God; many aspects of their feasts reminded them of their deliverance and deliverer.

We'd do well to take on that same attitude toward the Lord. In our emphasis on "becoming," which is so a part of our culture, let's never forget that we could never be "pressing forward" had we not first been delivered out of darkness.

> Lord, may I always be aware of where I have come from. May I always be aware of You as my deliverer. Please remind me of this when I lose sight of Your identity as deliverer. Thank You for my deliverance.

JANUARY 20
DELIVERED FROM AND DELIVERED TO

"So I have come down to deliver them out of the hand of the Egyptians, and to bring them up from that land to a good and large land, to a land flowing with milk and honey." (Exodus 3:8); "He has delivered us from the power of darkness and conveyed us into the kingdom of the Son of His love." (Colossians 1:13)

The longer we walk with Christ, the more we realize how much we've been delivered from: sin, judgment, satanic bondage, bitterness, unforgiveness—the list is nearly endless. As we become more familiar with His Word, we realize deliverance is at the heart of God's ministry to His people. The Lord delivered the Israelites out of slavery, and now in Christ we've been delivered from sin, its effects, and the judgments attached to it.

But for Israel, *deliverance from* was only step one. God didn't free Israel just to party in the wilderness. *Deliverance to* "the good and large land" was God's ultimate concern. It's the same with us. God didn't free us to simply spend the rest of our lives rejoicing over our freedom from yesterday's bondages. He frees us so we can enter our own Promised Land here on earth. In God's eyes, it's a continuous process; we're being delivered out of things as we're being delivered into other things.

There are our outward actions, where we give instead of take, love instead of judge, and serve others before we serve ourselves. Yet there's so much more that happens in our hearts and minds (Colossians 3:2). This process is a delightful deliverance that will take the rest of our lives.

There comes a point where our gratitude and joy for what we came out of becomes the impetus to press into those things that we've yet to receive as our inheritance. Let's never stop being grateful for what's past, but let's be energized to lean into our futures.

Lord, thank You for Your deliverance from and deliverance to. May I grow ever more grateful for the former and ever more encouraged to press into the latter.

MARK DUPRÉ

JANUARY 21

QUESTIONS WITH STRANGE ANSWERS: JOHN 6

"And when they found Him on the other side of the sea, they said to Him, "Rabbi, when did You come here?" Jesus answered them and said, "Most assuredly, I say to you, you seek Me, not because you saw the signs, but because you ate of the loaves and were filled. Do not labor for the food which perishes, but for the food which endures to everlasting life, which the Son of Man will give you." (John 6:25–27)

In John 6, Jesus fed the five thousand. Afterward, his disciples boarded a boat and crossed the Sea of Galilee toward Capernaum. On board, they encountered a storm. Meanwhile, Jesus was walking across the sea. At first, the disciples feared what they saw. But when Jesus identified Himself, "they willingly received Him into the boat, and immediately the boat was at the land where they were going" (John 6:21).

Some who'd been fed crossed the sea after the disciples. When they arrived in Capernaum, they saw Jesus. Justifiably confused, they questioned Him. Had there been any faith in their hearts, they might have asked, "How'd You get here? Did You perform a miracle?" Instead, their question reflected their fleshly thinking: "When did you come here?"

In His love, Jesus didn't directly answer their question. He worked to move them from earthly concerns (i.e., You gave us bread, so let's see what else you can provide.) to eternal things. In this case, the Bread of Life was standing right in front of them! They needed to be amazed, not answered according to their folly.

This is what God would love to do with us. Much of our thinking is limited by the mental boxes we feel must hold all our experiences. But God is always drawing us to new perspectives, to see things spiritually more than naturally and to understand that Jesus is the Alpha and Omega— what we need in any and all situations.

> Father, I confess that much of my thinking is like these people who were just curious about something they didn't understand. Help me hear Your reply when I ask foolish questions like this. Thank You for continual mercy and grace. Help me to see with the eyes of the Spirit instead of my own.

JANUARY 22

JESUS DOESN'T HAVE THE ANSWER; HE IS THE ANSWER

"Therefore they said to Him, "What sign will You perform then, that we may see it and believe You? What work will You do? Our fathers ate the manna in the desert; as it is written, 'He gave them bread from heaven to eat.'"... And Jesus said to them, "I am the bread of life. He who comes to Me shall never hunger, and he who believes in Me shall never thirst." (John 6:30–31, 35)

Read these words carefully. (For context, read John 6:24–35.) Jesus had miraculously fed the five thousand, and many of them sought Him out the next day. They'd enjoyed His extraordinary feat with the bread and hoped if He was indeed the Messiah, He might go one better than Moses, whom they credited with providing the bread-like substance for their ancestors.

When asked what they could do to gain food that lasts forever, Jesus told them to believe (an answer worthy of meditation for us all). Instead of believing in Him, they asked for yet another miracle. Jesus reminded them it was God who provided the manna, not Moses. He added that God was indeed going one better than Moses in bringing them the living Bread of Life Himself. Jesus was quite clear He was that Bread. Astonishingly, they asked Him to give them this bread, while He was standing right in front of them!

Graciously, patiently, He answered, "I am the Bread of Life." This became another moment of confusion instead of faith. Perhaps some couldn't make the connection between the earthly provision of the day before and the eternal, spiritual provision He was presenting to them.

Do we see Jesus as the source of our provision without realizing He is what we're looking for? He's our provision, our portion. That may fly in the face of our intellect, as it did for many of those in Jesus' time. But if we're open, it can fly into the center of our hearts.

Father, forgive me for the times when You are offering Yourself and I am looking for something else. Give me ears to hear You and eyes to see You in those moments. You're my sole provision in the next life; help me to see You like that in this one.

MARK DUPRÉ

JANUARY 23

BLESSED ARE THE "NOT OFFENDED"

"Jesus answered and said to them, "Go and tell John the things which you hear and see: The blind see and the lame walk; the lepers are cleansed and the deaf hear; the dead are raised up and the poor have the gospel preached to them. And blessed is he who is not offended because of Me." (Matthew 11:4–6)

If you're a serious believer, on occasion you'll be tempted to be offended by Jesus, His Word, and what He asks of us. A believer who's never been offended is someone who's probably not making much spiritual progress.

In Matthew 11, Jesus' words were directed at the imprisoned John the Baptist. Jesus quoted Isaiah 35 ("The blind see and the lame walk."), pointing to Himself as the fulfillment of the messianic prophecies. Then he urged John not to stumble over what was happening to him.

Jesus' words are also directed at us. What could offend us? Well, anything that crosses our expectations. God's ways are not ours. His timing is not ours. He answers prayer the way He chooses to, not according to our narrow expectations.

From a purely natural point of view, God can be confusing, confounding, and downright exasperating. In those moments, we'll either grow in faith and trust, pressing into what we know of His Word and the goodness of Jesus. Or, in our pride we'll allow ourselves to be offended—initiating a spirit of bitterness and cutting off the new spiritual growth the Lord wants to give us.

It's a choice. We may be "hard-pressed on every side, yet not crushed; we [may be] perplexed, but not in despair; persecuted, but not forsaken; struck down, but not destroyed" (2 Corinthians 4:8–9). Let's choose to believe and trust and not be offended.

Father, help me to see how this works. I don't want to be offended by You. I confess that I get confused and confounded sometimes. Help me in those moments to trust You more and trust in my own thinking and feelings less.

JANUARY 24

WHATCHA LOOKIN' AT?

"And the children of Israel said to them, "Oh, that we had died by the hand of the Lord in the land of Egypt, when we sat by the pots of meat and when we ate bread to the full! For you have brought us out into this wilderness to kill this whole assembly with hunger." (Exodus 16:3); Then [the spies] told [Moses], and said: "We went to the land where you sent us. It truly flows with milk and honey, and this is its fruit. Nevertheless the people who dwell in the land are strong; the cities are fortified and very large; moreover we saw the descendants of Anak there." (Numbers 13:27–28)

Experts tell us we often experience change as loss. They're right. When the Lord is moving us forward, we're often stymied by the same things the ancient Israelites were. We can become fixated on what we rosily remember about our past, back when things were "easier" or "simpler"—or at least clearer. At times, pressing into God can mean running into mental confusion and emotional disturbance. Trying to avoid this discomfort can result in a revisionist view of the past, leaving out details that made the past something we wanted to move on from.

The Israelites saw "giants" on their spy mission. They fell into the enemy's trap of believing the Promised Land "devours its inhabitants." But Caleb simply said, "Let us go up at once and take possession, for we are well able to overcome it" (Numbers 13:30). Caleb wasn't looking at yesterday's provisions in Egypt or focusing on the challenges ahead. He was considering something bigger than the giants: God's promise to give them the land. Yes, they were going to have to fight. But if God promised them the land, then He had the plan, the grace, and the power to make it happen.

So, whatcha lookin' at right now? Let's take our eyes off the past and the obstacles before us and put our eyes on Him. He's well aware of the challenges ahead, and He's the only One with the wisdom to know how to move around them or through them.

> Father, forgive me when I get lost in lamenting "the good ol' days." Help me to live in the present, allowing You to guide me by Your wisdom into my future. Thank You that You have a plan and that I can do all things You lead me to do through Christ who strengthens me.

MARK DUPRÉ

JANUARY 25

WHAT, ME COMPLAIN?

"Now these things [Old Testament stories of the Israelites in the desert] became our examples, to the intent that we should not lust after evil things as they lusted. And do not become idolaters as were some of them ... Nor let us commit sexual immorality, as some of them did ... nor complain, as some of them also complained, and were destroyed by the destroyer." (1 Corinthians 10:6–10)

Proverbs 10:19 says, "In the multitude of words sin is not lacking." That's because if we continue talking beyond a certain point, communication breaks down in value. Part of that breakdown is a fall into complaining.

From a purely natural, carnal viewpoint, complaining is fun. We get to push back against circumstances we don't like, and we can get people to agree with us. Both feel good. But in terms of efficiency, complaining is useless. It doesn't change the circumstance and isn't a good witness to others. But it's far worse than useless. It's wrong. First Corinthians likens complaining to lusting after evil things, becoming idolaters, and committing sexual immorality. It says because of these sins—including complaining—the Israelites were destroyed.

Why is such a "little" thing such a big deal to God? As the most efficient one in the universe, God knows we can't complain and listen to Him at the same time. When we complain, we're missing what God's trying to do and say in our circumstances and telling Him we resent His authority over us. Also, complaining to others isn't loving them or building them up.

There *is* a place for expressing complaints—to God. I'm not talking about whining, but pouring our hearts out to Him. Both David and Job did this. This is where the concerns, thoughts, frustrations, and heartaches we express as complaints need to go—to Him! So, let's close the complaint door to humans, and open the "pour out our hearts" door to God.

Father, forgive me for all the complaining I've done and still do. Help me to understand how useless and destructive it is. Lead me to develop new habits of taking those thoughts and frustrations to You— and help me to listen to You when I'm finished.

JANUARY 26
SEASONS AND CYCLES

"To everything there is a season, a time for every purpose under heaven: a time to be born, and a time to die; a time to plant, and a time to pluck what is planted." (Ecclesiastes 3:1–2)

All things on this earth come to an end. We know there's a hard stop to everyone's physical life, and most of us accept that. But within our lives are many seasons, all with their beginnings, and yes, their ends.

The same is true of the natural world. There are agricultural seasons and lunar and solar cycles. We work within their confines. We may note the passing of a beloved season with some degree of regret but quickly turn to the future as the cycles continue. We anticipate harvests and celebrate the New Year. Beginnings and endings are built into our cultures, and we make room to celebrate them.

Why not do the same with other cycles? In God's economy, some things will simply last a season: A relationship or the particular dynamics of a relationship. Your formal education. A ministry you enjoy. A way of living. A group involvement.

No matter how wonderful the season, God always moves on. The Old Testament sacrificial system had glory, but it was for a season. The life of King Solomon was so awe inspiring that the Queen of Sheba found "there was no more spirit in her" (1 Kings 10:5) when she experienced it. God had a certain shelf life planned for that, too.

Last year, something came to an end for you. In this coming year, something else will end. Some of these will be sad losses. Yet they're all part of life, where things begin and things end. Praise the Lord, there's grace for both.

> Lord, I recognize that You have built seasons and cycles in Your creation and into our lives. Help me to fully embrace each season and cycle You put me in. May I learn to enjoy what I can out of each, letting go of the passing seasons and joyfully anticipating the new ones.

MARK DUPRÉ

JANUARY 27

WAYS AND MEANS

"For My thoughts are not your thoughts, nor are your ways My ways," says the Lord." (Isaiah 55:8)

God is the chairman of our personal Ways and Means Committee. We know He's changing *what* we do, taking us from sin to righteousness, from fear to faith, from every lesser attitude to love. But He's also working continuously on the *way* we do things. God is concerned about outcomes, of course—our actions are important. But He's also concerned about process—*how* we do what we do.

Some of us don't even realize we *have* ways. We just do what we do in the most natural way possible—our way. But if the Lord is in our lives, our *ways* have to change. Malachi 3:6 says, "For I am the Lord, I do not change." Therefore, we're the ones who continually have to change as we're made into the image of Christ (2 Corinthians 3:18).

First, God wants to change our thinking about how we do what we do. Before we met Christ, we leaned on things we shouldn't have— our own strength, our own perspectives. We couldn't help ourselves. Now we're faced with a God who wants us to do His will His way— which isn't always logical to us. Walking around Jericho for a week, then seven times on the last day isn't logical (Joshua 6). But God's "illogical" way led to victory.

Our way of doing anything is never the best way; it's just our way right now. We can always learn a better way—of relating to people, communicating, solving problems, achieving a goal, and achieving spiritual victory.

Lord, as You change what I do, please change how I do things. Make me aware of Your ways in all I do. Bring me into the ways of grace, love, and godly wisdom.

JANUARY 28
THERE'S NO FORMULA

"For as the heavens are higher than the earth, so are My ways higher than your ways, and My thoughts than your thoughts." (Isaiah 55:9)

The best *way* of doing anything is to simply obey God. Yet even if we've clearly heard God's will, obeyed, and seen good fruit, we can learn the wrong lesson. We're to learn obedience to God, not a specific course of action. What worked yesterday isn't guaranteed to work tomorrow, even if we desire God's will.

In the business world, there are tools to help streamline processes: statistical process controls, Ishakawa diagrams, etc. In God's kingdom, only the Lord sees the whole picture. Only He can streamline the "production" of our walk in Christ. The most efficient thing we can do is lean into the Lord, find His will, and obey it.

God sees the whole "production." We don't. Perhaps God's end product isn't what we think it is. Maybe what we're working on at the moment involves someone else coming to a saving knowledge of Christ. Perhaps we're to learn something we don't even know we have to learn. Perhaps we're just a small part of a much bigger production God has in mind.

Perhaps everything you are is the missing piece in something God is working on. Don't assume you're either essential or unimportant. Yes, God can do anything He wants. But He wants, and has chosen, to use us! The way to do anything is to get as close as possible to Jesus and do what He shows us to do to the best of our ability. Then He gets His end product, and by His grace, we get a blessing!

Lord, forgive me when I look for the formula when I should just be looking for You. Thank You for working through me in the past. Help me to never take the attitude of "I'll take things from here, Lord." Let my lesson be that You are faithful and merciful and that You desire me to continue to come and seek You.d

MARK DUPRÉ

JANUARY 29

GOD'S PLAN OF TRANSFORMATION

"Let him who stole steal no longer, but rather let him labor, working with his hands what is good, that he may have something to give him who has need." (Ephesians 4:28)

This wonderful passage gives us the whole perspective of God when He's working to change our ways and means. When we become aware of sinful behavior, we think God wants us to stop it. That's true but woefully incomplete in terms of His plans for us. He wants to *transform* our sinful action into life for others and ourselves.

The theoretical thief Paul refers to here is encouraged to stop stealing so he can do something *else* with his hands, something positive, and finally, something beneficial. The goal isn't simply to stop what's bad but to let there be transformation.

Obviously, stopping the negative is the prerequisite to starting the positive. But it's just the beginning. The thief was told to put his hands to a different use, a constructive one. He was encouraged to do honest work. Then, after a while, those hands would have put him in a position to use his hands to give to others. The arc is complete— from stealing to creating to giving. That's the goal of God.

We're not called to live a life of frustration, always trying to stop doing things. If we're called to stop something, it's just the first step toward a positive expression of some kind that's designed to be an honest blessing to us and, ultimately, to others.

Do you have something you need to stop doing? Remember that stopping is only a part of a much larger plan to transform you. God has a positive plan and blessing in mind with all our sin.

Lord, help me see with the eyes of faith that my sins and weaknesses are the raw materials You use to bring life to me and others. Let me focus less on my sins and more on Your transforming grace.

JANUARY 30
OUR DEFAULT SETTINGS CAN BE CHANGED

"Then God said, "Let Us make man in Our image, according to Our likeness." (Genesis 1:26); "For all have sinned and fall short of the glory of God." (Romans 3:23)

Default settings on a computer are the hardware or software controls preset by the manufacturer. Incorrect default settings can result in strange-looking documents, messed-up applications, and bogged-down computers. Did you ever unthinkingly hit "yes" when the computer asked you something, then realize you'd made a mistake? The result can be chaos.

We have personal default settings as well. The default setting we have about an issue includes the position from which we operate, the mind-set that organizes our thinking, and the context we provide ourselves for dealing with problems and challenges.

These are determined by two realities: we're made in His image, and we've been infected by sin. Spiritually, we've all benefited from and struggled with some of our default positions. Some are great: Jesus is Lord; He is trustworthy; He works everything together for good. These are healthy default positions that bless God, others, and ourselves.

But other defaults can be damaging. Sinning, being wounded, or living in error can create default settings that make us react unrighteously, hear others incorrectly, and come to wrong conclusions. When we act on those conclusions, we can get in a world of hurt.

The good news is that, like computers, our default settings can be changed—by our choices and the blood of the Lamb. We'll talk more about these over the next few days. Today, let's realize that many of our "natural reactions" are based in wounds that God wants to heal and in wrong thinking He's working to correct.

Lord, thank You that in spite of my own sin and the work of the enemy in my life, I am still created in Your image. Thank You that You know how to heal me and correct my thinking, and that You're always working to transform me into the image of Christ (2 Corinthians 3:18).

MARK DUPRÉ

JANUARY 31

JESUS THE LOVING REALIST

"Now when He was in Jerusalem at the Passover, during the feast, many believed in His name when they saw the signs which He did. But Jesus did not commit Himself to them, because He knew all men, and had no need that anyone should testify of man, for He knew what was in man." (John 2:23–25)

What are your default settings? Over the next few days, we'll take a look at a few old settings that God's Word and His Spirit can address. Some will apply to you. Some may not. Some you may be aware of, others not so much. Some you may rationalize as "just the way you are." Ungodly default settings are not "us." They're getting in the way of us being who we're supposed to be.

Old default setting: "People always disappoint."

Cynicism has been described as "the wisdom of this age." This cynical statement is often used as an emotional survival strategy for those who've been hurt. Holding onto it can be a shield for hurt, but it doubles as a barrier for healing.

Jesus was the ultimate realist without being cynical. John 2:23–25 tells us Jesus knew man inside and out—the good, the bad, and the ugly. Yet He loved without measure, spoke boldly, and, ultimately, let people kill Him. He didn't live in disappointment with the responses of those around Him.

Our challenge is to not focus on the lack of trustworthiness in others, but to become as trustworthy as *we* can be. People fail. As fallen creatures, we all run that risk on a regular basis. But our God never does.

New default setting: Remember: 1) People are not God, 2) people will sometimes fail, 3) God is always faithful to us, 4) God is love (1 John 4:16), and love never fails (1 Corinthians 13:8).

Lord, help me to become the realist that You are. Help me to be wise in my dealings with people but openhearted and trusting above all in Your goodness. Help me to not be distracted from You by the failings of others.

FEBRUARY 1

WE ARE NEVER ALONE

"I am with you always, even to the end of the age." (Matthew 28:20)

Let's continue looking at how we can change our defective default settings ...

Old default setting: "I'm all alone in this."

Many of us feel this way, sometimes often. It's true that our trials and tribulataions are unique in some ways to us. No one has ever experienced the exact same combination of problerms and tests as we have. But we never experience them alone.

This is one area where our feelings can lead us into grievous error. If the idea that we're all alone in a circumstance becomes more than a quickly passing thought, we're wounding ourselves and calling God a liar.

Hebrews 13:5–6 tells us: "For He Himself has said, 'I will never leave you nor forsake you.' So we may boldly say: 'The Lord is my helper; I will not fear. What can man do to me?'"

If God has taken care of the biggest separator between Him and us—our sin—by the death of Jesus Christ, then He has clearly demonstrated His desire to be as close as we will allow Him to get to us.

New default setting: "If I have given my life to Christ, He is *always* with me."

Let's be persuaded along with Paul that "neither death nor life, nor angels nor principalities nor powers, nor things present nor things to come, nor height nor depth, nor any other created thing, shall be able to separate us from the love of God which is in Christ Jesus our Lord" (Romans 8:38–39).

> *Lord, help me to settle it forever in my heart and mind that You are always with me. I resist the lie that I'm alone just because I might sometimes feel that way. I believe what You say.*

MARK DUPRÉ

FEBRUARY 2

LEAVING OUR SURVIVAL STRATEGIES BEHIND

"Jesus answered and said to them, "This is the work of God, that you believe in Him whom He sent." (John 6:29)

Old default setting: My response to stress is, "What I need to do here is *survive*."

The survival strategies we've developed may have worked in the past, or seemed to work, from our perspective. But if our "saving grace" wasn't the Lord Himself, what got us through *then* is probably hurting us *now*. It can even be what keeps us from moving forward today.

In the past, we may have been too young or traumatized by hard times to turn to the Lord. We did our best to do what we thought would get us through. Most often, this is done subconsciously. But whatever we substituted for active faith in our God eventually has to go. We may have great affection for our old survival strategies. But over time they work less effectively and eventually become an impediment to spiritual progress.

What mental or emotional survival strategies did you develop when you were younger? Did you judge an entire group of people? Did you avoid certain things because they challenged your sense of safety? Did you vow to always do some-thing or make sure something never happened?

To get free from old bondages, we have to venture into places that may feel as if we'll be destroyed if we don't protect ourselves with old strategies. It's a painful necessity that will lead us to discover new grace and a stronger faith.

A new default setting is the work God requires: "I will believe in Jesus and seek Him for His will in each situation, even if it threatens my feelings of survival. Since He is my defender, I *will* survive."

Lord, I place my trust more in You, not in what I've developed up to now to survive. Show me how to do Your will in each situation, especially in those where I might be tempted to go back to my old ways. I declare that my continued survival is found in following You and Your ways.

FEBRUARY 3

NO LONGER A VICTIM!

"For whatever is born of God overcomes the world. And this is the victory that has overcome the world—our faith. Who is he who overcomes the world, but he who believes that Jesus is the Son of God?" (1 John 5:4–5)

Old default setting: "I am a victim."

This is a more common default setting than we might think. Hardly anyone says this aloud, but many of us harbor the thought sometime, somewhere. We almost certainly know folks who wrap themselves in this kind of identity. The reality is that we've all been victimized at one time or another. Some of us have been abused or libeled or cheated. The sins of others have affected us all.

But *being* a victim is not a matter of what another human has done to us. It's an identity issue—it's *how* we see ourselves. If you're a Christian, you may have been victimized, even at length. But if you're a believer, your primary identity has been changed, no matter what anyone has done to you.

You're now an overcomer, not a victim—simply because we're in Christ and He has overcome. Victims push people away to make sure they aren't sinned against. Overcomers don't enjoy rejection and abuse, but with Christ, they're no longer stopped by fear of them. Victims filter nearly every experience through their victimhood, distort reality by putting themselves at the center, and are always on guard. Overcomers can relax, knowing they're in His arms and that not everything is about them or going to hurt them.

New default setting: "People have sinned against me and will sin against me in the future. But I am in Christ, and I am not a victim, but an overcomer through the faith He gave me. This is my true identity!"

> *Lord, help me and my friends that struggle with this discover the reality of our new identity in You. Please strip away all the wrong thoughts and actions that go with seeing ourselves as victims. Help us to continue healing from where we've been victimized, and thank you that You changed our identities when we came to You.*

MARK DUPRÉ

FEBRUARY 4

FEARFULLY AND WONDERFULLY MADE

"For You formed my inward parts; You covered me in my mother's womb. I will praise You, for I am fearfully and wonderfully made." (Psalm 139:13–14); "If God be for us, who can be against us? He who did not spare His own Son, but delivered Him up for us all, how shall He not with Him also freely give us all things?" (Romans 8:31–32)

Old default setting: "I'm worthless (or stupid, or a jerk, or nothing ...)."

We have worth because we've been created in God's image. No one—absolutely no one—is worthless. No sin can erase the image that all of us are made in. No matter what you've done, you retain the dignity of being made in God's image. Take a moment and think about that. Let it sink in until you get to the point of never calling yourself stupid ever again.

Then take another look at Psalm 139, partially quoted above. We are all "fearfully and wonderfully made." Even you—you're not the exception. In God's eyes, in the eyes of your Maker, you are wonderfully made. Agree with Him on that, no matter how you may feel about yourself.

If you're a Christian, then God has made you worthy to not just be His creation, but His child. What the cross of Christ did was to make us worthy to be in Christ and share the benefits referred to in Romans 8 above.

Many of us catch ourselves when we disrespect others but freely call ourselves all sorts of names. If that's our habit, it's time to stop. Our worth is based on what He's done, not on anything in us or anything we've done. If we're in Christ, we've been made worthy.

Father, I stand in agreement with You that I am made in Your image, am fearfully and wonderfully made, and have been made worthy of partaking in the inheritance of the saints (Colossians 1:12). Help me change my thoughts about myself so that what I really feel and say aligns with Your truth about who I am.

FEBRUARY 5

A SEVERE MERCY

"But Peter said, "Ananias, why has Satan filled your heart to lie to the Holy Spirit and keep back part of the price of the land for yourself? While it remained, was it not your own? And after it was sold, was it not in your own control? Why have you conceived this thing in your heart? You have not lied to men but to God." Then Ananias, hearing these words, fell down and breathed his last." (Acts 5:3–5)

In 1977, Sheldon Vanauken published a book called *A Severe Mercy*, named after a statement to him from famous British author C.S. Lewis (*The Chronicles of Narnia*, etc.). It described a move of God that seemed unnecessarily harsh at first, but which Lewis described as a mercy, albeit a "severe" one.

This is what the Lord was doing in His church with Ananias and Sapphira. This young church faced persecution, but there was boldness and unity among its believers (Acts 4). In the midst of this came Ananias and Sapphira, who lied to church leaders. God judged them immediately and decisively.

Imagine the impact this must have had on the new church. A proper fear of God would have permeated everything. The reality of God would have come into sharp relief to everyone, perhaps especially to those wavering in their faith. Hypocrites would have left, purifying the church. The rest would have swallowed deeply and taken a solid assessment of their spiritual condition.

What a blessing for the church. What a cleansing and a strengthening! What a mercy to help the church strengthen its roots in God before more persecution came.

Has the Lord allowed something in your life you considered harsh? Take another look. God isn't arbitrary. While we'll never understand all the reasons for His actions until heaven, it may have been a lovingly merciful thing for Him to act that way at that time. He's a merciful God, so loving that He doesn't mind temporarily risking His reputation to extend His mercy to us. Time and spiritual growth are often the secret to seeing that mercy and love.

> Lord, I've judged You as harsh sometimes. Forgive me. I agree with Your Word that You are loving and merciful. Do what You need to do in me to help me see that anew. Thank you for all of your mercies.

MARK DUPRÉ

FEBRUARY 6

LOVING THE CHURCH

"A new commandment I give to you, that you love one another; as I have loved you, that you also love one another." (John 13:34)

Trends in the body of Christ come and go. Some are good; some aren't. One current trend is to criticize other Christian brothers and sisters without hesitation. (If it's not a trend when you read this, it will be again.) It must make the enemy happy.

Sometimes we disparage others because we're struggling with our own critical spirit. Sometimes we're so insecure we fall into the habit of trashing others so we can feel better about ourselves.

But the "religious" trap we can fall into is to believe we're somehow more mature because we're beyond others' viewpoints or feel we have a superior way of thinking or acting. Sometimes we mistake pride and judgment for spiritual maturity. We may be right in our discernment, but we can be wrong in our spirit.

If we truly love others as God loved us (1 John 4:7–11), the sins of others shouldn't distract us or lead us to criticize. Instead, we should reflect the glory of the great love story, extending God's love for us to our brothers and sisters. We can make a judgment call on an issue without condemnation.

The next time we're tempted to dump on a brother or sister or group, let's remember the command to love. It may seem like a good witness to point out others' errors, as if we're self-proclaimed defenders of the faith. But the stronger witness is to admit where something might be wrong and stay in a spirit of love. Now that's powerful and can change a life.

Lord, forgive me for how quickly I can judge my fellow brothers and sisters. Make me sensitive to the trap of trying to be cool and holy at the same time by criticizing Your church. Cause me to remember You based Your command to love on what You did for me and the rest of the body of Christ—not on how well we each respond to that love.

FEBRUARY 7

BREAKING THROUGH TO LOVE

"By this all will know that you are My disciples, if you have love for one another." (John 13:35)

The verse that follows the command to love (John 13:34) gives us one of many reasons to do so. The Lord has created reality in such a way that our genuine, heartfelt love for our Christian brothers and sisters helps others see we're disciples of Jesus Christ. That's the way He's made it, and He's graciously told us so. Let's give ourselves over to that glorious truth.

Perhaps you don't feel particularly strong at evangelism. One thing we can all do to share Jesus with others is to love His people. There's something about this love that shows Jesus to the world.

When we don't show love to other Christians, or we score points off other believers when they're wrong, we sometimes think we make ourselves, or even God, look better. Sometimes we do it to show we're not like other Christians. It might seem to make sense at the moment, but it's a trick of the enemy to divide us and compromise the gospel.

The stronger witness is to admit something might be wrong and stay in a spirit of love and unity. That can be difficult, but it's helpful to remember how much the devil hates Christian unity. He'll do anything to divide us.

We may have to do some dying to self to get there, but breaking through to love is powerful. Expressing genuine, even sacrificial, love for brothers and sisters shows the world to Whom we belong. How wonderful that obeying His command to love can lead to such life for others!

> Father, help me to love those that are in my spiritual family, locally and around the world. Help me discover how to express Your love when Your people act in ways that initially make it hard for me to do that. Thank You that Your command to love isn't restricted by anyone's behavior.

MARK DUPRÉ

FEBRUARY 8

LOVING "ESPECIALLY"

"Therefore, as we have opportunity, let us do good to all, especially to those who are of the household of faith." (Galatians 6:10)

How does the word "especially" in Galatians 6:10 make you feel? If we have a hard time loving the bride of Christ, the word can be shocking. Even if we don't, many of us recoil from the idea of having a *special* love for believers.

There's something special about the church of God—the people of God. It's dear to God's heart. Our love for our Christian brothers and sisters needs to be connected to our understanding of His heart. Acts 20:28 says He purchased the church with His own blood and, at Pentecost, filled it with His power. Ephesians 5 makes clear that the institution of marriage demonstrates how Jesus loves His bride.

Jesus identifies with His church, considering us closer to one another than we consider our natural families (Matthew 12:48–50). We have a family obligation to love. The first ministry collections were for the poorer believers in other parts of the world.

Yes, people mess up all the time. Yet God in His wisdom still chose to make us an integral part of His plan of salvation. He tells us to go out into the world and make disciples of those who hear and respond to God.

This kind of love is difficult because the church is made of people. It's easier to love the church as a whole, or humanity in general, than it is to love individual people. But Jesus died because of His love for individual people, not just a group, and we must set our hearts to love the family of God.

Lord, help me to have Your heart in loving Your church. Show me where my thinking and my heart may be off, and help me to have the special love for Your church that You have. Thank You!

FEBRUARY 9

PREPARING FOR MARRIAGE

"Prepare your outside work, make it fit for yourself in the field; and afterward build your house." (Proverbs 24:27)

Hidden among the practical gems of Proverbs is this advice. At first, it seems strictly agricultural and perhaps not pertinent to another kind of society. Look more closely, however, and it gives great advice for marriage and finances in general. Remember, the proverbs are often in the form of advice rather than prescription or proscription. They cannot always be taken as the only way to do things. But here's solid advice that would benefit marriages if it were followed more often.

Marriage is more than two people who love each other. We know it's a reflection of God's love for the church, and love and commitment form the basis of the relationship. Here the Scriptures give us direction in laying a practical foundation for that relationship.

There's a need for financial stability in a new marriage. Marriage isn't simply about a couple joining their lives together. It also forms a unit in society, one that needs a financial basis to thrive. There are always exceptions, but this Scripture indicates it's the norm for a family to be self-supporting, based on either a strong financial foundation or a reasonable expectation of one.

"Your outside work" can be your financial base or career. It's what enables you to establish "your house"—your family, and in some sense, even the inside of your home. It might not seem romantic to think about setting up a strong fiscal base for your relationship, but it helps provide a foundation for peace, easier communication, and love itself—all ingredients of a healthy marital relationship.

Lord, give me [them] patience and wisdom to set up a solid foundation for my [their] marriage. Grant me [them] the open doors and strength to lay a solid foundation for my [their] marriage, for our [their] sake and for Yours.r.

MARK DUPRÉ

FEBRUARY 10

JOSHUA: GOD'S PLAN IS HIS PRESENCE

"Moses My servant is dead. Now therefore, arise, go over this Jordan, you and all this people, to the land which I am giving to them— the children of Israel." (Joshua 1:2)

This is one of the great moments of Scripture. Everything changed for Joshua. His predecessor, the "great one," had passed. Joshua had been number two for a long time and was now being called to lead. Here was a "normal guy" called to fulfill a vision received by someone else--someone larger than life.

How was Joshua supposed to proceed? What plan would he adopt? Would he copy Moses? If not, what was the new strategy?

Joshua didn't lean on a plan, but a Person. God promised in Joshua 1:5, "No man shall be able to stand before you all the days of your life; as I was with Moses, so I will be with you. I will not leave you nor forsake you."

"God with Joshua" was the plan. God's presence *was* the strategy. In that context, what was God's first command to him? Verse 9: "Have I not commanded you? Be strong and of good courage; do not be afraid, nor be dismayed, for the Lord your God is with you wherever you go."

The first action Joshua was called to was a change of heart and mind: "Believe that I the Lord am with you, and let's begin this new relationship by encouraging and strengthening you with that assurance."

Have you ever had the rug pulled out from under you? Has your world ever suddenly changed? The best first response is to remember Emmanuel, God with us. Before we kick into action, let's kick into faith and believe that His presence is always our strongest asset.

Lord, when changes come quickly and I'm tempted to act before thinking, please remind me that You are with me. I want to know the wonder and power of that gift before making a move.

FEBRUARY 11

JOSHUA: THE COURAGE OF OBEDIENCE

"Have I not commanded you? Be strong and of good courage; do not be afraid, nor be dismayed, for the Lord your God is with you wherever you go." (Joshua 1:9)

As Joshua began to encourage himself in the Lord, he must have been quick to remember God's faithfulness in the past. God brought the children of Israel out of Egypt, gave them Moses for a leader, led them through the Red Sea, and provided manna and water in the wilderness. Plus, He'd made them victorious over the Amalekites.

Remembering how faithful God's been to us up until now is one way to stir our hearts to faith today. For Joshua, it was a good start. When he reviewed the challenges, obstacles, and seeming impossibilities, he saw that the battle was always the Lord's; the victories were all by His hand.

This led Joshua to a greater level of faith in following God's *command* to take courage. God wasn't giving a pep talk or trying to make Joshua feel better about his new challenges. He was giving him an order: be strong and of good courage. The courage Joshua needed—and received by believing God was with him—was the courage to obey God's next commands.

For Joshua, those next commands involved taking the Promised Land. That demanded a great deal of courage for battles within and without. We need courage for other things: being faithful to a call or a marriage covenant, reaching out to that one person, starting a new godly habit, facing a trial with grace. But our first command from the Lord is to take courage because He's with us. That's our starting point for obedience. Everything else is possible because of His presence.

Father, I take courage today because You are with me and because You are for me. Whatever else I face today for which I need courage, I first take courage because You are with me

FEBRUARY 12

LETTING GOD DIRECT

"And Lot lifted his eyes and saw all the plain of Jordan, that it was well watered everywhere (before the Lord destroyed Sodom and Gomorrah) like the garden of the Lord ... Then Lot chose for himself all the plain of Jordan, and Lot journeyed east. And they [Lot and Abram] separated from each other." (Genesis 13:10–11)

When Lot's uncle Abram offered him first choice of where he could live, Lot chose poorly. Note how he did it: "Lot lifted his eyes and saw ... that it was well watered," etc. Out of context, that doesn't seem like a problem. Lot chose what looked good to him and what he believed would make his life work. But Lot ended up in Sodom. Though Lot was "successful" in Sodom, he was a failure in most other ways, especially in regard to his daughters (Genesis 19:8, 30–38).

In contrast, the Lord said to Abram in Genesis 13:14, "Lift up your eyes and look from the place where you are." Abram responded to God's instruction to "lift up his eyes," meaning he allowed God to choose where he would live. Lot lifted up his own eyes, which tells us his judgment was based on his own perspective and observations.

We need to let the Lord direct our paths (Proverbs 3:6), as Abram allowed. Abram had his struggles, but he received many great blessings from God, which we all benefit from today. Lot's life was difficult and sinful and resulted in challenges that have affected us all (end of Genesis 19).

How are you making choices about your life? Do you base decisions on what looks good? Does God figure into the equation? Do you want Him to take your hand as you move forward with your life, or do you want to take His and let Him take you where He wants to go with you?

> Lord, please wean me from poor decision-making, something that's based on what seems good to me at the time. I realize I'm limited in what I can foresee. You are the great planner. You know all the details of what is ahead. I can only anticipate a few. Please direct my paths.

FEBRUARY 13

DOES GOD CARE WHERE I LIVE?

"Abram dwelt in the land of Canaan, and Lot dwelt in the cities of the plain and pitched his tent even as far as Sodom. But the men of Sodom were exceedingly wicked and sinful against the Lord. And the Lord said to Abram, after Lot had separated from him: "Lift your eyes now and look from the place where you are." (Genesis 13:12–14)

As we saw yesterday, there can be a big difference in how people determine their paths in life. But the specific decision each of these two men made holds another lesson: it matters where we decide to live. Lot chose to place himself among wicked men, and it had a terrible influence on him. Abram was determined to create a godly environment around himself. The first thing he did was build an altar (Genesis 13:18).

Many Scriptures warn us against surrounding ourselves with the ungodly. Lot may have been among the first who told himself he would have a positive spiritual influence on his environment. But the wickedness he surrounded himself with was too powerful, and it infected his spiritual life.

God cares where we live for many reasons. He knows what's best for us. He knows whom He wants as our neighbors. He knows what living situation will best work His purposes in our lives. Lot's future was greatly impacted by his choice of "neighborhood." None of us want to imitate that. It seemed to make sense to him at the time; it was "logical" and seemed an excellent choice. We'll never know how God might have directed him had Lot simply asked for His guidance.

The next time you move, even if it's within the same area, make sure to bring God into the process. We often ask for His help in opening doors and allowing us to find that good place. Let's start asking Him for direction even before the decision-making process begins.

Lord, thank You that You care enough about every detail of my life that You care where I live. Whether it will have a great impact on me or a little one, I ask You to direct me in my next move. I trust You to open every door of wisdom and provision.

MARK DUPRÉ

FEBRUARY 14

LAYING CLAIM TO OUR LAND

"For all the land which you see I give to you and your descendants forever. And I will make your descendants as the dust of the earth; so that if a man could number the dust of the earth, then your descendants also could be numbered. Arise, walk in the land through its length and its width, for I give it to you." Then Abram moved his tent, and went and dwelt by the terebinth trees of Mamre, which are in Hebron, and built an altar there to the Lord." (Genesis 13:15-18)

God made a powerful and meaningful command to Abram here. After pointing out the land Abram was to receive from God, and promising to make his offspring "as the dust of the earth," God told him to walk "the length and width" of the land.

It was apparently ancient custom for a person to finalize the transfer of property by visiting the land. Abram would be "staking his claim" prophetically by walking up and down the land, even if he didn't get to see the final possession of it in his lifetime. This is interesting history, but there is a huge lesson for us here.

The Lord has given us everything for life and godliness (2 Peter 1:3), and we're given an untold number of promises in the Scriptures, much more than we can detail here. Have you walked up and down the land of these promises, laying claim to them for yourself? Or are they part of a vast landscape that is impressive but unvisited?

The land wasn't finally Abram's until he walked the length and breadth of it. The promises of God aren't really ours in practice, aren't our real possession, until we walk through the length and breadth of them, claiming them as our own, agreeing with God that He has given them to *us*.

If you're a follower of Jesus, you have a great land of promises before you. You'll find most of them in the Scriptures. Have you taken possession of your land yet?

Lord, thank You for the kingdom of God, which You have brought me into. Thank You for the inheritance that comes with being Your child. Help me to take possession of what You are giving to me and not to leave any of it unexplored.

FEBRUARY 15
STRANGE ANSWERS: THE FIRST QUESTION

"Then the Lord God called to Adam and said to him, "Where are you?" (Genesis 3:9)

As preachers have pointed out throughout the ages, God didn't ask this question because He needed information. He's God; He knew exactly where Adam was. So, let's look at the question by itself. If you listen closely, you can hear the cosmic cry coming from God to his lost people.

Perhaps you're already familiar with the Law of First Mention and Adam's role as our federal head. If not, let me briefly explain. The Law of First Mention is a principle that helps determine the fundamental meaning of a doctrine by studying the first time it's mentioned in Scripture.

This principle is a treasure locator. Studying when something is first mentioned helps us arrive at a doctrine's deepest meaning. Being our federal head means Adam was more than simply an individual. He was head representative of the whole human race. God's test of Adam was therefore God's test of the human race; Adam's fall was ours as well.

This first question of Scripture is in some ways the great question of God throughout His Word. His call to Adam was His cry to the human race—"Where are you?" Can you hear God's broken heart? This wasn't a scolding parent searching for a lost child. It was a Father saddened by the separation His children's sin had caused. And the question itself was the beginning of the way back—for Adam and for us. I refuse to add to the Scripture, but in my imagination, I can hear a crack in His voice.

Lord, thank You that You searched for us and drew us to Yourself. Help me to remember that You are always, continually, drawing me. May I always be quick to say, "Here I am, Lord!"

MARK DUPRÉ

FEBRUARY 16

EVERY REASON TO BE HUMBLE

"Humble yourselves in the sight of the Lord, and He will lift you up." (James 4:10)

Social science research demonstrates that most people think they are better (more ethical, industrious, moral, etc.) than average. It sounds like Garrison Keillor, who reminded us that in Lake Wobegon, "all the women are strong, all the men are good-looking, and all the children are above average." That's statistically impossible, but funny. It's part of our fallen nature as a race that we don't—*can't*, actually—view ourselves (or our children) correctly.

We know humility is an attribute of being a Christian. But why is humbling ourselves so important—to God and for us? First and most importantly, it's because God says we should do it. Consider James 4:1. If we love God, we'll humble ourselves for that reason alone.

Humility is also part of God's design for us to be closer to Him. We often go through periods where we feel God is distant. That may be for many reasons, but one might be because there's an area where we need to humble ourselves.

Related to bringing us closer to God is the idea that humility often clears things up. Galatians 6:3 says, "For if anyone thinks himself to be something, when he is nothing, he deceives himself." Pride deceives; it takes us out of reality. Humility restores us to reality, bringing light and understanding to such issues of life as sin, love, grace, and mercy. The more we humble ourselves, the more we know God and understand ourselves.

Lord, thank You for Your reminders to stay humble. Please don't allow me to stray into deception and move to a place where we are far apart. Remind me by Your Spirit of who I am and who You are. Thank You that we have every reason to be humble.da

FEBRUARY 17
HE GIVES GRACE TO THE HUMBLE

"God resists the proud, but gives grace to the humble." (James 4:6)

We all desperately need God's grace. We need it to have faith to believe in Jesus Christ. We need it to receive anything at all from the Lord. We know we need it in relating to others.

If we want to find grace, we need to get humble or stay humble. According to James 4, humility is where God provides grace. Grace is like water—it flows to the lowest place. Those looking for water seek the low spots. Those looking for grace do the same thing.

If we want to be humble, we don't have to look far for good reasons. It comes down to two realities: we're deeply fallen creatures, and He is Almighty God. If we live in those two related truths, we'll find grace.

As a race, our fall into sin was deeper than our limited minds can comprehend and the effects more profound. We've been affected and infected mentally, emotionally, and physically as well as spiritually. This affects how we view ourselves.

Sin's consequences are present in our thoughts, our moods, our motivations, our lack of utter dependence on God, our incomplete desire for His glory, and our small ability to love God and others as we should. That may not be encouraging to contemporary self-image thinking. But it's really good news—because it's reality. It's the first half of understanding the first thing about humility.

Once we understand how deeply we've been reduced, wounded, and twisted by sin, the more likely it is that we'll humble ourselves before God and find His grace.

Lord, help me to realize how much sin has affected me on every level. Help me to realize how much I need Your Word and Your Spirit to bring light and truth to my mind and heart. Thank You that You loved us enough to draw us out of sin and into Your life.

MARK DUPRÉ

FEBRUARY 18

TAMING THE TONGUE

"In the multitude of words sin is not lacking, but he who restrains his lips is wise." (Proverbs 10:19)

Talking too much is not just a possible irritant; it easily leads to sin. In any conversation, there are only so many words that God intends. (I'm not being a legalist here—just speaking in generalities.) Have you ever felt that nudge that says, "You've said enough; wrap this up," then continued the conversation? What happened? It likely ended with things you wish you hadn't said or heard, or else devolved into silliness or worthlessness.

If you can't see this in your own life, consider a couple of phenomena. Listen to someone if he/she has unlimited time to talk or text. The conversation usually has a point in the beginning. But let the conversation go on too long, and it often moves to criticism, self-centeredness, or folly.

Or watch the scourge of reality television (but only for a few moments, lest you lose too many brain cells). Aside from creating unhealthy or manufactured conflict, the focus of reality TV is to get folks talking and talking and talking. Since actual *communication* isn't part of this talk, it often turns into unhealthy expressions of fear, anger, or judgment. This might make for good ratings, but it doesn't help the speaker or listener.

There are only so many things that "ought" to be said, even in light or humorous conversations. Not everything that enters the mind should exit the mouth. God desires to use our mouths for our benefit and for the blessing of others. Anything beyond that needs to be examined for its effect and effectiveness.

Lord, help me to look at my speech differently. Move me from simply expressing myself to blessing and edifying others. Lead me to express myself in ways that build others up.

FEBRUARY 19

LET'S MAKE JESUS MARVEL

"[The centurion said,] "Say the word, and my servant will be healed" ... When Jesus heard these things, He marveled at him, and turned around and said to the crowd that followed Him, "I say to you, I have not found such great faith, not even in Israel!" (Luke 7:7, 9) But Jesus said to them, "A prophet is not without honor except in his own country, among his own relatives, and in his own house" ... And He marveled because of their unbelief." (Mark 6:4, 6)

Jesus is said to have "marveled" twice. Once was in Capernaum—far outside Judah—and concerned a Gentile, a Roman soldier, whom readers would assume to be as far removed from real faith as possible. The second was in Nazareth, Jesus' hometown, among those who should have been "Jesus' people" in every sense of the word.

With the centurion, Jesus marveled at his faith. Among His people, Jesus marveled at their unbelief. Clearly, Jesus was struck deeply by the exercise of faith or the lack thereof. The centurion didn't need to see miracles or even have Jesus physically visit His house. The centurion understood authority and recognized it in Jesus. He knew the power of a command and had faith in the power of whatever Jesus would say.

How about us? Must we see new demonstrations of Jesus' power to believe? Do we trust in His word—especially those that have already been written down for us? The centurion added his faith to Jesus' spoken word, and his servant was healed.

Jesus also marveled at the unbelief of those who should have known Him best. Instead of responding to the presence of God, they were too distracted by their knowledge of Jesus as a son and sibling. Being too preoccupied and judgmental about the outside package, they missed the power of God within.

How about us? Have we missed God—and the blessings of His power and presence—because we know the person God's using too well? How sad for us, and how sad it was for Jesus.

> Father, help me to be like the centurion, recognizing the authority of God's Word as having real power. Forgive me for rejecting Your chosen vessels because I know them in an earthly sense. Help me to see Your power and presence wherever and in whomever You choose to display it.

MARK DUPRÉ

FEBRUARY 20

GOD OUR DEFENDER

"For the eyes of the Lord run to and fro throughout the whole earth, to show Himself strong on behalf of those whose heart is loyal to Him." (2 Chronicles 16:9)

We're probably first aware of God as Creator. As we meet Jesus, we come to know Him as Savior, the One who forgives, the deliverer, and either then or later, as Lord. As we walk with Him over time, we discover all those things He's looking to be for us. One of the most powerful is God our Defender.

Many of us have it deeply settled in our hearts that we are our own defenders. We may even think that's what God wants. Most of us know "God helps those who help themselves" isn't scriptural, but many of us act as if it is.

Let's focus on the big picture. Meditate on the fact that God *wants* to be our Defender. Read 2 Chronicles 16:9, as well as Psalm 34:7, Psalm 7:10, and Isaiah 31:5. It's a profound paradigm shift to let the Lord be our Defender. It raises all kinds of questions about what our responsibilities are and what are His.

Some of us run to the opposite extreme when challenged with a new perspective. For example, we may ask, "If God's my Defender, does that mean I don't do anything? Shouldn't I keep myself from harm?" We know these reactions are extreme, so we often throw out the new perspective because we're still in a reactive phase with it. What a tragedy to lose knowing Him better and having Him work more deeply in our lives because we don't "get" a new viewpoint right away.

Lord, I see that You desire to be the Defender of Your people. Please show me what that means to me individually. Please help me not to try to figure out the full implications of this now, but in faith I receive Who You want to be to me.

FEBRUARY 21
LETTING DOWN OUR DEFENSES

"But I will sing of Your power; yes, I will sing aloud of Your mercy in the morning; for You have been my defense and refuge in the day of my trouble. To You, O my Strength, I will sing praises; for God is my defense, my God of mercy." (Psalm 59:16–17)

What happens when we don't rightly fear God or trust Him to defend us? We have to find a way of protecting ourselves.

Here's a secret: We actually don't have the grace or wisdom to do that. When we defend ourselves, the strength and energy that God has purposed for other things gets sidetracked into making and executing a defense strategy. That's bad for two reasons: 1) That strength and energy was supposed to be used for something else, and 2) We can't defend ourselves as well as God defends us.

Failure to let God be our Defender results in building up walls that may work for defense against hurt and pain, but they also keep out His love and His voice. They also keep us self-directed instead of God-directed and others-directed.

Have you developed a defense strategy because of your history? Do you beat yourself up before others get the chance to? Do you keep people at what you feel is a "safe" distance? Have you developed a hard outer shell? (Good for candy, bad for people!)

To let God take the lead in this area can be terrifying to some folks. It isn't easy for anyone. We have to first believe His word, that He is interested, actually *invested*, in defending us. Then we have to abandon our plans, become uncomfortably vulnerable, and listen for His instructions. We can't anticipate what we might hear. So let's begin by agreeing that He is a wiser and stronger Defender than we are!

Lord, I believe Your word that You are my Defender. Show me what that means. Please take away those defenses I've created that keep me from you and others, and help me to understand that You are with me as Defender at all times.

MARK DUPRÉ

FEBRUARY 22

THE GOD WHO SEES

"The Angel of the Lord said to [Hagar], "Return to your mistress, and submit yourself under her hand." Then the Angel of the Lord said to her, "I will multiply your descendants exceedingly, so that they shall not be counted for multitude"... Then she called the name of the Lord who spoke to her, You-Are-the-God-Who-Sees; for she said, "Have I also here seen Him who sees me?" (Genesis 16:9–10, 13)

God has many names in the Old Testament, all testifying to different aspects of His character. He's called the God who heals, provides, and is our peace, among others. Used only once, however, is Hagar's appellation: You-Are-the-God-Who-Sees.

We might say, "Well, of course He sees!" Hebrews 4:13 tells us "there is no creature hidden from His sight." So what's so special about this particular act of seeing that preserves it as one of God's names?

We're given little explanation beyond Hagar's words. It's easy to understand her surprise that the Lord would truly see her. She was a slave, given to Abraham to help bear a child on which she'd have no claim. She'd developed a bad attitude toward her mistress, Sarah, who unfortunately responded in kind. To make things worse, Hagar disobediently ran away.

This is about as messy a situation as can be imagined. Yet God saw. He saw not at a cool distance, but saw her whole situation—her earlier mistakes, her despair, her precarious circumstances—with compassion. He did not come in judgment. Instead, He came with a soft word, direction, and a promise.

We make a real mess of things at times. Sometimes we reap what we sow. But God still sees. He sees everything. Nothing is so awful, or complicated, or sinful that He doesn't see and understand. And nothing is so messy that it's beyond His ability to rescue and restore.

Father, thank You that You "get" me and every circumstance I find myself in. Thank You that I can't mess up beyond Your ability to see and understand it. Thank You for having a plan to get me out. Help me to be humble enough to work with it.

FEBRUARY 23
DILIGENTLY SEEKING

"But without faith it is impossible to please Him, for he who comes to God must believe that He is, and that He is a rewarder of those who diligently seek Him." (Hebrews 11:6)

Hebrews 11:6 is such a familiar Scripture that sometimes it's hard to hear it with fresh ears. To help us do so, let's take a look at the inverse idea in the passage. If we thought God didn't exist, for instance, it would be foolish to try and please Him. If we thought seeking God would be painful or harmful, it would be the height of foolishness to even begin.

We do believe that He exists. But many of us no longer really believe that He's a rewarder of those who diligently seek Him. Our minds may not admit it, but our actions speak otherwise. Perhaps we've grown weary of seeking Him. What's really happened is that we've stopped believing Him on this point. Why work extra jobs for extra money? Because we believe there's a reward. God has told us there is a reward in seeking Him.

When you've lost something, how desperate are you to find it? For things we consider important—a document, a key, or if I can stretch the metaphor to the breaking point, a child—we search and search until we find it. How desperate are you to find Him? He tells us how to do that—by seeking Him with our whole hearts.

We have a certain storehouse of focus and energy in our lives. God has promised connection with Him and wisdom as we take that focus and energy from things that don't reward and begin to direct those attentions toward Him.

Father, help me to redirect my energies toward seeking You and Your wisdom. Show me where I've misdirected my focus and lead me to a renewed emphasis on You.

MARK DUPRÉ

FEBRUARY 24

STRANGE ANSWERS: GOD IS SEEKING YOU

"But the Lord God called to the man and said to him, "Where are you?" So he said, "I heard Your voice in the garden, and I was afraid because I was naked; and I hid myself." (Genesis 3:9-10)

God is the seeker, the One who goes after us. Scripture makes it clear that it was He who chose us (Ephesians 1:4), just as it was the Lord who chose Israel. Even from the beginning, directly after the first sin, it was God who came to us. We're the ones who run from Him until we're found by Him.

Being found is being honest enough to answer that question. Adam wasn't. Can *we* be? When God asks, "Where are you?", can you honestly tell Him?

Adam answered the way he did because he was deeply convicted of his sin but couldn't face it. He wasn't really answering the question—he was deflecting the discussion away from the question's implications.

The next time you feel that spiritual nudge from the Lord, listen closely. Is He asking you where you are? If so, answer Him honestly. Maybe your answer is, "Right here, Lord, in the middle of a mess I made." Or "Right here, Lord, filled with bitterness and anger, mostly at You." Or "Over here, Lord, on the sidelines, not really doing anything or going anywhere." Since He already knows where we are, just as He did with Adam, answering honestly is the beginning of connection. And that's the beginning of forgiveness and healing.

We can't cover ourselves and make things right without the blood of Jesus. And we can't have that forgiveness without turning to Him and looking at Him—and letting Him look directly at us.

Where are you today?

Lord, I confess that sometimes I deflect when You're beginning to speak with me. Forgive me for that. Help me to simply receive what You're saying and thank You that because of Your love and the blood of Jesus, I can be direct and honest with You.

FEBRUARY 25
USE YOUR WORDS

"And He said to them, "Go into all the world and preach the gospel to every creature." (Mark 16:15)

Remember Francis of Assisi? He's often revered for his love of animals and how he embraced poverty. A quote that's been attributed to him has become popular in recent days: "Preach the gospel; if necessary, use words." In other words, everything we do should be an expression of the gospel. Unfortunately, Francis never said that, and this was the opposite of what he actually did.

The quote was first attributed to Francis about two hundred years after his death. Recent biographers don't find a record of it anywhere during his life. What they do find is that Francis worked to express God's love in everything he did, and that included a good deal of preaching. Apparently, he used words a lot and is said to have died preaching on Psalm 141.

The gospel is good *news*. News isn't demonstrated; it's shared. To use the words *if necessary* is like telling television reporters to use words on their newscasts if need be—or telling people to feed the poor, and if necessary, use food.

Jesus, our great example, preached all the time. He never assumed someone would see a good work or a miracle and automatically "get" the gospel. Next time you read one of the Gospels, note how often Jesus took the opportunity to talk about some aspect of salvation or the kingdom of God.

We shouldn't make people guess about the power and love behind our lives. Let's preach the gospel at all times, and use our words often.

> *Lord, I want my walk and my talk to match. Help me to express Your truths with my words and to not let any good works substitute for sharing the good news.*

FEBRUARY 26

THE POWER IS IN THE GOSPEL

"For I am not ashamed of the gospel of Christ, for it is the power of God to salvation for everyone who believes, for the Jew first and also for the Greek." (Romans 1:16)

Yesterday's quote about preaching at all times has been used as a kind of escape clause for those who have a hard time sharing the gospel verbally. Many of us are reluctant to share the gospel for a variety of reasons. The Scripture above speaks to one of those. Some of us are simply ashamed of the gospel (if that weren't a temptation, Paul wouldn't have written that sentence). If that's our case, we need to repent and do some serious thinking about the wondrous nature of God, His power, and the fullness of the work of Christ.

But some of us are reluctant because we've believed a lie—that the power of the gospel is in us. The opposite is true: the gospel has the power to save no matter how much or how little of the Bible we know, how much evangelism training we've had, or whether or not we've had a spiritually victorious day. God's truth is no less the truth, with no less the power, even when we think we're not doing all that well with God.

Of course, we're naturally more excited to share the good news when we feel spiritually strong. But here is some good news about the good news: it is true and is the power of God to salvation every day. That's true when shared by vessels that are brilliant and educated and filled with God's love—and even by vessels that are having a bad day. In fact, sharing the good news sometimes gets us out of a bad day.

> *Forgive me for thinking that Your power is limited to my moods and the consistency of my walk with You. Help me to understand that the gospel, when shared with words, is powerful in and of itself. I resist in Jesus' name the taunts of the enemy that are working to keep me quiet. Help me to gafin a new level of boldness in sharing Your powerful good news.*

| ALONG THE WAY

FEBRUARY 27

REPENTANCE OVER TIME: JOHN NEWTON

"And do not be conformed to this world, but be transformed by the renewing of your mind, that you may prove what is that good and acceptable and perfect will of God." (Romans 12:2)

John Newton, author of the hymn "Amazing Grace," has a dramatic story of salvation. He was a notorious slave trader who came to Christ on a slave ship after a terrible storm. Later he became a minister, wrote hymns, and became an avid abolitionist. It's a great tale.

But Newton's story doesn't fit the modern narrative of becoming a Christian and getting things straightened out right away. When he returned safe and sound and saved to England after the storm, he signed on as a mate of another slave ship. He traveled back to America, studying his Bible as two hundred slaves lay captive beneath him.

Newton's writings make clear that the revelation of the evils of the trade came slowly to him as he read the Scriptures and lived in communion with the Spirit of God, who leads us into all truth. Newton later worked actively against the slave trade. But his transformation was a slow and oftentimes painful journey.

God often takes decades to complete a work in us—and in others. His goal with someone like Newton could just have been to convict him of the sin of slavery and renounce his part in it. But it was deeper and wider than that. Newton became a minister who was greatly influential in ending the trade and who also wrote the most popular, and perhaps powerful, hymn in the English language— one that still ministers to millions today. It took time, and amazing grace, to create that person.

God, help me to be patient with Your work in me and in others. Lead me to pray with wisdom for Your work in the hearts, souls, and minds of other people. Forgive me for judging them for not being transformed at the rate I think they should be. Thank You that You work deeply and providentially over time.

MARK DUPRÉ

FEBRUARY 28

REPENTANCE OVER TIME: JOSEPH'S BROTHERS

"Come and let us sell [Joseph] to the Ishmaelites, and let not our hand be upon him, for he is our brother and our flesh." (Genesis 37:27); "So [Joseph's brothers] sent messengers to Joseph, saying, 'Before your father died he commanded, saying, 'Thus you shall say to Joseph: "I beg you, please forgive the trespass of your brothers and their sin; for they did evil to you"' ... Then his brothers also went and fell down before his face, and they said, "Behold, we are your servants." (Genesis 50:16, 18)

As He did with John Newton, God used a good deal of time to bring Joseph's brothers to repentance. When we read the story of Joseph and his brothers (Genesis 37–50) we can see the small, but real, changes that occurred over time. In Genesis 42, the brothers display the first expressions of guilt over selling Joseph years before. They bring God into that process in Genesis 42:28. We can see at the dinner where little brother Benjamin was preferred that some kind of progress had been made in their hearts: "They drank and were merry with him" (Genesis 43:34).

As time and circumstances went by, they were dismayed in Joseph's presence, obviously feeling guilt at the uncovering of their sin. They probably made up the story about Jacob's message (Genesis 50:16), but it indicates a growing sensitivity to the wrong they'd done. We can't know the depth of genuine repentance in each brother's heart, but they ended up falling before Joseph and declaring themselves his servants.

It took years and a series of devastating events, but over time repentance was worked into their hearts. We can't forget that repentance is always God's intention and He is always working it into our hearts. He works through time, and He knows what He's doing—in us and in others.

Lord, thank You for the incredible model of Joseph's brothers. I see that You use time and circumstance to draw the sinner to righteousness and me to repentance. Help me remember You are doing this with others. Forgive me for judging You just because I often can't see it happening. Help me to be responsive to what You're doing in my own heart.

FEBRUARY 29

WHERE WAS GOD?

"II Kings 23:36-37 Jehoiakim was twenty-five years old when he became king…And he did evil in the sight of the Lord….; II Kings 24:8-9 Jehoiachin was eighteen years old when he became king…. And he did evil in the sight of the Lord…. ; II Kings 24:18-19 Zedekiah was twenty-one years old when he became king….He also did evil in the sight of the Lord…."

The story of the last three kings of Judah is a discouraging parade of failure. All three "did evil in the sight of the Lord," and the end result of their reigns was conquest and the Babylonian Exile. It's easy to wonder where God was in all of this. Had he stopped speaking?

Quite the opposite. We just need to look to another book to see the loving, warning voice of God during this time: Jeremiah. Though not alone, Jeremiah was the main prophet God had raised up to speak the word of the Lord to these kings.

Jeremiah actively preached repentance to the people. During Jehoiakim's reign, He predicted captivity and the 70-year exile. He predicted Jehoiachin would be conquered and die in a foreign land. (All that came true.) He counseled the people that exile was inevitable and not to resist. Yet he also told them exactly how to act during their time away (ch. 29) and promised the Lord would gather them back.

The question wasn't whether or not God was speaking; it was whether people were listening. Jehoiakim and Zedekiah both heard God's word and rejected it.

Thank God that the depravity and disobedience we see in II Kings 24 and II Chronicles 36 wasn't the whole story. Even in our dark age, God is speaking through His word, His Spirit and His anointed leaders. Many may ignore or even actively reject God's word. But for those who seek His word with the intent of obeying it, we are never without His voice.

Father, help me to not be distracted or discouraged by evil and failure. Thank you that even in the midst of it, You are speaking. Help me to seek and find Your voice.

MARCH 1

CAST YOUR CARES

"Cast your burden on the Lord, and He shall sustain you; He shall never permit the righteous to be moved." (Psalm 55:22)

What do you do when you're down or really upset? Many people drink or smoke or seek out destructive behaviors. But we're Christians now, and we don't do those things? Really? Maybe you have put those things behind you. If you have, praise God. But do you isolate? Eat too much? Close down inside?

God wants to take the heavy weights and concerns from us. We're not meant to bear them without Him. Too many of us are like the man carrying a heavy load along the road. A car picked him up, but he kept bearing the load. When the driver asked why he didn't put it down, he answered, "It's good of you to carry me. I couldn't possibly ask you to carry my burden as well." Let's not be that man.

What many of us miss is the word *cast*. This is crucial to the process of getting our worries and weights from our shoulders to His. Casting means to throw out, throw down, throw away—even to hurl something. Think of the energy of casting for fish. It's tossing something far away from you, with energy and focus directing where you want it to go.

Casting our cares is a three-part process. We have to know what we're casting, how to cast it, and where to cast it.

Today, let's remember the Scriptures use the word *cast* to talk about how we're to let God have our cares. Don't just lay them down—they're too easy to pick back up. Hurl them straight to Him; He's ready to receive them.

> Lord, help me to see that casting my cares upon You involves energy and focus. Your words about cares are not platitudes; they're real instruction. Help me to understand what You mean here.

MARCH 2

HE CARES ABOUT THE "LITTLE" THINGS, TOO

"But the very hairs of your head are all numbered. Do not fear therefore; you are of more value than many sparrows." (Luke 12:7); "Casting all your care upon Him, for He cares for you." (1 Peter 5:7)

What are the cares God wants us to cast upon Him? How big do they have to be to qualify for casting?

We usually think of these cares as our worries, our fears, and our serious situations. Those are included, but our cares cover a much wider territory than that. What about your *distractions*—the issues that capture your thoughts far too often, the nagging thoughts that weigh you down and that you wish you didn't keep thinking about? What thoughts keep getting in the way when you're trying to pray? These are cares, too, and ones we often keep to ourselves.

A dear friend once told me that her mother encouraged her to limit her prayers to the big things, as God was so busy that she shouldn't bother Him with "the little things." That's not our God. He sees everything and knows us as deeply as having the number of hairs on our head counted (and that must be an ever-changing number!).

Do an inventory of all things that weigh you down, that are always in the back of your mind. What are the unsolved issues, even if they don't dominate? What things lurk on the highest, farthest shelves in your mind and heart? God knows if you don't. Ask Him to reveal them, as they are there, affecting you and getting in the way.

> *I recognize that You are so big that You care about everything. Since Your thoughts and ways are not like ours, I can't judge what is a "big" thing and what's a "little" one. Help me to locate all my cares so I can cast them all upon You.*

MARK DUPRÉ

MARCH 3

WE'RE PART OF HIS PLAN

"Then the Lord said to Moses, "Now you shall see what I will do to Pharaoh. For with a strong hand he will let them go, and with a strong hand he will drive them out of his land." (Exodus 6:1); "But [Jesus] said to them, "You give them something to eat." And they said, "We have no more than five loaves and two fish ..." Then He took the five loaves and the two fish, and looking up to heaven, He blessed and broke them, and gave them to the disciples to set before the multitude." (Luke 9:13, 16)

The first Scripture above declares that the Lord is the One who will do what is necessary to Pharaoh. But we all know that Moses was instrumental throughout the entire process, from challenging Pharaoh to instigating the plagues themselves.

In Luke, we have the feeding of the five thousand. As in Exodus, it's God who provides the miraculous, but always with the full involvement of his servants. Once Jesus multiplied the food, He didn't directly feed the people, but He gave the food to His disciples to distribute the provision.

God doesn't always work alone. Many times He wants to work through His people. God could have arranged for the plagues to occur without any involvement from Moses. But He chose to critically involve Moses from beginning to end.

The feeding of the five thousand offers the same perspective. We remember the miracle-working multiplication power of God. But we can't overlook that it was the human disciples that actually did the feeding.

Sometimes we want God to do something all by Himself. But He may well want to accomplish His will with our full involvement. That involves our seeking Him, receiving His wisdom, obeying, and receiving His grace to do our part.

The next time you're asking God to do a miracle, or even a great work, be open to how He may want to fold you into the process.

> *Father, forgive me for the times when I haven't been open to being used by You as You begin to answer my prayers. I confess that sometimes I just want You to do something without me. Show me when You want me to be involved and help me let You work completely through me.*

MARCH 4

MADE IN HIS IMAGE: MALE AND FEMALE

"Do not rebuke an older man, but exhort him as a father, younger men as brothers, older women as mothers, younger women as sisters, with all purity." (1 Timothy 5:1–2)

Relating to the opposite sex may be the greatest source of joy, frustration, and humor mankind has known. It's practically a given in the non-Christian world that confusion and tension will never disappear from the male-female equation. But in Christ, we can break through the barriers and restore opposite-sex relationships to their original, fruitful intention.

Let's revisit Genesis 1:27: "So God created man in His own image ... male and female He created them." Can we hear what's in there? *Together* we're made in His image. Male-female relationships, rightly ordered, show something of God's character and nature more completely than a single gender. Deep down, rightly relating to the opposite sex is a desire in all our hearts—in singleness, marriage, the church, and the workplace.

There's no need to delve into the various ways men and women fail to relate rightly. We've all observed or participated in them. What's less obvious is God's kingdom intention for relating to our brothers and sisters: 1) no competition, 2) no flirting, 3) relating lovingly as brothers and sisters. First Timothy tells us how God wants His children to relate to one another.

You may have experienced all kinds of relational cluelessness, worldliness, or even abuse. There may not yet be a place in your heart for a godly vision of opposite-sex relationships. In the next few days, we'll look at ways to move in that direction. Today, let's recognize God has a holy, peaceful vision of His children relating in kindness, respect, and His love.

Lord, You've created us male and female for a reason. Forgive me for questioning Your wisdom here. I receive that the two genders have been created to present Your image to the world as we rightly relate to each other. Open my heart to learn and receive in this area.

MARK DUPRÉ

MARCH 5

THE OPPOSITE SEX: A KINGDOM PERSPECTIVE

"And [Jesus] answered and said to them, "Have you not read that He who made them at the beginning 'made them male and female.'" (Matthew 19:4); "Husbands ... dwell with [your wives] with understanding." (1 Peter 3:7)

Let me shock you: men and women are different! We're *supposed* to be different. There are books and articles galore that spell out the differences. They make informative, helpful, and occasionally amusing reading.

While there are plenty of exceptions, the fact is that men tend to compartmentalize more and women tend to be better multitaskers. Men are also more likely to have a success/competitive approach to life and relationships. Women lean more toward a relational, process-oriented approach. We could go on and on.

God made us male and female. He built differences in us from the start. We can make too much out of these differences, but most of us don't think enough about them.

The question for us as believers is: Are we committed to relating to the opposite sex (with their ways of thinking and acting that we might not fully understand) in a way that glorifies the Lord and expresses His love and life through us?

God has a kingdom way for us to relate to members of the opposite sex (see yesterday's reading). One way to get there is to humble ourselves in the area of understanding the other gender. Peter's exhortation to husbands in 1 Peter 3:7 has an application far beyond marriage. We're all to live in understanding with the other sex in every situation. Ultimately, we learn about the other sex not to reduce confusion, nor to gain control, but to serve the Lord by relating in the grace and wisdom that comes through true understanding.

Father, thank You that in Your wisdom, You made us male and female. Help me to understand the other sex in greater measure, not for myself, but that I may relate to them all in kingdom love and sincere appreciation for who they are.

MARCH 6

WHAT'S YOUR GOAL WITH THE OPPOSITE SEX?

"Do not rebuke an older man, but exhort him as a father, younger men as brothers, older women as mothers, younger women as sisters, with all purity." (1 Timothy 5:1–2)

What's your goal in relating to the opposite sex? Is it to relate lovingly as a brother or sister? Is it to express the love, joy, and grace of God in a way that blesses God and others?

Or are you shopping? Many guys are looking for someone to have sex with, or hang with, or be seen with. It's hoped most Christian men would run from this attitude. But men, are you shopping—for a wife, a girlfriend? Women, are you shopping—for a husband, security, a boyfriend, someone to have around on a Saturday night?

If it's human, or not available at Wal-Mart, Lowe's, or Amazon, don't shop for it. We should be receiving others for who they really are, then loving them as Christ loved us.

Single men and women: Can you handle being alone without a boyfriend or girlfriend? The irony is that if you can't, you're not yet ready for a mature relationship.

Here's the best advice anyone who's hoping/looking for a spouse could possibly receive: "But seek first the kingdom of God and His righteousness, and all these things shall be added to you" (Matthew 6:33). This sets a priority of action and thought, and promises that all these things (which includes a spouse) will *follow* that emphasis.

Let's free ourselves, and everyone else we relate to, from looking to people to fill needs God intends to fill. Let's free ourselves from the search for the kind of completion we can only find in Him.

Father, if I'm in Christ, I'm complete in You. Please show me what that means. Help me to be at peace with the opposite sex so that I can relate in love and wisdom to all, expecting nothing other than to bless them.

MARK DUPRÉ

MARCH 7

THE OPPOSITE SEX: HEALTHY BOUNDARIES

"I, therefore, the prisoner of the Lord, beseech you to walk worthy of the calling with which you were called." (Ephesians 4:1)

Most of us have a few "must-haves" and "thou shalt nots" in our relational tool bag when dealing with the opposite sex at work. There are things we do as a matter of course (e.g., treat co-workers with respect) and some things we believe we'd never do (e.g., pursue a sexual relationship with a coworker). But have we established clear and definable boundaries in terms of relating?

Ask yourself: Would my behavior or words change if my spouse/small group leader/pastor were around? Would I let any of them read my email communications with this person? Role-playing a few "what-if" scenarios with a trusted friend or spiritual adviser can help develop strategies that will free us to relate lovingly and openly.

Remember, proximity can lead to intimacy. For example, spending one-on-one time with a coworker of the opposite sex should be kept to a relative—and professional—minimum. It should be "in the light" in terms of everyone knowing that you're meeting.

The best boundaries are internal and emotional, not external or physical. The strongest and most effective standards are those held deep inside. They're more than what we do or don't do. They're part of who we are. A friend once had a co-worker tell him, "You are so married." Working in a business atmosphere of near-constant flirtation, someone carrying a virtual sign of unavailability apparently stood out. If we're content in Him and content with our various relationships, it shows—and we're safe from many possible hazards.

Lord, thank You that you care and have wisdom for all our various relationships. Show me how to act in a godly manner when I'm not in church or in a godly environment. Thank You that greater are You who is in me than he who is in the world.

MARCH 8

THE OPPOSITE SEX: GOD'S IN THE MIDDLE

"So God created man in His own image … male and female He created them." (Genesis 1:27)

Be grateful for the opposite sex. They help complete you as a person in ways that folks of your own gender cannot. This godly completeness is found in righteous male-female relationships, whether it's friend to friend, brother to sister, or coworker to coworker.

Of course, the ultimate male-female relationship is marriage. The New Testament reveals the full meaning of this particular relationship—that it is to be a reflection of the love Jesus Christ has for His church. So clearly, God is in that union. Yet since God is the center of the universe, He's also in the middle of all our relationships, including all those with the opposite sex.

The life, death, and resurrection of Jesus brought to light the ultimate purpose and meaning of marriage. It also brought healing to our gender differences. Consider what happened in Genesis. God made man and woman, but man and woman sinned. When God questioned them about it, a rift occurred between men and women. Adam's blame of Eve (and God!) is the root of all separation, anger, and even violence between the sexes.

It's easy to think of our own gender as the standard and judge from that vantage point. But Jesus is the only standard. In Christ, we recover what it means to be created in His image, male and female. As we act in a Christ-like manner toward the opposite sex, we present the image of the glory of God as He originally intended. Christ heals the break between the sexes and points us to the reality that, male and female, we're all fellow heirs of the grace of life.

> *Lord, thank You that You bring completeness to me in so many ways. I am complete in You (Colossians 2:10), and You bring healing to the gender differences, even revealing that marriage tells us more about Your love for us. Help me to be grateful for the opposite sex, and help me stop considering my gender's general ways as my standard.*

MARK DUPRÉ

MARCH 9

STRANGE ANSWERS: SEEKING KNOWLEDGE

"And [God] said, "Who told you that you were naked? Have you eaten from the tree of which I commanded you that you should not eat?" (Genesis 3:11)

Adam and Eve had been without clothes for a long time. It hadn't been a problem until now. Now "they knew" they were naked. Someone didn't have to tell them.

When the Lord asked, "Who told you?", He was probing into how they received information. He was rebuking them for seeking knowledge (and therefore, power and autonomy) on their own, apart from Him.

This question points to a sea change in humanity. Now people were seeking independently instead of receiving directly from God. The result was, and still is, fear, shame, and withdrawal from God. Seeking knowledge, a life, a career—anything—apart from a connection with Him leads to distorted perspectives coated with insecure pride. Seeking truth and salvation for ourselves outside of Christ is a vain attempt to cover ourselves with something—anything— that will minimize the hurt and stop the shame.

We can never add up simple facts and hope to come to the truth. The truth is in Jesus (John 1:17). Only the Lord can give us the proper context and perspective for what we learn or see. Knowledge is definitely power. That quest for knowledge and power apart from God was the opening salvo in the battle against His authority in our lives—and the weak spot exploited by the enemy of our souls.

Do you seek knowledge apart from God or recognize Him as Lord of all truth, including everything you learn? Let's allow God to continue redeeming Adam's sin by remembering that relationship with Him is both the foundation and capstone of everything we should ever know.

Lord, all truth is found in You. I confess that. Please forgive me for the times I seek knowledge and wisdom apart from You. Take what I know and give it meaning and context by adding and subtracting whatever You want.

MARCH 10

WRESTLING MATCH

"But I say to you, love your enemies, bless those who curse you, do good to those who hate you, and pray for those who spitefully use you and persecute you, that you may be sons of your Father in heaven." (Matthew 5:44–45)

How many enemies do you have? What makes them enemies? We know the Lord is our Defender and has His own ways of defeating our enemies. But what are *we* to do?

First, we need to reduce the number of our enemies. Many people we consider enemies might not be. For example, if someone's offended you, they may be insensitive—or perhaps you're overly sensitive. Maybe they were just having a bad day. That doesn't make them an enemy. Every parent who hears "I hate you!" from their child knows that child isn't an enemy.

The war-and-enemy model has been brought into areas where there used to simply be opponents and competitors. Today, *The Art of War* by Sun Tzu has become a business book, and politicians don't seek to win over opponents but to crush them.

Let's pull back to reality: Satan's our enemy. Disease, racism, and generational poverty are enemies. Someone with a different viewpoint or who's vying for the same position at work is not an enemy.

"We do not wrestle against flesh and blood" (Ephesians 6:12). Our real enemies are spiritual, and "the weapons of our warfare are not carnal" (2 Corinthians 10:4). That means we actually have very few enemies that are people.

Let's defeat our enemies by first reducing their number. Do an "enemy" reality check. Check off those who've simply hurt or offended you but are not set against you. Remember, our real enemies are unseen and fought with the spiritual weapons of faith, His Word, the blood of the Lamb, and the power of God.

> *Father, help me realize my enemies are few and mostly unseen. Forgive me for making some people my enemies who are not. Sharpen my spiritual vision to see my opponents and competitors as simply that. Thank You that You've given us spiritual weapons to fight our real enemies.*

MARK DUPRÉ

MARCH 11

FIGHTING WITH FORGIVENESS

"Then Jesus said, "Father, forgive them, for they do not know what they do." (Luke 23:34)

Once you've reduced your enemies to a real number (see yesterday's reading), then you can act. First, we must resist the temptation to bring judgment upon them ourselves. Remember Romans 12:19: "'Vengeance is Mine, I will repay,' says the Lord." Settle it in your heart that you have no right to seek revenge personally. This even extends to our thoughts. Fantasies about revenge need to be sacrificed to the Lord as well. Leave it in His capable hands to work something redemptive.

That's what we don't do—seek revenge. What we *do* is forgive. Jesus, radical as ever, is our model here. In the face of the worst injustice in the history of the universe, we have the most wronged person ever saying, "Father, forgive them." This had to have cut across the grain of every revenge-minded person that heard it at the time—and it still challenges us to the core. But it is our call.

The great challenge is releasing our enemies in forgiveness. As difficult as it is to say, "I forgive them," it's even harder to let them go in our hearts. Sometimes unforgiveness is our last attempt to maintain control over the situation. Sometimes it's our last false "comfort" when we've been wrongly treated. If that's the case, let God's Spirit soak into those corners of your heart so you can freely and completely release your enemies. Remember, too, that we're not releasing them into the ozone; we're releasing them *to* the Lord. He can be trusted with them.

Lord, help me forgive my enemies from the deepest part of my heart. I release to You control over what has happened in my life. I repent of taking any false comfort from holding them hostage in unforgiveness. You are trustworthy to receive every hurtful situation and wise and powerful enough to deal with those that have hurt me. Thank you for receiving it all.

MARCH 12

HOW TO LOVE YOUR ENEMIES

"You have heard that it was said, 'You shall love your neighbor and hate your enemy.'" (Matthew 5:43)

First of all, nowhere in the Old Testament does it say to hate your enemy. If it did, Jesus would have said, "It is written ..." But it wasn't written, only taught by some. What Jesus is saying here is to extend the honored commandment to love your neighbor (which he'd already expanded to the hated Samaritans) to loving your enemies. Once we've reduced our enemies and forgiven them, this is the command that remains: love them.

Remember, love is an action here, not a feeling. We are to do loving actions that reflect Romans 12:21: "Do not be overcome by evil, but overcome evil with good." Romans 12:14 tells us more specifically to "bless those who persecute you; bless and do not curse." Matthew 5 goes the next step and tells us to pray for them.

How can we love and bless? We can start by praying for their greatest needs. If they don't know the Lord, the greatest need by far is that they do. Pray for that, so that you may have another eternal brother or sister. God can do that. If your enemy is a believer and you have done all you can according to the principles of Matthew 18, then pray for their repentance, always staying humble that you might be a bigger part of the problem than you know. In both these situations, pray with the goal of blessing the other person(s), not asking God to vindicate you through what He does with them.

Lord, by faith and with Your grace and strength, I bless those that have hurt me. I bless them in Your name and pray for their greatest needs. Bring all of us to repentance.

MARCH 13

BEING A GOOD CITIZEN

"Remind them to be subject to rulers and authorities, to obey, to be ready for every good work, to speak evil of no one, to be peaceable, gentle, showing all humility to all men." (Titus 3:1–2)

As believers, we're citizens of heaven (Philippians 3:20), but God in His infinite wisdom has caused us all to be born in a certain place at a certain time. Can we honor that providential act by embracing our place and time? One of those ways is by fully engaging our roles as citizens of a country, a region, a state, and a town. If Queen Esther was born "for such a time [and place] as this" (Esther 4:14), so are we. Responsibilities will vary from person to person, but we're each called to rightly relate as citizens and members of our communities.

One simple way we do that is to "be subject to rulers and authorities." That means we obey the law, including paying taxes. Mark 12:17 couldn't be clearer: "Render to Caesar the things that are Caesar's, and to God the things that are God's." Taxation was no less intense a topic back then than it is today, especially since it was associated with the hated Roman oppressors.

Check your actions: Do you pay your taxes— all of them? Do you pay or receive payment "under the table"? That's simply another name for tax evasion, which is illegal. While there are real and understandable reasons why this is a challenge, we need to bring these concerns to God in prayer, believing Him for his power and direction. He can't bless disobedience.

Check your heart: Can you believe God is bigger than the government laws and that He'll bless your faithfulness?

> *Lord, I want to be effective in my place and time, as Esther and the sons of Issachar were (1 Chronicles 12:32). You are greater than all other forces in this world. Help me be faithful with my money, trusting You for all I need and for all You want me to have.*

MARCH 14
UNDERSTANDING OUR TIMES

"Of the sons of Issachar who had understanding of the times, to know what Israel ought to do." (1 Chronicles 12:32)

The sons of Issachar are famous for understanding what was going on around them. Ignorance, for them, was not bliss; they wanted wisdom. Ignorance is not bliss for us either, especially as those called to be faithful citizens.

How much do you understand about what is going on in your country, state, and region? Examples:

Country: In dialoguing with others, do you know that the phrase "separation of church and state" is not in the Constitution? Do you know that its original intent in Thomas Jefferson's letter of 1802 is the opposite of what many people think?

State: Do you know—for sure—what can and cannot be done in your state's schools in terms of prayer, carrying or reading a Bible, and forming a Christian club? Don't go only by what a fearful administrator might suggest.

Region: Do you know your local mayor (or congressman or state senators)? Do you pray for them?

You may or may not be called to political involvement. If you are, God bless you, direct you, and protect you—you'll need all three. But if not, you have the right and responsibility to vote. Educate yourself on the issues, and pray and vote in faith before God, which is pleasing to Him.

God has given most of us the gift of involvement in our various layers of government. We don't all have to become experts on politics or government, but we need to understand our times enough to be faithful stewards of our role as citizens.

Father, you know all my responsibilities and how much time they take. Lead me to become someone who understands the times I live in enough to be a force for truth and righteousness.

MARCH 15

A GOOD NAME

"A good name is to be chosen rather than great riches." (Proverbs 22:1)

We live in a world often ruled by marketing, branding, and polling. The truth of a person or a thing is often considered less important than what other people think is the truth. Some go so far as to say that even character isn't that important; performance is what really counts.

As Christians, we rightly back away from such concepts. We certainly can't let people's opinions hold too much sway, constantly second-guessing ourselves and keeping our eye on others instead of the Lord. But neither should we dismiss the importance of "a good name," as if reputation is of no consequence. If the Lord says it's better than great riches, there must be more to it than we might have thought.

So how do we get a good name? It's both a blessing from the Lord and the result of our actions. Take Ruth, for example, who has one of the best reputations in the Old Testament. Ruth chose to follow the one true God, leave idolatry, and honor her mother-in-law with years of kind deeds. Her reputation wasn't based on just one thing but was built step-by-step, based on her relationship with God and people. It took time, but the suspicious Moabitess living among the ancient Israelites came to be one of the most beloved and respected people in the community.

Tomorrow we'll discuss more about how the Lord uses good reputations. For now, let's agree with Ecclesiastes 7:1 that "a good name is better than precious ointment."

Lord, help me view my own reputation rightly. Help me to care about it to the degree that You do—and for Your reasons. Help me to value my good name over riches and to work to build that good name over time.

MARCH 16
A GOOD REPUTATION GOES A LONG WAY

"We give no offense in anything, that our ministry may not be blamed." (2 Corinthians 6:3)

Good reputations are important because God uses them. The first deacons of the New Testament church were chosen partly because they were men of good reputation (Acts 6:1–4). The church was able to minister with greater effectiveness because these people could be trusted to take over some duties that could free others.

Later in Acts 9, Saul, the church tormenter, is saved and becomes known as Paul. God chose a man named Ananias to explain spiritual truths to Saul. Ananias brought Saul to the other disciples and then to the synagogue to preach.

In Acts 22:12, Paul describes Ananias as "a devout man according to the law, having a good testimony with all the Jews who dwelt there." One reason Paul was so accepted in the Christian community (considering his former reputation) was the reputation of Ananias.

There are clearly some things God can trust us with if we've demonstrated enough good character to have a good name and reputation. There are special missions in the kingdom of God, like those described here, that depend on having a good name. Of course, God can use and choose whomever He wants for whatever task He appoints. But it's clear He has chosen many possessing a good reputation to do some of the most pivotal work in the early years of the church. May we have the kind of reputation that God could use for His work now.

Father, help me to develop the kind of reputation that would allow You to use me for anything. In the areas where my reputation isn't what You want, please change me so that it is.

MARK DUPRÉ

MARCH 17

WISDOM'S CRY

"Does not wisdom cry out, and understanding lift up her voice? She takes her stand on the top of the high hill, beside the way, where the paths meet. She cries out by the gates, at the entry of the city, at the entrance of the doors: "To you, O men, I call, and my voice is to the sons of men." (Proverbs 8:1–4)

Finding God's wisdom is something we all desire. But before we try to figure out a repeatable formula for how to find it, let's take a good look at the Scripture above. Wisdom isn't as elusive as it seems. In fact, it's looking to find us.

We often think wisdom is buried, like treasure. True, it's more valuable than silver, gold, and rubies (vv. 10–11). But it's not hiding. It's calling to us. Where does wisdom cry out? On a high hill, by the city gates (an especially populated and busy location). Wherever people gather or walk by, wisdom is crying out to be heard, lifting up her voice where we're most likely to be.

This isn't the conception we often have of God's wisdom. We're often so eager to find it that we forget what God's Word says about it. It's crying out to us, desiring to bring us blessings of every sort (read the rest of Proverbs 8). Maybe we're not listening. Or we're distracted. Perhaps we think attaining it is found at the end of a process of pros and cons or thinking through our options. But wisdom isn't attained by our work. It's heard and received.

Proverbs 8:34–35 says, "Blessed is the man who listens to me, watching daily at my gates, waiting at the posts of my doors. For whoever finds me finds life." Are we listening, watching, and waiting on God? Can you hear wisdom crying out to you?

Lord, as I seek wisdom throughout my life, help me to view it rightly. Thank You that wisdom is a gift that's received, not arrived at. Teach me to listen to You, to watch, to wait, and finally, to receive.

MARCH 18

PETER GETS RESTORED TO SERVE

"And the Lord said, "Simon, Simon! Indeed, Satan has asked for you, that he may sift you as wheat. But I have prayed for you, that your faith should not fail; and when you have returned to Me, strengthen your brethren." But he said to Him, "Lord, I am ready to go with You, both to prison and to death." (Luke 22:31–33)

In the Gospels, Peter's story is filled with more highs and lows than most people experience in a lifetime. He was in Jesus' inner circle, walked on water, saw Jesus transfigured, and was the first disciple to see the Lord after His resurrection. He also denied the Lord three times and "wept bitterly" at his sin.

Peter's restoration back to loving service is one of the most exquisite passages in all literature, not just the Bible. Yet the beginning of that restoration wasn't Jesus' call to Peter on the beach. It was an incident that occurred quite a while before the cross: "Now when Jesus had come into Peter's house, He saw his wife's mother lying sick with a fever. So He touched her hand, and the fever left her. And she arose and served them" (Matthew 8:14–15).

There's a lesson here, of course. We're called to serve. When we're raised up in any way, it is to continue serving. But this was for Peter, and for us, a prophetic occurrence as well. Peter saw someone laid out, unable to serve, counted out for the moment. Then Jesus touched her, and she was healed and restored to health and service.

Jesus did something He knew could bring hope to Peter later, in his darkest hour. How about you? What have you seen the Lord already do for you or others? Recalling a strong experience of God's power and faithfulness can be a valuable, encouraging memory for you someday when it's greatly needed.

Lord, thank You for the prophetic act of hope and encouragement You placed into Peter's life. I believe that's a picture of Your heart. Please bring to remembrance those things You've placed in my life, so that I'm reminded in the future of what You've done in my past.

MARCH 19

JESUS' FIRST QUESTION TO PETER

"So when they had eaten breakfast, Jesus said to Simon Peter, "Simon, son of Jonah, do you love Me more than these?" He said to Him, "Yes, Lord; You know that I love You." He said to him, "Feed My lambs." (John 21:15)

Imagine how Peter might have felt after Jesus' death—disappointed in himself and feeling like a failure. But the Lord had risen! And He was waiting on the shore. Peter put on his outer garment before jumping into the water. He was eager to see Jesus, but he wanted to be properly attired. Was he feeling ashamed, wanting to cover up? Was it simply a sign of respect? We don't know.

What we can know is the markedly different attitude Peter displayed next. Previously full of himself, Peter was humble, careful, and measured in response to Jesus' questions. We'll look at the first question today.

Peter's simple response was, "Yes, Lord, You know that I love You." He refrained from saying "more than these," dodging the question Jesus actually asked. A work has been done here. Peter might have expected a rebuke or to be relegated to the least of the apostles. So when asked this question, Peter humbly responded, "You know," acknowledging that Jesus knew everything—including Peter's foolishness, self-deception, and pride.

Then came three of the most profound words Peter would ever hear: "Feed My lambs." What stunning words of healing and redemption! No rebuke. No "you're forgiven, but...." No casting away. It wasn't over! He still had a call!

Have you ever felt that you lost your call because of a grievous sin? Then you can relate to Peter. Imagine the relief he felt that his disobedience—even denying the Lord directly—didn't cancel his calling. Here is the heart of God on display.

Father, You are forgiving and love to restore. Thank you for restoring me—all the many times You have. May I always remember that as I humble myself and come to You as Peter did, that I don't have to be afraid of what You will say to me. Help me to hold out that same hope to others who despair over what they've done.

MARCH 20

OPENING THE WOUND TO HEAL

"He said to him again a second time, "Simon, son of Jonah, do you love Me?" He said to Him, "Yes, Lord; You know that I love You." He said to him, "Tend My sheep." (John 21:16)

After Jesus told Peter to "feed My lambs," He threw him a major curve by asking him once again if he loved Him. Peter's answer was similar to his first. Jesus' response was similar but significantly different: "Tend My sheep." "Tend" means to keep as a vocation rather than a one-time event. It's the role of a shepherd. So, the call is more than to care for the young or spiritually immature "lambs." Perhaps Jesus was going to entrust Peter with greater responsibility than he initially thought.

The third time Jesus asked Peter if he loved him opened the deepest wound yet. John 21:17 says, "Peter was grieved." Three questions echoed the three denials, and Peter knew it. All the shame, guilt, and regret must have rushed to the surface. Peter might even have felt set up, with Jesus artfully pointing out Peter's great sin.

Then Jesus shocked him yet again: "Feed My sheep." Jesus opened the whole messy incident, but only to heal Peter and let him know he'd not only been forgiven but affirmed in his calling.

The Lord loves us enough to go to the deepest, most painful place with us. Yet it's never to condemn, only to heal. Jesus was subtle with Peter, indirectly recalling his three denials. Nonetheless, it must have cut Peter to the quick. The Lord may choose to open a wound more than we want. But let us see from this example His incredible tenderness in the process and His desire to heal what's behind it all.

Thank You for loving me enough to want to heal me completely. Help me to be as humble as Peter and accept your dealings with me, knowing that You are redemptive, and Your intentions are to restore completely. Go as deep as You want. Thank You that Your grace, love, and healing go deeper than my sin.

MARK DUPRÉ

MARCH 21

GOD TURNS OUR REGRET INTO SERVICE

"Most assuredly, I say to you, when you were younger, you girded yourself and walked where you wished; but when you are old, you will stretch out your hands, and another will gird you and carry you where you do not wish." This He spoke, signifying by what death he would glorify God. And when He had spoken this, He said to him, "Follow Me." (John 21:18–19)

In his three restorative questions to Peter, Jesus reopened a wound, then demonstrated His full forgiveness for Peter's denials and sins of pride. Jesus finished this talk with a prophetic word about how Peter was going to die. But there's more here than a simple look into the future. This was a promise that Peter was indeed going to be restored to service. He was going to glorify the Lord the rest of his life. The Lord's omniscience was turned from something shaded in sadness to a joyful light of promise.

To complete the work of restoration, Jesus simply said, "Follow Me." This was the call Jesus gave to the disciples in Matthew 4 and Luke 5. But "follow Me" was also a way of saying, "We're done with this now. Turn your regret into service. Leave your sadness, pick up your call, and walk with Me again."

Jesus wasn't content to simply say Peter was forgiven. Peter needed to know He was deeply known by the Lord and still forgiven for everything. Then he needed to be reaffirmed in his calling.

If the last thing you heard from the Lord is "I forgive you" and nothing more, continue the conversation. He has more to say and do. His words and touch bring us to the present and point us toward the future. He doesn't intend to leave us broken and forgiven, but forgiven, reinstated, and encouraged. That may take time and involve the wisdom of others, but restoring us to serve is the heart of God.

Thank you, Lord, that You have the heart to restore fully. Help me to hear everything You want to say to me when I fall. May Your work with Peter be a constant encouragement to go as deep as You want so that Your restoration may be as complete as You desire.

MARCH 22

PREPARING FOR THE FUTURE

"For I am God, and there is no other; I am God, and there is none like Me, declaring the end from the beginning." (Isaiah 46:9–10); "My brethren, count it all joy when you fall into various trials, knowing that the testing of your faith produces patience." (James 1:2–3)

Ever face a trial and wonder what you did wrong? Where did I sin? We try to make sense of things by looking for a direct connection from our past. A big part of why we can't make sense of things is because we keep looking to our pasts to explain what's going on in the present.

Think about Job. Scripture makes clear his friends were wrong. What Job endured had nothing to do with what he did wrong. God was doing a profound work in Job, one he learned to embrace. And millions have been encouraged by his words.

The point is that many, perhaps most, of our trials are because of what God sees in our futures, not what we see in our pasts. Yes, we reap what we sow, but even that is tempered greatly by God's grace and mercy.

The Lord sees the end from the beginning— our lives as much as the universe. What we call trials are often His preparations. We need training and preparation for what's ahead in this life and the next. He knows best how to do that.

Have you ever been able to look back and have some sense of how God used things in your past for your good and the good of others? The next time you're in a trial, remember you might be reaping, or you might be in the middle of a chastisement (Hebrews 12:5 6). But you might also be in the middle of an important preparation for your future.

Lord, thank You that You see my whole life and that You're a wise trainer who knows how to prepare us for our futures. Thank You for Your continued love and faithfulness, for Your training me for my future, and for Your ability to turn even a reaping or chastisement into good.

MARK DUPRÉ

MARCH 23

DO YOU WANT TO BE MADE WELL?

"Now a certain man was there who had an infirmity thirty-eight years. When Jesus saw him lying there, and knew that he already had been in that condition a long time, He said to him, "Do you want to be made well?" The sick man answered Him, "Sir, I have no man to put me into the pool when the water is stirred up; but while I am coming, another steps down before me." (John 5:5–7)

Jesus performed miracles for many reasons. Yes, He showed God's love and power in action. But God is always doing more than one thing. Explaining who Jesus is—and revealing the heart of God—is always a part of it.

This man's healing attracts our greatest attention. But there's far more here. Jesus knew he'd "been in that condition a long time." Jesus knows your condition, how long you've dealt with it, and the pain it's brought. He also knows where you are—not just physically, but spiritually, emotionally, and psychologically.

Also, this story tells us that divine opportunities that come our way may not come again. This man had to connect with Jesus to receive healing. When the Lord draws near, do we connect, listen, and do what He wants? Or do we push Him away, hoping to engage at a more convenient time? We hate it when people do that to us—and we hurt God and ourselves when we do that to the Lord.

This man also demonstrated patience and faith: certainly someone at some time would lower him into the waters. While his healing happened differently than expected (a lesson for us all!), it did happen. If he hadn't been there when Jesus visited, he wouldn't have been positioned to receive his healing.

Do you have a specific idea of *how* God is going to move? Let this man's story encourage you to continue trusting the Lord, but not to limit Him to answering in a particular way.

Lord, thank You that You answer prayers and heal. Help me to stay constant in faith and to be where You want me so You can meet me. I pray that You'll answer all that I pray in the ways that You want to, and that You'll give me the grace to see those answers.

MARCH 24

DO WE REALLY WANT WHAT WE'RE PRAYING FOR?

"Jesus said to him, "Rise, take up your bed and walk." And immediately the man was made well, took up his bed, and walked." (John 5:8–9)

According to Scripture, after this man was healed, he moved. He picked up his bed and made his way to the temple. He was willing to move on to the next stage of life as a healed man.

What did he give up? Perhaps a life of begging. Since he couldn't have gotten to the pool on his own for nearly four decades, he must have depended on others for nearly everything.

The question for us is: Do we really want what we're praying for? Are we ready to receive and act on God's answer? Healing or any similar deliverance can exact a price—we'll need to change.

Are you willing to leave your former dependencies? To redefine yourself? Are you ready to leave every excuse and take on the full responsibilities of life, as this man in John 5 appears to have done?

The world says familiarity breeds contempt. But familiarity breeds comfort as well. Many of us prefer to stay where we are rather than deal with the change and challenges answered prayer might bring. Some folks would rather complain than take that new job or remain lonely rather than risk the joys and challenges of forging relationships.

If God heals and delivers you, can you press forward into a new life? If He opens that door, are you ready to walk through it? Whatever old mat we may have—weakness, an old identity, or even the entire rhythm of your life—let's pick it up and walk when the Lord brings what we ask for.

Father, thank You for Your desire to heal and that You hear and answer old prayers. Help me to pick up my mat and walk when You answer mine.

MARK DUPRÉ

MARCH 25

THE CLASSROOM OF COMPARISON

"Imitate me, just as I also imitate Christ. (1 Corinthians 11:1) Therefore I urge you, imitate me." (1 Corinthians 4:16)

As long as there are people, there will be comparison. Unfair comparisons can hurt, of course. But comparison can also be a learning moment for us all.

For example, by comparing ourselves to others, we can learn how to be more loving, how to bring grace to difficult situations, and how to have godlier perspectives on any number of topics. If we consider ourselves lifelong learners, and everyone else as the source of life lessons, we can learn every day.

The challenge is resisting comparison that's accompanied by the enemy's attacks. Noticing someone is more gracious than you, for instance, can stir up voices that generalize and condemn: "See—you're a failure in this area." Whether it sounds like the devil or like us, that talk is straight from our enemy. The fault isn't comparison per se; it's listening to the negative voices that accompany it.

Let's learn from Paul and release the sanctifying power of comparison by redirecting our focus. Instead of listening to the enemy, let's cut a new mental pathway and embrace the many learning opportunities out there provided by God through the people around us.

When it comes to others, let's free them and us by taking on the role of the continual learner. Let's grab all the lessons of love, grace, and wisdom we can. Yes, a few folks may provide lessons of what not to do ("Wow—note to self: Don't ever do that!"). But if we have the right perspective and imitate others as they imitate Christ, we can grow every day.

> *Lord, the enemy has robbed me of so many learning moments because of his accusations. Help me to submit to You first and then resist the devil. Give me eyes to see and a heart to learn all the many lessons in the Spirit that You have out there for me*

MARCH 26
VICTORY AHEAD

"Now thanks be to God who always leads us in triumph in Christ, and through us diffuses the fragrance of His knowledge in every place. For we are to God the fragrance of Christ among those who are being saved and among those who are perishing. To the one we are the aroma of death leading to death, and to the other the aroma of life leading to life." (2 Corinthians 2:14–16)

God is leading us in victory—always. It's not evident everywhere yet. But don't be fooled—it's here! This Scripture says we're on a path of triumph! Because of His death and resurrection, the kingdoms of this world are becoming the kingdoms of our Lord and of His Christ! God is advancing!

To see the Lord leading in triumph, let's look at one of His Old Testament victories. The book of Joshua tells the story of the spies who scoped out the Promised Land. They told Joshua, "Truly the Lord has delivered all the land into our hands, for indeed all the inhabitants of the country are fainthearted because of us" (Joshua 2:24). In chapter 6, we have the resounding victory at Jericho.

We don't have to be afraid! Satan is the one running scared—the one who knows his time is short! (Revelation 12:12). He'll do anything to prevent us from living in that truth.

So does this mean we'll move forward in continual victory, no matter what? Well, "of the increase of His government and peace there will be no end" (Isaiah 9:7), so we know God's kingdom will always be moving forward. The question is whether or not we'll move with it. Either way, His path is one of victory.

The Lord never "tries" anything or "makes a stab" at accomplishing something. He knows what He's doing every step along the way. He always has a victorious end in mind, and His paths always lead to that end.

Lord, I haven't always seen that You're a victorious warrior. I believe in the "good end" of heaven, but I don't always see or understand Your victory before I get there. But Your word says You always lead us in triumph in Christ. I believe Your word, and I stand with You in what You say.

MARK DUPRÉ

MARCH 27

VICTORY OVER OUR SIN

"But the children of Israel committed a trespass regarding the accursed things, for Achan ... took of the accursed things; so the anger of the Lord burned against the children of Israel." (Joshua 7:1)

Joshua had just experienced the first triumph in the Promised Land—victory at Jericho. He'd followed God's lead in every detail, and the battle was a resounding success. Yet Joshua made a classic error with little Ai, a city which "should have been easy" to conquer. He presumed victory, never took time to seek the Lord, and proceeded with a plan that made sense to him. It was a terrible defeat.

When Joshua asked God why, He admonished Israel for transgressing His covenant through their deceit and theft of accursed goods (Joshua 7:1, 10-11). Later, when Joshua once again followed God's lead, Ai was taken.

The only thing that can slow down God's victory path in your life is sin. But Jesus paid the penalty for all our sin! Asking, "Lord, where am I missing it?" is one of the best prayers you can pray. The answer may be "nowhere," but it never hurts to ask—and to listen to God's answer.

If there is sin in our lives, this is where God's victory should be seen next. Our plan may have been for His triumph elsewhere. Yet on our way to that triumph, God wants us to experience the victory of repentance and forgiveness.

God knows we're going to stumble along the triumphal path. So after the initial shock of discovery, thank Him for revealing it and again for providing the victory. Remember, He knew it was there in the pathway all along—even before He called you to walk there!

Lord, I see that sin can prevent me from experiencing Your victories and slow me down from walking in triumph. Thank You that as I repent of the sin You show me, I can experience Your victory right away—over my sin and over the condemnation the enemy wants to bring along with it. Thank You that Your path of victory has always included Your provision for my sin.

MARCH 28
EXTENDING GOD'S GRACE TO OTHERS

"As each one has received a gift, minister it to one another, as good stewards of the manifold grace of God." (1 Peter 4:10)

Grace is often defined as "unmerited favor." Yet grace involves so much more. It empowers us to do the will of God, to forgive when it's hard, to do what would be impossible on our own—from walking in wisdom to building businesses to loving the unlovely.

The grace of God is extended to us in many forms: in salvation, in our spiritual and natural gifts, in our accomplishments, and in our experiences. As we're called to freely give because we've freely received (Matthew 10:8), we are called to both receive grace and to extend it to others.

How do we do that? One way is to be like Christ in His sacrificial love. Consider what He gave up (Philippians 2:7–8). He gave up the most for the sake of the least. If He extended that kind of selfless love to us, we're obliged to extend it to others.

Every gift of time, every act of service, every favor we do—these are reflections of the sacrificial love and grace of Jesus. By deliberately losing something (time, energy, focus, the chance to do something else) so that others may gain, we extend His grace.

If we say we want to be like Jesus, we need to look for ways we can be like Him. He gave up power, glory, and position because that is what He had. What do you have? Time? Money? Opportunity? Talent? Imitate our Lord by sacrificing that for others, and you will be a good steward of the grace of God.

Lord, Your sacrifice for me is beyond my comprehension. But I thank You for how much You sacrificed for me and for all You died to save. Let me show my gratitude to You by extending the grace You've given me to others. Show me how I can imitate You by forgoing things I call "mine" for the sake of another.

MARK DUPRÉ

MARCH 29

TAKING THE LOW PLACE OF GRACE

"And being found in appearance as a man, He humbled Himself and became obedient to the point of death, even the death of the cross." (Philippians 2:8)

One way we extend grace to others is by positioning ourselves rightly. This is called humility. Taking the low place puts us in a place where we can receive God's grace. Once we receive grace, it's easier to extend it.

We don't "achieve" humility. It's a matter of getting real—knowing that God is God, we're not, and there's nothing in us apart from Christ than can extend God's kingdom or bring genuine spiritual good to anyone else. Thankfully, we have the great model in Jesus.

When we live in gratitude for His amazing grace, we remember how unworthy we are for His sacrifice on our behalf. When this is real to us, we're open to extending that awesome grace to anyone.

We all have people we relate to that are difficult to deal with. There's a special code for them: EGR (Extra Grace Required). When our response is based on their works rather than our received grace, we get irritated and annoyed. When they behave as we think they should, it's generally easy to be kind and gracious. But if we continue to receive God's grace and let it flow through us, it doesn't matter how they behave. Here we find the classic tension between grace and works—their works draw forth our received grace.

We never see Jesus acting small, impatient, or condescending. He took the eternally low place, received grace from His Father, and extended it to everyone in His path. We have His example. Once we find our own low place, we can do the same thing.

Jesus, if You died for me and gave so much, and I've received that gift, then I have it within me to extend the grace You extended to me to others. Help me to deeply understand the manifold aspects of Your sacrifice so I can rightly minister the manifold grace of God to others (1 Peter 4:10).

MARCH 30

EXTENDING GRACE THROUGH OUR MOUTHS

"Let no corrupt word proceed out of your mouth, but what is good for necessary edification, that it may impart grace to the hearers". (Ephesians 4:29)

Here's another opportunity to extend grace—through our speech. To understand Ephesians 4:29, we need a little context. In the previous verse, Paul says: "Let him who stole steal no longer, but rather let him labor, working with his hands what is good, that he may have something to give him who has need."

Note the progression. Some individuals used their hands to steal, to take things. Now they use their hands to work, to create, to earn a living. In turn, the former thief now has something to give those in need.

Like the thief who starts to do honest work, we can repurpose our speech to bring blessing. We all know what damage we can inflict with our tongues (check out James 3). We need to actively think before speaking, aligning our will and our hearts to edify and impart grace with our words. We have a great opportunity to build the kingdom, to extend Christ's love, to help others achieve their spiritual destiny, and to express the truth in a situation. We can do great good through our mouths!

What do we have to lose? There are sacrifices: the great feeling of expressing ourselves, telling other people off, and unloading. Sometimes we simply enjoy the sound of our own voices.

Yet look at what others may gain. They can be built up, encouraged, made wiser, shown a better way—all through the fruit of our lips. Remember the repentant thief's journey—and that God purposes our mouths to follow that same path.

> *Father, help me to make my mouth an instrument of righteousness (Romans 6:13) and an avenue of Your grace that builds up the hearer. I don't always think of verbal expression that way. Please change my thinking and my way of communicating to reflect Your purposes for me.*

MARK DUPRÉ

MARCH 31

BEING CONTENT

"Let your conduct be without covetousness; be content with such things as you have. For He Himself has said, 'I will never leave you nor forsake you.'" (Hebrews 13:5); "Not that I speak in regard to need, for I have learned in whatever state I am, to be content." (Philippians 4:11)

These verses give us a command to be content and present a model of contentment in Paul. We read these verses, nod in agreement, and wish we were like that. We know we should cultivate gratitude and express it regularly to the Lord. We admire (or are jealous of) people who are content and have a deep desire to be like them. Yet counting our blessings and expressing our thanks hasn't proven to be enough.

Being content sounds simple, yet it's comprised of many elements, some seen and some not. We try dealing with these elements one at a time. But the enemy plays with this approach, usually adding the lie that our real joy is connected to something found in the natural world.

There's one more thing to be done: repent of our discontent. If we're in Christ, we have no real reason to be discontent. It's our portion in Christ to have the peace and joy contentment brings.

If you're not content, why not ask God to forgive your discontent? Take on contentment in the name of the Lord, in faith, as a gift from God gratefully received. Then hold onto it like the most stubborn kid playing King of the Hill—just let God be the Defender of it instead of you.

Contentment is a matter of the heart, a place we find in the spirit. It's not a result of possessions, achievement, or waiting for that one more thing to happen. It's ours now in Christ, and we may be just one real repentance away from enjoying it.

Lord, I recognize You have called me to contentment. Forgive me for living in discontent. I take on contentment as a gift from You and ask that You show me how to stand still and see Your salvation as I hold it against any attack from the enemy. Thank You that those battles are only meant to strengthen my ownership of that place of contentment.

APRIL 1
LEAVE YOUR GIFT AT THE ALTAR

"Therefore if you bring your gift to the altar, and there remember that your brother has something against you, leave your gift there before the altar, and go your way. First be reconciled to your brother, and then come and offer your gift." (Matthew 5:23–24)

Matthew 5 paints a picture of the moment when an Israelite would hand a sacrificial offering to the priest at the temple, seeking the Lord's forgiveness, but then remembers someone has a complaint (a legitimate one, from the context) against him. Quite inconveniently and going against conventional views of common sense and efficiency of time, the Lord tells him to leave the gift there—in the middle of the process of sacrifice—and go get reconciled.

First, notice the urgency that defies our logic. Why not finish out the process of sacrifice and then go to the offended brother? Stopping a sacrifice in mid-offering is a dramatic move. Jesus must think that division in the body of Christ is such an important issue it should be tended to immediately. There are many lessons we can learn from this, but let me reduce them to two:

Take care of personal relationship conflicts quickly. While there are no more animal sacrifices to interrupt, this picture tells us that speed and direct action are of utmost importance.

This also reminds us that growing spiritually with Jesus is inextricably interwoven with our relationships with our brothers and sisters. He's placing personal relations—and their reconciliation—smack dab in the middle of our worship of the Lord.

We offer sacrifices of worship, love, and service. Let's be open to hearing from the Lord that a human situation must be attended to if we're to complete the sacrifice we are offering to God.

Lord, help me see the deep connection You see between how we worship You and how we are to love our neighbor, specifically our Christian brothers and sisters. I repent from artificially separating them or for letting my idea of convenience and ease override what Your Word is telling me.

MARK DUPRÉ

APRIL 2

WILL YOU PASS ON YOUR INHERITANCE?

"And if you are Christ's, then you are Abraham's seed, and heirs according to the promise." (Galatians 3:29); "I will make you a great nation; I will bless you and make your name great, and you shall be a blessing. I will bless those who bless you, and I will curse him who curses you; and in you all the families of the earth shall be blessed." (Genesis 12:2–3)

Christians are dynasty builders. We have the family name, the wealth, the wisdom, the keys to the kingdom, the armies, the supplies, and most importantly, the mandate. Our biggest problem is that we often don't even know it.

We have a priceless spiritual inheritance in Christ. The reason stories as diverse as *The Prince and the Pauper* and *The Princess Diaries* resonate so deeply is that there's a desire and a recognition that we have something—some position, some wealth—that has our name on it that we can own and even pass on.

What's our inheritance in Christ? To begin with, we're forgiven and have peace with God. (We could just stop here.) But we're also justified, sanctified, given hope, and granted perseverance through trials. The love of God has been poured into our hearts, we're saved from wrath, given grace that abounds, and transferred from slavery to freedom. We are alive to God, free to obey Him, delivered from condemnation, and adopted as His children. We've received spiritual gifts to serve others, and we have access to the throne of grace and the protection of the Most High.

Don't think for a moment that you're not a king or queen with great possessions. To use a powerful Old English word, *reckon* it to yourself that you indeed have a mighty inheritance. You may not yet know what to do with it, but if you're open to it, you'll learn how to use it well and how to pass it on.

Lord, I acknowledge that in You I have a great inheritance, one that's so large I admit that I don't know how to handle it. Open my eyes to see all You've given me, and train me to steward it well.

APRIL 3

RECEIVING OUR INHERITANCE

"O Lord, You are the portion of my inheritance and my cup; You maintain my lot. The lines have fallen to me in pleasant places; yes, I have a good inheritance." (Psalm 16:5–6)

This psalmist checked out his inheritance. He was familiar enough with it to ascertain its dimensions, its boundaries, and the "pleasantness" of what he saw. Do you consider your "inheritance" what your family, or life, has handed you? Or are you focused on what God's given you and who He says you are?

We read about Esau despising his inheritance and shake our heads in disbelief. But to some extent, we're guilty of the same thing. Esau's pathetic substitute for his father's blessing and a double portion of his estate was some bread and red lentil stew (Genesis 25:29–31).

What have you received from God so far? If you're a believer, you have a testimony. You have the Word in your mind and in your heart. You have salvation, the demonstrated faithfulness of God, and an understanding of what the truth is. You have God's presence with you at all times. You have His power and grace. That's a great inheritance—and it's just the beginning!

What is your "red stew"? Is it a moment of pleasure—drinking, drugs, or sex? Is it dating or planning to marry an unbeliever (someone without an inheritance)? Is your "red stew" money, the desire for fame, or always being focused on having a good time? Is it laziness? Jacob knew Esau's weaknesses, and he exploited them. Our enemy knows our weaknesses too. He wants to use them as sorry replacements for the greater things God has in store for us to receive.

Lord, please identify my "red stew" weaknesses, the things I substitute for Your inheritance to me. Open my eyes to see the birthright my new birth has provided for me, and teach me to be more assertive in receiving what You're giving.

APRIL 4

YOU HEAD UP A DYNASTY

"He who overcomes shall inherit all things, and I will be his God and he shall be my son." (Revelation 21:7)

Did you inherit something negative from your family? Is it divorce, drinking, drugs, fornication, the curse of illegitimacy, or a spirit of control? The issue isn't what we've inherited. What's important is the question "Is it going to stop with me?" Or are you going to pass it on? We're all going to pass on an inheritance of some kind. What kind will ours be?

We need to have the vision of being dynasty builders—concerned with more than just our own lives. Will the mudslide of anger, hatred, sloth, or other family weaknesses get passed down, or will I overcome in the name of Jesus and put an end to it in my life and generation? It's not what I inherited from my parents that counts—it's what I'm continually inheriting from my heavenly Father!

How do we overcome? Read the Word with focus—find out what you don't need to be living under! Learn the rules of this kingdom. Dorothy's amazement at being in Oz should be a pale picture of our amazement of being in a new kingdom where the rules are different, the enemies more defined, and the rewards far greater than the world we came from.

Where is your inheritance going? Even if you're single and childless, you're part of an extended family that you could affect for generations. Let's live and overcome not just for your sake, but also for theirs.

You are at the head of a dynasty. Know that. Overcome for your spiritual descendants. Continue to receive His inheritance. Then pass it on.

Lord, forgive me for seeing myself so individually. You see me as the head of a dynasty, much of which I'll never see in this lifetime. Teach me to overcome for their sakes and pass on all that I've inherited from You.

APRIL 5

RESTORE AND MORE

"And the Lord spoke to Moses, saying: "If a person sins and commits a trespass against the Lord by lying to his neighbor about what was delivered to him for safekeeping, or about a pledge, or about a robbery, or if he has extorted from his neighbor ... then it shall be, because he has sinned and is guilty, that he shall restore what he has stolen, or the thing which he has extorted." (Leviticus 6:1–2, 4)

When we sin against someone, we should do whatever it takes to not only ask for forgiveness, but to restore. If we lie, or simply find out that what we shared with others wasn't the truth, we should work to set the record straight. If we take, we should give back and more. Simply saying "sorry" isn't usually enough to make up for the damage caused by our sins against others. Genuinely repentant people want to restore and bless those they've hurt. The Old Testament principle of restoration should be our guide to any kind of sin we've committed against another person.

Yet there's a precious addition here to the issue of restoration. Leviticus 6:2 reminds us that sins against others are also sins against the Lord Himself. While we should be aware of the effect our sins may have on others, and work diligently to honor the principle of restoration, we need to remember that we have to connect directly with the Lord as well. People can forgive our sins against them, but only God can wash away our sins. Sometimes realizing our sin against others can be so difficult to handle that we forget that getting things right includes seeking God's forgiveness as well.

If we've sinned against someone else, there are things we need to hear, learn, and do that we can only receive directly by going to the Lord and opening our repentant hearts before Him. Let's never leave Him out of the process of repentance and restoration involving others.

Lord, forgive me for not seeking Your forgiveness as well as others' when I sin against someone else. You have something You want to do in me when I sin. I want to be faithful in my repentance toward others and toward You—for their sake, my sake, and Your sake.

APRIL 6

RUBBLE ROUSER

"Then I said to them, "You see the distress that we are in, how Jerusalem lies waste, and its gates are burned with fire. Come and let us build the wall of Jerusalem, that we may no longer be a reproach." ... So they said, "Let us rise up and build." Then they set their hands to this good work. (Nehemiah 2:17, 18)

Nehemiah's story of returning to Jerusalem and building up the city walls is full of reality checks and encouragements. He faced opposition from outside enemies and even his own people. Yet he was consistently patient and prayerful, and his mission was crowned with success.

Hidden within his story is a beautiful picture of how God works with our lives. Nehemiah 2 tells us how he went to survey the damage that had been done. After assessing the damage, Nehemiah repaired, restored, and rebuilt using parts of the wall and other structures that were already there.

When we come to Christ, God begins to do the same thing. God "surveys" the damage the enemy has done (and that we, to be honest, have contributed to by our sin). His plan is then based on what is reusable and what needs complete replacement.

What kind of rubble did you have when you came to Christ? What rubble remains? Broken relationships, abortion, disappointment, abuse, loss? God knows your rubble and knows exactly how to sift through it all, using parts of that rubble to build you up.

God can take anything we've done or that's been done to us and use it in His rebuilding program. If God created us, doesn't He have the wisdom and power to know how to re-create and rebuild us? He takes our sin and washes it away. He takes our sorrow, defeats, and disappointments and uses them in our rebuilding process. Nothing—nothing—is wasted once God gets His hands on it!

God, I have a lot of rubble in my life. Take away what is hurtful to me and others. But please transform and redeem the rest. Thank You that You know exactly how to rebuild, restore, and repair.

APRIL 7
ANOTHER TOUCH

"Then He came to Bethsaida; and they brought a blind man to Him, and begged Him to touch him. So He took the blind man by the hand and led him out of the town. And when He had spit on his eyes and put His hands on him, He asked him if he saw anything. And he looked up and said, "I see men like trees, walking." Then He put His hands on his eyes again and made him look up. And he was restored and saw everyone clearly." (Mark 8:22–25)

Sometimes context is everything when we work to understand what the Lord is saying. Yes, Jesus gave the blind man sight here, demonstrating his power to heal and encouraging us to not despise gradual healings.

But there's more. There's a reason this story of physical healing is placed right after a story about his disciples' spiritual blindness (Mark 8:13–21). For one, Jesus was healing their spiritual blindness step by step, teaching by teaching, miracle by miracle.

For another, the story suggests that we might make the mistake of believing we've received everything from God because we've genuinely been touched in an area. Could we hear Jesus if He asked us the same question he asked the half-blind man? Could we admit the truth, that we realize we only see in part and need another touch from His healing hand? Perhaps there is a clue in how Jesus finished the healing: He touched his eyes again and *made him look up.*

Let's be honest with God about our continual need for Him. Let's be real in knowing that we're on a journey of spiritual sight and growth. And let's look up and behold Him as He puts His hands on us. What patience He has with us, and what grace!

Lord, put Your hands on me again. I admit I only see in part and need more of You. Until I see You face-to-face, I'll always need another touch. Until then, I look up to behold You, the giver of every good gift.

APRIL 8

DON'T JUDGE – HELP!

"And why do you look at the speck in your brother's eye, but do not perceive the plank in your own eye? Or how can you say to your brother, 'Brother, let me remove the speck that is in your eye,' when you yourself do not see the plank that is in your own eye? Hypocrite! First remove the plank from your own eye, and then you will see clearly to remove the speck that is in your brother's eye." (Luke 6:41–42)

This well-known Scripture is often used to discourage us from judging others. After all, we have our own "stuff" to deal with. But a closer look at this passage reveals that it doesn't simply say, "Don't judge others."

It really says that while we're noticing others' weaknesses, we need to do two things. First, we need to let God deal with our problems and weaknesses, which are often far greater than those of the folks around us. (Planks are a lot larger than specks!)

But it's part two of the Scripture that tends to get overlooked. Once we've placed ourselves in a humble position and seen our own weaknesses in His light, we're now positioned to actually help the other person. A plank in our eye will obviously distort our vision, and removing a speck from someone else's eye will take all the visual acuity and accuracy we can muster.

There are many ironies in the tension between our sinful world and the kingdom of God. One is that our own sinfulness causes us to view others' sins inaccurately. This renders us unable to help. Once we take a low place and let God work in us, we're equipped—and called—to help others. Once the plank is gone, our spiritual perspective is cleared up. Then we have the grace, love, and wisdom to know how to help others. If we don't have that grace, love, and wisdom, perhaps we might still have that plank.

> *Lord, help me see the many planks that I have, not just so that I don't judge, but so I can actually help someone else. Please remind me by Your spirit when my planks are getting in the way.*

APRIL 9
POSITIONED FOR BLESSING

"Then the Lord spoke to Moses, saying: "On the first day of the month you shall set up the tabernacle of the tent of meeting" ... So Moses finished the work. Then the cloud covered the tabernacle of meeting, and the glory of the Lord filled the tabernacle." (Exodus 40:1–2, 33–34)

The Lord gave Moses precise instructions on how to set up the tabernacle in the desert. It was a complex task. It took time to prepare everything and to put each item in its proper place. (Look at Exodus 40 for the details.) After Moses finished the work, the glory of the Lord filled the tabernacle.

We often want the glory of the Lord without doing the work that Moses did. He was obedient to the Lord and had put everything into His order. It appears clear from the Scriptures that nothing that God asked was left undone. Everything in the sphere Moses was responsible for was in order.

How about you? Is your life in God's order? As far as you know, is there order in your relationships—with your husband, your wife, your children, your parents, your friends, your pastor, your boss, your neighbor? Is there a relationship that has gotten too big and overly important, or is there one that's been neglected and is in need of repair?

Is everything in its right place? The Lord told Moses exactly what to put in the tabernacle and where to put it. Do you have an assurance that the various elements of your life are what should be there and that they're in God's order?

Our Lord wants to bless us. Are we rightly positioned to receive those blessings? His glory falls as we fall into His order. Start putting in order those things that are askew and just watch what happens.

Lord, I believe that You desire to bless Your people. Please show me anything that is out of order in my life so that You can bless me—not only for my sake, but because You clearly want to.

APRIL 10

STEWARDSHIP, NOT OWNERSHIP

"Know that the Lord, He is God; It is He who has made us, and not we ourselves; we are His people and the sheep of His pasture." (Psalm 100:3)

Then God blessed them, and God said to them, "Be fruitful and multiply; fill the earth and subdue it; have dominion over the fish of the sea, over the birds of the air, and over every living thing that moves upon the earth." (Genesis 1:28)

Everything belongs to the Lord—everything! He's not only Creator, but owner. This isn't a hard concept. So what's the problem? The famous seagulls in *Finding Nemo* remind us of the problem with their calls of "Mine, mine, mine!"

We can have a hard time with God's Word in this area. We might theoretically agree that everything is His. But if we look deeper into the spiritual truths of ownership, we realize that if we're not owners, we must have another role. We're stewards, those who manage someone else's property, finances, or household affairs.

Being caretakers brings a change in perspective and course of action. If someone else owns something, they get to decide how it's used. A good steward makes certain every resource is used in a way that reflects the owner's interests.

Consider the earth. Contrary to many a bumper sticker, we don't belong to the earth. The earth belongs to the Lord. As stewards, He's given us authority over the earth. We need to have the same respect for our planet that we would give to anything lent to us for safekeeping.

Somewhere in the debate on climate change, global warming, and fracking lies a principle of stewardship. We're called to have dominion, not to pillage, strip areas bare, or dump toxic chemicals. This call brings with it a call to respect the earth as belonging to the Lord, which means we must approach our responsibilities with humility and a desire for God's wisdom.

> *Lord, please help me be influenced more by Your Word and Your thoughts than the dialogue swirling around me. Thank You for the call to have dominion over the earth. Give me Your heart and Your mind to have proper dominion over the part of the earth You've put in my hands.*

APRIL 11
SUCCESS IS FAITHFULNESS

"Moreover it is required in stewards that one be found faithful." (1 Corinthians 4:2); "He who is faithful in what is least is faithful also in much; and he who is unjust in what is least is unjust also in much." (Luke 16:10)

In some ways, stewardship is what life's all about. The principles of stewardship are simple: 1) Nothing's so small that it's exempt from our responsibility to be faithful with it, and 2) Fidelity depends not on the amount entrusted, but on our sense of responsibility toward the trust.

Look at the life of Joseph, the master of stewardship. Sold as a slave to the Amalekites, he's sold again to Pharaoh. As "overseer of the house," everything related to Pharaoh's household was put under Joseph's authority. Then Joseph was framed and thrown into prison. There, he became the keeper of the prison.

Nothing here was "fair," but Joseph continued being a good steward with whatever he was given. Ultimately, he gained stewardship over Pharaoh's house and was second in command of his kingdom. Joseph was moved up by God not only to demonstrate how God rewards faithful people, but to be trained to steward resources that would keep God's chosen people from being destroyed. This wasn't about one man getting rewarded; it was about preserving the people of God.

In Joseph's various trials, he was being trained for greater and greater stewardship. So are we. Today is preparation for tomorrow, a tomorrow we co-create with God by our faithfulness now.

Look at your life. You're stewarding everything "in your possession"—time, material things, talents, abilities, skills, relationships, money. You're in training for your future, right to the end of your life and beyond. The question is never what we have; it's how faithful we are with stewarding it.

> Lord, help me to realize that success in Your eyes is how faithful I am with the things You are allowing me to steward. Help me to take a fresh new approach to all that I have in my sphere, being grateful for what I have and embracing Your call to be faithful in stewarding everything.

MARK DUPRÉ

APRIL 12

USE IT OR LOSE IT

"For the kingdom of heaven is like a man traveling to a far country, who called his own servants and delivered his goods to them. And to one he gave five talents, to another two, and to another one, to each according to his ability; and immediately he went on a journey." (Matthew 25:14–15)

This parable is so familiar it's easy to forget its continual application in our lives. (Read Matthew 25:14–29 if you need a refresher.) The man who received five talents traded them, made five more, and was made a ruler over many things. Same with the two-talent man. Notice that God was looking for how faithful they were—not what they started and ended with. Their reward was based on faithfulness, not on results.

Then there was the one-talent man. Ultimately, his talent was taken from him and given to the ten-talent man. He wasn't a squanderer or a prodigal son. Many of us can identify with his reasoning, but it contains a wrong idea about God. He called his master hard, blaming him for his own unfruitfulness.

The worldly phrase "Use it or lose it" applies in the spiritual realm when talking about stewarding. This story illustrates the importance of stewarding whatever we have, especially if we think it's only "one talent." Maybe you don't think you have enough time—just a talent's worth. Are you using your free time wisely and in submission to God?

Do you think you aren't talented? If so, apologize to God, who made you fearfully and wonderfully (Psalm 139). Tell the devil you're not going to listen to his lies anymore. Take some serious prayer time and effort (take a gifts test or talk to someone who knows you well) to find your talents. Then use them! Be like the five- and two-talent people. Start investing!

> Lord, all gifts are from You—everything. I confess that I have given too much time to wanting gifts I don't have and comparing myself to others. Please forgive me and help me see and connect with what You've put inside me. Help me to see where to start using my gifts and give me the necessary kick in the pants to get going in the right direction. Thank You!

APRIL 13

ISOLATING

"Whoever isolates himself seeks his own desire; he breaks out against all sound judgment." (Proverbs 18:1 ESV)

This Scripture can be read two ways. Both are true. The one who self-isolates seeks his own desire to be alone over the Lord's desire for him to enjoy connection and fellowship. Also, the person who pulls back from others is being selfish and doing so to pursue selfish goals.

It's far too easy in our culture to become isolated. There are all kinds of electronic devices that provide the illusion of real connection. Social media can allow us to isolate and seem (or even *feel*) connected at the same time.

We were created by God to need people and connect with them regularly. We can't obey the 150-plus "one anothers" in the New Testament if we isolate. How can we prefer one another, love one another, or carry one another's burdens if we withdraw? How can our spiritual gifts edify the body if we don't show up? How can we be a blessing to others if we don't avail ourselves of human contact? Conversely, we may be waiting on God for an answer that He intends to bring through a human being.

If you are an isolator, take a good hard look at the consequences of isolating. Review some of the "each other" and "one another" Scriptures in the New Testament. Then starve the monster by going to church or fellowship when you least want to. Go knowing God is with you and will work on your behalf. He'll have His hand in yours the whole time.

Father, I recognize that You want Your people to be together, work things out together, and enjoy one another. Forgive me for the times when I isolate. Draw me close to You when I'm tempted and remind me of the blessing of Psalm 133.

MARK DUPRÉ

APRIL 14

JESUS BELIEVES IN PRAYER

"But when you see the abomination of desolation standing where he ought not to be (let the reader understand), then let those who are in Judea flee to the mountains. ... Pray that it may not happen in winter." (Mark 13:14, 18 ESV)

"Pray that your flight may not be in winter or on a Sabbath." (Matthew 24:20 ESV)

These are extraordinary Scriptures. Jesus is quoting Daniel, who predicted the desecration of the temple in Jerusalem in 168 BC by Antiochus Epiphanes, then the Romans' destruction of the temple in 70 AD. His warnings are dire with portents of great suffering and tribulation.

In the middle of his admonitions stands an amazing command: "Pray that it may not happen in winter." In the midst of great judgment, the Lord offers the Israelites a lifeline. We casually use the phrase "I pray that ..." or "Please pray that ..." so that it becomes an expression of a wish or a thought rather than a specific request for prayer. When Jesus says, "Pray that ..." He's not suggesting those listening toss the thought around their minds for a while. He's telling them to present the request before the Almighty, in His Name, for their own good.

Furthermore, Jesus grants His listeners the opportunity to change the future. The Lord of All tells His followers that their prayers can move a date from one timeframe to another! Doesn't He tell us to pray for many things? We know we ought to pray, but rarely does a Scripture tell us what to pray for so specifically, with such a focus on a single future event.

These two things tell us more about our God. One, how gracious He is in throwing out a lifeline, even in the midst of judgment! May we see every lifeline He brings our way. Two, apparently Jesus believes prayer works and can change things. Do we agree with Him?

> Lord, thank You for mercy in the midst of judgment. Give me eyes to see and a heart to appreciate Your lifelines. Help me remember that You often tell us to pray and You wouldn't have told Your followers to pray unless You knew those prayers would be effective (James 5:16).

APRIL 15

THE QUEEN OF SHEBA: THE HARD QUESTIONS

"Now when the queen of Sheba heard of the fame of Solomon concerning the name of the Lord, she came to test him with hard questions. She came to Jerusalem with a very great retinue, with camels that bore spices, very much gold, and precious stones; and when she came to Solomon, she spoke with him about all that was in her heart. So Solomon answered all her questions; there was nothing so difficult for the king that he could not explain it to her." (1 Kings 10:1–3)

The Queen of Sheba is a mysterious figure that pops up in the Old Testament, the Quran, Ethiopian history, and Jesus' words. It's estimated she traveled about 1,200 miles to see Solomon, considered the greatest king on earth at the time.

That trip would be arduous. She could have sent an envoy but clearly wanted to see things firsthand. Camels, spices, precious stones ... she came as an equal to the king. She was ready to bequeath Solomon the traditional gifts and present to him the "hard questions." She came to impress—and to test.

Life is filled with hard questions. Do we ever ask God to answer them? We may ask why, but often we're just expressing our frustration; we're not positioning ourselves to actually *expect* and *receive* God's answer.

The Queen of Sheba knew Solomon's reputation—for wealth, greatness, power, and wisdom. What great expectations she must have had as she approached Jerusalem. How impressed Solomon must have been with her commitment to see him and receive his wisdom. What a blessing to share that wisdom with one so eager to receive it!

In the same way, God can handle us and all our difficult questions. But let's remind ourselves of what she did first—invested a great deal of personal emotion and energy into getting to the King. Nothing—not time, not inconvenience—was going to stop her. And once there, she was certainly going to pay attention.

Father, I confess that I don't make anywhere near the effort the Queen of Sheba made to come before You. I so often take Your presence for granted and treat it lightly. You paid a high price for me to be able to get into Your presence. Help me to make my own "twelve-hundred-mile-trip" to You past my own thoughts, distractions, sins, and cares of this world. Put in my heart the same desire to receive what we see in her.

MARK DUPRÉ

APRIL 16

THE QUEEN OF SHEBA: MORE THAN IMPRESSED

"And when the queen of Sheba had seen all the wisdom of Solomon, the house that he had built ... there was no more spirit in her...." "Blessed be the Lord your God, who delighted in you, setting you on the throne of Israel!" (1 Kings 10:4, 5, 9)

After spending time with Solomon, the Queen of Sheba was more than impressed. "There was no more spirit in her" means "she gave up." She came with a huge posse and a great deal of personal power, but she stopped competing, let go of her own sense of self, and let herself be properly overwhelmed.

Have you seen how amazing, wonderful, and full of wisdom God is? Have you gotten close enough to be dazzled? If this queen can let go of all she had, can we?

How aggressively do you pursue God's wisdom? We need to make it to the court of the king, look around, and press in to see what He has to say. Go—pursue God until you get His answer. When you receive what He is saying, it will satisfy! When you really connect with God, you'll respond like the queen and have no more spirit in you. Anything short of our proclaiming "Blessed be the Lord MY God" falls short of His call to us.

Have you come to the end of yourself, where there's no more spirit in you—no more questioning, fighting, trying to keep it all together, or holding on to what you understand, lest you somehow be proven wrong?

The Queen of Sheba let her world get rocked. Will we let God rock, undermine, and shake ours? He wants to take our breath away. What Solomon provided for the queen is what God wants to do for us. Let's draw close enough to let Him!

Lord, I know You're amazing and wondrous. Help me to seek You so closely that I get to see that for myself. Help me to let go of all that I bring to You so that I may fully know the wonders of Your ways and Your words.

APRIL 17

THE QUEEN OF SHEBA: OUR ROLE MODEL

"The [Queen of Sheba] will rise up in the judgment with this generation and condemn it, for she came from the ends of the earth to hear the wisdom of Solomon; and indeed a greater than Solomon is here." (Matthew 12:42)

In Matthew 12, the scribes and Pharisees asked Jesus for a sign. In rebuking them, Jesus said the Queen of Sheba would rise up in the end times to rebuke and bring judgment against those who were in the very presence of God and rejected Him. She went 1,200 miles to see Solomon—a mere man—and they had Jesus right in their midst!

What does that say to us?

I don't want to be rebuked by the Queen of Sheba. But I confess I'm guilty—how greatly do I treasure God's chosen ways of connecting with us through Scripture, worship, and prayer? Have you ever thanked God that we live now instead of in Old Testament times? We have the Holy Spirit living within our hearts. How the old prophets would have treasured that opportunity!

Solomon was the greatest king of his time, the epitome of wisdom in Israel's eyes, providing answers to the most difficult questions. In contrast, Jesus doesn't just have the answer—He *is* the answer! The Queen of Sheba went to great pains to get to Solomon. But God went through great pains—literally and figuratively—to come to us!

Let's take the queen as a model. The pains she took to get to Solomon, the time spent, the expectations—she was rewarded for all of that with answers and a vision of kingship and worship that overwhelmed her. She was gifted not only with answers to her deepest questions, but with a permanent change of perspective.

Thank you, Lord, for this example. The Queen knew what she had to do and where she had to go to find what she was seeking. I know too. Help me to have her drive and expectation for the greater treasures that lay on the other side of my seeking You.

MARK DUPRÉ

APRIL 18

FAULTY THINKING

"When either a man or woman consecrates an offering to take the vow of a Nazirite, to separate himself to the Lord ... All the days that he separates himself to the Lord he shall not go near a dead body ... All the days of his separation he shall be holy to the Lord." (Numbers 6:2, 6, 8)

The Nazirite vow was a voluntary, temporary vow to the Lord. While abstaining from several things, the one taking the vow also had to avoid contact with anything that would make him unclean, specifically a dead body. Today we could look at the vow as a call to holiness to every Christian, a model for denying oneself temporarily to seek the Lord.

Among many countercultural elements of this vow is what happens when the person taking the vow is defiled, even accidentally. Today's culture would find that grossly unfair. After all, it wasn't the vow-taker's fault if someone died too quickly for him to get away. But God says he still needs to remove the defilement. What grace, mercy, and wisdom we find here.

How often are we defiled—by a dirty joke, an image we didn't choose to see, or a thought sparked by someone else's gossip? That doesn't even begin to take into consideration the more serious abuse folks impose on others.

What we learn here is that fault isn't the issue. What's important is getting healed, getting cleansed, and getting right with God. We don't have to make sin offerings or burnt offerings, but we know what those offerings pointed to—His future sacrifice. We go to Him, ask for the cleansing of His blood and the healing touch of His hand. We forgive, thank Him for the provision, and go on—leaving the issue of injustice in His capable, merciful hands.

> *Father, thank You that there is a provision for defilements—big ones and little ones. Please move me on quickly when I get stuck in the injustice phase and carry me quickly to the grateful phase of accessing and appreciating Your cleansing.*

APRIL 19
LET'S MAKE JESUS MARVEL

[The centurion said,] "Say the word, and my servant will be healed" … When Jesus heard these things, He marveled at him, and turned around and said to the crowd that followed Him, "I say to you, I have not found such great faith, not even in Israel!" (Luke 7:7, 9) But Jesus said to them, "A prophet is not without honor except in his own country, among his own relatives, and in his own house" … And He marveled because of their unbelief." (Mark 6:4, 6)

Jesus is said to have "marveled" twice. Once was in Capernaum—far outside Judah—and concerned a Gentile, a Roman soldier, whom readers would assume to be as far removed from real faith as possible. The second was in Nazareth, Jesus' hometown, among those who should have been "Jesus' people" in every sense of the word.

With the centurion, Jesus marveled at his faith. Among His people, Jesus marveled at their unbelief. Clearly, Jesus was struck deeply by the exercise of faith or the lack thereof. The centurion didn't need to see miracles or even have Jesus physically visit His house. The centurion understood authority and recognized it in Jesus. He knew the power of a command and had faith in the power of whatever Jesus would say.

How about us? Must we see new demonstrations of Jesus' power to believe? Do we trust in His word—especially those that have already been written down for us? The centurion added his faith to Jesus' spoken word, and his servant was healed.

Jesus also marveled at the unbelief of those who should have known Him best. Instead of responding to the presence of God, they were too distracted by their knowledge of Jesus as a son and sibling. Being too preoccupied and judgmental about the outside package, they missed the power of God within.

How about us? Have we missed God—and the blessings of His power and presence—because we know the person God's using too well? How sad for us, and how sad it was for Jesus.

> Father, help me to be like the centurion, recognizing the authority of God's Word as having real power. Forgive me for rejecting Your chosen vessels because I know them in an earthly sense. Help me to see Your power and presence wherever and in whomever You choose to display it.

MARK DUPRÉ

APRIL 20

GOD OUR DEFENDER

"For the eyes of the Lord run to and fro throughout the whole earth, to show Himself strong on behalf of those whose heart is loyal to Him." (2 Chronicles 16:9)

We're probably first aware of God as Creator. As we meet Jesus, we come to know Him as Savior, the One who forgives, the deliverer, and either then or later, as Lord. As we walk with Him over time, we discover all those things He's looking to be for us. One of the most powerful is God our Defender.

Many of us have it deeply settled in our hearts that we are our own defenders. We may even think that's what God wants. Most of us know "God helps those who help themselves" isn't scriptural, but many of us act as if it is.

Let's focus on the big picture. Meditate on the fact that God wants to be our Defender. Read 2 Chronicles 16:9, as well as Psalm 34:7, Psalm 7:10, and Isaiah 31:5. It's a profound paradigm shift to let the Lord be our Defender. It raises all kinds of questions about what our responsibilities are and what are His.

Some of us run to the opposite extreme when challenged with a new perspective. For example, we may ask, "If God's my Defender, does that mean I don't do anything? Shouldn't I keep myself from harm?" We know these reactions are extreme, so we often throw out the new perspective because we're still in a reactive phase with it. What a tragedy to lose knowing Him better and having Him work more deeply in our lives because we don't "get" a new viewpoint right away.

Lord, I see that You desire to be the Defender of Your people. Please show me what that means to me individually. Please help me not to try to figure out the full implications of this now, but in faith I receive Who You want to be to me.

APRIL 21

RUTH: GODLY ABANDONMENT AND COMMITTED LOVE

"Where you die, I will die, and there will I be buried. The Lord do so to me, and more also, if anything but death parts you and me." (Ruth 1:17)

Ruth's final state—as a woman married to a godly, successful Israelite, a foreigner who became an ancestor of Christ—can be taken as a romantic "happy ending." But that obscures the passionate commitment Ruth lived by, its sacrifices and its rewards.

Ruth committed herself to Naomi's God and to that God's people, but she also committed herself to her former mother-in-law until the end of Naomi's life. "Where you die, I will die" is a monumental promise to a widow who would otherwise be alone and without any prospects.

How easy it is to miss Ruth's continued commitment as we watch and wait for the romance with Boaz to blossom. Ruth wasn't hoping for a husband; she was thinking there might be favor bestowed on her that would benefit the household. Her commitment to Naomi was foremost in her mind.

There are so many wonderful lessons here. In committing herself so completely to the good of another, to letting go of any personal agendas and even putting her own name on the line, Ruth is a model of godly abandonment and committed love. She lost her life (for Naomi) and found it (Matthew 16:25). God honored that commitment by bringing to Ruth a godly, rich husband, respect, and finally, a place in the lineage of our Savior.

When we make commitments, how long do they last? Do we carry them through to the end or do we get "interrupted" by life? May Ruth's example be a deep and lasting encouragement to us.

> *Lord, help me to be wise in my commitments and carry them through to the end. Thank You for preserving the story of Ruth for us. May her love and commitment to Naomi remind us of what You call us to do and what You've already done for us.*

MARK DUPRÉ

APRIL 22

RUTH: SMALL ACTIONS AND EVERYDAY EVENTS

"So Boaz took Ruth, and she became his wife." (Ruth 4:13)

God has everything under control. Ruth gleaned in the fields to help Naomi. She "happened to come to the part of the field belonging to Boaz" (Ruth 2:3). There are customs and laws in this story that may seem like obstacles. They weren't. They were opportunities for God to show what He could do.

God can work through natural disasters, miracles, or dramatic turns of events. But He mostly works through everyday situations and even our culture's customs. It was the custom of the day to allow gleaners the opportunity to gather a little extra by leaving some grain after the first pass through. An ancient Near Eastern custom of the "redeeming relative" is also mentioned in Ruth as a moment of suspense and anticipation, but the result was always in God's hands. It was always going to be Boaz.

Ruth is the story of small actions and everyday events that God worked like an orchestra conductor. No one in the book of Ruth has a dream, commands the elements, gets a revelation from God, or strikes out with a large, bold action. Nothing is outside of the norm or outside of the culture.

Do you believe God is big enough to work through normal channels? Do you believe He's strong enough to use simple things, everyday events, and "normal" ways? God never once calls attention to Himself in the book of Ruth, yet His steady, loving, providential hand is everywhere to be seen. Take a step back and you'll see it in your life too.

Lord, thank You for reminding me that You're often found in the still, small voice rather than in the strong wind, earthquake, or fire (1 Kings 19:12). Help me to see You—and trust You—when You're being quiet.

APRIL 23
RUTH: GOD THE GREAT ARTIST

"Thus both the daughters of Lot were with child by their father. The firstborn bore a son and called his name Moab; he is the father of the Moabites to this day." (Genesis 19:36–37)

Take a moment to review the sordid story of Lot and his daughters in Genesis 19. Now what does this have to do with Ruth? More than we might think. As much as Ruth is a beloved and instructive story in and of itself, it reaches forward to Jesus Christ and backward to the ignoble story of the beginning of the Moabite nation.

Part of the wonder of Ruth's story is redemption—of fleeing Israel and returning, of "bitter" Naomi becoming the blessed grandmother, and of the lost foreigner (part of an enemy people) becoming a child of God with a place in the lineage of Jesus. Yet in the midst of Ruth's story is something else—a powerful, prophetic image of the redemption of the sin of Lot and his daughters.

In a powerful way, Ruth's actions "undid" the sins of Lot's daughters. In a sense, her actions mirrored the actions of those disobedient ones. But this time things were done in righteousness, "reversing" the previous actions. If you look at Numbers 25:1–3, you can see even more sins connected with Moab, sins also "reversed" by the obedience and faithfulness of Boaz and Ruth.

God is a great artist. Part of the beauty He creates is painting images of redemption for us to see if we look (and study) closely enough. He weaves circumstances, opportunities, and acts of obedience into a tapestry of grace and restoration. We won't see all of them until heaven, but it wouldn't hurt to start keeping an eye open for them now.

Lord, thank You for the image of redemption that Ruth shows us. Help me see how You have created these images and are in the process of creating them in my life and in the lives of others. You are the Great Artist. Use my life, even the bad parts, to create images of love and grace.

MARK DUPRÉ

APRIL 24

RUTH: LEARNING TO WAIT IN PEACE

"So she [Ruth] went down to the threshing floor and did according to all that her mother-in-law instructed her. And after Boaz had eaten and drunk, and his heart was cheerful, he went to lie down at the end of the heap of grain; and she came softly, uncovered his feet, and lay down. Now it happened at midnight that the man was startled, and turned himself; and there, a woman was lying at his feet." (Ruth 3:6–8)

God has everything under control. Ruth gleaned in the fields to help Naomi. She "happened to come to the part of the field belonging to Boaz" (Ruth 2:3). There are customs and laws in this story that may seem like obstacles. They weren't. They were opportunities for God to show what He could do.

God can work through natural disasters, miracles, or dramatic turns of events. But He mostly works through everyday situations and even our culture's customs. It was the custom of the day to allow gleaners the opportunity to gather a little extra by leaving some grain after the first pass through. An ancient Near Eastern custom of the "redeeming relative" is also mentioned in Ruth as a moment of suspense and anticipation, but the result was always in God's hands. It was always going to be Boaz.

Ruth is the story of small actions and everyday events that God worked like an orchestra conductor. No one in the book of Ruth has a dream, commands the elements, gets a revelation from God, or strikes out with a large, bold action. Nothing is outside of the norm or outside of the culture.

Do you believe God is big enough to work through normal channels? Do you believe He's strong enough to use simple things, everyday events, and "normal" ways? God never once calls attention to Himself in the book of Ruth, yet His steady, loving, providential hand is everywhere to be seen. Take a step back and you'll see it in your life too.

Lord, thank You for reminding me that You're often found in the still, small voice rather than in the strong wind, earthquake, or fire (1 Kings 19:12). Help me to see You—and trust You—when You're being quiet.

APRIL 25

MONEY MATTERS

"Thus both the daughters of Lot were with child by their father. The firstborn bore a son and called his name Moab; he is the father of the Moabites to this day." (Genesis 19:36–37)

Take a moment to review the sordid story of Lot and his daughters in Genesis 19. Now what does this have to do with Ruth? More than we might think. As much as Ruth is a beloved and instructive story in and of itself, it reaches forward to Jesus Christ and backward to the ignoble story of the beginning of the Moabite nation.

Part of the wonder of Ruth's story is redemption—of fleeing Israel and returning, of "bitter" Naomi becoming the blessed grandmother, and of the lost foreigner (part of an enemy people) becoming a child of God with a place in the lineage of Jesus. Yet in the midst of Ruth's story is something else—a powerful, prophetic image of the redemption of the sin of Lot and his daughters.

In a powerful way, Ruth's actions "undid" the sins of Lot's daughters. In a sense, her actions mirrored the actions of those disobedient ones. But this time things were done in righteousness, "reversing" the previous actions. If you look at Numbers 25:1–3, you can see even more sins connected with Moab, sins also "reversed" by the obedience and faithfulness of Boaz and Ruth.

God is a great artist. Part of the beauty He creates is painting images of redemption for us to see if we look (and study) closely enough. He weaves circumstances, opportunities, and acts of obedience into a tapestry of grace and restoration. We won't see all of them until heaven, but it wouldn't hurt to start keeping an eye open for them now.

Lord, thank You for the image of redemption that Ruth shows us. Help me see how You have created these images and are in the process of creating them in my life and in the lives of others. You are the Great Artist. Use my life, even the bad parts, to create images of love and grace.

MARK DUPRÉ

APRIL 26

MONEY MATTERS: GOD'S UNUSUAL PROMISE

"A faithful man will abound with blessings, but he who hastens to be rich will not go unpunished." (Proverbs 28:20)

We love God's promises. They're everything to us: His promises of faithfulness, strength, and help in time of need, His unfailing and unending grace, His mercies that last forever. There's almost no end to the Bible's promises that are obvious blessings to us.

However, some Scriptures are just as strong a promise and don't seem like a blessing. Yet they most certainly are. Proverbs 28:20 is one such promise. It can be a lifesaver, a word of direction that can save us untold miseries.

It's a blessing to know a certain path contains guaranteed dangers and punishments. Then we can avoid it. The good, alternate road? Being faithful.

Of course, this addresses two of the central themes of Scripture: that we're called to be faithful (as opposed to successful) and that riches are not to be sought in place of seeking the Lord.

Even the phrasing is colorful and specific enough to be a blessing. We know folks who hasten can trip and fall. They can move blindly past their real responsibilities. They can even run into people and hurt them. These are things God wants to save us from. Since He wants to bless us, he directs us toward faithfulness instead.

Obviously, we can work to make money, but only in the context of being faithful to Him. As we thank God for His promises, let's remember this one and the merciful assurances and warnings it provides.

Lord, thank You for all Your promises. Thank You for the direction of this word and Your heart that we see in it. Please stop me if I start to hasten in the wrong direction and let me joyfully rest in the blessings that come with being faithful to You.

APRIL 27

READY TO GO?

"The Lord spoke to Joshua …: "Moses My servant is dead. Now therefore, arise, go over this Jordan, you and all this people, to the land which I am giving to them—the children of Israel. Every place that the sole of your foot will tread upon I have given you, as I said to Moses." (Joshua 1:1–3)

Consider the background of this command to the Israelites: They'd been slaves for four hundred years in Egypt. About a year after the Exodus they received the Ten Commandments, then camped at Mt. Sinai for another year. Then they wandered in the wilderness for about thirty-eight years, encamping for a final year before they were commanded to enter the land.

During that time, the tabernacle was erected. They learned how to worship according to the sacrificial system. They learned about tithing, handling various social and family difficulties, sexual morality, and fairness in business and legal matters. For those who only knew those wilderness years, they might have thought life consisted of settling down and following the rules. Then came the call to move. Imagine how much had to change!

They'd set up ways of cooking, raising children, and gathering manna. Their homes and habits worked for their accustomed lifestyle. Life was good. Now they had to cross the Jordan and take the Promised Land.

Are you ready for the next call? Have you grown comfortable in your present circumstances to the point where a call from God would be intrusive? Paul said he was "content" in all circumstances (Philippians 4:12), not comfortable. He knew his current circumstance was only a temporary one.

God had a work to do in His people before releasing them to take the land. God is continuing to work in us to help us expand His kingdom. He's always looking ahead to the next phase with an eye to what He has for us in the future.

Father, forgive me when I get so used to the blessings, rhythms, and habits of my life that I miss Your voice moving me forward. Thank You for yesterday's blessings and the blessings I see as I look around. I pray they don't distract me from You and Your call. I confess that while You loved me yesterday and love me today, You're always preparing me for tomorrow.

MARK DUPRÉ

APRIL 28

GOD PREPARES US FOR CHANGE

"Then Joshua commanded the officers of the people, saying, "Pass through the camp and command the people, saying, 'Prepare provisions for yourselves, for within three days you will cross over this Jordan, to go in to possess the land which the Lord your God is giving you to possess.'" (Joshua 1:10–11)

After forty years in the wilderness, the people of Israel were now called to go in and take the land. Their lives abruptly changed from settling and wandering to one of focused warfare. Those who moved the tabernacle were called into action. Skills related to traveling and warfare now became more important as skills related to settling were put on the back shelf. Some folks found their familiar strengths unimportant in light of new challenges. Some had to face fears and responsibilities they might have been avoiding. Others found they were needed as never before, using strengths and gifts they hadn't previously known about or used.

God not only knew the radical change was coming, but He had already prepared them for the change. Telling them to prepare their provisions tells us that He had given them those provisions already.

When God changes our circumstances, we may feel blindsided and unprepared. But God is sovereign. A change of outside circumstances is no surprise to God. If we've been walking with Him, we're not unprepared. We may have to employ previously unused skills and call on strengths we're not sure we have. But we are prepared, even if we don't feel it.

If the Lord gave the children of Israel only three days to prepare their provisions, He knew things were "ready to go." If God gives us a challenge that seems absurd or impossible, it's because He knows we're "ready to go" too.

Father, help me to be more flexible and trusting when circumstances change quickly. Thank You that nothing is a surprise to You, and that You have given me everything I'm going to need to face every new challenge.

APRIL 29

OBEDIENCE MAY BE THE KEY!

"But be doers of the word, and not hearers only, deceiving yourselves. For if anyone is a hearer of the word and not a doer, he is like a man observing his natural face in a mirror; for he observes himself, goes away, and immediately forgets what kind of man he was. But he who looks into the perfect law of liberty and continues in it, and is not a forgetful hearer but a doer of the work, this one will be blessed in what he does." (James 1:22–25)

God is so gracious, and has shown us so much mercy, that we can underestimate the power of obedience. But if we ask Him for direction and hit the proverbial "brick wall," we may need to ask if there's anything getting in the way of receiving direction for the next step.

The story of Achan in Joshua 7 is the classic example of disobedience getting in the way of God's plan. Achan disobeyed Joshua's directions, which had come from the Lord. Israel's progress was stopped short and there were terrible consequences for Achan and others. When we have problems hearing God, we need to review our actions to see if we need to repent of an active wrong like Achan's.

But sometimes that wrong is a sin of omission rather than commission. Achan disobeyed God's command by doing something. We may have disobeyed by not doing something. Perhaps we simply didn't want to do it or found it too hard. Maybe we were afraid of what would happen if we did it. Whatever the reason, disobeying the Lord by omission is as great a sin as doing something against His express command. A special danger of disobeying by omission is that we often try to resist it by forgetting about it, making it harder to see than an obvious sin of commission.

The next time you're seeking His direction and things remain unclear, consider what God's told you to do that hasn't yet been done. It may be the key to releasing His wisdom for the next step.

> *Father, please bring to mind what I haven't done that You've told me to do. Forgive me for resisting Your command and letting things go. Thank You for Your Holy Spirit that can bring all these things to mind and then empower me to move forward in strength and wisdom.*

MARK DUPRÉ

APRIL 30

RESPONDING, NOT REACTING

"And they rose early in the morning and went up to the top of the mountain, saying, "Here we are, and we will go up to the place which the Lord has promised, for we have sinned!" And Moses said, "Now why do you transgress the command of the Lord? For this will not succeed. Do not go up, lest you be defeated by your enemies, for the Lord is not among you." (Numbers 14:40–42)

Years before the lessons of Ai, the children of Israel demonstrated another way of mishandling the judgments of the Lord. The men who'd spied out the land brought back a negative, faithless report that caused a great deal of dissension and rebellion. After Moses' intercession, the Lord didn't destroy His people but sent a plague on those who brought the report.

After mourning, the people of Israel made a classic error: they *reacted* instead of *responding*. They took their direction into their own hands. Their knee-jerk reaction was believing they could reverse things by aggressively doing what they thought they should have done earlier—and what they assumed God wanted them to do now.

The people of Israel should have humbled themselves before the Lord and received their direction from Moses. Instead, they made reactive assumptions, went against his counsel, and made a mess of things.

When we've made a mistake and experienced negative consequences, it's tempting to react and try to "fix" things. But only God really knows how to do that. We have His Word, prayer, and godly leaders to help us discern our "next steps" after we mess things up. Take advantage of them!

The point wasn't what Israel thought should be done—in this case, taking over the land. The point was obedience to the Lord. Their first sin was not believing God was going to give them the land. Their second mistake was after seeing their sin, they relied on their own thinking instead of seeking the Lord.

Lord, help me to humble myself enough after I sin that I don't compound the problems I've created. Help me to respond to Your Holy Spirit's leading rather than reacting and trying to correct situations by doing what I think best. Thank You that You always have wisdom for me when I ask.

MAY 1
WHAT'S MY RESPONSIBILITY?

"Moreover it is required in stewards that one be found faithful." (1 Corinthians 4:2)

False responsibility is a problem that's so pervasive that most people who suffer from it have no idea they have this spiritual disease. They think it's simply part of their personality when it's actually a demonic pressure from the outside. It's one of the great problems of this age, bringing untold misery to millions—from those who struggle under it to those who interact with those who are struggling.

It's characterized by misreading the Scripture above in one of these ways:
- It's required that I make sure certain things happen.
- It's required that I bear the responsibility for guaranteeing certain outcomes.
- It's required that I worry—and I have good reasons for doing that.
- It's required that I make everyone happy and like me.
- It's required that I make sure my wife/husband/children are never unhappy or angry.
- It's required that I be responsible for someone else's walk with Christ.

Doesn't that list get ridiculous? It doesn't seem that foolish when it remains inside and unstated. It only looks that way when it's brought into the light.

The simple truth is we're only called to be faithful. We're not responsible for anything other than our own actions. We're not God, and we're not to take over the areas that are His. Getting free from false responsibility doesn't mean we let everything go; the choices are not control vs. a lack of responsibility. We simply need to learn to fulfill our real responsibilities and leave the rest in His capable hands.

Lord, please show me where I'm operating under false responsibility. I can't see it if You don't show me. Minister to my fears that keep me operating this way. Show me where and how I'm to be faithful and help me see how much You want to be God in my life and in the lives of those around me.

MARK DUPRÉ

MAY 2

GRABBING THE BRASS RING

"No temptation has overtaken you except such as is common to man; but God is faithful, who will not allow you to be tempted beyond what you are able, but with the temptation will also make the way of escape, that you may be able to bear it." (1 Corinthians 10:13)

Grabbing the brass ring on a vintage carousel required looking for it, good timing, and proper placement. The reward was often a free ride. Finding the "way of escape" promised in 1 Corinthians 10:13 is like grabbing that ring.

We have to look for the way out that God promises. That involves faith that it's there and a heart that wants to find it. Timing was also key for those looking for the ring. There was usually only a moment or two during the ride where all the circumstances came together to allow the rider to grab the ring. God's way of escape is often like that. Yes, He's incredibly merciful and full of grace. But His way of escape from the temptation may not last forever, nor always be easily available.

But God promises to make a way. It's up to us to locate it and grab it. The brass ring didn't fall into the hands of the people looking for it—they had to grab it. It's often the same with our God-given opportunities to escape our temptations. God may open a door, but we have to walk through it.

The next time you're faced with temptation, start looking for the way of escape. God promises it will be there. Then don't presume on His grace. Take advantage of the way out as soon as possible. Only heaven will reveal the pain you'll avoid. But the joy of obedience will be your portion in this life!

Thank You, Lord, for this beautiful promise. Help me to get better at seeing Your way of escape for me, and help me to move quickly and take advantage of the way You provide.

MAY 3
SPEAKING THE TRUTWH IN LOVE

"But, speaking the truth in love, [we] may grow up in all things into Him who is the head—Christ."(Ephesians 4:15)

Some Scriptures are directed at certain kinds of people: church leaders, husbands, wives, children, or those who find themselves in certain circumstances. Others sit gloriously on the page applying to everybody—and challenging us all. This is one of those. It sets up a spectrum that includes everyone. On one extreme are the people who have no trouble speaking the truth, no matter how harshly it comes out. On the other are those who want to express love and acceptance to everyone.

Then there are the rest of us in between. We don't want to intentionally hurt anyone, yet we know there are things that sometimes need to be said and situations that need to be firmly addressed.

Speaking something in love requires a sensitivity to the person hearing the truth and to the circumstances around both that person and the issue at hand. Speaking the truth keeps us from being hypocritical or acting out of fear of rejection.

This Scripture challenges us to hold two things in active suspension—love and truth. This can only be done under the power of the Holy Spirit. No one is automatically good at doing this; it takes practice and a heart leaning on the Lord.

There's no set formula for speaking the truth in love, but setting the goal always before us reminds us of our utter dependence on the Lord to follow His word here. We'll never find "the method" with practice, but we'll learn to grow in strength and grace to help us find "the way" each time.

Lord, if You call us to speak the truth in love, then You have a way for us to do that each time. Help me to move away from either extreme that excludes the other and give me a greater understanding of Your heart, a heart that always joins truth with love.

MAY 4
RADICAL FORGIVENESS

"And be kind to one another, tenderhearted, forgiving one another, even as God in Christ forgave you." (Ephesians 4:32)

There's a spiritual disease that affects us all to one degree or another. It's called RU— residual unforgiveness. The Latin name is *notquitelettinggo-ius*. These are the areas of unforgiveness that try to hide like children who don't want to go to bed.

Want to find them? Ask yourself: Whose name causes me to shut down? Who have I put in a "judgment box" that tends to stay there? Is there someone I heard bad news about and I was kind of glad—just a little? Who's the person I would have a hard time extending grace to, even if I hadn't seen them in years?

Radical means "at the root." Radical forgiveness gets to the root of things. If you've ever had any "radical" work done, you know it's serious, it can hurt, and it takes commitment. Radical forgiveness is no different. The experience changes us, but for the better.

As He is the author and finisher of our faith (Hebrews 12:2), let's look to Jesus as our example. He forgave His murderers on the cross (Luke 23:34) and died for us while we were still sinners (Romans 5:8). Colossians 3:13 says, "Even as Christ forgave you, so you also must do." What Jesus has provided for us, we must provide for others, even when it hurts.

Just because you've been able to "move on" or you don't feel angry anymore doesn't mean very much. Many diseases are unfelt or in remission. If we're honest, there's usually some work to be done—which we'll continue tomorrow.

Lord, You set the example for us. If You could forgive with all that was so unfairly done to You, and You call us to forgive, then we can do it through You who strengthens us. Soften my heart; make me real in this whole area.

MAY 5
WHY UNFORGIVENESS REMAINS

"Beloved, do not avenge yourselves, but rather give place to wrath; for it is written, "Vengeance is Mine, I will repay," says the Lord." (Romans 12:19)

Unforgiveness remains in us because of a stubborn truth or a stubborn lie. For example: If I forgive, the person will "get away" with it. (Justice is in God's hands.) If I forgive, it's like saying what happened wasn't a big deal. (The issue's unforgiveness, not the size of the offense.) It's the last bit of control I have over the situation. (An illusion—it's unforgiveness that has control over you.) I've moved on, so it must be okay. (Surviving isn't forgiving, and moving on doesn't mean your heart is free.) I don't want to revisit the pain. (No one enjoys the process, but the redemptive work of Jesus' grace and power are only found in reality, not avoidance.) If I forgive, I have to trust that person again. (Trust is earned. It may take time or never happen again. Trust and forgiveness are separate issues.)

Comedienne Lily Tomlin is attributed with saying: "To forgive is to give up all hope for a better past." If we haven't forgiven completely, there's something to be faced, but even more so, a treasure awaiting us in God. The enemy wouldn't put up such a fuss if there weren't something worthwhile to be gained.

Even the world knows the foolishness of unforgiveness, which is often compared to drinking poison and expecting the other person to die. We weren't created originally nor were we born again to hold on to offenses. There's only grace to forgive, not to hang on to hurt.

Father, I give up my choice not to forgive. Take me to the painful place if it will bring about forgiveness. You tell us to forgive, and I am yours. Thank You that while I fear and avoid at times, I know that there is a blessing awaiting me as You take me through the process.

MAY 6

FORGIVING AS HE FORGAVE

"Let all bitterness, wrath, anger, clamor, and evil speaking be put away from you, with all malice." (Ephesians 4:31)

All true revelation of who God is comes after meeting Him as the One Who Forgives. If God put forgiveness at the forefront of His contact with us, then we need to keep forgiveness at the forefront of our concerns. After setting our hearts to forgive because "God in Christ forgave" us, here are a few things that may make it easier:

Realize the folks who hurt you are people, like you. They're not monsters. If they've hurt you, they carry a burden too. Either they carry around the weakness that inadvertently hurt you or the sinful behavior that led to your hurt. Negative character traits have their own built-in punishment.

Realize you've hurt people as well. That can be hard to hear when you're in pain, but we need to realize we've done damage too.

Change your focus from the offense, the offender, and the pain, and let this one truth grow in your mind and heart: Jesus forgave you everything! Everything! Stop rehearsing the unfairness. Stop the internal conversations you'd have if given the opportunity. Put your energies into remembering His great sacrifice for you.

Long-held emotions won't change right away. But remember, God regularly presents us with commands that can't be accomplished in our own strength. His "impossibilities" help us learn about His abundant grace and power.

God's grace and strength are there. They always will be. When you're ready to conquer RU (residual unforgiveness), remember who called you to forgive and who will lead you through it.

Lord, I confess it's sometimes hard to move my heart and mind away from the hurts and betrayals. Help me see Your sacrifice for sin for what it is—the greatest act of love and sacrifice set against the greatest, most unfair betrayal of all time. And thank You for reminding me of Your power to finish what You begin.

MAY 7
IT ALL POINTS TO JESUS

"You shall not sacrifice to the Lord your God a bull or sheep which has any blemish or defect, for that is an abomination to the Lord your God." (Deuteronomy 17:1)

A passage such as Deuteronomy 17:1 can seem either obscure beyond understanding or appear to be an Old Testament law we don't have to pay attention to anymore. (And therefore don't have to think about.) Or it could be seen as an example of something God asks us to do that's practically impossible—such high standards!

Animal sacrifices to God, as well as the priests themselves, had to be without blemish (Leviticus 21:16–23). The Israelites were to be reminded regularly of God's holiness, purity, and perfection.

Can you imagine the work that went into having to check over each animal to make sure it didn't have any defects? Depending on the condition of one's heart, that activity could have been a burdensome, even irritating, task. On the other hand, it could have been a joyful search for the right sacrifice to please the Lord.

What's your attitude toward the commandments of God? Do you see them as limiting, restricting your freedom and self-expression? Or do you see His commandments as loving sacrifices to Him? Of course, we aren't sacrificing for sin here, as the ancient Israelites did. We're merely sacrificing the desires of our flesh. Do we see that God's commandments are not difficult, but are meant to protect us and ultimately be a blessing to us?

God's commandments are meant to be a joy (1 John 5:2–3). They also have incalculable benefits (Psalm 19:7–11). Let God get ahold of your heart in the areas that you don't see yet.

Lord, what You tell us to do is for Your glory, but it's also for our good. Help me to see that in the areas that I don't. Cleanse me and touch my heart, that all my rebellion to Your Word will eventually dissolve in the knowledge of Your love and care for me.

MAY 8

EVERYTHING TESTIFIES OF JESUS!

"You search the Scriptures, for in them you think you have eternal life; and these are they which testify of Me." (John 5:39)

Yesterday's reading reminded us that God's commandments are meant to be joyful—yes, even the commandment about unblemished animals for sacrifice. This is a truth we should treasure and hold onto our whole life long.

Yet there's another treasure hiding in Deuteronomy 17:1. Like every other part of the Old Testament, it points to Jesus. As we look back on this ancient law from our New Testament perspective, we can see it's a foreshadowing of the great sacrifice that was to come—the sacrifice with the perfect, sinless, unblemished Lamb of God. In reality, that "obscure Scripture" has Jesus right at its center.

In fact, Jesus is in the center of everything. If we can't see that, we just need to keep looking. If we seek Him, we'll find Him. And when we find Him, we'll see that He's in the middle of it all, as well as at the beginning and the end. (Check out Colossians 1:16 and Ephesians 1:10.)

So it all begins, and ends, with Him. All is "through Him and for Him," including every commandment, every Scripture. Deuteronomy 17:1 points to His perfection and the great worth of His sacrifice for us. Other Scriptures point to His life, His obedience, His death, His love, His character, His care for us. Some are easy to see, and some are head-scratchers at first. But behind everything we see, hear, know, and read is the Lord Jesus Christ.

> *Lord, let the rest of my life be like the road to Emmaus story in Luke 24, where You spent time showing others all those things that pointed to You. Heal my heart and take the scales from my eyes, that I might see You in all the places You are, in Your Word and in Your world.*

MAY 9
UNSEEN FOOTPRINTS

"When the waters saw you, O God, when the waters saw you, they were afraid; indeed, the deep trembled. Your way was through the sea, your path through the great waters; yet your footprints were unseen." (Psalm 77:16, 19 ESV)

This psalm begins as a lament and ends as an encouraging recollection of God's deliverance of His people from Egypt. The Exodus was the single greatest work in Israel up to this point. It was how the nation of Israel recalled both their beginnings as a nation and the power of their God.

If God's footprints are through the sea, then He has immense powers over everything, over every circumstance that can be thrown our way— even our most difficult trials. If God can make His way through all that, then we're guaranteed victory in Him.

If His footprints are through the great waters, then how big our God must be! Footprints (with the marvelous and instructive exception of Jesus and Peter) are usually found on the bottom of a body of water. What we have here is a picture of the almighty God striding through the strongest forces of nature, delivering us without leaving a trace of His efforts. Leaving no footprints can imply that the victory comes from above, of course. But it can also imply how He can bring victory without showing us where He's been and how He has done it. Not a trace. No evidence. Not even a footprint. Yet He was there, delivering His people.

Sometimes God graciously lets us see a trail of His activities and we can rejoice in how marvelously He brought something about. But sometimes God graciously hides where He has been, deliberately not leaving a trail. Either way, He knows best and we praise Him for it.

Lord, thank You that You often let us see how You have moved to bring Your will about. And thank You that sometimes You prefer to hide Your footprints. Help me to understand that You hide them for good reasons and for Your purposes. Help me to rejoice in Your will being done, no matter how evident You make Yourself.

MARK DUPRÉ

MAY 10

STRANGE ANSWERS: THE DANGER OF CATERIES

"And it came to pass, when Joshua was by Jericho, that he lifted his eyes and looked, and behold, a Man stood opposite him with His sword drawn in His hand. And Joshua went to Him and said to Him, "Are You for us or for our adversaries?" So He said, "No, but as Commander of the army of the Lord I have now come." (Joshua 5:13–14)

This exchange is one of the most electric in the Bible. (Read verses 14-15 for more.) Joshua is, understandably, in a military mind-set. War and survival have given him a pinched perspective where there are only two categories of being— with him or against him.

What happened with Joshua is often what happens with us: he was unable to discern the Lord, even when He was right in front of him. The answer of the Angel of the Lord, considered by most to be a pre-Christ manifestation of God, jogged Joshua out of his paradigm. Then he was able to see.

Have your experiences led you to categorize people or circumstances? If it's not "A," it must always be "B"? It's an easy temptation. It makes thinking simpler and easier to put everything into boxes and categories. But, like Joshua, we miss God when we think this way.

The next time you're tempted to make assumptions about someone because they don't fit into an expected pattern or to make up your mind about a circumstance that was surprising or confusing, can you resist making a quick judgment until you get the mind of Christ on it? As this passage in Joshua shows, there are always other categories and perspectives than the ones we're comfortable with. In fact, those categories not only limit us and others, but they can eventually become idols.

If we, like Joshua, back up and stay open, we might begin to think more clearly—and may actually see the Lord!

> Lord, forgive me for how quickly I put people and events into boxes. I see how I can miss You when I do that. Help me the next time I'm tempted to do that and cause me to see the reality of the situation— and You.

MAY 11
BUT I HAVE TO UNDERSTAND!

"The secret things belong to the Lord our God." (Deuteronomy 29:29)

Perhaps nothing other than direct sin has slowed down our walks more than our stubborn insistence on having to understand what's going on. Most Christians readily admit they believe God's thoughts are not like ours, and neither are His ways. Yet many Christians don't really act as if this is true.

Our minds were created by God to seek coherence and try to "add things up." This is a great gift in our natural lives, a gift that brings us safety, understanding, and enjoyment. But in the spiritual realm, it can be somewhere between a demonic trap and an idol.

We can't fully understand what God's up to for many reasons. After all, what's going on is not just about us. It involves many others (some we know and some we don't) in and around our lives. God's also not just working in the moment, but over time. His timeframe might be months, years, decades, or more.

Most importantly, He is almighty God. He doesn't look at anything like we do. Our perspectives are so affected by sin, brokenness, and simply being human that we can't even come close to grasping a true understanding of what He's doing at any given moment.

God's Word is full of wisdom that helps us understand all we need in most circumstances and trials. Spending time with Him, praying, listening—these will bring us perspective and peace. Let's sacrifice our drive to understand when things get hard—and replace the stress of this mental and spiritual strain with trust in His power and goodness.

Lord, please stop me short when I'm heading down the road of seeking to understand things that are truly beyond me. Help me to understand what I need to understand and give me a waiting heart that is poised to hear whatever You want to speak to me.

MARK DUPRÉ

MAY 12

MOVING FORWARD WITHOUT UNDERSTANDING

"And it came to pass, when Joshua was by Jericho, that he lifted his eyes and looked, and behold, a Man stood opposite him with His sword drawn in His hand. And Joshua went to Him and said to Him, "Are You for us or for our adversaries?" So He said, "No, but as Commander of the army of the Lord I have now come." (Joshua 5:13–14)

Insisting on understanding what God's doing is not only frustrating, but can be detrimental to our spiritual health. If we focus on trying to figure out what's beyond our comprehension, we may slow down the work of God to a snail's pace because we're determined not to proceed faster than our understanding. An even greater danger comes from forcing ourselves toward an "understanding" that may be woefully lacking or completely wrong—an unstable and inaccurate starting point from which to proceed.

When we insist on understanding before we move forward, we're creating an idol. Reason was the idol that began to replace faith hundreds of years ago. It's still an attractive replacement when we're weak.

It's only natural to seek understanding. But we have to be willing to move forward in obedience, whether we understand or not. That's called walking by faith. What do we have faith in? That God is good, that He's trustworthy, that He has things in control and, best of all, that "all things work together for good" (Romans 8:28).

Once we let go of our need to understand, we're forced to simply trust and obey. Can we trust that if we let go, He's still in control, still operating in wisdom, power, and love?

That may take some time, and it involves a leap of faith. But such a switch will save a great deal of time in the long run. It may open the door to hearing what God wants us to hear next.

God, I don't want to go in circles. I don't want to wander into spiritually dangerous waters by locking down on a false "wisdom." I give You permission to shake me out of that phase when I get stuck there. Give me a heart that always wants to hear what You have to say next. Thank You!

MAY 13
HEZEKIAH'S HERITAGE

"Now it came to pass in the third year of Hoshea the son of Elah, king of Israel, that Hezekiah the son of Ahaz, king of Judah, began to reign. And he did what was right in the sight of the Lord, according to all that his father David had done." (2 Kings 18:1, 3)

Is there anything in your family background you'd rather not repeat in your life? You're not alone. One of ancient Judah's greatest kings faced that challenge and won victory over it. So can we.

Hezekiah was Judah's thirteenth king and had one of the longest reigns in Judah's history. His father, Ahaz, practiced child sacrifice, worshipped idols, and didn't trust God even when the prophets had direct words from God for him.

Yet when Hezekiah came to power, God made an encouraging distinction between him and Ahaz. Note how 2 Kings 18:1 says Hezekiah was the "son of Ahaz." But when it mentions "father" in verse 3, it mentions David. What God saw in Hezekiah was someone acting in the spirit of his ancestor David, not after the spirit of his natural father.

What about you? Do you think your natural inheritance was so bad you can't overcome it? Ask yourself, "Who is my father?" Your natural parents gave you your genetics, but it was your heavenly Father who gave you a new heart. Your parents might have loved you very much, but it was your heavenly Father who loved you enough to send His son to die for you. He's the One "who called you out of darkness into His marvelous light" (1 Peter 2:9).

Your strongest identity is being a child of God. Let that flow into the deepest recesses of your heart. Once you do that, God's influence will grow greater than the strongest member, and greatest sins, of your natural family.

> *Lord, help me not to be distracted by the sins of my family and my ancestors. Help me to continually put my eyes back on You. No matter what I struggle with, You are my Father and I want that relationship to be stronger than any in my natural family.*

MARK DUPRÉ

MAY 14
HEZEKIAH: RUTHLESSLY PLEASING

"[Hezekiah] removed the high places and broke the sacred pillars, cut down the wooden image and broke in pieces the bronze serpent that Moses had made; for until those days the children of Israel burned incense to it, and called it Nehushtan. He trusted in the Lord God of Israel, so that after him was none like him among all the kings of Judah, nor who were before him." (2 Kings 18:4–5)

How did Hezekiah undo what his earthly, natural father Ahaz had done? It wasn't just that Hezekiah had a different spirit, patterning himself after his ancestor King David. God actually used Hezekiah to reverse the sins of his nation.

Numbers 21 tells how God responded to the Israelites' incessant complaints by sending venomous snakes. When Moses prayed for the people, the Lord told him to make a bronze snake and put it on a pole. Whenever anyone looked to it, they'd live. This is a foreshadowing of Christ. But over time, the serpent became an idol. What began as good and holy turned into a kind of false god.

What's in your family line or history that began well but has turned into an unhealthy habit? Is a sense of guilt preventing you from breaking away from an old custom or ritual when you know deep down there's no more life left in it?

Hezekiah was ruthless in destroying the bronze serpent—and was ruthlessly pleasing to God. Are we? When things that began in God no longer have the life of God in them, we need to seek the Lord for wisdom in how to move away from them. Some we simply have to drop. Others involve people we need to dialogue with, always with love and grace. But if we want to break away from the spirit of Ahaz and move in the spirit of David, our desire to please the Lord must be our greatest motivation.

> *Lord, I don't want to keep participating in any spiritually lifeless activities. If there are traditions and habits I've received that are no longer Your portion for me, please show me. Show me how to move away from them in Your righteousness and love.*

MAY 15

HEZEKIAH: LEARNING FROM HIS MISTAKES

"And so it was, when King Hezekiah heard it, that he tore his clothes, covered himself with sackcloth, and went into the house of the Lord. Then he sent Eliakim, who was over the household, Shebna the scribe, and the elders of the priests, covered with sackcloth, to Isaiah the prophet, the son of Amoz." (2 Kings 19:1–2)

This incident occurs after one of the low points of Hezekiah's reign, politically and spiritually. He'd failed to seek and trust the Lord, and compromised terribly, stripping God's temple of its gold and silver to bargain with Sennacherib, king of Assyria. He acted in the spirit of his father, Ahaz (2 Kings 16:8). If the story ended here, it's unlikely Hezekiah would be remembered so positively.

But Hezekiah broke off his past by learning from his mistakes.

When Sennacherib wasn't persuaded to back off, Hezekiah began to act differently, as shown in the passage above. Instead of continuing to compromise, he began to act like David. In 1 Samuel 30:8, David sought the Lord. Here, Hezekiah does. Hezekiah sends his emissaries straight to the prophet Isaiah, asking him what the Lord was saying—a complete turnabout from before.

The result was as different as the approach. Hezekiah would be tested once more with this invader, but now he had God's promise: "I will cause him to fall by the sword in his own land" (2 Kings 19:7).

Yes, Hezekiah made a big mistake. But he learned from it and got it right the second time. He broke with the ungodly pattern of his father and sought the Lord. It wasn't too late.

We all make mistakes, some of them big ones. The question is whether we learn from them or not. Few mistakes were as devastating as what Hezekiah did earlier. Few actions were as godly as what he did next.

Lord, help me learn from the things I do wrong—mistakes and sins alike. Thank You for the example of King Hezekiah. Help me break old habits when I get into trouble and seek You first during those times.

MARK DUPRÉ

MAY 16

HEZEKIAH: THE FOLLY OF APPEASING THE ENEMY

"And in the fourteenth year of King Hezekiah, Sennacherib king of Assyria came up against all the fortified cities of Judah and took them. Then Hezekiah king of Judah sent to the king of Assyria at Lachish, saying, "I have done wrong; turn away from me; whatever you impose on me I will pay." And the king of Assyria assessed Hezekiah king of Judah three hundred talents of silver and thirty talents of gold. So Hezekiah gave him all the silver that was found in the house of the Lord and in the treasuries of the king's house." (2 Kings 18:13–15)

We stop in the middle of our look at Hezekiah to look at how the enemy attacked him—and attacks us. Sennacherib exacted a heavy toll on the Judean king, who stripped silver and gold from the temple to appease him.

This shows us the folly of appeasing the enemy of our souls with "tribute." Hezekiah compromised, giving up precious things—things from the holiest places in the land. This is the enemy's first attack. If he can't get us to reject the Lord, he'll scare us—or entice us—into compromise.

What is our silver and gold, the treasure of our house? The enemy would like all of us—body, soul, and spirit. But if he can't get us to reject God and embrace sin, then he'll nibble away at the connections we have with our God—the precious things, like our gratitude, our peace, our time reading God's Word or praying and communing with Him. Because they directly connect us to our life with God, these precious things are the areas the enemy first hopes to see us compromise, as this will hurt both us and God.

Where are you quick to compromise? These areas may not seem like much in the beginning, as with Hezekiah and the temple's treasures. The relative insignificance of the compromise is part of the enemy's plan. But if we can see quickly where the enemy is nibbling away, and realize what he's trying to do, we'll submit to God, reject fear, move past disappointment, and beat the enemy back.

> *God, help me see more of the enemy's plan, including where I compromise. Help me find You in those places that have been spiritually vulnerable up until now. Help me to take my compromises seriously and to bring Your serious victory to them.*

MAY 17

HEZEKIAH: HOW TO HANDLE THE ENEMY'S TAUNTS

"But do not listen to Hezekiah, lest he persuade you, saying, 'The Lord will deliver us.' Has any of the gods of the nations at all delivered its land from the hand of the king of Assyria?" (2 Kings 18:32–33)

Hezekiah had compromised earlier with Sennacherib. Now, it was time for a flat-out attack of Judah. It began with a verbal taunt (2 Kings 18:28–35) that contained some common areas of attack. Sennacherib's envoys went after Judah's leadership, Judah's God, and then recounted all of Judah's enemies' successes. Our enemy does the same thing.

Attacking the leader—of a church, a family, a prayer group—is the first, easiest thing to do. Leaders are people, and people are flawed. This is really an attack against God's order, not an individual.

After Sennacherib's man undermined Judah's leader, he tried to discredit Judah's God. He wanted God's people to forget His faithfulness and earlier victories. Then, he began listing Assyria's conquests. Yes, Assyria had been successful militarily. But God wasn't using them to bring judgment to Judah.

Have you heard taunts such as these? None of them are from God. They're all attacks, whether based in truth or not. Yes, leaders can fail, but Hezekiah was God's man for the job. God is faithful, no matter what we feel. And Satan's successes take nothing away from God's ability to save and rescue.

We need to learn to recognize these subtle attacks of the enemy—the ones that get under our skin and into our brains. A lot was at stake in Judah at this time. What's at stake for us is a more vibrant relationship with God. Let's do what Hezekiah did: ignore the enemy's taunts, and instead turn to God with open and trusting hearts.

Father, help me see what the enemy is trying to do when he attacks my leaders and Your reputation. Help me to resist the distractions that put my thoughts and energies on the enemy's work to the point that I'm forgetting You and Your promises. By Your grace, I set my heart back on You.

MARK DUPRÉ

MAY 18

HEZEKIAH: THE GOOD EXCEPTION

"So the servants of King Hezekiah came to Isaiah. And Isaiah said to them, 'Thus you shall say to your master, 'Thus says the Lord: "Do not be afraid of the words which you have heard, with which the servants of the king of Assyria have blasphemed Me. Surely I will send a spirit upon him, and he shall hear a rumor and return to his own land; and I will cause him to fall by the sword in his own land."'" (2 Kings 19:5–7)

In these Old Testament times, seeking the Lord meant two things. Going to the temple was one of them. The temple was where the ark was, the presence of the Lord among His people. It was where a person could have access to the forgiveness and presence of God.

Hezekiah wisely sought the word of the Lord, which was done by seeking out the recognized prophet. The Old Testament is full of stories about prophets and kings, many of which feature frustrated, resistant kings and prophets who aren't listened to or who're running for their lives. Hezekiah was the happy exception who sought the word of the Lord, received it, and let it guide him to wisdom and victory.

Hezekiah was in a crisis situation, yet he'd clearly learned how harmful it was to use his own thinking and follow the world's pattern. So, under pressure, he acted in faith. He entered the temple and sought God's word.

Have we learned our own lesson about the dangers of using our own thinking and doing what the world does? Seeking God is always the best way to begin. Being in prayer and going to church both put us in the presence of the Lord. Entered into with faith, this will give us a more accurate spiritual perspective. And in our New Testament times, we have God's Word—so full of wisdom and godly direction—and the advice of godly leaders, elders, and counselors. We have a great many spiritual riches available to us when we turn to Him.

Father, help me see what the enemy is trying to do when he attacks my leaders and Your reputation. Help me to resist the distractions that put my thoughts and energies on the enemy's work to the point that I'm forgetting You and Your promises. By Your grace, I set my heart back on You.

MAY 19

HEZEKIAH: WHAT A PRAYER!

"Then Hezekiah prayed before the Lord, and said: "O Lord God of Israel, the One who dwells between the cherubim, You are God, You alone, of all the kingdoms of the earth. You have made heaven and earth. Now therefore, O Lord our God, I pray, save us from his hand, that all the kingdoms of the earth may know that You are the Lord God, You alone." (2 Kings 19:15, 19)

Earlier, Hezekiah entered the temple and sought the word of the Lord through the prophet Isaiah. Then he prayed one of the most heartfelt, instructive prayers in the whole Bible. (You can read his entire prayer in 2 Kings 19:15–19.) Jesus told His disciples how to pray with what we call The Lord's Prayer. In the Old Testament, Hezekiah provided another great model.

Notice how the king begins not with his request, or even his situation, but with God. He's recalibrating his own heart as he first connects with the Lord, giving Him the honor He deserves. See how similar to Jesus' words: "Our Father, who art in heaven; hallowed be thy name."

Then, Hezekiah gets honest about the reality of his situation. He doesn't get "religious" or try to minimize things to seem holy, but continues pouring out his heart about the real danger in front of him: without God's help, Judah would be another Assyrian conquest.

After focusing on the Lord and getting real about what's going on, then and only then does Hezekiah ask the Lord for anything. He lifts a simple but powerful request up to God. No torrent of words, no begging. After connecting with God, Hezekiah knows who God is to him and his country. He knows God's power.

To cap it off, look at Hezekiah's reason for his request: that others would know that the Lord, alone, was God. Not just that he and his nation would be saved—but that God would be glorified. This is a powerful prayer from a transformed heart!

> Father, may I learn from Hezekiah how to pray. Let me see You in Your glory and power before I pour out my heart to You. May my honest prayers be motivated by a desire that You be glorified above all else.

MAY 20

HEZEKIAH: GOD'S FINAL WORD WASN'T FINAL

"In those days Hezekiah was sick and near death. And Isaiah the prophet, the son of Amoz, went to him and said to him, "Thus says the Lord: 'Set your house in order, for you shall die, and not live.'" Then [Hezekiah] turned his face toward the wall, and prayed to the Lord, saying, "Remember now, O Lord, I pray, how I have walked before You in truth and with a loyal heart, and have done what was good in Your sight." And Hezekiah wept bitterly." (2 Kings 20:1–3)

Here's one last, tender lesson from Hezekiah. If God told us to put our house in order because we were going to die, we might have any number of reactions. We know getting angry with God or walking away from the Lord wouldn't be the right response. Many of us might think simple resignation would be the most spiritual thing to do. Hezekiah did something else.

Like Moses before him, Hezekiah was quick to connect with God on every point—even the difficult ones—and pour out his heart before Him. Like Moses, Hezekiah even brought God's word right back to Him (see verse 3 above).

Hezekiah's weeping wasn't his reaction to the news. It was his response to the Lord. Like his heartfelt prayer of 2 Kings 19, Hezekiah is honest with his emotions—and his implicit request of God to reconsider in light of his obedience. Without attitude or rebellion or disappointed resignation, Hezekiah leaves the door open for God to have the last word. And through Isaiah, He did—God added fifteen years to Hezekiah's life.

Instead of closing down, Hezekiah kept his heart and his connection with God open, even after hearing what we might take as God's "final word." Of course the Lord had a right to say no, but we'll never know what God might have done if Hezekiah hadn't prayed openly with the Lord. What an example to us. When faced with trials, enemies, or death, the one right response is to get right back into communion with Him.

Lord, thank You for the many examples of Hezekiah's life. Help me to learn from my mistakes, as he did, and to bring everything to You in prayer. You are worthy of all my trust and of an ever-open heart.

MAY 21
JUMPING TO CONCLUSIONS

"Now the children of Israel heard someone say, "Behold, the children of Reuben, the children of Gad, and half the tribe of Manasseh have built an altar on the frontier of the land of Canaan, in the region of the Jordan—on the children of Israel's side." And when the children of Israel heard of it, the whole congregation of the children of Israel gathered together at Shiloh to go to war against them." (Joshua 22:11–12)

Ancient Israel's tribes on the eastern side of the Jordan River had been fighting alongside their western counterparts to take the land God had promised them. One of the first things these two-and-a-half tribes did after crossing the Jordan was build an altar. That's all the rest of Israel knew, but look how quickly they assumed the worst. They assumed this was a sacrificial altar in violation of God's law. (Read Joshua 22:13–20 for the whole detailed accusation.)

The opposite was true. The altar was supposed to be a teaching tool, an altar of remembrance called an "altar of witness." Thankfully, when their accusers heard the explanation, war was averted.

How quickly we sometimes attach accusation to information and assume others' motivations. There are a couple of possible steps to take here. One is simply to find out the real story. Proverbs 18:17 says: "The one who states his case first seems right, until the other comes and examines him" (ESV). The first story can seem complete; it usually is not. If we do this first, we can stop at step one.

If we've been too quick to judge and assume, we have to take a second step: repent and do some self-examination. If we've been wrong about something, we need to ask the Lord to search our hearts and show us why we're so quick to judge—and what needs dealing or healing. This second step is one that too many of us skip over, but it's necessary on the way to spiritual maturity.

Lord, help me hold back from making judgment calls until I know all the facts. Please show me those things that lead me to judge others and assume their motivations and work to remove any tendency toward that in my heart.

MARK DUPRÉ

MAY 22

KEEP THE FRUIT TREES

"When you lay siege to a city for a long time, fighting against it to capture it, do not destroy its trees by putting an ax to them, because you can eat their fruit. Do not cut them down. Are the trees people, that you should besiege them?" (Deuteronomy 20:19 NIV)

At first glance, this relatively obscure Scripture can seem to be something modern sounding and environmental in tone. It's not. This passage has to do with warfare and God's loving heart for his people. God was offering a rule for war. As opposed to the slash-and-burn approach of some of Israel's enemies, the Lord's people were to use wood from non-fruit-bearing trees to wage their warfare. They were to protect the fruit trees for the sake of their future.

What does this mean for us? We have battles where we're tempted to fight with all we have, including rage. We end up hurting people, relationships, or our consciences.

While we know we battle against principalities and powers, we sometimes make the mistake of battling flesh and blood (Ephesians 6:12), which can leave a trail of blood and tears. Damaged relationships can be our destroyed fruit trees if we don't use all of God's ways on our way to victory.

In our focus on spiritual victory or even our concept of "making things right," we are to leave protected those things that will provide fruit in our futures, including a clean heart. God wants us to emerge from spiritual battles with a clear conscience and preserved relationships. It may seem more challenging and limiting, as leaving fruit trees alone must have seemed to those in the midst of battle. But God wants to bless us. He's looking at our futures when He gives us such commands. It's for our blessing. He does know best.

Father, thank You that You care enough for our futures to give us such guidance and wisdom in the midst of battle. Help me to keep all Your commands in the fight so that I emerge with a clear conscience and unscathed relationships.

MAY 23

COUNTING THE COST—LATER

"For which of you, intending to build a tower, does not sit down first and count the cost, whether he has enough to finish it—lest, after he has laid the foundation, and is not able to finish, all who see it begin to mock him, saying, 'This man began to build and was not able to finish'?" (Luke 14:28–30)

Luke 14:28–30 is a question, but contains great direction for anyone starting a project. In context, of course, it's about what we need to do to follow the Lord to the end. (See verse 33.)

We might think we took care of this once and for all when we made that first commitment to God. But this commitment, like forgiveness, is more of a stand of faith than a one-time event. It's a position we stake out that we may need to go back to time and time again. When we're younger, and/or newly saved, how can we know what life will be like? We grow in wisdom and understanding over time.

If we grow discouraged or spiritually weary along the way, this can turn into self-blame, because we may believe we didn't count the cost accurately. But the great news is that the reason we made the first commitment is the same as the reason we can recommit: we have Jesus—and that's enough. "God with us" is the reason for our success, the one thing we can always count on and the cornerstone of our ability to persevere.

Don't let the enemy blame you if you find yourself counting the cost again—or have done so several times. Life and trials may cause us to rethink our ability (or even desire) to make it to the end, but the presence of Jesus in our lives brings us reassurance, the power and the very reason to finish the race.

> *Lord, thank You for helping me count the cost all along the journey with You. Thank You for all Your encouragements along the way, and for reminding me that it's Your power that takes me through and Your presence with me that makes me want to finish with You.*

MARK DUPRÉ

MAY 24

GOD GOES BEFORE US

"Therefore understand today that the Lord your God is He who goes over before you as a consuming fire. He will destroy them and bring them down before you. (Deuteronomy 9:3); I will send My fear before you, I will cause confusion among all the people to whom you come, and will make all your enemies turn their backs to you." (Exodus 23:27)

Like the Israelites, we're called to go into areas of this world filled with unbelievers, false idols, sinful behaviors, and ungodly thinking. Some of the areas into which God wants to expand His kingdom include business, government, the arts and culture, and every country and people group in the world.

The Scriptures are replete with stories of what happens when God's people mistakenly or sinfully tried to invade an area without the direction and presence of God. But there are just as many stories of the great successes God's people made when they followed Him. One of God's most precious promises to His people was His assurance He was going before them. He wasn't just with them; He would go on before them to prepare the way, just as modern warfare often includes "softening the target" with air power before a land invasion.

Look at how God describes His work here: as a consuming fire sent to destroy and bring down the enemy, as something He calls "My fear" that will cause confusion among the people.

Are you being sent into a new land, one filled with giants and enemies? If God is calling you to go into the land, it's because He has a plan for victory. Part of His plan includes preparing the land for you. Only God knows where to aim His weapons and at whom. But since these Old Testament examples are for us to learn from (1 Corinthians 10:11), let's seize them in prayer as godly weapons for the extension of His kingdom.

> *Father, thank You that You never send us into a place that is unprepared for us. Remind me to partner with You by praying ahead of time that You would fully soften the spiritual target before sending me in.*

MAY 25
LITTLE BY LITTLE

"I will not drive [the enemy] out from before you in one year, lest the land become desolate and the beasts of the field become too numerous for you. Little by little I will drive them out from before you, until you have increased, and you inherit the land." (Exodus 23:29–30)

This passage can be discouraging to those of us who love the idea of a dramatic, swift victory over our spiritual enemies. But the completeness of the Lord's victory at Calvary and with His resurrection does not always translate into instant victory. God, in His eternal wisdom, has generally chosen to give us victory over time, step-by-step.

Gradual victory keeps us in a state of awareness of spiritual warfare and is a precaution against letting our guards down. We also have to keep depending on the Lord. As for what the "beasts of the field" might represent, it might be best to start with a literal interpretation. These were untamed, dangerous elements that could attack at any moment. Taking possession "little by little" helped prevent God's people from being overwhelmed by all the dangers the land posed.

For us, these "beasts" could be the temptations of this world. They could be unseen spiritual forces we're not aware of, which might overwhelm us if they were released against us all at once. Remember, justification is an instant event. Sanctification takes the rest of our lives. In the same way, God's advance in our lives first comes with a grand victory (salvation) followed by incremental steps of holiness and dominance over sin and self.

No matter how slow the progress may seem, God is still moving, still bringing His victory. God never leaps ahead foolishly, but wisely and strategically possesses the land—the land of our hearts, our minds, our souls, and every place He sends us into.

Lord, thank You for instructing us in the way of full victory. Lord, help me not to be discouraged by slow progress. Help me instead to stay focused on what You want me to do as You work through me to extend Your kingdom and hold Your victory.

MAY 26

GOD KNOWS YOUR ENEMY'S STRENGTHS

So the Lord was with Judah. And they drove out the mountaineers, but they could not drive out the inhabitants of the lowland, because they had chariots of iron. (Judges 1:19); They fought from the heavens. The stars from their courses fought against Sisera. The torrent of Kishon swept them away, that ancient torrent, the torrent of Kishon. O my soul, march on in strength! (Judges 5:20–21)

Hidden in these little-read passages is a story of God's ability to overcome our enemies, even when they have a so-called "advantage." We can see from Judges 1 that iron chariots were considered such a powerful weapon that the Scriptures almost give Judah a pass for not being able to drive out the inhabitants of the lowlands. If we read Judges 4:3, we see that having such a weapon put that army in a position of great strength and superiority.

Yet when God sends His people out to wage warfare, He's fully aware of what they're facing. Judges 4:15 tells us the Lord "routed Sisera and all his chariots." How did that happen? Judges 5 explains in such a poetic way that it nearly hides God's method. The heavens opened and God sent a flash flood. Simple and easy. No chariot, no matter how powerful, can operate in muddy ground.

God knows how to bind your enemy, no matter how strong his advantage may seem to be. Facing an enemy possessing chariots must have seemed insurmountable for Judah. Yet how little it took for God to turn the enemy's "strength" into a disadvantage.

Judah didn't try and figure out how God was going to give them the victory. They just moved forward in faith and God moved. Let's be like that. Our God knows exactly what it will take to stop our enemy in his tracks. Let's step out in faith when He directs and watch Him move.

Lord, You know my enemies and all their so-called "strengths." I believe You're wiser and stronger. Thank You that I don't have to figure out how You might bring the victory—I only have to step ahead when You direct me.

MAY 27

SAMSON: THE LORD, THE MAN, AND THE MYTH

"Then [Delilah] lulled [Samson] to sleep on her knees, and called for a man and had him shave off the seven locks of his head. Then she began to torment him, and his strength left him. And she said, "The Philistines are upon you, Samson!" So he awoke from his sleep, and said, "I will go out as before, at other times, and shake myself free!" But he did not know that the Lord had departed from him." (Judges 16:19–20)

Samson has somehow slipped from Scripture into legend. He's become a kind of ancient god with superhuman strength who's defeated by his own hubris. Part of the "myth" of Samson is that his strength was in his hair. If we believe that, we're making the same mistake Delilah and the Philistines made.

Numbers 6:1-20 tells us about Samson's Nazirite vow. In brief, it says no wine, no haircuts, no contamination through contact with dead things, and a call to holy living. In Judges 13–16, we see Samson breaking every last condition of the vow and more.

Yet Samson's story is really more about the Lord. The Lord's presence accounted for Samson's strength, not something as random as the follicles on his head. How regrettable Samson didn't realize this—and how foolish for us not to see that the arm of the Lord is greater than any aspect of a person's physical body.

Misunderstanding the source of Samson's strength can make God seem arbitrary or the story more like a fairy tale. God didn't invest Samson's hair with anything. The Lord waited until every condition of his vow was broken before He "left him." Then we see how graciously the Lord restored Samson's strength when Samson began to reverse the pattern of his sin.

How patient God is to keep working with us, demonstrating His faithfulness by His mercies toward Samson. Let's leave the myth of Samson behind and embrace the story of God's great faithfulness, forbearance, and love we find there.

You were so patient with Samson, not bringing any kind of judgment against him until he violated the last part of the covenant. Help me to be encouraged to keep loyal to my covenant with You, thanking You with my obedience to Your word.

MARK DUPRÉ

MAY 28

OBEDIENCE BEFORE EXPERIENCE

When He had stopped speaking, He said to Simon, "Launch out into the deep and let down your nets for a catch." But Simon answered and said to Him, "Master, we have toiled all night and caught nothing; nevertheless at Your word I will let down the net." And when they had done this, they caught a great number of fish, and their net was breaking. (Luke 5:4–6)

Experience and wisdom count for something. These fishermen were experienced at their craft. They knew nighttime was the best time for catching fish in their area. They knew when to dry their nets and how best to let them down into the waters.

But in this situation, wisdom and experience almost stood in the way. Simon Peter, who made his living as a fisherman, argued with Jesus when He told him to let down their nets. But then Peter added the all-important response, "nevertheless at Your word I will let down the net."

Peter wasn't guaranteed a successful catch at the word of the Lord. He was just being obedient. If no fish had been caught, Peter would still have been a faithful follower of Jesus. At this point, Peter wasn't concerned with nets and fish; he was concerned with being obedient. Ending up catching so many was an added bonus.

Peter didn't "bring God" into his fishing through prayer or any other means so he'd be a successful fisherman. He was seeking first the kingdom of God and His righteousness (Matthew 6:33). This one thing—a successful day of fishing—was added unto him as he was obedient.

May we never let experience and our own "wisdom" get in the way when the Lord is working to direct us. What makes ultimate sense is not what makes sense to us, but doing the Lord's will. Remember, He's more concerned with our obedience and the faithfulness of our hearts than worldly success.

Lord, I argue with You sometimes when I think I know better. Sometimes I talk myself out of obeying You because I think I have reasons not to. Forgive me for that. Help me to simply attune myself better to Your direction and promptings, believing that obedience is more important than any other action.

MAY 29
JE NE REGRETTE RIEN

"For even if I made you sorry with my letter, I do not regret it; though I did regret it. For I perceive that the same epistle made you sorry, though only for a while. Now I rejoice, not that you were made sorry, but that your sorrow led to repentance. For you were made sorry in a godly manner, that you might suffer loss from us in nothing." (2 Corinthians 7:8–9)

Today's title, *Je Ne Regrette Rien* (which means "I Don't Regret Anything") is the name of the signature song from France's most famous singer of the last century, Edith Piaf. It's considered an assertive act of independence and defiance. It's also foolish and shortsighted. (Piaf died of ill health and drug addiction at forty-seven, hardly a proper symbol for the perspective of the song.)

Usually, we use this phrase as a defense mechanism because we haven't figured out what to do with our regret. Regrets weigh us down, etched in marble in our hearts and minds. The Lord doesn't want us to live in regret and has given us ways to properly deal with it.

One level of regret is: we didn't do what we wanted to do. Yes, the past is gone, but maybe you can still move forward. Bring your regret to the Lord. Lay it at His feet. Let go of your old interpretations and explanations surrounding it. Battle to not pick it back up again. Let the Holy Spirit flow through you, healing, bringing light and perhaps conviction. The Lord's good at getting to the bottom of things and clearing away debris.

Many of our regrets surround our gifts and callings from the Lord. Since these are irrevocable (Romans 11:29), they still reside within us, often tugging and stirring. Regret binds these gifts and callings, holding them back from godly expression. Let's let Him clear away the regret so the word He's put in us can come forth. He'll make room for it in your life.

Father, I give you my regrets for the things I didn't do. I lay them at the feet of Jesus and ask You to take away the chaff and leave the wheat. I want to see what You put in me originally. I ask that You would release my gifts and callings for Your glory.

REGRET: GETTING TO GODLY SORROW

"For godly sorrow produces repentance leading to salvation, not to be regretted; but the sorrow of the world produces death." (2 Corinthians 7:10)

If regret is rooted in your own sin, the Lord may well be working a godly sorrow within you. Perhaps you're not sure if that's the case. But God knows. As you lay out the regret and every accompanying sentiment at His feet, ask God directly if there's sin in the midst of all those feelings.

If there's sin involved, many kinds of sorrow might be attached: 1) if we regret things because they didn't work out—that's worldly sorrow, 2) if we're sorry because we messed things up for ourselves—that's worldly sorrow, 3) if we're sorry because we messed things up for others—that's a mix of godly and worldly sorrow, and 4) if we regret something because we sinned against God, and in the process hurt others and perhaps ourselves—that's godly sorrow.

It may take a while to get to the point of godly sorrow. We often develop fortresses of defense around our regrets, as we don't want to compound our hurt with the added pain of repentance. We need to remind ourselves of God's promise that godly sorrow is not to be regretted. It leads to salvation. It doesn't lead to increasing amounts of pain—that's the enemy speaking.

Once we realize our first offense was against God Himself (like David in Psalm 51:4), we bring that sin and regret to the Lord for forgiveness. Godly sorrow is a gift from God, not something to be feared. Only our enemy tells us it will crush us. God knows it will liberate us.

Lord, please move from within and without to lead me to godly sorrow for those sins that have caused my regrets. Sift through every thought and feeling attached to them. I trust You that this is for my building up and my sanctification. Thank You that You work all things together for my good.

MAY 31

REGRET: FORGIVING OURSELVES

"Not that I have already attained, or am already perfected; but I press on, that I may lay hold of that for which Christ Jesus has also laid hold of me. Brethren, I do not count myself to have apprehended; but one thing I do, forgetting those things which are behind and reaching forward to those things which are ahead, I press toward the goal for the prize of the upward call of God in Christ Jesus." (Philippians 3:12–14)

Sometimes we're working things out well spiritually and hit a familiar brick wall that stops us in our tracks. It's called the "I can't forgive myself" syndrome. Almost all of us have this condition on occasion, but there are sure cures.

One is to bow, without argument, to God's command to forgive—including ourselves. If we can't forgive ourselves, we're setting a higher standard for forgiveness than Jesus did. His sacrifice on the cross was enough for all of us.

But perhaps there's another reason for this. Sometimes, we're so appalled at what we did that we're still in a state of spiritual shock. We may have had a view of ourselves that didn't include the behavior we exhibited. We're shocked at the depth of our sinfulness. If that's the case, we need to repent of our pride and overestimation of ourselves. It turns out we're not "all that" after all. We need to bow low—deeply humble ourselves—and receive His free gift. The reality may well be that, against what we really believed and hoped and all that made sense to us, we, like everyone else, sinned.

The good news is that God knew that all along. He was leading you to this point and stands ready—because of what Jesus did two thousand years ago—to forgive you and cleanse you of all unrighteousness. Remember, you may be the only one who's surprised by what you did. The One who loves you most knew all about it—and He still loves and still forgives.

Father, move me past my feeling that I can't forgive myself. I repent of my pride that would raise up a higher standard than Your cross for forgiveness. Thank You for Your patience with me.

JUNE 1

WHEN LOVED ONES SIN

"But [Samuel's] sons did not walk in his ways; they turned aside after dishonest gain, took bribes, and perverted justice." (1 Samuel 8:3)

Eli was a priest and leader in ancient Israel. God chose him to mentor Israel's great prophet Samuel. Yet Eli was a grossly ineffective spiritual leader in his own family. His sons were also priests, but they were wicked (1 Samuel 2:12–17). Samuel apparently didn't learn his lesson from Eli, as Samuel's two sons were also perverse.

It's hard when loved ones sin, especially members of our own family. In our loyalty, we tend to either overlook sinful behavior or justify it. Sometimes our own moral code gets compromised. When we do this, we not only injure ourselves spiritually, but take ourselves out of the place where we can be effective in helping them.

We may say we don't want to be judgmental and unloving—and want to keep relationship. Or we may let our righteous fear of God slide into the vat of tolerance. Neither path is a godly one.

We're strongly challenged when a loved one falls away, especially when they self-identify as believers with a "slightly different" theology or clearly unbiblical views on a matter. Our call is always to love. But our call is also to pray. This is where we find our peace, receive wisdom for the situation, and can be effective in changing things.

It's heartbreaking and painful to live in this kind of circumstance. But God has strength and wisdom for it. He can also change things if we take our hands off, pray with faith, and love as He directs.

Father, this is a hard one. Show me a new place where Your love replaces earthly tolerance of sin, and show me how to pray for the situation. Thank You that in You, I can be at peace, knowing that You have this in Your hands.

JUNE 2
GUILTY! TRUE OR FALSE?

"For when I kept silent, my bones wasted away through my groaning all day long. For day and night your hand was heavy upon me; my strength was dried up as by the heat of summer. I acknowledged my sin to you, and I did not cover my iniquity; I said, "I will confess my transgressions to the Lord," and you forgave the iniquity of my sin." (Psalm 32:3–5 ESV)

There's a significant problem with mankind and the issue of guilt. There's too little acknowledgement of real guilt and far too much receiving of false guilt. (We'll begin talking about false guilt tomorrow.)

David beautifully describes the effects of true guilt in Psalm 32. He opens this psalm with his feelings of joy when his guilt led him to the Lord: "Blessed is the man against whom the Lord counts no iniquity and in whose spirit there is no deceit" (Psalm 32:2 ESV).

As much as modern psychology sometimes views real guilt as a pathological problem, we know instinctively that sinning brings guilt because we've broken God's law. Guilt is like pain—it shows us where the problem is. And like pain, we can either live with it or get help. David gave us the example of acknowledging and confessing sin and being forgiven by the Lord.

In a world that tells us the feelings of guilt are the real problem, we know sin is the problem. We also know that true guilt leads us to stop covering our iniquity and acknowledge our sins, leading us to the Forgiver and forgiveness. When we've sinned, feeling guilty is a gift from God whose purpose is to lead us to the gift of repentance.

The next time you struggle with real guilt, thank God you're being led to the source of cleansing and forgiveness. Since He loves us, He doesn't leave us in our sin. Glory to God!

Lord, thank You for the pain of guilt that leads me back to You. By Your grace, let me stay sensitive to the working of Your hand that leads me to forgiveness and deliverance.

JUNE 3

FALSE GUILT IS AN ENEMY

"But with me it is a very small thing that I should be judged by you or by a human court. In fact, I do not even judge myself. For I know of nothing against myself, yet I am not justified by this; but He who judges me is the Lord." (1 Corinthians 4:3–4)

False guilt has nothing to do with what's true or real, or with actual sin or repentance. It's a harsh master, partly because of its subtlety. It's been rightly called "fear of disapproval in disguise," driving those who carry it with the constant threat of condemnation.

When we carry false guilt, we're sinning by judging ourselves. But with false guilt, there's nothing to judge or repent of (other than the sin of self-judgment), so we're dealing in unreality. We're bearing false witness against ourselves. We know it's wrong to judge others, especially when they've done nothing wrong. It's just as wrong to judge ourselves, especially when it isn't sin, but the feeling of falling short that we're fighting.

Furthermore, isn't it up to the Lord to be our judge? If we're His, He's already judged our sin at the cross. We don't have the wisdom, grace, power, or calling to judge ourselves correctly. Our duty is to remain open to the genuine conviction of the Holy Spirit when we sin, and to let God correct us when we're mistaken.

What keeps false guilt alive is sin, but not the sin we think or that we're being accused of internally. It's the sin of fear of man, which lays a trap (Proverbs 29:25), plus the sin of judging ourselves, an audacious presumption of authority. We need to exchange our fear of man for the fear of God and repent of our pride in taking over God's place as rightful judge in our lives.

> *Father, forgive me for caring more for what others think—or might think—about me and what I do. Help me to trade this concern for a genuine desire to please You first. Forgive me for judging myself, taking over Your role and stepping into Your shoes. I repent and leave such actions to You.*

JUNE 4
RIDDING OURSELVES OF FALSE GUILT

"There is therefore now no condemnation to those who are in Christ Jesus, who do not walk according to the flesh, but according to the Spirit." (Romans 8:1)

Do you know someone (perhaps yourself) who keeps saying, "I'm sorry" when they haven't done anything wrong? That's not sensitivity; that's false guilt.

Some people take pride in not doing certain things because they'd feel guilty if they did, even if the thing itself isn't sinful. That's not something to be proud of; it's letting false guilt rule us instead of Christ.

Perhaps the problem is that some of us privately believe our perfection is our "salvation," the way to find freedom from guilt and shame and finally possess peace. Of course, we'd never say that. But that's what some of us believe deep down.

We need a better belief: Jesus is the true way to salvation. His perfect life and sacrifice on the cross were enough to take care of our guilt. We don't have to be perfect. We never did! If we sin, we just bring ourselves to the One who's already perfect and accept the free gift of forgiveness. If He said it was finished on the cross, then it's finished—the payment for guilt and sin has been made!

Forgiven but don't feel it? That's not uncommon. But if we let that determine our actions, we're putting our feelings before what the Lord has said. These lies and their attached feelings are our enemy and need to be driven out as much as the Old Testament tribes occupying the Promised Land. We find victory not by pretending they aren't there, but by moving forward in faith regardless.

Father, please help make false guilt a nonfactor in my life. Thank You that You don't just forgive, but You also set us free from guilt! In Jesus' name, I receive that forgiveness and the freedom from guilt that comes with it.

MARK DUPRÉ

JUNE 5

JESUS IS THE GUILT REMOVER

"Therefore submit to God. Resist the devil and he will flee from you."(James 4:7)

Satan loves counterfeits. He can't create, but can only twist, pervert, and imitate what God's created. He takes real things and bends them out of shape until they become a destructive mockery of the real thing. Guilt is a real thing, the condition that separated all of us from God as a race and as individuals.

So the enemy has twisted it and offered it back to us in the form of a demonic imitation, a painful parody of the real thing, scorning the work of Jesus on the cross. Satan is saying, "It's not finished" when Jesus said it was. He says we're not free to do the will of God because he's fanned the dying embers of real guilt into a fire of false guilt.

If we've received forgiveness, it's only the voice of Satan that would stir up feelings of guilt. Would Jesus ever tell us to feel guilty when He's removed our guilt? Of course not! So the voice must come from the enemy.

What to do? James 4 has the answer. So how do we submit to God? By saying, "Yes, Lord, what You say is true, even if I don't feel it. I'm not going to agree with my enemy anymore when he suggests that just because there are leftover feelings of guilt, that I am actually guilty. I know You've made full provision for taking my guilt away and that Your will is that Your children walk in liberty."

Lord, how quickly I can become inundated with a tidal wave of false guilt. Please show me where the enemy has gained a foothold in my life by fooling me into accepting his accusations as my own voice. I renounce his voice by faith and accept what Your word says about You, the cross, and how completely forgiven I am in You. Sift through my heart and mind by your Spirit. Correct my thinking and stir my heart to believe Your glorious truth.

JUNE 6

THE PATH OF HOLINESS

"And they were both naked, the man and his wife, and were not ashamed. (Genesis 2:25); But as He who called you is holy, you also be holy in all your conduct, because it is written, "Be holy, for I am holy." (1 Peter 1:15–16)

This is a simple but profound and powerful truth: we can't go back to innocence, but we can go on to holiness.

Some segments of our world want to go "back to the garden," as if there were a way outside of Christ to regain the innocence they instinctively know we've lost. Some try to adopt some of the external expressions of living in the garden (of Eden). Others emulate children's behaviors to try and get back to innocence.

We can't go back. We, in Adam, were expelled from the garden. We can't return to the pure state of innocence. We're dead and lost in our sins, having forfeited our innocence forever. Yet God has called us to something greater than innocence. He's called us to share in His holiness.

We need to stop trying to regain and instead start working to attain. Let go of the thought of recapturing innocence. We're called to something greater. Innocence was always intended to be directed toward holiness. Part of the glory of forgiveness is that we're positioned, even with our lost innocence, to go on to holiness.

We need to press on toward our goal (Philippians 3:13–14). Grieve the loss of innocence if you must. Then pick yourself up and move, with God's grace and strength, into the path of holiness.

Lord, I let go of all dreams of regaining my innocence. Thank you for restoring me and setting me on another, better road—the road toward holiness. Help me to be poised to receive all that You have for me on that road.

MARK DUPRÉ

JUNE 7
ONE OF GOD'S GREAT PLEASURES

"A fool takes no pleasure in understanding, but only in expressing his opinion." (Proverbs 18:2 ESV)

Most of the discussion of this verse is on the fool, who prefers expressing himself to anything else. But hidden in the verse is a gift for all of us. It's the pleasure that comes with understanding. There's a joy to "getting" something, to having true enlightenment and wisdom about things.

The Scriptures give us more wisdom on the subject than simply contrasting the pleasure of understanding with the folly of the over-expressive. For example, Psalm 119:130 says, "The unfolding of your words gives light; it imparts understanding to the simple" (ESV). Proverbs 14:29 tells us, "Whoever is slow to anger has great understanding, but he who has a hasty temper exalts folly" (ESV).

In revisiting Proverbs 18:2, we can rightly infer that close listening—rather than expressing—is yet another key to receiving the pleasure of understanding. Of all of God's many pleasures to us, have you counted gaining understanding among them? God calls it a pleasure; we should start considering it one, too. Let's talk less and listen more. Let's get into His Word and let Him show us all its colors. Let's stay of a calm spirit; we'll not only avoid conflict, but we'll grow in understanding. And finally, let's lean into the Lord on the subject, seeking understanding as a hidden treasure (Proverbs 2:3–5).

Lord, I've never looked at understanding as a pleasure. Thank You that it's one of Your enjoyable gifts to us. Help me to learn how to seek it, stay cool, and do a lot more listening.

JUNE 8

ENTERING THE LAND WITH FAITH

"And the Lord spoke to Moses, saying, "Send men to spy out the land of Canaan, which I am giving to the children of Israel." (Numbers 13:1–2)

Every Sunday school student remembers this Bible story. The children of Israel bring back a bad report of the Promised Land—all, that is, except Joshua and Caleb, who bring back a positive one. What accounts for the difference?

It's a matter of faith and unbelief. Nearly hidden in Numbers 13:2 is the crux of the instruction: "the land of Canaan, which *I am giving* to the children of Israel." The purpose in checking out the land was so they could see what the Lord would be dealing with—not to question the viability of receiving the Lord's promise to them.

Joshua and Caleb saw the same good land, the same milk and honey, the same fortified cities, the same descendants of Anak. But they saw them in the context of faith. They saw something beyond what their eyes reported: to them, the land was going to be theirs, plain and simple. They saw warfare was going to be necessary, but had no doubt they'd win. This was their inheritance from God. Nothing would be able to stop Him. Though others lost out and time went by, they indeed received their inheritance.

What has God promised you—either by His whispers or in His Word? If He promises it, our main challenge is to believe it. We might all see the obstacles, but we can't see them as showstoppers. For us, they should be occasions for God to show His power and receive glory.

Lord, help me to receive Your promises so deeply that I don't see obstacles as showstoppers. Help me to be like Joshua and Caleb. You are well able to accomplish Your word.

MARK DUPRÉ

JUNE 9

BIRTH ORDER

"In Him also we have obtained an inheritance, being predestined according to the purpose of Him who works all things according to the counsel of His will." (Ephesians 1:11)

These last few decades have seen an emphasis on birth order and how it affects us as individuals. There's no doubt that our place as the oldest, the youngest, or the one in the middle places us in different circumstances. The problem is when there's an implication that you're a victim of your birth order, that birth order determines your destiny, or that it explains (or excuses) the way you are.

While there's data that seems to suggest birth order carries a certain degree of importance, there are scientists who feel the effects of birth order are somewhere between negligible and nonexistent.

Look at some of the Bible's examples: King David was the eighth and youngest son. Adam and Eve's third son led to Noah, whose third son led to Abraham. Isaac's second son, Jacob, was the father of the twelve tribes. Jacob's eleventh son saved the nation from starvation because of his high position in Egypt. Moses was the second son.

Clearly birth order didn't prevent any of these people from fulfilling the call of God in growing into great leaders.

God's put us in the families He's chosen, in the order He's decided. Every position has its benefits and challenges. God is sovereign in placing us in those positions and in working those opportunities for our good (Romans 8:28). As with every circumstance we face, we must handle it with His grace, power, and wisdom. And we can rejoice because He's in charge and He knows what He's doing!

Father, help me and those I love to accept our place in the birth order as we would accept any other circumstance. Forgive me for whining, complaining, or using my position as an excuse for anything. Thank You for placing me where You did, as that is Your will for me.

JUNE 10

THE PILGRIM'S PATH

"The Lord shall preserve your going out and your coming in from this time forth, and even forevermore." (Psalm 121:8)

Psalm 121 is the second of the fifteen "Psalms of Ascent," sung by pilgrims traveling to Zion to worship the Lord. These are also called Songs of Degrees, the Gradual Psalms, or Pilgrim Songs. Psalm 121 is the "Just Getting Started On The Journey" psalm.

Where are you going right now? For most of us, that's an oddly phrased question. It's much easier to ask, "What are you doing?" as we tend to view our lives in terms of activities and events. Psalm 121 reminds us that we, like the ancient Israelites, are on a journey.

Remember how you got into the kingdom of God in the first place—God drew you to Himself. It was a journey to Him. We're still being drawn to Him. Sometimes we think of our journey as a series of checkpoints: Education, Marriage, Kids, Career (or just keeping the job), Retiring, Playing with Grandkids, Dying, and going to Heaven.

God forgive us for this. He has so much more! He's determined a far greater journey for us: "For whom He foreknew, He also predestined to be conformed to the image of His Son" (Romans 8:29).

That's the journey we're on—a journey of being conformed to the image of His Son! We've been on that journey since the day we met Jesus, and it's what's going on now in our lives. God knows where we started and every obstacle along the way. But He also knows His appointed goal and the strength of His power to accomplish His will.

> Lord, help me remember that You have me on a journey. I don't want to get caught in the day-to-day plans and activities that would distract me from Your pathway for me. Thank You that You've made every provision to bring me along this journey to this almost unimaginable appointed end.

MARK DUPRÉ

JUNE 11
THE LORD WILL GET YOU THROUGH

"I will lift up my eyes to the hills— from whence comes my help?"(Psalm 121:1)

We're on a journey to becoming more and more like Jesus, with each pilgrim's path as individual as we are. Yet Psalm 121 applies to everyone; it describes a pilgrim who knows where he's going but doesn't exactly know what he's going to run into. Isn't that all of us?

As the pilgrim began, he looked up and saw the hills. That was where the Lord had chosen to dwell (Psalm 132:13) and where the pilgrim could most directly meet God. So why did he need help? Because the hills between him and Zion were dangerous. There were lions, bears, robbers, and enemy soldiers who could easily hide in the craggy terrain. There was too much heat during the day and not enough at night. These were legitimate concerns.

As you look at your own hills—those things standing between you and Zion—what brings you fear? What are you upset about, confused about, struggling with? Whatever it is, it's just the latest thing you're running into on your journey to being like Jesus.

Rest assured, whatever is in the hills is part of the journey. Don't be distracted from your destination because of might face. Remember, our help comes from the One who made heaven and earth. Since He's the One drawing you to Himself in the first place, it's in His interest to get you through whatever is ahead so you can get to Zion. He wants you to continue your journey more than you do!

Lord, thank You that You're the One who will get me through every possible obstacle and danger. You have the plan to get through everything that slows me down. Thank You that You care more than I do that I make it to Zion.

JUNE 12

GOD OUR HELPER?

"My help comes from the Lord, who made heaven and earth. The Lord is your keeper; the Lord is your shade at your right hand." (Psalm 121:2, 5)

What a promise to those on a journey—that the Lord (the more personal, covenant name of our God) promises to be with us, as close as our shadow. He's also promised to be our helper. We tend to think of "helpers" as assistants, less important than the person doing the main task. There is the "real do-er," and then there is "the helper." It's hard sometimes to see that God has put Himself in that role for us. If we're honest, we know we need help on our Christian walk. And our helper is God Himself.

We've all had "helpers" in the kitchen, on our taxes, and in our personal lives. Some were of genuine help, some weren't. Some cared but didn't really have the power or wisdom to help. God cares more than any human could. He describes Himself as the One who made heaven and earth. That's real help and real power. It puts into perspective any need we might have along our journey.

Our culture sometimes makes us feel guilty for needing help. It takes the experiences of life and the power of the Holy Spirit to show us how much we need it. And that's good! We're created to need help— and created to have that main helper be the God who created the universe!

God's goal is not our self-sufficiency. That should never be our goal, either. We need to accept we're in constant need of help. Our Creator has made it this way. The good news is He Himself is our helper.

Lord, You are my helper. Please remind me of this until I get a complete understanding of it. Forgive me for my independence and self-sufficiency. Help me learn how to work with You as my Lord, Savior, and helper.

MARK DUPRÉ

JUNE 13

HE DOESN'T SLEEP – EVER!

He will not allow your foot to be moved; He who keeps you will not slumber. Behold, He who keeps Israel shall neither slumber nor sleep. The Lord shall preserve you from all evil; He shall preserve your soul. (Psalm 121:3–4, 7)

Are you ever afraid that you won't "make it" if you try to move forward spiritually? If you try to break a habit? Or start a new one? We so easily forget that God is with us—He's our helper all along the way. Our steps, directed by our own wisdom and will, can be unsure at times. But every step we take in Him is secure.

On the way to Jerusalem, pilgrims had to sleep in the hills, aware of what lurked in the dark in those dangerous places. But they could rest securely if they knew God was their helper, because God Himself never sleeps. Do you sleep peacefully like this? He keeps us safe during the day, where "the sun shall not strike," and at night, where the moon shines over all activities. It is all under His hand of protection.

The psalm says the Lord keeps us. "Keep" and "preserve" (the same word in the original Hebrew) are used six times in this short psalm! His hand may be invisible to us, but He's always there, helping and keeping us, making sure nothing stops us on our journey to Zion. What an exciting "replay" this will be for us in heaven, to see all the keeping and preserving that went on of which we were unaware!

So look unto the hills without fear. There may be dangers, toils, and snares. But He's there, too, actively helping, actively preserving, actively working to free us from all obstacles and help us on our way.

Please remind me all along the way how very close You are and that You've designated Yourself as my helper and keeper along the way. I am never alone and never left without help. I can rest because You never do.

JUNE 14

QUESTIONS WITH STRANGE ANSWERS: SAMSON

"When [Manoah] came to the Man, he said to Him, "Are You the Man who spoke to this woman?" And He said, "I am." Manoah said, "Now let Your words come to pass! What will be the boy's rule of life, and his work?" So the Angel of the Lord said to Manoah, "Of all that I said to the woman let her be careful. She may not eat anything that comes from the vine, nor may she drink wine or similar drink, nor eat anything unclean. All that I commanded her let her observe." (Judges 13:11–14)

The story of Samson begins with his parents. After his mother discusses her angelic visitation with her husband, Manoah questions the angel about the boy's future. We expect an answer that begins with "He will be" or "He will do." Instead, to ensure God's word will come to pass, the Angel of the Lord (whom many feel is God Himself) gives instruction to the mother.

In his Bible commentary, Matthew Henry points out that the mother's habits will directly affect the health and strength of her son. True enough, and the best preparation for a Nazarite would be to have a mother who followed Nazirite laws while pregnant, including no alcohol or contact with dead bodies.

Here we have another example of the human desire—Manoah's—to *understand* something, answered by a divine command to *do*. It's as if the Angel answered Manoah by reminding him of a command He'd already given Manoah's wife. This answer can also be the response to Manoah's earlier prayer in Judges 13:8.

How well do we remember what we've asked of the Lord? Have we been distracted by events that followed our prayer to the point where we're no longer expecting an answer? Have we simply forgotten what we've prayed?

We may forget, but the Lord doesn't. Maybe what's happening today is an answer not to yesterday's prayer, but to last week's, last month's, or last year's. Or perhaps He's *instructing* you to do something instead of satisfying your curiosity about what He's doing. Wouldn't you rather have it that way?

Lord, as much as I want to understand, I want Your will to take place. Keep me focused on Your words to me. Thank You that You hear my prayers and remember them long after I've forgotten them.

MARK DUPRÉ

JUNE 15

NOT EXACTLY "AS AT THE FIRST"

"So Joshua arose, and all the people of war, to go up against Ai ... And he commanded them, saying: "Behold, you shall lie in ambush against the city, behind the city. Do not go very far from the city, but all of you be ready. Then I and all the people who are with me will approach the city; and it will come about, when they come out against us as at the first, that we shall flee before them." (Joshua 8:3, 4–5)

Joshua had tried to take Ai earlier, but was defeated because there was sin in the camp (see Joshua 7 and the sin of Achan). Once that sin was taken care of, God gave new instructions to take the city, which was a successful effort. In his instructions, Joshua tells the people to flee when the inhabitants "come out against us as at the first." Notice what's not in Joshua's reference to that painful incident: no reproach, no guilt, no taking anyone to task. It's a simple reference to a historical fact with nothing else attached.

On one hand, Joshua's words are a simple instructional reference to the soldiers going into battle. But it's more than that. It's an inclusion of a past "failure" into the plan for a successful future. Joshua's reference here to "as at the first" is an example of God's redemption.

What do you have in your past that you would rather forget? Remember, as the Lord wiped all guilt away from His people by a complete judgment of Achan, He's wiped away all our guilt by the judgment that fell upon Jesus Christ.

If you have experienced the forgiveness of Jesus, your sins have been forgiven and forgotten. In fact, He's redeemed our pasts so that He can actually use our sinful pasts to help us because He's stripped it of all guilt and judgment. Don't be afraid of remembering if God turns your attention to your past. If it's been forgiven, the sin and guilt of it has been forgotten in God's heart.

Lord, I confess I've often pushed away memories because I haven't believed that I've been fully forgiven. I repent of my unbelief and thank You that when You say that You've forgiven and forgotten, You mean it.

JUNE 16

LOOKING AHEAD

"And truly if [Abraham, Isaac, and Jacob] had called to mind that country from which they had come out, they would have had opportunity to return. But now they desire a better, that is, a heavenly country. Therefore God is not ashamed to be called their God, for He has prepared a city for them." (Hebrews 11:15–16)

Like our spiritual forefathers who looked ahead to a time they'd never see here on earth, we need to let God be "the glory and the lifter of our heads" so that we too are looking at something beyond ourselves, something we'll never see in our lifetime.

Generations of believers. Family curses broken. A healthy church that changes its community over decades. Placing spiritual seeds in the world of law, government, business, or the arts. Missionary outreaches that change tribes and nations. Writing that will live and continue to bear fruit.

Perhaps this verse in Hebrews is the most helpful (and overlooked) passage on looking forward—and back. There's a real danger spoken here as well: "If they had called to mind that country from which they had come out, they would have had opportunity to return." They could have chosen to stop believing God, give up on the dream, and settle back into what they knew. What a loss that would have been—for them and for us.

Let's not just not look back. First, let's determine that there is no going back, even if we could. Then let's look ahead in faith (after all, Hebrews 11 is the great "faith chapter"), let Him lift up our eyes, and take a look at where we're going—our upward call, our inheritance in Him. Once we catch that vision, we won't even want to think about yesterday.

> *Father, I don't want to go back to any kind of old life. Help me see the future You have for me—in this life and far beyond it. A full picture would probably overwhelm me, so please give me enough of a glimpse of the future to motivate and excite me. Be my glory and the lifter of my head.*

MARK DUPRÉ

JUNE 17
CHEERING US ON

"Therefore we also, since we are surrounded by so great a cloud of witnesses, let us lay aside every weight, and the sin which so easily ensnares us, and let us run with endurance the race that is set before us." (Hebrews 12:1)

Hebrews 11 tells us about those who looked ahead to "a heavenly country," reminding us of those who've successfully gone before. Their faith encourages us to run our own race as they ran theirs, believing that, like them, what God is working in and through us will bear fruit long after our lives end here on earth.

The beginning of chapter 12 builds on that thought and gives us one of the most inspiring and emboldening images we could have: "so great a cloud of witnesses." What a glorious thought! We know we're never alone because God is with us. But He's not the only one! We have so many cheering us on that they look like a cloud!

If you've ever attended a race, you know the importance and power of the "witnesses." They cheer, encourage, provide refreshment along the way, and help runners make it through to the end. Their goal is to see the runners finish strong.

The witnesses in Hebrews 12 are not only waiting for Jesus, but for us. The previous verse (Hebrews 11:40) says, "Apart from us, [the Old Testament witnesses] should not be made perfect." They get it—we're all in this together. Their lives were recorded in part to cheer us on. As those who successfully ran the race, they are now happy to encourage us by example.

They are with us; they are part of us. May we begin to see this as clearly as they do.

Father, thank You that I'm part of a huge group of believers all over the world and throughout history. Thank You that the lives of others are for our encouragement.

JUNE 18

RUNNING A GOOD RACE

"Therefore strengthen the hands which hang down, and the feeble knees, and make straight paths for your feet, so that what is lame may not be dislocated, but rather be healed." (Hebrews 12:12–13)

If we're running a race, we need to make certain the path we're on is clear of obstacles and headed in the right direction—and that we're healthy and ready to move forward. We can't run our race if our hands are hanging down (this imagery is taken from a race where a runner receives a baton from those who ran before). Feeble knees also make for poor running. In addition, we can't run a good race on a muddy road or one in disrepair. It may slow us down or injure us along the way.

Straight paths are the paths of God's wisdom. Specifically, Scripture warns us against sexual immorality and being unholy, which takes us from the path God has for us and onto dangerous ground.

So before we continue our race, we need to make sure our pathway is clear and that we're healed from past injuries. Otherwise, as the runner with drooping hands and feeble knees painfully demonstrates, we can do damage to ourselves and others. We must continue our race from a place of strength and wholeness; otherwise we might become spiritually dislocated—technically able to move forward, but painfully continuing to injure ourselves as we move.

As anyone who has surgery can attest, the healing process can be painful. The point isn't to stop moving forward because it hurts. The point is to fix what's broken—or heal from what's hurting us—and exercise our way back to continue the race, this time from a place of health and strength.

Lord, thank You that You are so invested in us and in our walk that You encourage us to stop and strengthen ourselves, to get the healing we need to move forward again. Show me where I need Your healing and how to get it.

MARK DUPRÉ

JUNE 19
LEFTOVER COVENANTS

"I said, 'I will never break My covenant with you. And you shall make no covenant with the inhabitants of this land; you shall tear down their altars.' But you have not obeyed My voice. Why have you done this? Therefore I also said, 'I will not drive them out before you; but they shall be thorns in your side, and their gods shall be a snare to you.'" (Judges 2:1–3)

The Lord made a covenant with His people and He'd done His part: He'd delivered them out of Egypt and brought them into a new land. Their part of the covenant was to drive out the inhabitants of the land, avoiding its idolatry. Judges 1:27–36 tells how the tribes failed to dislodge the previous dwellers.

Those unholy inhabitants became "thorns," and their gods became a snare. Since ancient Israel's struggles and victories are an example (1 Corinthians 10:11), it's easy to see the applications to us.

God's made His covenant with us, His people. Our part of the covenant is to gratefully allow God's Spirit to conform us into the image of Jesus Christ (Romans 8:29). That means dislodging whatever holds us back from that process: sins, habits, and demonic strongholds within.

Like the Israelite tribes, some of the dislodging has occurred. Perhaps we've conquered anger, lust, or unkind speech. But perhaps the enemy's presence remains. Or perhaps, like the people of Dan, we've allowed the enemy to press us into a corner of our inheritance, preventing us from taking all that God's given us.

We may have made a covenant with the previous inhabitants of the land (e.g., greed, lust, control, etc.). Perhaps we've accommodated particular sins to such an extent that they've made a place in our lives that can't be easily dislodged. We must be constantly open to God's revelations about where we've made these largely subconscious agreements, so we may begin to work with God to dislodge them.

Lord, open my eyes and heart to be convicted of where I have made even unspoken covenants with sin. I receive Your call to renounce these covenants and take all the spiritual land You have granted me.

JUNE 20

THORNS

"And lest I should be exalted above measure by the abundance of the revelations, a thorn in the flesh was given to me, a messenger of Satan to buffet me, lest I be exalted above measure. Concerning this thing I pleaded with the Lord three times that it might depart from me. And He said to me, "My grace is sufficient for you, for My strength is made perfect in weakness." (2 Corinthians 12:7–9)

There are other reasons God has allowed—or even placed—thorns in our lives than what we read about yesterday. We see at the end of Judges 2 that while disobedience may be a reason the "enemies" are in "our land," God uses their presence to test us. This isn't simply a matter of pass/fail, as with academic tests. This is to make us stronger, to fortify our side of our covenant with the Lord, to grow our character.

Paul's experience tells us another reason for the presence of a thorn: to learn how powerful God's grace can be. Our weakness combined with God's strength is more than enough to meet any challenge.

No one likes thorns, no matter why they're there. But they point us powerfully to our Savior. We want Him to be our deliverer, and ultimately, He wants that too. But having a thorn can be uncomfortable enough to rouse us from our spiritual stupor, which is always a good thing. In seeking the Lord, we press in closer to Him.

Most of us want to know the reason for the thorn, and sometimes He tells us. Yet we can at least ask for wisdom for how to respond. Since He gives liberally and without reproach (James 1:5), we can always count on receiving that wisdom as we wait on Him. Thorns aren't fun. The gold is in seeking Him about them.

Father, I want to know why my thorns are still here. I trust that You know what You're doing. If I'm not in a place where I can receive and understand Your wisdom, then please show me what You'd like me to do about them right now. Thank You!

MARK DUPRÉ

JUNE 21

OUR GREATEST TREASURE

"Thus says the Lord: "Let not the wise man glory in his wisdom, let not the mighty man glory in his might, nor let the rich man glory in his riches; but let him who glories glory in this, that he understands and knows Me." (Jeremiah 9:23–24)

What's your greatest treasure? What are the things you hold most dear? Spouse? Children? Other loved ones? Great friends? Your health? Your job? Memories? Be honest—what are the things you're happiest about having in your life?

We might be tempted to say, "knowing the Lord." We can all agree that's a good answer. But to be completely honest, while we know He's our greatest treasure, at least in theory, knowing Him isn't usually experienced as our greatest treasure. The good news is there are things we can do to change that.

First, let's remember it's God who began a relationship with us, not the other way around. Just as He knew how to draw you to Himself in the first place, He knows how to draw you closer to Him now. It's up to you to simply keep responding to His leading. He has the plan to get you there.

We can also position ourselves correctly before God for this work to be completed. For instance, if you wanted to get to know someone better, you'd probably tell them. Then you'd offer some opportunities to help make that happen.

How God longs to hear these words from you! So tell Him. Then make steps toward getting to know Him better while being sensitive to how He would like to continue the relationship. We can know with complete confidence that He's more than ready to deepen the relationship. In fact, by the time you come around to asking, He's actually been asking the same thing of you for a long time.

Lord, I realize You want to know me more deeply and that You want me to have that same, deeper relationship with You. I want to know You more. Show me how to begin from where I am.

JUNE 22
HE COMES TO US IN HIS WORD

"You search the Scriptures, for in them you think you have eternal life; and these are they which testify of Me. But you are not willing to come to Me that you may have life." (John 5:39–40)

Continuing our theme of getting to know God better personally, what are some practical things we can do?

1. Spend time with Him and be yourself (just like you would with a human!). Be honest about who you are. Pour out your heart. Expect a response. When He speaks, pay attention, just as you would in a human conversation.

2. Read His book. This is not a legalistic exercise or something to check off your to-do list. It's not a duty, as the Pharisees might have viewed it. This is probably the only book you'll read with the author actually present with you. He longs to lead you spiritually into understanding what you're reading—not just with your mind, but also with your heart and spirit.

This is our book. It's not written for unbelievers. It's written for us. It's written to enlighten us, correct us, and transform us. We can read it quickly, dutifully, or intellectually. Or we can read it faithfully, with an open, teachable heart and a mind that's looking to know God better.

Just as we know we can't really know other people until we're with them and they talk to us, we can't really know who God is until we hear and receive His words.

Yes, a lot of the Bible is about our faith and the history of God's covenant relationship with His people. It's good to know this. Yet we also catch God's heart when we read it. His Spirit is eager to show us Jesus as we read.

Lord, deliver me from reading Your Word carelessly. Help me see the love behind it and help me to be open to Your Holy Spirit as I read it.

MARK DUPRÉ

JUNE 23

OUR GREATEST TREASURE: GROWING IN COMMUNITY

For I say, through the grace given to me, to everyone who is among you, not to think of himself more highly than he ought to think, but to think soberly, as God has dealt to each one a measure of faith. For as we have many members in one body, but all the members do not have the same function, so we, being many, are one body in Christ, and individually members of one another. (Romans 12:3–5)

If we want to get to know God well, we'll be a devoted, integral part of His people. We can see from the entire chapter of Romans 12 that one of the manifestations of a prideful spirit is not recognizing the Body of Christ or participating in it with God's love. Look at what He instructs us to do: love, give preference, rejoice and weep with others, associate with the humble. These can't be done alone. They're only done in relationship with others.

If we love God, we'll obey Him (1 John 2:3). So if we love Him, we'll obey all the Scriptures that have to do with interrelating with His people. When we struggle with people, we need to remember that when Jesus was asked about the greatest commandment, He answered with two, not one. Why? Because He sees the unity of them. He sees them as one commandment.

In God's heart, loving Him means loving His people. Loving Him means getting in there, letting iron sharpen iron (Proverbs 27:17), letting God use people to shape us into the image of Jesus, and letting Him use us to minister to His people (Romans 12:6). If we pull back from His people, we're pulling back from God.

There are aspects of God's character and heart we're only going to learn in community. As we connect with others and experience the bumps and bruises of human interaction, we learn more and more about Him. We learn His patience, His longsuffering, and, especially, His great love.

Lord, it's easy to love You and often hard to love others. But thank You that You want me to live in relationship with others. Use them in my life. Use me in theirs. And help us all to come to know You more in the process.

JUNE 24

WHO ARE YOU WEARING?

"Do not lie to each other, since you have put off your old self with its practices and have put on the new self, which is being renewed in knowledge in the image of its Creator." (Colossians 3:9–10 NIV)

There's a question that used to be heard at nearly every awards show. Reporters inevitably asked celebrities, "Who are you wearing?", referring to the name of the designer of their gown or tux.

That's a great question to ask ourselves as we go out to face the day. We've been made new in Christ. We're new creations with new hearts. But we have a choice as to who we're going to put on. Are we going to slip on the "old us," which is comfortable, familiar, and "perfectly" broken in? Yes, it's like a second skin at times, but if we're believers, this old nature has been dealt a deathblow at the cross. In spite of its apparent "comfort," it's no longer a good fit.

Scripture gives us a lot of direction on how to put off the old and put on the new. Colossians 3:8 tells us to put off things like anger, malice, slander, and filthy language. Colossians 3:12 tells us to "clothe" ourselves with compassion, kindness, humility, gentleness, and patience. But that just scratches the surface. Putting off the old and putting on the new is a lifelong study.

Who are you wearing today? Are you putting off the old man, the old nature, the old habits, the old identity? By faith, are you putting on the new man—which is who you really are—supported by God's Word, His grace, and His power? Clothing ourselves daily in Christ is the greatest clothing choice we can make.

Lord, thank You that because of what You've done, we can put off the old, which is dying anyway, and put on the new. Thank You that we're being renewed every day and we can help that process by what we "wear."

MARK DUPRÉ

JUNE 25

OUR VICTORY OVER SATAN: GOD'S WILL

"For this purpose the Son of God was manifested, that He might destroy the works of the devil." (1 John 3:8)

"Put on the whole armor of God, that you may be able to stand against the wiles of the devil." (Ephesians 6:11)

Our victory over our enemy has been bought with a great price, and Satan will do anything to undermine our confidence in that victory. If we doubt its reality or power, we miss part of our destiny and the enemy gains a temporary upper hand.

There are several reasons we have this victory, all beginning and ending in God. The first is simple: it's God's will for us. It's more than a hope or a wish. God intends for us to stand against the schemes of the devil (Ephesians 6:11). And Jesus came to destroy the enemy's power over us (1 John 3:8).

As Jesus sent His disciples out to minister in Matthew 10:7-8, He instructed them to cast out demons. The devil has clearly had his successes. But it's just as clear that it's God's will for us to reverse those successes while advancing His kingdom.

This is God's heart, as well as a presentation of His plan to strip Satan and free those held in bondage to him. Hebrews 2:14-15 says Christ's death on the cross will destroy "him who had the power of death, that is, the devil, and release those who through fear of death were all their lifetime subject to bondage."

Don't ever doubt that our victory over Satan is the will—and plan—of God. Rest assured the Lord will "take from [the devil] all his armor in which he trusted, and [will] divide his spoils" (Luke 11:22).

Lord, help me to not be distracted in extending Your victory over Satan. I declare my faith in You, that this victory is Your will and Your heart. Help me rest in that truth while I continue to seek You for my role in it.

JUNE 26

OUR VICTORY OVER SATAN: GOD'S SOVEREIGNTY

"You are of God, little children, and have overcome them, because He who is in you is greater than He who is in the world." (1 John 4:4)

Our victory over Satan is the heart and will of God for us. Yet more than that, God also has the sovereign power to win and extend this victory. It would mean little more than wishful thinking if the power we received to fight the enemy wasn't from the God who's above all and has all power. The One who wills victory also has the power to make it happen.

God's sovereignty and power is a theme flowing through the entirety of Scripture. One of the most commonly quoted encouraging "promises" of God is powerful in its direct simplicity (John 4:4, above). This is our "bottom line" for the issue of authority: God's power is greater than Satan's, no matter what we experience, feel, or see around us.

Yet nearly hidden in this powerful word is another jewel. Not only can we see that God's power is greater than our enemy's, this Scripture makes the direct comparison of God's power with Satan's. We can see where the main contest lay— between God and Satan. This is not just a statement of how powerful God is; it's also an indication of how God's power is being applied.

Greater is He who is in us (God) than our enemy. This is a great encouragement when we feel overwhelmed by Satan's power and victories. It's also an encouragement to use that superior power where it's best applied—against the wiles and schemes of our enemy.

Father, I confess that I'm sometimes disheartened and distracted from You by the temporary victories of our enemy. Please remind me that Your power is always greater than his. Remind me, too, that Your great power isn't meant to be simply admired, but to be used to destroy the enemy's kingdom and to increase Yours.

MARK DUPRÉ

JUNE 27

OUR VICTORY OVER SATAN: SIN AND DEATH

"[God] wiped out the handwriting of requirements that was against us, which was contrary to us. And He has taken it out of the way, having nailed it to the cross. Having disarmed principalities and powers, He made a public spectacle of them, triumphing over them in it." (Colossians 2:14–15)

It's God's will that we have victory over Satan. He can accomplish that because He has all power But this sovereign power has not been reserved for heavenly application only. It's been brought to earth and manifested in the cross and resurrection of Christ—the direct source of our authority over the enemy.

We see victory over Satan throughout the ministry of Jesus. His casting out demons in Mark 1:39 is just one example. Similar examples abound in the four Gospels. Through Jesus' death, He paid to have this same conquering power available to us. In predicting His death and its effects in John 12:31, Jesus says, "Now is the judgment of this world; now the ruler of this world will be cast out."

Tied to Jesus' life and death is the resurrection, whereby Jesus conquered death, first for Himself and then for us (1 Corinthians 15:54-57, Acts 2:24). This victory also includes victory over sin. Romans 6:5-7 makes that victory and its source clear.

The life, death, and resurrection of Jesus have purchased complete victory over the enemy. We have heaven, an intimate knowledge of God, and, ultimately, victory over death and sin. Jesus paid it all and bought it for us. His final step was to hand over to us this victory for which He so dearly paid.

Father, thank You that so much has been accomplished in the life, death, and resurrection of Your Son, Jesus. Help me never to take it for granted and to grow constantly in an understanding of what that purchased victory means for You and for me.

JUNE 28

OUR VICTORY OVER SATAN: THE GREAT TRANSFER

"And Jesus came and spoke to them, saying, "All authority has been given to Me in heaven and on earth. Go therefore and make disciples of all the nations, baptizing them in the name of the Father and of the Son and of the Holy Spirit, teaching them to observe all things that I have commanded you; and lo, I am with you always, even to the end of the age." Amen." (Matthew 28:18–20)

If this power had remained with Christ for forgiveness of our sins and eternal life only, we should be the most grateful of people. But God has gone beyond that, first declaring that all power has been granted to Jesus Christ, and then that He has given that power to us who believe. The transfer began even before His death and resurrection when He sent out the seventy on the first "missions trip." (See Luke 10:19 to see the limited but real authority He granted them.)

After His death and resurrection, things changed for the more powerful. Jesus spoke of His own authority directly in Matthew 28:18. The rest of the passage says two things about that authority: He expects His disciples to move in that authority as He sends them out, and it will always be available to them.

Almost hidden in Jesus' prediction of the end times is a prophetic story (Mark 13:34) that speaks of the same thing. Jesus talks about a man leaving his house and authority to his servants while he's away. Perhaps the first listeners focused on the waiting part of that story. For us, we see God's plan to give His authority to us while He goes away (i.e., back to heaven), with the idea of our using that authority in His (visible) absence.

If we believe, we have His mighty authority over our enemy. It's a gift. It's a weapon. May we use it according to His wise direction.

Lord, You paid a dear price to hand this great authority over to us. May we live in that authority every day as You continue to send us out to make disciples. Thank You for such a marvelous gift and weapon of warfare.

MARK DUPRÉ

JUNE 29

LIFT UP YOUR EYES

"Lift up your eyes and look to the heavens: Who created all these? He who brings out the starry host one by one and calls forth each of them by name. Because of his great power and mighty strength, not one of them is missing." (Isaiah 40:26 NIV)

How often we lose our perspective! Our heads get bowed down, by real or imagined weights and cares. We get confused and Satan has a heyday. Isaiah, writing prophetically to his nation 100 years in the future, addressed this very situation. The nation was going to be exiled, which would pull the proverbial rug out from everything they thought they knew. They were going to be confused, heartbroken, devastated, and depressed.

Throughout Isaiah 40, the prophet combats this new confusion with a reminder of old truths. While God's people were still reeling from current events, Isaiah reminds them of something they already knew. God's saying, "Hey, I know nothing makes sense right now. But remember what you know about Me: I created everything. If I'm bigger than creation, I am bigger than your circumstances."

God's response to His aching, confused people is not an explanation or more information. Instead, God's answer interrupts their thought process and gets them refocused. The beginning of the way out was to lift up their eyes to the Lord and let what they knew about Him sink more deeply into their hearts and minds.

Did you ever been thrown by events? Have you been equal parts upset and confused? Lift up your eyes to the Lord, even if you're upset with Him. Let Him remind you of what you know. It's times like this when we need to be recalibrated in heart and mind. God's good at this. Look to Him and let Him begin the process.

Lord, I need to be reminded regularly to lift up my eyes to You, in good times and in bad. Thank You that You're in control. There's nothing too big or difficult for You. In Your mercy, draw me back to You when events take my attention away from You.

JUNE 30

LIFT UP YOUR EYES: GOD'S TENDER HEART

"But Zion said, "The Lord has forsaken me, the Lord has forgotten me." "Can a mother forget the baby at her breast and have no compassion on the child she has borne? Though she may forget, I will not forget you! Lift up your eyes and look around; all your children gather and come to you. As surely as I live," declares the Lord, "you will wear them all as ornaments; you will put them on, like a bride." (Isaiah 49:14–15, 18)

In the second Scripture of this series on lifting up our eyes to the Lord, God's tone has changed and is more personal. Instead of calling attention to His everlasting nature and power, He calls attention to His tender heart.

If you read the rest of Isaiah 49, you'll see God go far beyond comforting Israel. He even promises more than restoration, granting Israel a future status undreamed of and not prayed for. While fully answering the prayers of the weary and downtrodden, God goes beyond answering prayer to accomplishing His eternal plan, which looked forward to the first and second coming of Christ.

There are two things to consider here. One is that in answering our prayers, God, the great multitasker, is simultaneously working out a plan of far greater and eternal scope that happens to fold in all our concerns and supplications. If we lift up our eyes, we'll see answers that go so far beyond the answers to our specific prayers as to be almost unrecognizable in their greatness.

While this shows His awesome power as Creator and Sustainer of the universe, the Lord doesn't point to this aspect of Himself in these promises. He points to a Father's heart that would never forget His children.

Yes, as Creator and sustainer, God has the power to do what He wants. But as our caring Father, He has the heart to comfort us and hear our prayers because He loves us and would never forget us or forsake us.

> Father, the love You describe in Isaiah 49 is almost impossible to comprehend. But I lift up my eyes to see You and ask that You open my eyes and heart to receive Your tender Fatherly heart. Thank You that You have great power but You operate out of great love.

MARK DUPRÉ

JULY 1
LIKE A WEANED CHILD

"Lord, my heart is not haughty, nor my eyes lofty. Neither do I concern myself with great matters, nor with things too profound for me. Surely I have calmed and quieted my soul, like a weaned child with his mother; like a weaned child is my soul within me." (Psalm 131:1–2)

This short psalm is such a tender picture that it sometimes hides the power of what's being presented here. The psalmist's soul has been through a process that leaves him like a weaned child. When a child is weaned, there's a new independence. The child's no longer directly dependent upon the mother for sustenance.

How about you now? Is there a dependence upon your parents? For example, do you need the affirmation of your mother or father to feel good about yourself? How about guidance? Our parents have lived longer than we have, and many have a wealth of wisdom to share. But God has also supplied His Word, His Spirit, pastors, counselors, and godly friends—sent to guide us into all truth (John 16:13). If a parent's word ends up having the same weight as God's, then we haven't been weaned.

Are you financially independent from your parents? If you're forty and still leaning on Mom and Dad financially, you haven't been fully weaned. If that sounds awkward, it should.

How often do you speak to your parents? Scripture tells us to honor them. But if you can't go a couple of days without communicating with them because there's an emotional need, then there is a weaning that needs to be done.

Parents can be the best and the worst aspects of growing up. We have to find the "right place" for them in our lives. We'll talk about this more tomorrow. But for now, do you think you're completely weaned from your parents?

> *Lord, help me to be completely free from dependence on my parents. Show me where I might still be leaning on them in the wrong way. I bless You that You call me to honor them. Help me to do that in every aspect of my relationship with them.*

JULY 2
RIGHTLY RELATED TO OUR PARENTS

"Surely I have calmed and quieted my soul, like a weaned child with his mother; like a weaned child is my soul within me. O Israel, hope in the Lord from this time forth and forever." (Psalm 131:2–3)

Yesterday, we focused on the word *weaned* in Psalm 131:2. Today we put our attention on the word *with*—"like a weaned child *with* his mother." Children who are not yet weaned often expect—and sometimes demand—attention and feeding from their mothers. The picture Psalm 131 gives us is of a child next to a parent, peaceful and content, free from the need to pull on Mom, yet also free to relax right next to her.

This speaks to our emotional connection with our parents. Being able to be calmed and quieted with our parents means we've worked out our feelings about them. If we once had problems with them, now we don't hate them, need them in the wrong way, or resent them, nor have we hardened our hearts against them. We've worked through our attitudes and issues enough that we can be with them in peace.

Being able to be "with" our parents means we've come to terms with the reality that they are/were people, people who succeeded in some things and might have failed in others. If they are abusive, of course you don't have to have them in your life. But you do have to work through unforgiveness and resentment so you can talk (or even think) about them and be at peace.

No matter what happened with our parents, whether they are still here or exist only in memory, God calls us to a place of peace where we can be "with" our parents, established in peace, able to honor, and free to express His grace.

Lord, in Your sovereignty, You arranged for me to have the parents I had. I thank You for the blessings, and I thank You for the grace to work through the difficulties. Help me to take my eyes off of them and put them on You and Your call for me to come to know this secure place of peace and quiet in my soul.

MARK DUPRÉ

JULY 3

MARY: OUR EXAMPLE

"Then Mary said, "Behold the maidservant of the Lord! Let it be to me according to your word." (Luke 1:38)

Mary is one of the most beautiful, humble, and godly figures in Scripture, and her life is worthy of serious study. Yet because the medieval church put some unbiblical associations on her (e.g., she was conceived without sin, remained sinless throughout her life, was taken directly into heaven, is some kind of mediator between man and God), Christians after the Reformation have been reluctant to put any serious attention on her, lest we swing the pendulum too far back in the other direction.

To set the record straight, let's settle a few things: Mary isn't God's mother; she gave birth to the man who was the incarnation of the Son of God. She also had other children than Jesus (Matthew 13:55), likely including James and Jude, authors of the New Testament books bearing their names.

There's far too much for us to learn from Mary to put her in the shadows. Her words in Luke 1:38 exhibit a heart of complete surrender and trust. Mary had just been told she'd be pregnant out of wedlock, which meant shame and possible stoning. At the least, her child would have suffered from questions about the legitimacy of his birth, which Jesus probably faced (see John 8:41, possibly a sarcastic reference to questions surrounding Mary's pregnancy).

Mary wasn't naïve about what this pregnancy would mean, which makes her trusting response all the more remarkable. Not only is she an example of faith and obedience, but her life demonstrates what God can do in the life of a willing servant.

> *Lord, thank You for such an example of humility and godliness as Mary. Help me to have the open and trusting heart she demonstrated, believing that You knew best even when she knew what some of the repercussions of her obedience might be. That's the kind of trusting heart I want.*

JULY 4

MARY: WHERE WE COME FROM DOESN'T MATTER

"Now in the sixth month the angel Gabriel was sent by God to a city of Galilee named Nazareth, to a virgin betrothed to a man whose name was Joseph, of the house of David. The virgin's name was Mary. And having come in, the angel said to her, "Rejoice, highly favored one, the Lord is with you; blessed are you among women!" (Luke 1:26–28)

Mary was a poor, teenage girl living among a disrespected people, at a time when spirituality was generally associated with men. Even among her people, her town was of low reputation: "Can anything good come out of Nazareth?" (John 1:46). If Mary were in a Jane Austen novel, it would be said that "she had no prospects."

Yet, as Acts 10:34 reminds us, "God is no respecter of persons." If anyone could have been considered "out of the running" to be used by God, a lowly teenager from the middle of nowhere would be. Nothing in her gender, circumstances, family, or position in society would qualify her for greatness in this world. For those who want to look for some great act of faith on Mary's part that might have qualified her spiritually for this great role, we're given nothing. Yes, Mary was "highly favored" and "blessed," but that is all because of God's love and grace extended toward her.

If God could choose Mary and grant her "high favor," then He can choose and use anyone. We can never think that where we came from, our social status, our youth, or our gender could ever disqualify us from being mightily used by God. Anything that tries to convince us otherwise is not of God.

Scripture doesn't reveal why God chose Mary. But the Bible does reveal that Mary's view of herself overrode all the natural "limitations" she might have possessed: she was a "handmaid of the Lord" (Luke 1:38 KJV) who gave free reign to whatever God wanted for her.

> Lord, I confess that I've thought You were limited in using me because of the outward circumstances of my life. I see from Mary's life that her circumstances were no limitation to Your working powerfully through her. Help me to grow in faith and trust that I can come to the point of complete openness to whatever You have for me. "Let it be to me according to Your word."

MARK DUPRÉ

JULY 5

MARY: GOD USES THE TROUBLED AND THE FEARFUL

"But when she saw him, she was troubled at his saying, and considered what manner of greeting this was. Then the angel said to her, "Do not be afraid, Mary, for you have found favor with God. And behold, you will conceive in your womb and bring forth a Son, and shall call His name Jesus." (Luke 1:29–31)

Mary's life has shown us that God can choose anyone He wants, from any place at any time to any background and circumstance. He doesn't just choose those who don't feel troubled or get scared. Look at Luke 1:29. Mary didn't live in a spiritual state of ecstasy; she lived in the real world into which an agent of God came to speak to her. It's only natural to be "troubled" at what he said; anyone would be. It was a normal response to try to understand what was going on.

Since conception without "knowing a man" (Luke 1:34) was physiologically impossible, Mary had a logical question about how this was going to happen. Her doubts, thoughts, questions, and fears were natural, and God was gracious enough to deal with them.

God can handle our questions, thoughts, confusions, and fears. He isn't put off by them, as long as our heart is poised to obey. Mary's spiritual posture was to say yes to God. She just possessed a few questions. She didn't need answers to decide whether or not to obey. She didn't need to "think things through" to make up her mind about whether or not to embrace His will.

How encouraging to know that God uses people who have questions and fears as well as logical minds. How gracious of God to show Himself to Mary by meeting her at her level. If we position ourselves to do His will as Mary did, who knows how God may meet us at ours!

Lord, You have shown us that You use normal folks—people who get troubled, have questions, and ponder things. Thank You that You were gracious enough with Mary to answer her questions and calm her fears. Let my questions be like hers and not arising from unbelief. May they come from a heart of faith that is ready to obey.

JULY 6

MARY: POISED TO DO HIS WILL

"But Mary kept all these things and pondered them in her heart. (Luke 2:19) Then [Jesus] went down with them and came to Nazareth, and was subject to them, but His mother kept all these things in her heart." (Luke 2:51)

What we don't see or read in Scripture is often as important as what we do. We don't see Gabriel asking Mary how she felt about the situation God was presenting. He doesn't even try to convince her to respond a certain way. He simply came and announced what God was going to do.

The Scriptures above paint a picture of a thoughtful woman and a tender heart. Yet nowhere do we see Mary sorting through her feelings before declaring herself "the handmaid of the Lord" (Luke 1:38 KJV). It's clear that while she had many feelings, working through those feelings was a task to do after saying yes to God.

In our society, a great percentage of media coverage involves how people feel about things— when they win a race, when they lose a race, when someone has disappointed them, when a victory is gained. We can receive the mistaken impression that fully expressing and working through all of our feelings is a prerequisite to doing anything.

But as noted in yesterday's devotion, Mary was poised to do God's will, no matter what it might involve. That spiritual position is the best position to take regarding our feelings. Being ready to do His will positions us to deal in wisdom with every manner of feeling we might have. Feelings should never lead us, but they can be a great joy in the wake of our obedience.

Lord, my feelings can tempt me into unhealthy directions at times. Help me to put them in their proper place in my life, enjoying what You want me to and having Your wisdom to know what to do with the rest.

MARK DUPRÉ

JULY 7

GOSSIP'S TASTY TRIFLES

"The words of a talebearer are like tasty trifles, and they go down into the inmost body. (Proverbs 26:22) A dishonest man spreads strife, and a whisperer separates close friends." (Proverbs 16:28 ESV)

Gossip is a scourge of this age. It's always been a common sin, but there are so many ways of spreading untruths and unauthorized information these days that the damaging power of gossip is often unrestrained. Our call as believers is to understand what gossip is, be aware of its negative consequences, and to refrain from participating in it.

Gossip is powerful. We think it's a matter of our ears and our minds, but that isn't what Scripture says. It goes down into our "inmost body." It spreads strife and separates close friends. We recoil at the idea of deliberately doing that, but that's the effect of sharing these "tasty trifles."

One mistake we make is thinking something isn't gossip if it's true. Yet truth is only part of the picture. First, there's gossip's intention. Is it to make the talebearer feel stronger, better, smarter, or "there first" with the information? We need to be brutally honest with ourselves as to why we should be sharing any information. To say we're sharing for purposes of prayer can be a destructive self-deception.

Lastly, there's the question of appropriateness and authority: Is this your information to share? Do you have the right to share it? Is it your story or someone else's story? You have someone else's reputation in your hands, and a person's good name is valuable. Gossip goes down deep into the hearer, so we need to be aware of what we're placing into another person's innermost parts.

Father, gossip is so common in this world that I don't often notice when I'm doing it. Show me when I don't have the authority (or Your permission) to share what I hear. Please open my eyes and remind me of Your word about its powerful effects.

JULY 8
RESISTING GOSSIP'S EFFECTS ON US

"An evildoer gives heed to false lips; a liar listens eagerly to a spiteful tongue." (Proverbs 17:4) "Where there is no wood, the fire goes out; and where there is no talebearer, strife ceases." (Proverbs 26:20)

While we may be diligent to not spread gossip ourselves, the presence of gossip around us may cause its effects to come our way. Our response? Guard against it. But if we hear it, we need to know what to do with it.

Scripture's quite strong in describing those who listen to gossip and enjoy doing so. The Bible calls them evildoers and liars—harsh terms. The problem with gossip is we often don't recognize the fruit of "false lips" or see evidence of a "spiteful tongue." "Giving heed" and listening "eagerly" can be a trap if information isn't presented truthfully and righteously or if a talebearer's intention is less than honorable.

If we realize we've listened eagerly to gossip, we need to repent and ask forgiveness. If we heard it with a good, open heart, we still need to acknowledge something has gone deeply into us—something that takes the power of God to get out. Gossip is like an ugly irritant that grows a deformed pearl of judgment unless it's removed. We need to bring what we've heard, and any judgment we may have had against another person, before the Lord, and ask Him to remove it.

If you've spread gossip and later found out it wasn't true, you need to set the record straight. If you tend to be a gossiper, that's a lot of people and a lot of work. The good news is that if you're not, there's very little work to be done! Let's determine that as far as gossip's concerned, "the fire goes out" and "strife ceases" with us.

Lord, help me to do the work that needs to be done when I've received gossip, either eagerly or accidentally. Even when I've been defiled by gossip, let me do what needs to be done to destroy its effect. Let the fire die in me so that strife will cease with me.

MARK DUPRÉ

JULY 9

A THANKFUL HEART

"Rejoice always, pray without ceasing, in everything give thanks; for this is the will of God in Christ Jesus for you." (1 Thessalonians 5:16–18)

Giving thanks to the Lord "in everything" can be a sticky thing if we don't understand God's power, purposes, and heart. Why should we give thanks for pain or trial or persecution? Is God really that perverse?

First Thessalonians 5:16–18 presents almost a bird's-eye view of how to move through our whole lives, always (deep down) rejoicing, praying and giving thanks in all things (or "circumstances," in some translations). It's an attitude that should color our entire existence, not just pop up occasionally when we're feeling especially spiritual.

This passage says, "in everything," not "for everything." God isn't saying we should thank Him that others sin, that someone died, or that we're suffering. We give thanks because He can redeem it all. He's always working everything together for our good (if we're in Christ), eventually working everything together for His glory. We give thanks because He's with us in our circumstances. We give thanks because we can see beyond the short-term pain to the long-term victories. We give thanks because, no matter what's right in front of us, He's in control, and His covenant love to His people never ends (Psalm 107:1).

Without God and His promises, we have no reason to be thankful in anything or for anything. But because He's with us, working on our behalf, we have reason for thanks. We may have to seek His face for the proper perspective from which to give genuine thanks, but there's ample reason to have a thankful heart.

Father, help me look beyond what's temporary in my circumstances so that I can see what is eternal and give You thanks for how You work all things to my good. Help me have a grateful heart, so I can see more things to thank You for and more reasons to be thankful for You and Your love

JULY 10

DAVID AND UZZA: GETTING ANGRY WITH GOD

"Uzza put out his hand to hold the ark, for the oxen stumbled. Then the anger of the Lord was aroused against Uzza, and He struck him because he put his hand to the ark; and he died there before God. And David became angry because of the Lord's outbreak against Uzza." (1 Chronicles 13:9–11)

At first glance, it might seem David had every reason to be angry. He was trying to bring the ark of the Lord back to Jerusalem. That was a good thing. He'd even bought a new cart for the occasion. That, however, was a rash and thoughtless decision (read the entire chapter of 1 Chronicles 13 for the big picture).

Was David angry with God? If so, was it for ruining his celebration or for hurting Uzza? Perhaps he was angry with himself. Certainly David had a mess on his hands and was angry about that. While Scripture doesn't say specifically that David was angry with God, David knew God's sovereignty. He knew God was ultimately responsible for what happened that day.

Have you ever been angry with God? (Don't be religious or polite here.) What things come up when you get angry with Him? Are they the same things again and again? If so, there's something that needs His touch, your repentance, or both.

Responding in anger toward God requires repentance, yes, but it also requires some soul searching. Bring your reasons out into the light and to the cross. The enemy may say they're too silly or too sinful to bring into the light. That's because he wants us to hang onto hurtful things.

When you find yourself angry with God, take a good look at what's coming to the surface. Bring it all to the cross, even the "silly," embarrassing things. Release it. Repent and cry out for healing and wisdom. This is redemption at work.

> Lord, help me see why I get angry at things and especially at You. If there are patterns, I want to see them, get healed, and learn from them. You died for everything, including all the things underlying my angry responses. May Your death not be in vain for them.

JULY 11

DAVID AND UZZA: COMING AROUND TO GOD'S WAYS

"David was afraid of God that day, saying, "How can I bring the ark of God to me?" (1 Chronicles 13:12)

Here David asks an excellent question, and one that should have been asked earlier. David's fear of the Lord was becoming the beginning of wisdom for him (Proverbs 9:10).

We must assume that once David's heart was quieted and his anger quelled, he began to ask himself and others what happened. A healthy fear of the Lord led him to realize he'd completely missed the will of God in how to transport the ark. The ark, as one of the "holy things," needed to be carried by the right people in the right way—and not directly touched under penalty of death. It was all right there in God's Word: Numbers 4:15, 7:9, 18:3.

The ark was only supposed to be carried on poles resting on their shoulders, but David had placed it in a cart—the exact treatment the unknowing, idol-worshiping Philistines had used when they returned it to Israel. Using a new cart was hardly a proper substitute for doing things God's way.

God has His ways of doing things. His will and ways need to be sought. Sometimes, God's quick judgment can be seen as harsh. But David was helping set up the worship of God in Jerusalem. It was a key moment. Calling attention to His ways and His holiness was a mercy in the long run. This act of God's judgment resulted in the fear of God and called attention to the importance of obeying His Word. What wisdom came of it!

Lord, help me remember that You have ways You want to be worshiped. There are things You love and things You hate. May a healthy fear of You be my constant companion, leading me to greater and greater wisdom.

JULY 12

HE GUARDS, WE GUARD

"O Timothy! Guard what was committed to your trust. (1 Timothy 6:20) But I am not ashamed, for I know whom I have believed, and I am convinced that he is able to guard until that Day what has been entrusted to me. By the Holy Spirit who dwells within us, guard the good deposit entrusted to you." (2 Timothy 1:12, 14 ESV)

Here Paul is writing to Timothy, his disciple and son in the faith. He's writing about holding onto the sound doctrine imparted to him by Paul, doctrine now endangered by false teachers bringing in an early version of what would become the gnostic heresy.

There's a beautiful tension in the words Paul writes. On one hand, he expresses his full confidence that God will guard what was entrusted to him right through to the day of the second coming. At the same time, Paul charges Timothy with guarding the same things. God's power will enable Timothy to keep the godly deposit safe. But even with God's power, it's still Timothy's responsibility.

There's no contradiction here. There are simply two truths that are both true at the same time: God will guard what was committed to Timothy, and it's up to Timothy to guard it too.

Like Paul, we can rest knowing that God is well able to guard those things entrusted to us. It's His desire to do so. It's also up to us to guard those same things, using the power of His Spirit. Within God's greater power to guard, we join Him in guarding. His ability and power take nothing away from our duty to guard these things. And our call to guard these things is not an action outside of Christ, something we do independently or in our own strength. It's what we do with Him. Our minds might have trouble with that, but our spirits understand.

Lord, let me be more like Jesus in looking to what You do and doing what I'm called to do with You. Help me to be diligent to guard what You've deposited in me as I thank You for guarding it as well.

MARK DUPRÉ

JULY 13
WEIGHING IN ON TRIALS

And the Lord said to Satan, "Behold, all that [Job] has is in your power; only do not lay a hand on his person." (Job 1:12)

I know a man who arrived at the airport and set his suitcase on the scale at the airline counter. To his great surprise, the scale showed it was overweight. "Only kidding!" the airline attendant said with a devious smile. She'd put her thumb on the bag, weighing it down beyond its proper weight. At that moment, he heard the inaudible but clear voice of the Lord: "This is what Satan does in real life."

Our trials have a true and necessary weight in life. It's the perfect, appropriate weight for us. Its goal is to transform us into Christ's image (Romans 8:29, 2 Corinthians 3:18) and work for our good (Romans 8:28). It produces good fruit.

Yet we find other weights, extra burdens that can lead to discouragement, even despair. That extra weight originates in the enemy's attempt to maintain the remnants of his kingdom and hurt those God loves. It's given life (more weight) from the enemy's lies. Its goal is bad fruit.

We need to take a second look at our trials. Yes, God is sovereign and allows the trials, as He did with Job. But some of the weights we experience may come from the enemy and need to be removed. We may need to renounce the enemy's lies and embrace God's truths.

Look at the fruit of your current trial. Where there's anger, judgment, depression, or discouragement, there's an added weight not from God. We may not be able to remove the trial, but with God's wisdom and guidance, we may be able to lighten it by removing Satan's thumb.

Lord, help me to discern what is of You and what is from the enemy in my trials. Help me not to accept weights that are from my enemy. Help me to recognize bad fruit and remove it at its root.

JULY 14
GOD OF ALL

"Praise the Lord, all you Gentiles! Laud Him, all you peoples! For His merciful kindness is great toward us, and the truth of the Lord endures forever. (Psalm 117:1–2) Or is He the God of the Jews only? Is He not also the God of the Gentiles? Yes, of the Gentiles also." (Romans 3:29)

In Old Testament times, most people worshiped their local gods. They might have been gods of natural phenomena, such as fire or fertility, or the ruling god of the area. Most nations outside of Israel assumed that Yahweh (the Lord) was simply the name of that region's particular local god.

God continually reminded Israel that while He was their God, He was also Lord of the whole earth. He wasn't their tribal god, local god, or god of their religion. He was the One who created the universe and everything (and everyone) in it.

Sometimes when we evangelize, we come from a place where we're asking people to take our local/personal/religious God as their God. But the truth is: God is already their God. They may not have "personalized" that or acknowledged it. But because God is the Lord of the whole earth, He is their God. Their personal relationship with Him—either nonexistent or vibrant—has nothing to do with that fact. When they come to Christ, they're making everyone's God their own personal Lord. But He has always been and will always be their God.

This is something we need to "personalize" deeply in our hearts when we pray for others and share the saving love of God with them. God is Lord over all, calling everyone to repent. He who could do anything did the supreme act of sacrifice for those who choose to receive it. But He is not just our God. He is their God and everyone's God.

Lord, help me remember as I share Your gospel message that You are everyone's God, even before You become their personal Lord. Let that change the way I share Your incredible love and the way I view the unsaved in general.

MARK DUPRÉ

JULY 15

QUESTIONS WITH STRANGE ANSWERS: SHOWING, NOT TELLING?

"Then Manoah [Samson's father] said to the Angel of the Lord, "What is Your name, that when Your words come to pass we may honor You?" And the Angel of the Lord said to him, "Why do you ask My name, seeing it is wonderful?" (Judges 13:17–18)

This exchange is similar to Jacob's with the Angel of the Lord that appeared to Him in Genesis 32. After wrestling with the Angel all night, Jacob asked the Angel his name. It was logical to ask, as Jacob had just been granted a new name—Israel—by the Angel. But Jacob's request was denied. In that culture, revealing a person's name was believed to give insight into that person and considered an attempt to gain leverage in dealing with him. Considering Jacob's history of deception and misuse of authority up to this point, it isn't surprising the Angel withheld his name. Instead, he asked Jacob another question: "Why is it that you ask about my name?" Then he blessed Jacob.

Manoah seems to exhibit more faith than Jacob here. He's less self-concerned and more intent on giving proper honor. Yet the Angel responds by asking a question similar to the one asked of Jacob: "Why do you ask My name, seeing it is wonderful?"

Manoah's response to that answer was sacrifice and worship, after which the Angel did something "wonder-full," ascending in the sacrifice's flame toward heaven, *showing* rather than *telling* Manoah and his wife whom they'd been dealing with—God. A name, no matter how profound, wouldn't have sufficed. God demonstrated His power, a much greater encouragement to Manoah than revealing a name he wouldn't have understood.

Is God *showing* you things rather than *telling* you things right now? Are you asking to hear when He'd prefer that you ask to see?

> Lord, lead me in asking the right questions to match the answers You're desiring to give me. Forgive me for pressing for one kind of answer when You're graciously giving me something better. Give me eyes to see what You're doing and a heart to understand.

JULY 16
THERE'S ALWAYS HOPE

"Now when Ahithophel [counselor to King David's rebellious son Absalom] saw that his advice was not followed, he saddled a donkey, and arose and went home to his house, to his city. Then he put his household in order, and hanged himself, and died." (2 Samuel 17:23)

Suicide is never presented as anything but negative in the Scriptures. Ahithophel, Saul, Abimelech, Zimri, and Judas all took their lives— and Scripture is clear they all made the wrong choice. Sadly, suicide is one of the scourges of our age, with the suicide rate among believers almost the same as unbelievers.

For those who are struggling, and those who want to help, remember: No matter how bad things seem, there's hope, because God's taking us forward into His plan. He never leaves us alone or where we are. He works through time to lessen pain and is described as the lifter of our heads. (Psalm 3:3).

Help is available. God gives us everything we require for life and godliness (2 Peter 1:3). If first attempts at getting help didn't work well, give it another try. God never leaves us in the lurch.

If you believe in God, this is a terrible way to meet Him. Thoughts that guide us in the direction of suicide are either lies or partial truths all twisted around. The devil comes to steal, kill, and destroy (John 10:10).

Suicide is also deeply hurtful—to others. It only kills the person, not the pain. Instead, it *transfers* that pain to other people. It lives on, most often magnified, tormenting others, sometimes for the rest of their lives.

For those contemplating suicide, give God time and look for help. The darkness you feel is the devil's smokescreen. For those helping others, pray against deception, and be the one to provide the help needed.

Lord, I pray for those struggling with this terrible temptation. Release hope in them and may they reach out for help—to You or to someone else. Strengthen me to be the encourager and hope-giver You want me to be.

MARK DUPRÉ

JULY 17
THE FREEDOM TO SAY NO

"Receive one who is weak in the faith, but not to disputes over doubtful things. For one believes he may eat all things, but he who is weak eats only vegetables. Who are you to judge another's servant? To his own master he stands or falls. Indeed, he will be made to stand, for God is able to make him stand." (Romans 14:1–2, 4)

If you have enough deep conversations with fellow believers, you'll find no two Christians view everything the same way. There are differences in interpretation, in emphasis, in practice, and in perspective. Since the Lord's ways and thoughts are so very far above ours, we can rightly assume that we all fall short of understanding the almighty God. No one could hope to have full comprehension of all of His ways.

The word *receive* in Romans 14:1 is also translated "accept" and "welcome." These words speak to the attitude of our hearts. We often "tolerate" and "endure" others with whom we disagree, but these attitudes keep us from enjoying Spirit-led fellowship. Receiving and welcoming them is another level of blessing, one that benefits us and glorifies God.

Paul does, however, call this particular group of believers "weak." In context, Paul is describing those who haven't understood the liberty we have in Christ and are tied to old legalistic methods of relating to God. Most of us come from some point of legalism before we come to Christ, and we bring that baggage with us. We all need others to receive, accept, and welcome us as we come to understand our freedoms in Christ.

The last verse in the passage above ("Who are you?") contains a slight rebuke as well as an encouragement. Clearly, we need to repent of judging others. The same wonderful God who helps us grow from weakness to strength will help others do the same thing. He's Master of us all, and helping us stand strong is His business, responsibility, and pleasure.

Lord, forgive me for closing my heart to those who think differently, and especially those who are genuinely weak. Help me to welcome, receive, and accept them. Cleanse those things inside that prevent me from doing that.

JULY 18
FREER THAN WE THOUGHT

"But beware lest somehow this liberty of yours become a stumbling block to those who are weak. But when you thus sin against the brethren, and wound their weak conscience, you sin against Christ."(1 Corinthians 8:9, 12)

We can read the Scripture above as a limitation on our Christian liberty. Or we can see just how expansive and grand our liberty is. Here Paul continues the discussion about whether believers should eat meat sacrificed to idols when in the presence of a weaker brother or sister whose beliefs differ from their own.

Paul hits the nail on the head for most of us when he says in 1 Corinthians 10:29, "For why is my liberty judged by another man's conscience?" He then goes on to tell us not to give any offense to anyone else for their conscience's sake, the sake of the gospel, and the glory of God.

Our liberties are not impinged by such a circumstance. In fact, our liberties are more affirmed than ever. Yes, you're free to eat the meat in good conscience before God in one circumstance. In another circumstance, you don't have to, because you're free to love and "in honor [give] preference to one another" (Romans 12:10). That's love in action. And it's our freedom in action as well.

Most of us don't face the idol situation today. But having an alcoholic drink or seeing a movie may well be a stumbling block for others, either for doctrinal or personal reasons. It may feel that there are limits placed on our freedom when faced with situations like these, but in actuality, these scenarios just confirm how very free we are.

Lord, help me to love You and others enough to give up a right or two for the sake of the gospel and loving others. Remind me that I'm free in You to do that with grace. Thank You for that freedom!

MARK DUPRÉ

JULY 19

A FATHER'S COMFORT

"And he recognized [Joseph's bloody tunic] and said, "It is my son's tunic. A wild beast has devoured him. Without doubt Joseph is torn to pieces." Then Jacob tore his clothes, put sackcloth on his waist, and mourned for his son many days. And all his sons and all his daughters arose to comfort him; but he refused to be comforted, and he said, "For I shall go down into the grave to my son in mourning." Thus his father wept for him." (Genesis 37:33–35)

Like any loving parent, when Jacob was presented with the so-called "evidence" of his son Joseph's death, he grieved. Although his other children tried to comfort Jacob, for reasons left unexplained, he refused to be comforted. Perhaps he didn't believe Joseph was dead and hoped he'd return. Perhaps he felt leaving his grief behind would dishonor the memory of his beloved son. Whatever the reason, Jacob made it clear he planned to mourn this loss until the day he died.

For some of us, refusing to be comforted may be a stand we take to maintain control over a situation over which we have no real control. Clearly this isn't what God has for us. Holding on to grief too long isn't healthy, and it's not God's will for us. God is our Comforter. Turning away from His comfort is turning away from Him.

Eventually, we need to bow before our Lord and let Him comfort us. As a loving Father, it's a role He wants to take. Not only does He love us and desire to free us from tormenting grief, He's chosen to use us to be comforters to others as we learn to receive His comfort—either directly from Him, through others, or both. This is how He equips people to bless others in time of sorrow. Let's allow our Father to comfort us. In time, we can pass on His gift and use it to comfort others.

Father, thank You that You are a Comforter. You know exactly how to touch us in our grief. Help me to receive Your comfort when I need it and help me to see how I can be used to bless others in the same way when they need it.

JULY 20
VOWS

"Make vows to the Lord your God, and pay them; let all who are around Him bring presents to Him who ought to be feared." (Psalm 76:11)

Vows are a solemn promise or pledge that binds us to perform a specific act or behave in a certain manner. Vows in Scripture were made to God as a promise in expectation of His favor or in thanksgiving for His blessings. All were voluntary, but after the vow was made, it had to be performed. Perhaps the most famous vow in Scripture was made by the prophet Samuel's mother (1 Samuel 1:10–11) and the most notorious by Jephthah in Judges 11.

We live in an age that encourages loose and thoughtless speech. It can be easy to make a vow and not even realize it. Jesus preached simplicity of speech: "But let your 'Yes' be 'Yes,' and your 'No,' 'No.' For whatever is more than these is from the evil one" (Matthew 5:37). Remember that vows, once made, are expected to be fulfilled.

We want to make sure that whatever we utter as a vow is godly and realistic. Here are a few things to keep in mind:

- Be real. Never make a vow beyond your source of strength or ability to fulfill it.
- Once you make the vow, commit yourself to keeping it.
- Never make a vow to do anything against God's Word.
- Never make a vow as part of a "deal" with God.
- Never let a vow about tomorrow substitute for obedience today.

Vows are serious expressions, and we need to view them with sincerity and a desire to honor God.

> *Father, help me not to utter the wrong kind of vow. Help me understand how serious a spoken vow is and how it fits in with my relationship with You. May I never make a vow as part of a deal, but only as thanksgiving and honor.*

JULY 21
INNER VOWS

"I am the vine, you are the branches. He who abides in Me, and I in him, bears much fruit; for without Me you can do nothing." (John 15:5)

Perhaps more powerful than spoken vows are the inner vows we make. Some we may have said aloud; others remain hidden in our hearts. We know a vow's been made when something—a person or circumstance—contests that vow. We might get defensive, protective, and angry, and maybe don't even know why.

Maybe you've never vowed a vow like Jephthah in Judges 11. But how about one of these: "I'm not going to treat my kids like my parents treated me." "No one's going to get me to lose my cool." "I'll never be dependent on anyone again—I'll make it on my own."

The tricky part of making inner vows is that our goal is usually a good one, perhaps even a godly one. Peter vowed to remain faithful to Jesus (Mark 14:29), yet it was no time at all before he betrayed him. It was a vow of good intention, but there was one fatal flaw: he relied on his own strength to fulfill it.

It's not the vow itself that's usually wrong. It's the *how of the vow*. Every inner vow begins with "I will" or a similar sentiment. It's based on our strength and determination, not on God's grace.

Identifying inner vows is a Spirit-led endeavor. For permanent change, we need the power of His Spirit combined with a humble heart. We need to give God free reign to touch old memories and get into tender places. We'll learn how to undo these vows tomorrow. For today, let's agree with David's prayer:

"Search me, O God, and know my heart; try me, and know my anxieties; and see if there is any wicked way in me, and lead me in the way everlasting" (Psalm 139:23–24).

JULY 22

UNDOING UNGODLY VOWS

"The Lord is my strength and my shield; my heart trusted in Him, and I am helped." (Psalm 28:7)

Old ungodly vows can be a great impediment to our spiritual progress. They must be identified, repented of, and renounced. Inside an inner vow are hurts waiting to be healed and prayers waiting to be released.

For example: "No one's going to tell me what to do again." This clearly comes from a desire not to get hurt. It's time to forgive the offense and the offender. Then we can ask the Lord to heal any hurt left over from the experience and undo all the mental and emotional tangling that goes with making ungodly inner vows.

Next, we repent and renounce the vow. This can be confusing or maddening. After all, someone else hurt me! What do I have to repent of? We sinned in making a vow before forgiving, before asking for God's wisdom, and doing it in our own strength. Bottom line: We left God out of things and moved ahead. We didn't let Him be our defender! That needs to be repented of.

When we pray, "I want to let You become Lord of this whole situation. I take my hands off of it!" that puts us in a place that seems very vulnerable. But it's where we discover God's strength and covering.

It's time to release the prayers that have been waiting—sometimes for years—to be prayed. Oh, the freedom and joy that awaits us in the Lord as we go from grace to grace and glory to glory! There's more power to this process than you can know. It's work and it's worth it.

Lord, help me work with Your Spirit in bringing to light every ungodly inner vow I've made. Help me replace vows and judgments with new trust in You. Help me replace my hurts with Your healing, and release every prayer that these vows have locked up all these years. Thank You!

MARK DUPRÉ

JULY 23

ARE YOU STILL WORSHIPPING AT THE HIGH PLACES?

"Asa did what was good and right in the eyes of the Lord his God, for he removed the altars of the foreign gods and the high places." (2 Chronicles 14:2–3)

High places in ancient Israel were a combination of godly worship and idolatry. Some were centers of idol worship and stayed that way. Others began to be used for worshipping the one true God. But they were always a temptation for God's people. Even when the high places were replaced by the permanent temple in Jerusalem and worship was to be centralized, high places remained.

They remained because some people wanted to worship the Lord the way they wanted to worship the Lord. It was what they'd gotten comfortable with. Traveling to Jerusalem was so … inconvenient.

Are we still worshipping at our own high places? Our homes can be places of true worship. But they can turn into a high place when we skip church and tell ourselves God is just as happy with our Bible reading and prayers that day. Or we can substitute enjoying God's beautiful creation for worshipping with God's people. Nature is beautiful, but we can let it become a high place for us.

Israel had the hardest time getting rid of its high places. We do, too. The remnants of our fallen nature insist we can worship God however, and wherever, we choose. That's simply independence, which is first cousin to the sin of rebellion. God's ways aren't always "convenient." If we love God enough, we'll long to worship Him in a way that pleases Him.

Lord, please cleanse me of "my own ways" when it comes to worshipping You, obeying You, and giving You the glory. I want to make a divine exchange of my ways for Yours. Where I'm substituting my wisdom for Yours, please show me. Thank You that You know best.

JULY 24
SECOND CHANCES

"Now Barnabas was determined to take with them John called Mark. But Paul insisted that they should not take with them the one who had departed from them in Pamphylia, and had not gone with them to the work. Then the contention became so sharp that they parted from one another." (Acts 15:37–39)

Did you ever fail in a ministry situation— either as a "crash-and-burn missionary" or someone who simply couldn't get the hang of being an usher? Perhaps you couldn't sing well enough with the choir or just didn't find your place in children's ministry.

John Mark was one of those people. After an auspicious beginning accompanying Barnabas and Paul on a great missionary trip, Mark left before the trip was over and returned to Jerusalem (we're not told why). The tension was so great over this event that when Barnabas wanted to take Mark on his second trip with Paul, Paul disagreed so sharply that he and Barnabas split up and went their separate ways.

What would you have done if you'd been Mark? Would you have given up on ministry, assuming the Lord was done with you? Would you have let discouragement take you out of the race? Would you have let bitterness into your heart? Would you have stopped serving Him?

We're not given a lot of detail on what Mark thought, but we can follow Paul's ever-softening heart toward him. As we see Paul move from anger and rejection to full acceptance of Mark and his ministry, we also see a minister who didn't give up.

From Paul's acceptance, we also see the Lord's. Mark hung in there, trusting the Lord to heal, open doors, and continue using him. Not only did he become a useful missionary after all, but working with Peter's material, he became the author of the second Gospel. That's hardly a failure!

Lord, thank You that You look past—and can actually build on—my failures. When I fall, help me get back up and get back into a place of service. I trust You will keep working with me as I make myself available to You.

JULY 25

PAUL LEARNS A LESSON

"Only Luke is with me. Get Mark and bring him with you, for he is useful to me for ministry." (2 Timothy 4:11)

The story of Mark (see yesterday's devotion) is one of the most powerful, subtle, and encouraging secondary stories of the New Testament. But it's not just Mark's story. It's part of Paul's story as well.

It's understandable that Paul didn't want to have John Mark go along for the second trip when he'd left them during the first trip. But was Paul too harsh? Was he trying to avoid further inconvenience on a challenging trip? Was he not very forgiving?

We don't know his thinking, but we do know Paul loved the Lord and, eventually, his heart softened toward John Mark. But what about his attitude toward Barnabas? One might think from Acts 15 that their relationship was irretrievably broken.

But as he did with John Mark, Paul seems to have softened toward Barnabas. By the time we get to 1 Corinthians 9:5-6 (written about a half dozen years after Galatians), Paul seems to consider Barnabas a fellow minister, an equal, and a man of respect whom Paul can turn to as an example of godly ministry.

We don't know exactly what changed. But how good it is to know that two great ministers eventually reconnected, even if just in heart, and that differences didn't win over spiritual unity and common ministry.

Are you presently disconnected from anyone you used to serve with? Can the Lord touch that situation without a negative reaction from you? Are you open to the moving of His Spirit in that area? Since you've changed over time, is it possible they have, too?

Father, help me have fresh spiritual eyes for those who have separated from me. Help me see what You're doing now, not just what the enemy might have done in the past. Since You changed Paul's heart, I pray You'd change mine.

| ALONG THE WAY

JULY 26
BARNABAS: THE POWER OF ENCOURAGEMENT

"And when they had read [the letter], they rejoiced because of its encouragement." (Acts 15:31 ESV)

Barnabas is a relatively minor character in the New Testament. After separating from Paul over the issue of bringing John Mark, Barnabas tends to fade out after Acts 15. But like most encouragers, Barnabas seems content to have served a role of cheering on and reinforcing others.

Barnabas was the one who paved the way for the feared Paul to come into Jerusalem's Christian community. When the word of the Lord began to spread from the Hebrew-speaking Jews to the Hellenists (Greek-speaking Jews), it was Barnabas who was sent to speak and preach to them. The result? "He exhorted them all to remain faithful to the Lord with steadfast purpose, for he was a good man, full of the Holy Spirit and of faith. And a great many people were added to the Lord" (Acts 11:23–25 ESV). What a great contribution to the early, growing church—and a significant development for the spread of the gospel!

When the new converts in the Antioch region were being taught falsehoods, Barnabas was sent with Paul to deliver a letter of correction. The response? The verse above. They rejoiced not because of its doctrinal accuracy (which was important), but "its encouragement."

Are you an encourager or a critic? Critics and encouragers see the same things. But encouragers are concerned with, and connected to, others. They want to help them. Critics are motivated by pride. They stand alone. If you're tempted to criticize, give God what you see, and find a way in Him to become a Barnabas.

Lord, I want to be an encourager. Help me see things the way Barnabas did. Use me as You did him. Help me not to back off in judgment when I see things, but help me continue to remain connected with people and find Your way of encouraging them.

MARK DUPRÉ

JULY 27

BREAKING THROUGH TO LOVE

"Beloved, let us love one another, for love is of God; and everyone who loves is born of God and knows God. Beloved, if God so loved us, we also ought to love one another." (1 John 4:7, 11)

What goals do you have at the moment: a house, a better job, a degree, marriage, children, retirement, getting out of debt? If you have these goals, chances are you're willing to endure the pain of sacrifice and the denial of other things. You're also probably willing to take on things like extra work or student loans.

If there's a goal, there's pain involved. Cars generally mean car payments. Houses have monthly mortgage payments. Athletic records demand focus and a good degree of physical pain. But if the goal means enough to us, we're willing to sacrifice for it.

What's your goal in relating to other people? Have you ever put it into words? Here are some popular options: Be polite/social only. As much as possible, keep minimal contact. Be kind and helpful. Don't let them hurt me. Fight temptation to look at them as potential customers. Don't really think about it ...

There's only one human relationship goal in the kingdom of God, and that is to love one another. Every other duty falls under that one central idea. Do you deliberately, intentionally love your Christian brothers and sisters, even at your own expense? Have you made it your own personal goal? If we call Him Lord, how determined are we to obey the Lord in this area?

We'll look at other aspects of this goal in the next days. For now, can we move "loving one another" onto our list of goals?

Father, I confess that I haven't made loving my brothers and sisters the goal You want it to be. Open my eyes to see Your heart in this matter, and to see what You're doing in my life to work in me to express more of Your love.

JULY 28

JESUS BROKE THROUGH

"Though I speak with the tongues of men and of angels, but have not love, I have become sounding brass or a clanging cymbal." (1 Corinthians 13:1)

"Though I am successful, though I have a good family, though I'm well respected in my church, though I'm considered a good neighbor, though I found a cool boyfriend/girlfriend, though I am financially secure, though I'm moving up in the company, though I have a successful ministry, *but have not love* ... I have become sounding brass or a clanging cymbal."

Taking that Scripture seriously should give us great pause. Usually we're flowing so well in what we're good or practiced at that we forget it means nothing if we do not love. To begin to apply God's Word, let's look at our own lives and our great model: Jesus Himself. We weren't asking for His love (Romans 5:8). In fact, as a race, we put up every resistance possible to it. Yet, He was persistent and knew how to break through to bring His love to us.

How about you personally? Has God interrupted your life? If so, think about what He had to work through to get His love to you: religious traditions, pride, stubbornness, misperceptions about God, fear, anger. What did He work through to bring you His love?

These are the same things we have to work through with others. Love wasn't easy for Him, and it can be challenging for us. Yet Jesus sets the example of love—sacrificial, self-denying, and going all the way—and then He tells us to follow that example. He fought to get that love through. We're called to that same fight!

Lord, remind me that it wasn't simple or easy for You to bring Your love to this earth—or to me. If You loved us with effort, sacrifice, and pain, that's what You call me to do. Thank You that I can draw on Your strength to do that which I can't do on my own.

MARK DUPRÉ

JULY 29
THE POWER OF CHRISTIAN LOVE

"And may the Lord make you increase and abound in love to one another and to all, just as we do to you." (1 Thessalonians 3:12)

One of the reasons we find it hard to love—and to do the necessary work to break through the many barriers we encounter—is that we haven't realized how important this is to God, and that He clearly calls us to love our Christian brothers and sisters.

Aren't we to love everyone? Of course, but even in a Scripture that reminds us to do just that, there's still a special clause directing us to love "one another" (referring to those in the church of Jesus Christ). "To one another" and "to all" are two different groups.

God calls us to a special love for believers. So why is this so difficult at times—even when we understand it's our call, we have His example, and we understand that what we have in Christ is meant to be expressed in love? Of course, some people are challenging and difficult, and we often expect more from our Christian brothers and sisters, which sometimes leads to disappointment.

But the greatest reason we find it hard is spiritual resistance. There's too much at stake for the enemy to lose when we love one another. When we love from the heart, Jesus is pleased, we're moving in the Spirit, and there's a great power released for good. Satan, desperate to hold on to whatever he can of his ever-dwindling kingdom, knows the power of Christian love more than we do. He'll do whatever he can to stop it. Let's disturb him and his diabolical plans.

Lord, help me to love my brothers and sisters from the heart. I want to frustrate the devil and glorify You. Renew my thinking, free my heart, and change my attitudes, that I may love others as You love me.

JULY 30
SHARING THE GOSPEL BY LOVING

"Since you have purified your souls in obeying the truth through the Spirit in sincere love of the brethren, love one another fervently with a pure heart." (1 Peter 1:22)

Satan hates it when we love one another. That's because the love we show to our fellow believers is one of the main ways other people "hear" the gospel. As John 13:35 reminds us, "By this all will know that you are My disciples, if you have love for one another."

If the devil can stop up one of the main expressions of the gospel, he'll do it. He'll do it with fear, selfishness, unforgiveness, jealousy— whatever it takes to stop our hearts from loving our Christian family members.

We need to remember this is not a matter of people. It's a spiritual battle. Between our weaknesses and those of others, the enemy has plenty to work with when it comes to stirring up barriers to love.

Love, demonstrated in service, has to be the goal. We've all been hurt, and we all have our reasons why we find it hard to love one person or another. But if we set our eyes on loving—really loving with His love—then what awaits us is healing, understanding, and a revelation of God that we've never had.

Perhaps you're not the evangelist you'd like to be. Perhaps you struggle to figure out how best to share the gospel with those around you. Yet you share the gospel in part when you love your brothers and sisters. His love, shared among us, is so attractive, so different from the world's "love," so full of grace and forgiveness, that it calls attention to its author and our King.

Lord, help me to remember that expressing Your love is a spiritual matter, one that has opposition. Thank You that loving Your children shows others that we are Your disciples. Magnify Your love among Your people.

MARK DUPRÉ

JULY 31

THE POWER IN OUR LOVING UNITY

"You shall chase your enemies, and they shall fall by the sword before. Five of you shall chase a hundred, and a hundred of you shall put ten thousand to flight; your enemies shall fall by the sword before you." (Leviticus 26:7–8) How could one chase a thousand, and two put ten thousand to flight, unless their Rock had sold them, and the Lord had surrendered them? (Deuteronomy 32:30)

As we look at the many reasons we have for loving one another, the final reason is purely strategic. It relates to Satan's battle against us.

Remember, our enemy doesn't hate us as much as he hates God. He knows that if he hurts us, that hurts God. But he's primarily invested in keeping his kingdom, so he'll resist whatever begins to compromise that.

The devil can do the math. If one of us can damage him to the human equivalent of one thousand men, and two can put ten thousand to flight, can we see why he's so interested in making sure we stay unloving and divided as a church? It's clear there's great spiritual power in our loving unity. Our enemy works overtime to keep that unity from happening.

Think of the power presented here! A loving husband and wife, united in serving the Lord and raising their children. Loving, supportive friends who help one another put an end to the enemy's victories in their lives, replacing them with God's healing and attributes. A loving church, putting offenses aside and forgiveness front and center, impacting a community with God's saving grace and power. Think of what the Lord could do to combat the many physical and moral scourges of our age if we could come together in love.

We have great power at our disposal. It's called the love of God. This is not a matter of sentiment or even human harmony. It's about striking down the power of the enemy with our God-received unity and love.

Father, when I'm tempted not to love, help me remember who is doing the tempting. May my love for Your people bring both great destruction to Satan's kingdom and great growth to Yours. Amen.

AUGUST 1
ONE NARROW WAY

"All things have been delivered to Me by My Father, and no one knows the Son except the Father. Nor does anyone know the Father except the Son, and the one to whom the Son wills to reveal Him." (Matthew 11:27)

For those who want to prove from Scriptures that Jesus is the only way to God, John 14:6 and Matthew 7:13 have always been go-to verses. Yet Matthew 11:27 shines a bright, clear light on who Jesus is and His connection with the Father. It's a great companion verse to help settle the issue of how to know God.

The verse reveals Jesus as administrator of God's grace. The "all things" delivered to Him include authority, judgment, and saving grace. Here, Jesus positions Himself as the one and only mediator, the only true, living connection with the God of the universe.

Most serious students of God's Word have settled in their hearts that Jesus is the only way to the Father. But this is anathema to current thinking, which trumpets the spiritually dangerous idea that there are many ways to God, insisting only one way isn't "tolerant" of other opinions.

Can it really be that surprising that the one true God might only be reached by one true path? If God is truly God, He can lay out the path before Him any way He chooses. In this case, He's chosen Jesus. That's not intolerant; it's God being specific. God hasn't hidden the way to Himself. He's made it clear. If you don't know Jesus is the one and only way to God the Father, ask Him today to show you. If you do know, take joy that He's revealed that to you.

Father, thank You that You've made it clear in Your Word who Jesus is. I thank You that You've shone a bright light on the path to salvation. I pray for those who are confused by the world's idea of many roads leading to God and ask that You clear away clouds of deception and reveal Jesus.

MARK DUPRÉ

AUGUST 2
BUILDING IN PEACETIME

"And [Asa] built fortified cities in Judah, for the land had rest; he had no war in those years, because the Lord had given him rest." (2 Chronicles 14:6)

How should we handle times of peace? This may seem like an odd question, as we are much more sensitive to what happens in times of war. In times of spiritual war, we have a strong sense of what's necessary. We must defend, fight, and respond to attacks. We dig into the Word. We pray. We let the Holy Spirit search our hearts. We're open to repentance, and we search for God's wisdom, often crying out to Him for help.

We often feel alive in spiritual warfare, as the things of God become very real to us during these times. But what about when we're not at war? For a while, we might need some time to recuperate, reflect, and get our spiritual bearings back.

But when things get back to "normal," then what? King Asa gives us an example: we should build. Is there a weakness in your character that needs fortifying? Is there a relationship that needs repair, restoration, or strengthening? Are there areas of study (theology, doctrine, history, famous Christians) that you finally have the time to dig into? Ask the Lord to show you how best to use the downtime you might be blessed to have.

We should take advantage of these times when we're not fighting a specific battle to build up others and ourselves. We never know what's in store for us or how long we have. We often see our lives as spiritual battles with points of rest in between. Can we begin to look at it as times of building interrupted by occasional warfare?

Lord, help me see that You've given me periods of rest when You do. I confess that sometimes I don't recognize them as opportunities to build. Direct me in how and where I can build during those seasons, and thank You that You use those times to prepare me for what's next.

AUGUST 3

VICTOR, NOT VICTIM

"For whatever is born of God overcomes the world. And this is the victory that has overcome the world—our faith." (1 John 5:4)

We've all been victims: people on the receiving end of something hurtful. But that has nothing to do with who we are.

Our culture, with help from our enemy, has succeeded in creating and sustaining a "victim mentality" for too many of our citizens. This is detrimental to society and even worse for the church. Once a Christian embraces "victim" as an identity, the enemy has won a fearsome battle. Not only has the Christian repositioned himself spiritually into an errant, damaging state, but certain changes occur that keep God's grace at a distance.

Those that self-identify as "victim" are inwardly focused; they become black holes of grace, always receiving and destroying and never expressing outward life. Victims are also often deceived into thinking they can sin with impunity—being harsh, judgmental, and unkind—without having to repent, because they feel they're justified, since they've received that kind of treatment. It's a replacement of the blood of Jesus—as well as real repentance—with an excusing covering created by their pain. Even modern psychology has recognized how the victim easily shifts to the role of persecutor in many disorders.

The other great sadness is living a lie. We are victors if we are in Christ! No matter what happens to us, that identity cannot change. As we live in Him, we live in victory. It has nothing to do with outward circumstances. It has everything to do with what He's done and who we are now in Him.

Father, I receive that identity anew by faith. If I'm in You, I am walking in Your victory. Deliver me from all sense of victimhood and self-pity, and help me to keep my eyes on You. I am not who I am based on what has happened to me; I am who You say I am.

MARK DUPRÉ

AUGUST 4

COMPLETELY FORGIVEN AND TRULY FORGOTTEN

As far as the east is from the west, so far has He removed our transgressions from us. (Psalm 103:12) "I, even I, am He who blots out your transgressions for My own sake; and I will not remember your sins." (Isaiah 43:25)

This is one of the most straightforward concepts in Scripture, and one of the hardest to understand and apply to our lives. There are two parts to it.

One is that as we repent, God removes our sins so far from us they can't touch us anymore. "As far as the east is from the west" indicates a distance as far as we can imagine and then some. When forgiven, our sins are separated from us, cut off from us, and removed too far away from us to come back.

Closely related is the idea of God "forgetting" our sin. To be more specific, God says that He won't "remember" our sins. "Remember" in the Bible doesn't refer to God bringing something to mind that He "forgot" intellectually. To remember means God moves on someone or something in alignment with what they've done or what He's promised. God not "remembering" our sin means He doesn't associate that sin with us anymore, and His actions toward us reflect that.

Not remembering our sins means He doesn't hold those sins against us anymore. Since they're gone, He doesn't bring them up again. (It's the enemy of our souls that is so good at that.) It also means that His love, His mercy, and His grace are poured out on us just as if we hadn't sinned. In terms of relationship, God is able to forget our sin when it's brought to the cross. We'll never understand it, but may we appreciate and rejoice in it!

Lord, I rejoice in Your Word even as it challenges me on so many levels. Thank You for no longer remembering my sin once it's forgiven. Help me see the grace and power behind that reality, and help me be more like You with others in that same way.

AUGUST 5

GODLY VS. WORLDLY SORROW

"Now I rejoice, not that you were made sorry, but that your sorrow led to repentance. For you were made sorry in a godly manner, that you might suffer loss from us in nothing. For godly sorrow produces repentance leading to salvation, not to be regretted; but the sorrow of the world produces death." (2 Corinthians 7:9–10)

Paul had sent an earlier letter to the church at Corinth, one that caused some pain and, thankfully, repentance. Here he says that while he's sorry for the pain involved, he's not unhappy about it, for it led to a godly sorrow.

What is godly sorrow? We all "feel" bad when we've been rebuked, or a sin is exposed, or when we realize we've made a mess. But that's worldly sorrow. If we're genuinely sorry because we've hurt others, that's better. That's a combi- nation of godly and worldly sorry. But it's not yet the kind of sorrow that brings true repentance and heartfelt change.

True godly sorrow has God at its center. It's aware of the impact of our sin on our lives, but it's more focused on the negative effect it's had on others—and even more on how it's hurt God. This produces real repentance, because the ultimate root of sin is rebellion against God.

Perhaps the greatest biblical example of godly sorrow is King David. After murder and adultery, David is cut to the quick by a word from the prophet Nathan (2 Samuel 12:7) and pours out his heart in Psalm 51. His awareness of God—and of his violation of God's laws—is so acute that he sees how all his sins have ultimately been against the Lord, even those that involve others.

This kind of repentance is probably the most painful, yet it's the only one that leads to cleansing. Once godly sorrow is in the heart, there's nowhere to go but to the Lord.

Father, move me past worldly sorrow when I sin. Help me to be sensitive to the effect of my sin on others, but most sensitive to when I hurt You. I give You permission to go deep in my heart to produce the kind of "repentance that leads to salvation, not to be regretted."

MARK DUPRÉ

AUGUST 6

TOO BIG FOR YOUR BRITCHES?

[King] Joash did what was right in the sight of the Lord all the days of Jehoiada the priest. (2 Chronicles 24:2)

Now after the death of Jehoiada the leaders of Judah came and bowed down to the king. And the king listened to them. Therefore they left the house of the Lord God of their fathers, and served wooden images and idols; and wrath came upon Judah and Jerusalem because of their trespass. (2 Chronicles 24:17–18)

God put prophets and priests into the lives of Old Testament kings. They were often His way of keeping them from pride and the deceptions that came with their position. But when the wise men died and weren't replaced, worldly success went to the kings' heads, and they veered away from God's wisdom and direction. Ironically, humility was what first led to their successes. Yet after those successes, pride in their achievements (that is, in what God had given them) was what led them to throw off their godly covering. Joash paid dearly for this, suffering military defeat and his own murder.

There's an old phrase used when someone grows proud and overreaches in a self-important way. We used to say he's "too big for his britches." It's a common danger not only to kings but to us all. But there's a way to prevent it.

Do you have a Jehoiada in your life, someone ministering God's words, keeping you humble, checking your ego, and preventing your successes from going to your head? Large or small, we all have our successes. We need spiritual people who are unimpressed with us and not afraid to challenge us when we need it. Kings fared badly without their spiritual coverings. We're no less susceptible.

Let's learn a lesson here. If you have a covering that helps keep you in line with God, be grateful. If circumstances change, find a way to get that covering back. If you don't have such an influence in your life, pray for one.

Father, help me see the need for people in my life to keep me grounded in You. Thank You for their influence in my life. Thank You for those I've recognized as specifically sent by You, but also let me hear Your word no matter who it comes through.

AUGUST 7

BUILDING BLOCK OR STUMBLING BLOCK?

"[Jesus] said to them, "But who do you say that I am?" Simon Peter answered and said, "You are the Christ, the Son of the living God." Jesus answered and said to him, "Blessed are you, Simon Bar-Jonah, for flesh and blood has not revealed this to you, but My Father who is in heaven. And I also say to you that you are Peter, and on this rock I will build My church, and the gates of Hades shall not prevail against it." (Matthew 16:15–18)

Much has been written about the meaning of the word *rock*, which is the same word as *Peter* in this passage. But there's another "rock" connection that has a lesson for us. Jesus calls Peter the "rock" on which He'll build His church. The most commonly agreed-upon interpretation (outside of Catholicism) is that Peter's revelation of who Jesus really is (given to Peter by God)—is the rock upon which Jesus will build His church.

But the impetuous apostle follows his holy revelation with a horrible suggestion—that Jesus not go to the cross to die for us (Matthew 16:21–23). Jesus makes it clear that this time, God isn't behind Peter's words: "Get behind me, Satan!" Then, Jesus continues the "rock" analogy by calling Peter "an offense to Me."

The more accurate, literal translation of the word *offense* or *hindrance* is "stumbling block." Peter had shifted from being a building block to a stumbling block. What's the difference, since it's the same person? It's the motivation and the power behind him. When Peter's led by the Holy Spirit, he's a building block. When he's led by the enemy, he's a stumbling block.

What an example! When we're leaning on the Lord and His understanding, God can use us to build His kingdom. When we speak and act (or react, as Peter did) on our own understanding, we become a stumbling block. Peter serves as a warning but also an encouragement to hear what God's saying to us, speak it, and be used by God to build.

> Lord, I want to be used by You to build and never to be a stumbling block. Deliver me from thinking out of my own heart and mind. Teach me to hear and receive Your word and to speak it in an edifying way.

AUGUST 8

FREE TO LAY DOWN OUR RIGHTS

"Jesus anticipated him, saying, "What do you think, Simon? From whom do the kings of the earth take customs or taxes, from their sons or from strangers?" Peter said to Him, "From strangers." Jesus said to him, "Then the sons are free. Nevertheless, lest we offend them, go to the sea, cast in a hook, and take the fish that comes up first. And when you have opened its mouth, you will find a piece of money; take that and give it to them for Me and you." (Matthew 17:25–27)

Some of the jewels found in God's Word are instances where Jesus does something profound and then we find leaders of the New Testament church doing the same thing. One such occurrence addresses the issue of giving offense.

Here, Jesus begins a theological discussion about the believer's freedom as it relates to the demands of government and society. Jesus' instruction: Go do what prevents the community of nonbelievers from being offended. In this case, Jesus even performed a miracle that took care of any possible offense by respecting the law of the land.

During the years of the early church, Paul shows us the same principle in action. Timothy, who had a Jewish mother and Gentile father, didn't need to be circumcised to become a full-fledged Christian believer. But since Timothy was ministering to Jews, Paul didn't want that to be a stumbling block to the gospel (Acts 16:3). Later, in Romans 14:13, Paul emphasizes the importance of not putting any kind of stumbling block in another believer's way.

What a contrast to current thinking, which puts individual rights above love and grace. How quick we are to assert our "liberties" and even— God forbid!— think we're operating in the Holy Spirit's power by doing so. Jesus and Paul thought otherwise. They demonstrated that true freedom in the Holy Spirit is being sensitive to possible offense and free enough to know that as children of God, we're at liberty to lay down our rights for love.

Father, thank You that You've made us Your people and that we have a special relationship with You. You've made me Yours and made me free. May I use that freedom to keep the door open for Your truth and saving grace.

AUGUST 9

THE MISSING INGREDIENT?

Therefore since a promise remains of entering His rest, let us fear lest any of you seem to have come short of it. For indeed the gospel was preached to us as well as to them; but the word which they heard did not profit them, not being mixed with faith in those who heard it. (Hebrews 4:1–2)

In Hebrews 4, the author is talking about those who left Egypt with Moses in the Exodus. They were unable to enter into God's rest because of their sin and disobedience, stemming from their unbelief. They heard God's Word; they just didn't believe it. The Lord offers us that same rest in Christ, and we're also challenged to add faith to our hearing of God's word.

Anyone who's spent any time in the Scriptures knows those moments when God's word leaps from the page into our hearts and minds. Perhaps we're illuminated or convicted. Those moments are gifts, and we receive them gratefully.

Yet those *rhema* words are generally few and far between. It's our responsibility the rest of the time to mix what we read with our faith, personally receiving His Word. When you read the Bible, are you simply looking for the word that jumps off the page, or are you bringing your faith to what you read, receiving His Word as truth and believing that it has some spiritual application, at least somewhere?

How about at church? Do you bring your faith to sermons? Do you expect to hear a word that edifies and encourages, or even challenges? Or has familiarity bred not contempt, but complacency, or even judgment, where our pride leads us to place ourselves over the Word instead of under it? If you do the latter, you're mixing the Word with unbelief, and you'll receive little. If you do the former and mix your hearing with faith, you'll receive His Word and be changed.

Father, I've read far too much of Your Word and heard far too many sermons and teachings that I haven't mixed with faith. Please forgive me for that. I want to enter into everything You have for me. Show me how to mix my faith with every category of word from You that I hear.

MARK DUPRÉ

AUGUST 10
AMAZING GRACE, NOT SIMPLE JUSTICE

"Jesus anticipated him, saying, "What do you think, Simon? From whom do the kings of the earth take customs or taxes, from their sons or from strangers?" Peter said to Him, "From strangers." Jesus said to him, "Then the sons are free. Nevertheless, lest we offend them, go to the sea, cast in a hook, and take the fish that comes up first. And when you have opened its mouth, you will find a piece of money; take that and give it to them for Me and you." (Matthew 17:25–27)

Matthew 20:1-15 recounts a story that many tend to think is about salvation. However, it goes against the central core of the gospel if that's the primary interpretation. Our salvation isn't earned, as the wages are in this story. It's a gift, received through faith by the grace of God.

This story is actually about the kingdom of heaven and those who work in it. As the first round of workers should have been happy to get work and rejoicing in the work all day, those of us serving God for a long time should rejoice in what we've received. Just knowing we're loved, saved, and being used by God should be a continual blessing. When all's said and done, we really don't want simple justice (as the workers here did). We should be rejoicing in God's amazing grace.

The concluding words of Matthew 20:15 can cut and cleanse if we let them: "Don't I have the right to do what I want with my own money? Or are you envious because I am generous?" (NIV). Can you hear the heart of God here? He wants us to understand He's a sovereign God who can do what He wants. He is more gracious than we can imagine, and He acts out of wisdom. Who are we, as mere humans, to question that?

God's plan for everyone is unique, and to us, full of mystery. We can rejoice that He's wise and knows exactly what He's doing with everyone.

Father, forgive me for begrudging others Your blessings and grace. I confess that I don't know what You're doing with others and that my focus should instead be on following You to the best of my ability. Thank You for the grace and mercy I have not deserved but nevertheless have received from You.

AUGUST 11

STEWARDSHIP, NOT JEALOUSY

"Now if the foot should say, "Because I am not a hand, I do not belong to the body," it would not for that reason stop being part of the body. But in fact God has placed the parts in the body, every one of them, just as he wanted them to be." (1 Corinthians 12:15, 18 NIV)

When we become jealous of others, especially our fellow believers, we're defiantly questioning the wisdom of God. It's a trick of the devil, as we have no reason for jealousy. God loves us equally; we know that in our heads, if not quite in our hearts. But God also knows what He's doing when He gives gifts. They're all given by the Holy Spirit for different reasons, most of which we'll never fully understand.

The real issue is that we're called to be good stewards of what we have, being faithful to God in how we use what He's given us. For many of us, moving into godly stewardship has to wait while we adjust to not having what we want or being gifted in areas we might not particularly like. That's part of our growing in sanctification.

It's true that sometimes God's blessings seem to fall greatly on some and less on others. We'll never know the inside story involving anyone else. But Scripture makes it clear that obedience is rewarded, diligence produces good results, and God answers the prayers of His people. Truth be told, if we were allowed to look deeply into the trials and challenges of some we're jealous of, we might be shocked into silence and gratitude for our own lives.

What we have from God is up to God. Our focus should be off of others (except for love) and on our own hearts, our own diligence, and our own faithful stewardship. That's what God expects, and that's what His grace is for.

Lord, thank You for what I've received from You. Help me to develop all You've given me for Your glory. Forgive me for being jealous of others. I release them all and pray Your blessing on them.

MARK DUPRÉ

AUGUST 12
GOD'S WORD TRUMPS CIRCUMSTANCES

"Then the men of David said to him, "This is the day of which the Lord said to you, 'Behold, I will deliver your enemy into your hand, that you may do to him as it seems good to you.'" And David arose and secretly cut off a corner of Saul's robe. Now it happened afterward that David's heart troubled him because he had cut Saul's robe. And he said to his men, "The Lord forbid that I should do this thing to my master, the Lord's anointed, to stretch out my hand against him, seeing he is the anointed of the Lord." (1 Samuel 24:4–6)

What a setup for David! King Saul had been trying to kill him for years. One day David and his men were in the far recesses of a cave when King Saul entered to relieve himself. Surely God had delivered Saul into David's hand! Getting rid of the man trying to kill him would be justified by nearly everyone and would "move things forward" in David's ascent to the throne.

But there was something more powerful than logic, legal justifications, or even the appearance of an "open door" where circumstances seemed to all line up. It was the simple word of God. David recognized that Saul, in spite of his actions, was chosen by God as Israel's king. David knew he had no right to injure him. No action by Saul, no set of circumstances could persuade David to violate a law of God he'd so deeply internalized. David was even "troubled" by having cut off a corner of Saul's robe!

The reality of the situation was not that Saul was being delivered to David, his eventual successor. The reality was God was testing David's heart.

It's easy to be deceived by circumstances that appear to be to our benefit. But God's Word always trumps our circumstances. Whether it's one of the Ten Commandments or simply the demands of love, we can walk in the wisdom of God when we live by His Word. Circumstances can confuse. God's Word is "a lamp unto [our] feet" (Psalm 119:105 KJV), making our path clear through any set of circumstances.

Father, I'm easily swayed at times by circumstances. Help me to live by Your Word and the principles I find there. May I have Your Word deeply in my heart, like David, that I may not sin against You (Psalm 119:111).

AUGUST 13
WE LEARN OBEDIENCE, TOO

"Though [Jesus] was a Son, yet He learned obedience by the things which He suffered. And having been perfected, He became the author of eternal salvation to all who obey Him." (Hebrews 5:8–9)

We know Jesus was the Son of God, that He was sinless and that He performed miracles. We can respect that, but it's often hard to relate to it. Hebrews 4:15 tells us Jesus sympathizes with our weaknesses, being tempted in all points as we are.

Hebrews 5 goes one further, telling us Jesus wasn't "perfect" until His struggle in the garden was complete. That doesn't mean He wasn't sinless; in Bible language, it means He had to be made the sacrifice for sin, which involved spiritual battles and obedience.

Part of the goal of our suffering is to learn obedience. It's not a natural trait. It must be learned like a subject in school. How did Jesus learn obedience? Not by reading the Torah or even praying. According to God's Word, He learned it through what He suffered. In essence, He let His sufferings teach Him what God was asking of Him and allowed it to both soften and strengthen His heart so He could rise to the yes God was calling Him to.

What can we learn from this? We are, as He was, constantly being matured in obedience by God's actions and His call on our lives. Jesus had an appointed earthly end in God's plan; so do we. God worked His plan in Jesus. He's working His plan in us.

Regarding suffering: Instead of complaining or enduring, can we allow our sufferings to teach us greater levels of obedience? That's a wholly different perspective on what we go through, one that's redemptive beyond words.

Father, I receive the truth that You have a plan for me that involves my continuing to grow in obedience to You and Your call. Help me to see that and see my sufferings in a new and more redemptive way.

MARK DUPRÉ

AUGUST 14

USE WHAT YOU HAVE

"Having then gifts differing according to the grace that is given to us, let us use them: if prophecy, let us prophesy in proportion to our faith; or ministry, let us use it in our ministering; he who teaches, in teaching; he who exhorts, in exhortation; he who gives, with liberality; he who leads, with diligence; he who shows mercy, with cheerfulness." (Romans 12:6-8)

This section from Romans encourages us twice over. Both encouragements call us to action. The first is that no matter what we think or feel, as members of the body of Christ, we've each been gifted by God according to His wisdom and grace.

This may seem obvious. But the church is filled with people who don't realize they're gifted, or how they're gifted, or that they need to take steps to use their gifts to help build up the church and show Christ's love.

Notice how the gifts here involve relating to others: prophesying, ministering, teaching, exhorting, giving, leading, and showing mercy. We have to "get in there" if we're going to use our gifts to bless God and build up others.

The second encouragement pertains to the "how" of using our gifts. We're called to prophesy "in proportion to our faith," which should take off a lot of pressure. We're to lead "with diligence," give "with liberality," and show mercy "with cheerfulness." All these inspire us to express our gifts with energy, focus, and enthusiasm.

A famous marketing motto is "Just do it!" Here, God says, "I gave you gifts; now use them." If we look at this from God's perspective, He's given us part of Himself in His gifts to us. He's done this because He loves us, He wants the gifts to help us grow into the image of His Son, and He wants everyone to work together to build up the church in love (Ephesians 4:16). What a divine vision!

Father, thank You for giving us gifts that reflect Your character and show us Your love for Your people. Open my eyes to see how You want me to use them. Please help me get past my personal barriers to being used, that I may grow spiritually and be used fully to bless others and bring You glory.

AUGUST 15
GRADUAL HEALINGS

Then [Jesus] came to Bethsaida; and they brought a blind man to Him ... And when He had spit on his eyes and put His hands on him, He asked him if he saw anything. And he looked up and said, "I see men like trees, walking." Then He put His hands on his eyes again and made him look up. And he was restored and saw everyone clearly. (Mark 8:22–25)

Jesus' gradual healing of the blind man has many applications. First, it encourages us to keep looking for completeness in anything the Lord begins. We should never be hesitant to ask the Lord to "put His hands on [us] again." This might be the next prayer He's hoping to hear from us.

Yet perhaps the most significant aspect of this healing is its placement in God's Word. It's preceded by the feeding of the four thousand, a request for a sign by the Pharisees (ironic that this unfulfilled request comes right after the miracle of the feeding!), and a conversation with the disciples about their failure to understand what Jesus called "the leaven of the Pharisees." Jesus asks his disciples, "Do you not yet perceive nor understand? Is your heart still hardened? Having eyes, do you not see?" (Mark 8:17–18).

In the next passage of Scripture, Jesus asks His disciples who men say He is, and Peter makes his groundbreaking, revelatory proclamation that He's the Christ. After so much confusion among His followers, the light has finally broken through; like the blind man, they can see! There was once partial understanding about who this Man was, until more time with Jesus brought true and clear comprehension.

Let's remember the placement of this story when we look to God for healing in any area. It may take more than one touch of His hand. Whether it's a physical healing we're looking for, or an understanding we're seeking (the disciple's challenge), it's the Lord's will to finish the works He's begun.

Lord, help me see things I don't see. Heal my spiritual sight. If I need to "look up" as part of the healing, please make it clear what I need to do. And, Lord, in every area that needs to be completed, touch me again.

MARK DUPRÉ

AUGUST 16

LORD, TOUCH ME AGAIN

"Then [Jesus] came to Bethsaida; and they brought a blind man to Him, and begged Him to touch him. So He took the blind man by the hand and led him out of the town. And when He had spit on his eyes and put His hands on him, He asked him if he saw anything. And he looked up and said, 'I see men like trees, walking.' (Mark 8:22–24)

We're repeating yesterday's Scripture but stopping mid-story to make a point. When Jesus was halfway done with healing the blind man, he asked if he saw anything. He responded, "I see men like trees, walking."

Now if you'd witnessed this, your first thought might have been, "Hey, we're halfway there. But this isn't complete yet." Why not? Because people aren't trees, and this man viewing them as trees doesn't make them trees.

Can you imagine what this person would have concluded about men, trees, and other things in nature if he'd only received a partial healing? What conclusions—silly, dangerous, or otherwise—might he have come to? His view of man would have been skewed and his view of nature distorted. Would you have trusted any conclusions that arose from such distorted perceptions?

If we're not completely healed by God in an area, we're like this man. Of course, Scripture makes clear that we know and see only in part (1 Corinthians 13:9–12). But when the Lord really shows us something, it's usually characterized by its clarity. Many of us have been wounded and abused or beaten down by life. We may have received some healing, but in terms of God, others, and ourselves, we may still "see men like trees, walking."

Jesus' second touch involved putting His hands on the blind man and asking him to look up. We may well need that two-part touch to be able to see things correctly and come to godly conclusions about our Lord and life.

Lord, touch me again so that I can see clearly. Show me where I'm still seeing things vaguely, or even wrongly. Touch my heart and heal my spiritual sight. For areas in which I've come to wrong conclusions because I saw things so inaccurately, please help me backtrack, repent if necessary, and allow You to "recalibrate" me correctly.

AUGUST 17
COMPASSION OR FOOL'S GOLD?

"As a father pities his children, so the Lord pities those who fear Him." (Psalm 103:13)

In the same way that self-pity produces bad fruit, so does feeling sorry for someone. In the psalm quoted above, the word translated "pity" literally means "have compassion for," which is a biblical concept. Our Lord is a God of compassion, and we're called to be compassionate to others. So if by having pity we mean having compassion, then we're bearing the right heart attitude toward others.

But "feeling sorry" for someone is different. As self-pity locks people into a victim mentality, feeling sorry for others places a kind of victim mentality on them. There's actually a smidgen of a lack of faith combined with a slight lack of respect here. Compassion should lead us to action of some kind. Feeling sorry for someone tends to lock them into their condition and fails to bring faith for change into the scenario.

Feeling sorry for someone also demonstrates a (perhaps invisible or unfelt) lack of respect for that person, as if they were unable to better their circumstances. If folks around the "victim" continue to feel this way, they may not search for a way out of the situation or a path toward healing.

God is a God of redemption. He's working to redeem every situation. Feeling sorry for someone is the fool's gold of emotions, causing us to feel a distorted version of compassion while actually working to prevent growth. Let's bring all of God's compassion to those who need it, while keeping faith and hope alive in our hearts as we do.

Father, show me my heart in this area. If I fall into self-pity, please do what is necessary to get me out of it. If I fall into a faithless state of feeling sorry for anyone, help me to move over to genuine, hopeful compassion for them.

AUGUST 18

BUILDING ON THE ROCK

"Therefore whoever hears these sayings of Mine, and does them, I will liken him to a wise man who built his house on the rock: and the rain descended, the floods came, and the winds blew and beat on that house; and it did not fall, for it was founded on the rock." (Matthew 7:24–25)

The three passages we'll look at over the next three days are often viewed individually. But let's take a look at their connections and similarities. First, we'll notice there are three sets of two—two foundations, two gates, and two trees. Jesus isn't only comparing each element within the pair, but He also presents them in a row so we can see a bigger picture.

The culmination of the two smaller stories is the one above, the story of two men who build. One can either build foolishly or with wisdom. The preceding stories give us some guidance as to how to build wisely: on the rock.

When we admire someone else's spiritual building, we sometimes make the mistake of trying to build what they have. Instead, it's better to ask, "*How did you build?*" When we build in the Spirit, the *how* is usually more important than the *what*. God's ultimately in charge of what's being built; we have great responsibility in the how.

But I'm not building, you might say. I'm working, or raising children, or involved in a ministry. You might be doing one or all of those things. But you're also building a spiritual edifice of some kind at the same time. Every day, in all that you do, you're building. God is faithful to make sure that a day is never wasted and that our activities are never without purpose.

In the next few days, we'll see what other insights Matthew 7 provides to help us build wisely.

Father, help me realize that I'm always building something in the Spirit, especially when I don't realize I'm doing that. Open my eyes to see the difference between foolishness and wisdom in the building process, and help me build wisely.

AUGUST 19
MORE EQUIPPED THAN WE KNOW

"Enter by the narrow gate; for wide is the gate and broad is the way that leads to destruction, and there are many who go in by it. Because narrow is the gate and difficult is the way which leads to life, and there are few who find it." (Matthew 7:13–14)

How do we build with wisdom, making sure we build on the rock (meaning the Rock of Christ) and not on sand? The two short stories in Matthew just before the parable about building on the rock shed light on that.

Jesus presents us with two gates, one wide and one narrow—and only one leads to life. Our first step onto the path of life was our step into salvation, which for many of us was a faith-filled, trepidation-filled one, packed with wonder and too many questions to even express. The path that followed was like that gate of life, narrow and difficult. In other words, every real step of faith along that road is similar to that first step.

It's true that some steps only happen once. Becoming a Christian happens once. But then we have to work out our salvation.

Our first step involved repentance, a change of thinking, a surrender, and a dying to self and the idea that things have to make perfect sense before we proceed. Every genuine step forward follows a similar pattern.

That may seem daunting, but when we're born again, we have the Spirit of God within, which tunes us into His voice and makes His Word come alive. The path may indeed be narrow and difficult, but we're now equipped as never before. We now know Christ as our Strength, our Comforter, our Protector, and our Wisdom.

Our knowledge of His love and faithfulness makes every step easier. And the closer we press in, the more aware we become of how well equipped we are.

Lord, I want to walk in the Spirit. Help me see the narrow, difficult path, and then help me to continue to walk down that road. Thank You that You are with me, directing, supplying, and comforting all along the way.

MARK DUPRÉ

AUGUST 20
TAKE A LOOK AT THE FRUIT

"Beware of false prophets, who come to you in sheep's clothing, but inwardly they are ravenous wolves. You will know them by their fruits. Do men gather grapes from thornbushes or figs from thistles? Even so, every good tree bears good fruit, but a bad tree bears bad fruit. A good tree cannot bear bad fruit, nor can a bad tree bear good fruit." (Matthew 7:15–18)

The other comparison Jesus makes before speaking about building on the rock is between a tree that bears good fruit and one that bears bad. After showing us that all our steps of faith are similar to our first one, Jesus shows us another helpful bit of direction: look at the fruit of what you're doing.

Galatians 5 helps us see if we're building on the rock or sand, bearing good fruit or bad. Galatians 5:19-20 gives us fruits of the flesh, including adultery, lewdness, idolatry, hatred, jealousies, outbursts of wrath, selfish ambition, envy, and drunkenness. Not a pretty list, but it can be a helpful one. If we see these kinds of fruit in our lives, we're not building on the rock in that area.

Galatians 5:22-23 presents us with the fruit of the Holy Spirit: love, joy, peace, longsuffering, kindness, goodness, faithfulness, gentleness, and self-control. To the extent that we can see these in our lives, our relationships or activities, we're building on the rock.

There is fruit that comes from all we do. To know how we're building, let's take a look at what fruit we're producing. God's Word in Galatians helps us identify the specific fruit Jesus is talking about in Matthew. God's Holy Spirit helps us by convicting us of sin as we produce bad fruit and by encouraging us with His joy and peace as we produce good fruit.

Father, I want to produce good fruit. Please show me where I produce good fruit, that I might be encouraged and continue. Please show me where I'm not, that I can turn toward You for forgiveness and help. Thank You for this valuable direction in helping me to build on the Rock.

AUGUST 21
THE REST OF THE STORY

"Into Your hand I commit my spirit; You have redeemed me, O Lord God of truth. (Psalm 31:5); My God, My God, why have You forsaken Me? Why are You so far from helping Me and from the words of My groaning?" (Psalm 22:1)

When Jesus cried out, "My God, my God, why have You forsaken Me?" (Matthew 27:46), it was far more than a personal cry. Jesus was quoting a psalm that most of the Jewish listeners would easily have recognized. Unlike today, most students of God's Word back then spent a great deal of time in study and would easily have recognized the opening words to one of the most devastating and heartfelt psalms in the Scriptures. Jesus knew the opening words of the psalm would remind the more attentive listeners of the whole psalm, not just its plaintive first line.

The same goes with Jesus' bookend cry, "Father, 'into Your hands I commit my spirit'" (Luke 23:46). Again, these words could stand on their own as an individual cry to His heavenly Father. But once again, Jesus knew the attentive listener would know from that one line that He was reminding them of the entire 31st psalm. If you read both psalms in their entirety, you can see hints of "the joy that was set before Him" (Hebrews 12:2).

The two lines quoted by Jesus are but a small and painful part of each psalm. When we read the whole psalm, we can see the power, glory, and victory Jesus was ultimately pointing to in His words! He was giving much more of a story to us than these simple quotations might indicate at first.

Father, help me to understand the whole message Jesus was giving here. Help me to see something of what He was looking to in the future, that I might share in that joy that was set before Him on the cross.

MARK DUPRÉ

AUGUST 22
THE QUIET, COURAGEOUS HERO

"Joseph of Arimathea, a prominent council member, who was himself waiting for the kingdom of God, coming and taking courage, went in to Pilate and asked for the body of Jesus. Then he bought fine linen, took Him down, and wrapped Him in the linen. And he laid Him in a tomb." (Mark 15:43, 46)

The actions of Jesus' followers provide a contrasting story around his death. Peter, James, and John all fell asleep during Jesus' agony in the garden. Peter denied him three times. Nearly all of Jesus' immediate disciples forsook him and fled. Only John was there at his death.

Once He rose, the first people the angel spoke to were so afraid they didn't do what he asked. When they did tell the disciples, the disciples were filled with "unbelief and hardness of heart" (Mark 16:14).

Then take a look at Joseph of Arimathea, a minor figure in the Gospels. Unlike the better-known disciples, Joseph "took courage" when others feared, and he asked Pilate for Jesus' body. (Some translations say he went in "boldly.")

Joseph, "a prominent council member," put his reputation at risk by not agreeing with the Sanhedrin about Jesus (Luke 23:50–51). He put his money where his mouth was by supplying everything for Jesus' burial. He risked political and possible legal problems by asking the local governmental ruler for the dead body of a perceived criminal, one that had a questionable reputation among the religious leaders.

What a contrast Joseph provides! While the more visible disciples were failing, God had a quiet, courageous follower in the midst of the most trying time of our Savior's life, a person who discreetly and unobtrusively followed the Lord under desperately trying circumstances. No matter who might visibly fail, God always has His faithful followers.

Lord, let me be like Joseph, who took courage when others were bound by fear. Let me move forward when others are too frightened or distracted to obey. No matter what famous disciple may disappoint or fall, may my eyes be on You as Joseph's were, quietly but completely doing Your will.

AUGUST 23

INVESTMENT LOST?

"But a man of God came to him, saying, "O king, do not let the army of Israel go with you, for the Lord is not with Israel—not with any of the children of Ephraim." Then Amaziah said to the man of God, "But what shall we do about the hundred talents which I have given to the troops of Israel?" And the man of God answered, "The Lord is able to give you much more than this." (2 Chronicles 25:7, 9)

King Amaziah was putting his army together, which included a huge number of mercenaries from Israel's northern kingdom to assist in fighting. The tab was a hefty one—100 talents of silver, a huge investment.

Then a prophet of God cautioned him against using the mercenaries. Amaziah responded with a mixture of faith and unbelief that reflected his original description as one who "was right in the sight of the Lord, but not with a loyal heart" (2 Chronicles 25:2). His response indicates a desire to obey the word of the Lord, but it lacks a degree of trust. Amaziah asks, "But what shall we do about the hundred talents which I have given to the troops of Israel?"

Have you ever made an investment you knew had to end? It could be a job, a relationship, or a path of some kind? Most of us want to obey the Lord. But how do we recoup what we've invested? Has all that time, money, ministry, or energy been completely lost?

The prophet could have answered the king's question in any number of ways. But his answer to Amaziah is also ours: "The Lord is able to give you much more than this." This wasn't an assurance that the Lord would, but that He was able to. If God's able to give more than we've invested, then we have to let go and trust that His command to stop the investment is the perfect wisdom of God. No other explanation is needed.

Father, help me to hear You clearly when I need to stop investing in something. May I resist the temptation to come up with a logical possible scenario as to why if it's not clear to me. Help me to simply trust in Your good character. If You speak something, I trust that You know what You're doing

MARK DUPRÉ

AUGUST 24

NOT JUST ME AND JESUS

"And the Lord God said, "It is not good that man should be alone." (Genesis 2:18)

The first thing God says about man is that it isn't good for him to be alone. Of course, that leads directly into the creation of Eve. But the Lord's words reverberate far beyond the marriage relationship.

We're not meant to be alone, live the Christian life alone, or serve God alone. We were created, wired, and programmed from the start for community, fellowship, and relationship. In fact, we need other people to be all God calls us to be as individuals and to do all God's called us to do.

Why can't it just be me and Jesus? Why can't I serve God in my own way, by myself? We can do that, but it goes against God's design and plan for us. How can we obey the Lord's command to "be kindly affectionate to one another with brotherly love, in honor giving preference to one another" (Romans 12:10) if we don't connect—really connect—with our Christian brothers and sisters? How can we answer the many calls to spiritual unity in Scripture if we stand alone?

Our enemy hates unity and its power. He'll do whatever he can to isolate us, even just mentally or emotionally. He knows that embers set apart from the fire of coals will cool quickly and that the pride that forms with independence is a fertile breeding ground for all kinds of ungodliness.

Yes, God's people can be difficult and occasionally infuriating. They can also be lovely, kind, and reflective of the heart of Jesus. But they are His people. And we are among that people.

Father, forgive me when I retreat from Your people for the wrong reasons. Lead me in Your paths of connection and service. Give me Your mind to understand Your plan for me with others and Your heart to love others like You do.

AUGUST 25

HERE ARE MY MOTHER AND MY BROTHERS!

"And a multitude was sitting around Him; and they said to Him, "Look, Your mother and Your brothers are outside seeking You." But He answered them, saying, "Who is My mother, or My brothers?" And He looked around in a circle at those who sat about Him, and said, "Here are My mother and My brothers! For whoever does the will of God is My brother and My sister and mother." (Mark 3:32–35)

One of the most healing, wonderful, challenging realities of being a Christian is that we automatically become part of another family. There are really only two kinds of families: the "nuclear family" of parents and children (including variations of that, such as natural-born, adopted, single moms, single dads, etc.), and the family of God.

Romans 8:15 tells us that we've "received the Spirit of adoption by whom we cry out, 'Abba, Father.'" Hebrews 2:11 tells us Jesus is our brother. These are not metaphors; this is reality. The body of Christ is not *like* our family; it *is* our family. Our heavenly Father is a real father and the best one. Other Christians—they are our real brothers and sisters.

The spiritual bond we share with our Christian family is a more precious connection than even the natural family connection, in part because we take it into eternity with us. Our natural bonds pass away with our death. Heaven won't know natural connections—only spiritual ones, ones we are blessed to enjoy on this side of the grave.

Locking this truth down in our hearts and minds can release a new level of love, understanding, and support. We come to see that we're constantly inheriting the gifts of our family members—in their gifts, talents, and acts of love.

Yes, we have responsibilities when we're members of a family. But when there's a great, mighty, loving family like the body of Christ, belonging is a joy.

Father, thank You that You've placed me in such a magnificent family. May all the good things I learned from You through my natural family be turned into blessings toward all my brothers and sisters. Help me see with Your eyes the riches I have in belonging to the household of God.

AUGUST 26

THE BENEFITS OF TEAMWORK

Two are better than one, because they have a good reward for their labor. Though one may be overpowered by another, two can withstand him. And a threefold cord is not quickly broken. (Ecclesiastes 4:9, 12)

Belonging to the body of Christ is a gift from God to us as individuals. For the more pragmatic among us, living and serving together has another benefit: we get more done that way!

Teamwork multiplies effort. You can't be a choir alone or a soccer team by yourself. Musical solos are wonderful, but there's nothing like a group singing together in perfect harmony. Watching individual athletes demonstrate their skills is a joy, but there's something uniquely enjoyable about watching a good team sport. Jesus worked with a team of twelve and a sub-team of three. Paul and Peter, though we think of them as striking individuals, functioned as team members in their ministries.

Working together brings out gifts and callings in ways that operating individually can't match. Some skills only develop when working together, such as learning to lead, delegate, and receive from others, developing trust or becoming trustworthy ourselves, learning to mentor or being mentored ... the list goes on and on.

There's also the joy of different perspectives. We need one another's varying ideas and we need to bring our understanding to those ideas so we can properly receive and internalize them. This broadens our world immeasurably. (We're almost always smarter together than we are individually.) Connecting with and serving with others is worth more than taking ten college courses and studying dozens of educational and training books. Teamwork takes us farther than we could ever go on our own.

Father, help me to be completely open to those that You have called me to work with so that You can maximize our connection. Thank You for their differing gifts, perspectives, and personalities. May our service together bring us great change and bring You great glory.

AUGUST 27
THE MYSTERY OF GOD'S SOVEREIGNTY

"For by Him all things were created that are in heaven and that are on earth ... All things were created through Him and for Him. And He is before all things, and in Him all things consist." (Colossians 1:16–17)

The sovereignty of God used to be a given in the church and was a common subject of preaching. It was even understood to a limited extent by the unsaved. That's not the case anymore.

Take the time to read and take in Scriptures like the one above (Hebrews 1:3, Ephesians 1:11, Psalm 115:3). God has unlimited power, does what He chooses, and has sovereign control over the affairs of men, nature, and history. His power is absolute and infinite. He's the potter and we're the clay. Being God and being almighty, He has the power and the right to do whatever He wishes and is under no obligation to us.

There are aspects of God's sovereignty we can see and even experience, but we'll never truly understand it on this side of the grave. Digging into the Word, being led by the Spirit, allowing God to have His way in our trials—these will shed light on these aspects, but our hope in putting the pieces together will have to wait until heaven.

The scientists among us have a good example. In this life, God's sovereignty is like a chemical suspension. We see the various pieces, but they don't blend into a cohesive whole. When we're in His presence, and "[we] shall know just as [we] also [are] known" (1 Corinthians 13:12), we'll see it as a chemical solution and will finally perceive how it all blends together into something new and, in this case, wondrous.

Lord, help me accept and receive those things that I don't yet understand, but that Your Word makes clear. Let me never use as an excuse the fact that I will never fully understand some aspects of You before I see You face to face, but let me continue to grow in understanding of Your will and Your ways.

MARK DUPRÉ

AUGUST 28

GOD CARES ABOUT THE LITTLE THINGS

"Are not two sparrows sold for a copper coin? And not one of them falls to the ground apart from your Father's will." (Matthew 10:29)

How big does something have to be for God to care about it? Or do something about it? Can we even make that kind of judgment call?

A dear friend once confessed her mother had cautioned her that God was busy with big things. She was told to not bother Him with little ones. There's a teaching about the value of priorities in there somewhere, but what a misrepresentation of the heart of God!

Jesus tells us His heavenly Father takes care of the birds and therefore must be fully aware of what they're all doing. In His time on earth, Jesus took time for little children and spoke to people on the outskirts of society. We put our own human perspectives on God when we say He isn't concerned with the "smaller things." Ironically, it ends up making God smaller to us. Who gets to judge what is smaller and what is greater? In God's economy, a very small thing—like a random shot of an arrow—can have a great effect (1 Kings 22:34).

God is so powerful and loving that He doesn't have the same divisions we have between small and great things. He sees every "little" and "big" thing with equal clarity.

Like any good parent, He cares about the things we care about. He may always be working on maturing our priorities, but His love and concern are so great that they break out and flow over every boundary we try to put on them.

Father, forgive me for every time I've limited Your love and concern in my thoughts and prayers. Show me continually how You are not like humans, and that Your love is not only higher, but deeper than I've ever imagined.

AUGUST 29

HE CARES ABOUT EVERYTHING THAT AFFECTS US

"Casting all your care upon Him, for He cares for you." (1 Peter 5:7)

Imagine speaking with a young child who's distressed over something that seems inconsequential to you. If you love him, you'll be genuinely concerned over what's distressing him. What hurts him touches you.

God is like that. He cares about what we call the "little things" because He cares for us. Like a good parent, He may try to comfort us or shift our attention away from the problem, but these actions show His concern about the things that touch us, not His lack of it.

Letting God direct us every day means we become increasingly sensitive to His whispers, to the "still small voice" that directs us in such "little things" as to what route to take to a destination or to make that stop at the grocery store. If God's directing us to do something, how could we call it a small thing? Small-seeming divine appointments have changed lives and nations.

Certainly, it's important to listen to God and obey Him in what we call the "big things." However, there are dangers in limiting our thinking to that. We may think we have God's mind on what's big and what isn't. We may also allow Him the big things, but use our own wisdom and strength for the rest. We don't want to live by the Spirit in some categories and by the flesh in others.

If we really want to be like Jesus, we'll allow God to direct us in the little and big things. After all, He cares about all of them.

Father, thank You that You lead us in what we experience as the big things and the little things. Forgive me when I've kept You out of parts of my life. Help me to make You Lord over them all.

AUGUST 30

GOD'S CARE NEVER WAVERS

And a great windstorm arose, and the waves beat into the boat, so that it was already filling. But He was in the stern, asleep on a pillow. And they awoke Him and said to Him, "Teacher, do You not care that we are perishing?" Then He arose and rebuked the wind, and said to the sea, "Peace, be still!" And the wind ceased and there was a great calm. (Mark 4:37–39)

How quickly we question whether God cares about us when we're threatened or perturbed! Perhaps our situation is life and death, like that of the disciples. Or perhaps it's less dire, centered on heartache, disappointment, or even inconvenience. The question asked of our Lord often remains the same: "Does He care?"

This is the real question of the heart. It's at the center of the disciples' insecurities. And ours. If the issue of caring hadn't been underneath, the disciples might have gone right to "Help us!" rather than questioning God's concern for them. How often do we do the same thing? When challenged or confused or threatened, our insecurities rise up and our prayers reflect the unspoken query: "Lord, do You not care?"

When we first come to Him, we learn quickly that God cares for us. Finding and continually rediscovering God's love and concern is part of the ongoing joy of walking with Jesus. Yet as we grow spiritually and are faced with greater trials and temptations, that belief is often challenged— and we're given the opportunity to deepen our faith in His love.

When the next trial, inconvenience, or challenge comes our way, let's reaffirm that yes, even in this situation, God cares for us. We may not know God's plan, but we can rest assured that no matter what we understand, He loves us, understands exactly what we're facing, and is working everything out for our good because of His love.

Father, I believe that You always care and are actively caring for me. Help me believe it more deeply. When that belief is challenged, please help me to stand on what Your Word says and what I know is true about You.

AUGUST 31

OUT OF SIGHT AND EARSHOT

"And the temple, when it was being built, was built with stone finished at the quarry, so that no hammer or chisel or any iron tool was heard in the temple while it was being built." (1 Kings 6:7)

In the middle of the description of the building of Solomon's temple is an obscure passage about where the hammering and chiseling was done. It was done a distance away, out of sight and earshot. When the finished pieces were brought into the temple area, they could be laid down relatively easily and quietly. It was almost as if they appeared from nowhere, ready to be perfectly placed.

If we're to be fitted together with others in worship and ministry (i.e., in the body of Christ), a good deal of chiseling and hammering may need to be accomplished. During that time, God may choose to lower the noise level of ministry and worship, waiting until our rough edges are gone and stony areas hammered into tenderness—all at a distance from the ministry itself.

God may be calling you into areas of service and ministry beyond what you're doing now. But perhaps He's doing the more painful transformational work in you away from the crowd, in a way that won't negatively impact your brothers and sisters and His work. We'll need to stay in community during the process, but we can rejoice that the noise of the hammering and chiseling often occurs away from the eyes and ears of others. It's better for us; it's better for others.

If you're being hammered and chiseled right now, perhaps God's simply preparing you for proper placement in His body, the temple of the Holy Spirit. Let's allow Him to complete the noisy work in us, then watch how He puts us in place, perfectly formed by Him for His purposes.

Father, thank You that You lead us in what we experience as the big things and the little things. Forgive me when I've kept You out of parts of my life. Help me to make You Lord over them all.

MARK DUPRÉ

SEPTEMBER 1
THE PRODIGAL, REVISITED

"Then [Jesus] said: "A certain man had two sons. But when [the younger son] came to himself, he said, 'How many of my father's hired servants have bread enough and to spare, and I perish with hunger! I will arise and go to my father, and will say to him, "Father, I have sinned against heaven and before you."'" (Luke 15:11, 17-18)

The story of the prodigal son is so well known in Western culture that many unbelievers could provide the basics of the story. Yet its simple interpretation of a selfish, straying child who comes home after a rough time is both off-kilter and woefully incomplete.

First, we think of it as a story of a son. It's actually the story of a father and his two sons. In some Middle Eastern cultures it's known as the "The Father With Two Sons" story. Seen from this perspective, we see an aggrieved father treated badly by his younger son. The term "prodigal" doesn't mean one who's run away. "Prodigal" means reckless, wasteful, or foolish in terms of money and/or time. When the son finally comes to himself, realizing the bad state he's in, he decides how he'll get back in his father's good graces.

That plan is interrupted, however, by the father, who's been waiting and watching. He goes running after the son (something a man of his age and dignity wouldn't normally have done in that culture). The son can't even get his plan out before the father completely receives him and showers his love and acceptance on him, which was always the father's plan.

It's our Father's plan as well. God is patiently waiting, looking, and longing for the rebel to come to him. This parable gives us a glimpse into the heart of our heavenly Father, who waits to receive us and shower us with family blessings.

Father, help me see You in this famous parable. Thank You that You were waiting and watching for me and that when I came to You, You received me graciously and generously. May I present to others that same picture of You.

SEPTEMBER 2

THE PRODIGAL: NOT A SERVANT, BUT A SON

"And the son said to him, 'Father, I have sinned against heaven and in your sight, and am no longer worthy to be called your son.' But the father said to his servants, 'Bring out the best robe and put it on him, and put a ring on his hand and sandals on his feet. And bring the fatted calf here and kill it, and let us eat and be merry; for this my son was dead and is alive again; he was lost and is found.'" (Luke 15:21-24)

With so much traditional emphasis on the son's decision to come home after his "wake-up call," a great deal of understanding is lost. "Coming to oneself" isn't about salvation. The son's decision to come home was wise, but his plan was not God's. He wanted to admit his mistake, but he doesn't ask for forgiveness. Even worse for our understanding of salvation is his end goal: to be working for his father again, but in a lowly, servant position (Luke 15:18).

How many have followed this line of thinking—that if we could just get back into God's good graces, we'd take a new, safe position as his worker or servant? This isn't humility. It's another offense against the father, but one that the father quickly moves past. He has no desire to make his younger son pay for his sin by moving him from son to hired hand. He's received only as a son. The son may feel he's "no longer worthy" to be called "son," but the father's love and acceptance have made him worthy of it.

When we stray, we sometimes come back timidly, safely, and indirectly—as a kind of worker. God is like this father, who wants us back as sons and daughters who relate to Him as Father. To receive the grace necessary for this takes true repentance and humility.

Can we hear the word of the Lord to us? "I don't want you as an employee or servant, no matter what you've done. Be my son. Be my daughter. Let's relate again."

Lord, You are our Father. Jesus' prayer model to His disciples makes it clear that that is what we are to call You. Don't let me fall into being just a servant or employee. Help me to continually receive Your Fatherhood.

SEPTEMBER 3

THE PRODIGAL'S OLDER BROTHER

"But [the older son] was angry and would not go in. Therefore his father came out and pleaded with him. So he answered and said to his father, 'Lo, these many years I have been serving you; I never transgressed your commandment at any time; and yet you never gave me a young goat, that I might make merry with my friends. But as soon as this son of yours came … you killed the fatted calf for him.' And he said to him, 'Son, you are always with me, and all that I have is yours.'" (Luke 15:28-31)

No look at this parable would be complete without paying some attention to the older son. Many a sermon has warned not to be like him. It's obvious why—he's unloving, judgmental, petulant, stubborn, and refuses to welcome back his formerly rebellious brother. (His ugly phrase "this son of yours" insults both his brother and his father.)

But there's more. Again, it's the father who initiates the entire exchange. Since the older son wouldn't go in to join the festivities, the father went outside to see him. This is similar to the father running to meet his younger son upon his return. For those of us who can relate in some way to the older son's feelings, it's good to know God doesn't leave us outside, alone in our misery, but draws near to engage us. May we be more open to our Father's words and heart than this son was.

Both sons were struggling with the same issue—relating to their Father as boss/employer. The older son didn't even speak to his father as a father, but instead pointed to his many years of diligent service. How tragic that the older son never enjoyed the father-son relationship that existed or experienced the blessings that accompanied it. What a loss!

We have a loving, patient, relational Father. Whether we're rebellious or sinking into a low-level relationship with Him, our Lord reaches out and draws us back into the kind of connection He died to create. May we always see that and be encouraged when we read this parable.

Father, thank You that You not only take back the repentant rebel, but You also reach out to the legalists and the tired workers who've lost sight that they are an adopted child of God who has all the benefits of that relationship. May I always self-identify first as a loved child of God.

SEPTEMBER 4

THE PRODIGAL STORY IN CONTEXT

"Or what woman, having ten silver coins, if she loses one coin, does not light a lamp, sweep the house, and search carefully until she finds it? And when she has found it, she calls her friends and neighbors together, saying, 'Rejoice with me, for I have found the piece which I lost!' Likewise, I say to you, there is joy in the presence of the angels of God over one sinner who repents." (Luke 15:8–10)

To understand the parable of the prodigal son, we need the context of the two parables that precede it. The first (Luke 15:4-7) tells the story of a man who's lost a sheep. Instead of "writing off" that one sheep or being content with the ninety-nine he has, he goes after the lost one. The parable's last line is one we're encouraged to embrace: "There will be more joy in heaven over one sinner who repents than over ninety-nine just persons who need no repentance." This is the heart of God, showing us how He pursues the lost—us included.

Next, we read about a woman who's lost a coin and searches diligently to find it. The "commentary" at the end of the story is nearly identical to that of the lost sheep. The lost sheep already belonged to the man, and the lost coin already belonged to the woman. This is God's heart as He continues to go after those He already considers His.

By the time we get to the parable of the waiting father who had two sons, we have a new perspective on the story. This is the third parable in a row about something/someone that was lost. The same terminology is used in all three: what was lost is found.

As we read and reread those parables, let's keep in mind the central character in each—the One who seeks that which was lost. That's our Father, and all three parables are an illustration of His loving heart.

Father, help me see Your loving, searching heart here. When I step back from all three stories, I see a God who is patient but always seeking us, one who keeps searching for us when we're lost. Help me, too, to see other connections in Your Word that I haven't seen yet.

MARK DUPRÉ

SEPTEMBER 5

SKEET SHOOT

Knowing this first: that scoffers will come in the last days, walking according to their own lusts, and saying, "Where is the promise of His coming?" (2 Peter 3:3–4)

The subject of scoffers is an unhappy one. Since the Scriptures address it so frequently (Proverbs 13:1, 19:29, 22:10), the Lord must want us to be aware of scoffers, how they work, and what to do. Many associate the scoffer with the end times. Second Peter makes it clear they will indeed arise at that time, heaping doubt and scorn on believers and belief.

But there are other kinds of scoffers that are subtler in their sin. The simple definition is one who derides, scorns, or heaps ridicule. For Christians, this isn't the person who simply disagrees with you. It's the one who actively engages with you so that they can make fun of you or what you believe, even to the point of showing disdain.

We mustn't dismiss the argumentative person outright; perhaps they're struggling with God on their way to faith. But we can't be naïve about the reality of the scoffer.

Scoffers don't want to learn. They ask questions prepared to contest what comes out of your mouth. Their questions have nothing to do with curiosity, but are designed like a skeet shoot, to create something they can shoot at.

Unhappier than the existence of scoffers outside the kingdom is the occasional scoffer inside, the one who truly knows Jesus but is bound in a behavior pattern that continually contends with others and always seems to find an opposite position to take from yours. For them, we show love but avoid the arguments. And if we notice a pattern, we pray for them.

Father, help me avoid getting caught in the scoffer's argument, whether the scoffer is a believer or not. Give me wisdom in that moment to show love but to follow Your leading out of contention. Please cleanse me of any tendency in that direction that might exist in me.

SEPTEMBER 6

TRUTH ISN'T RELATIVE

"Oh, send out Your light and Your truth! Let them lead me; let them bring me to Your holy hill and to Your tabernacle." (Psalm 43:3)

"If you abide in My word, you are My disciples indeed. And you shall know the truth, and the truth shall make you free." (John 8:31–32)

The devil is working overtime these days— with cooperation from the current culture—to make truth a relative thing. We hear that it's not important what happened; it's how you feel about what happened. It's not what really is; it's how you feel about it.

Certainly our perspectives are important. How we feel about people, God, events, and even God's Word are significant. God pays a great deal of attention to how we feel about all these things—usually not to indulge, but to change. But feelings don't change the reality of anything external to us. I can be the sincerest atheist in the land, but it doesn't negate the existence of God. I can react strongly to God's Word—even reject it—but that will never change its truth.

What we have to reject is the idea of "my truth" and "your truth." My belief, yes. My perspective, yes. My perceptions, yes. But truth stands by itself. We should do our best to die to ourselves to approach a fuller understanding and apprehension of the truth in all its facets.

Truth doesn't ultimately abide in us. Truth is in God and His Word. We can find a firm foundation and stability there. Praise the Lord, we're not left alone with our perceptions of truth! Psalm 43 is a cry to be led into the one truth—God's truth. John 8 gives us a way to continue to come to truth—by abiding in Christ. That leads to discipleship, which leads to truth, which leads to freedom.

Father, lead me to truth the rest of my days. May I always recognize my feelings and interpretations as only that and nothing more. May I have a heart that looks for and submits to truth, and that seeks to abide in You, to be Your disciple, and to live in truth.

MARK DUPRÉ

SEPTEMBER 7
SKEET SHOOT

"For this reason a man shall leave his father and mother and be joined to his wife, and the two shall become one flesh." This is a great mystery, but I speak concerning Christ and the church. (Ephesians 5:31–32)

Today's entry is not for the married, the hope-to-be-married, or the single. It's for everyone. Marriage, a reflection of the love of Christ for His beloved people (among many other things), is being assailed in an unprecedented manner. We need to get God's perspective on marriage and obey Hebrews 13:4 and honor marriage in our lives.

The first thing we need to consider is God's view on marriage. Clearly, it's important to God. He created it and has made it the foundation of our society. He gave provision for newlywed men in ancient Israel to refrain from war or any business that would take them away from home for a full year so they could better establish their marriage. He spends a lot of time in the New Testament telling husbands, wives, and children how to behave with one another.

Of course, nothing comes close to the truth of Ephesians 5. All we need to do is look at that truth, coupled with the stability marriage brings to society and child raising, and it's easy to see why the enemy's so intent on destroying it.

We need to make sure we're not part of that attack. This is not a political statement; it's addressed to the heart. No matter what our parents experienced, what we've seen, or what we might have experienced ourselves, marriage is to be honored by all. We need to side with God—not man, not experience—and proclaim the worth and goodness of the first institution created by God.

Lord, forgive me for disparaging statements I've made about marriage. Help me see marriage with Your eyes and Your heart. Thank You that You've given us a picture of Your love for Your church, right here on this earth. May I honor that image of Your love, no matter where I am personally in relation to marriage.

SEPTEMBER 8

MARRIAGE: GOD'S IDEA FIRST

"But did He not make them one, having a remnant of the Spirit? And why one? He seeks godly offspring. Therefore take heed to your spirit, and let none deal treacherously with the wife of his youth." (Malachi 2:15)

Marriage is an individual experience—one we have, one we lost, one that hurt, or one we want. But marriage is much larger than our own personal experience. It's a precious institution for society, God's church, and all mankind, created by God, with many purposes.

Certainly it's meant to bring us personal joy. But as Gary Thomas, author of *Sacred Marriage*, asks on his book's cover, "What if God designed marriage to make us holy more than to make us happy?" Note he doesn't say, "instead of," but "more than." That question immediately takes marriage out of the realm of what's simply personal and elevates it to something grander. God has a plan for married people that's consistent with every other move of His Spirit within us—to transform us into the image of His Son.

We rightly lament marital breakdown and dysfunction in our society because we know the damage it causes. Fatherlessness alone has given rise to untold crimes and personal misery. We also see the heart of God in Malachi (above) that seeks godly offspring. Solid marriages are the foundation of a stable society, and godly stable marriages are the best way to bring godly offspring to God.

Sometimes marriage is such a deeply felt, personal experience that we forget it was originally God's idea. He has purposes for it beyond our own enjoyment. For these reasons, we need to respect and honor marriage wherever we see it.

Lord, help me see the role of marriage in society and especially in Your kingdom and in Your purposes in the life of the married person. May my life be one of respect for every marriage, first in my own and then in everyone else's.

MARK DUPRÉ

SEPTEMBER 9

MARRIAGE: FOR HIS SAKE, TOO

"Then He said to them all, "If anyone desires to come after Me, let him deny himself, and take up his cross daily, and follow Me." (Luke 9:23)

Because marriage was created by God, we cannot redefine it, reshape it, or drain it of its meaning. It will stand against every onslaught the enemy throws against it, no matter how man tries to bend, break, or distort it. There won't be marriage in heaven, but until then, we need to honor it as God's creation.

If you're married, it's worth every effort to make it work. If doing it "for the children" gets you refocused on making it work, then start there; at least that's a goal outside of yourself. But if you know Christ, then let's make our marriages work for His sake. For all He's done for us, it's the least we can do to do everything we can to make our marriages work, even if we must "die daily."

If friends come to you with marital challenges, the best way to show love is to pray for them, lead them to the Scriptures that pertain to them, and help them find the internal and external resources to make their marriage work. Encourage them in God and what He can do. Statistics show that those that weather even severe marital storms end up happier in the long run. It's worth working things through.

If there's abuse or rampant infidelity, these are other matters. But for the most part, marital problems arise when we stop obeying God somewhere, become selfish, and/or were improperly prepared for the realities of marriage. It's in everyone's best interest to support marriage, especially the Lord's.

Lord, thank You for all the many things that marriage is. Help me to deny myself and follow You in my life and in my marriage, and to help others do the same.

SEPTEMBER 10

THE FRUIT OF REPENTANCE

"Create in me a clean heart, O God, and renew a steadfast spirit within me. Restore to me the joy of Your salvation, and uphold me by Your generous Spirit. Then I will teach transgressors Your ways, and sinners shall be converted to You." (Psalm 51:10, 12–13)

David's words in Psalm 51 paint perhaps the best-known picture of repentance in the Scriptures. Most of us have mined this psalm for its manifestations of the various aspects of repentance. David first cries out for mercy, leaning on God's lovingkindness for the boldness to pray. He realizes the depth of his sin and the cleansing he needs. Though he's clearly sinned against both Bathsheba and Uriah, David also sees the depth of his rebellion against God Almighty.

Many of us think David's prayer essentially ends with verse 12, as if the full fruit of repentance were connecting with God's presence and being restored in the joy of our salvation. But the psalm goes on, and the next verse gives us a fuller picture of what the fruit—the end result—of real repentance looks like: "Then I will teach transgressors Your ways, and sinners shall be converted to You."

It's tempting to believe that we've come full circle from sin to a right relationship with God when we feel reconnected and forgiven. But David's fruit of repentance was in reaching out to others in ministry.

The final expression of our repentance is outward. We may feel God has completed a work in us when we're no longer sinning, or we feel close to Him again. But He's done when we're flowing in a new and deeper ministry to others. May we not stop short in the work of His Spirit in our lives.

Father, help me continue to follow You through the end of Your work in me as You lead me in repentance. I see that Your final goal is not just rightness with You, but ministry to others. May I see it, be open to it, and allow Your work to be completed in me.

MARK DUPRÉ

SEPTEMBER 11

HUMILITY BEFORE HONOR

"And he went into all the region around the Jordan, preaching a baptism of repentance for the remission of sins ... saying: "The voice of one crying in the wilderness: 'Prepare the way of the Lord; make His paths straight.'" (Luke 3:3–4) The fear of the Lord is the instruction of wisdom, and before honor is humility." (Proverbs 15:33)

We rightly remember John the Baptist as the one sent to prepare the Jewish people for the arrival and message of Jesus. We also rightly remember that he was direct, occasionally rough, and a nonconformist. Part of the outrage over John's work was his baptism. He directed it at Jews, at a time when it was generally only for Gentiles converting to Judaism. For a Jew to be baptized took a great deal of spiritual humility and an openness to God that was uncommon in those days (and still is today).

While his outward call was to humble repentance, John himself demonstrated his own personal humility in the midst of it. In referring to the coming Lamb of God, John said he wasn't worthy to loosen His sandal strap (Luke 3:16). Loosening a sandal strap was the job of the lowest slave. This is right where John was placing himself in relation to his cousin and Messiah, Jesus.

Historically, we can easily see how John's call to a spiritual awakening was a preparation for the ministry of Jesus. Can we also see it as a working principle for how God operates in nations, churches, and individuals?

Perhaps the Lord has honor prepared for you. If so, humility will have to come first. Without that humility, the Jews would have seen and heard Jesus with their *natural* eyes and ears, but would have missed the blessing of knowing who was in their midst and the joys of receiving His message.

Lord, may I humble myself in Your sight constantly. When I need to be humbled, may I see it as preparation for receiving more of You and, perhaps, more from You.

SEPTEMBER 12

QUESTIONS WITH STRANGE ANSWERS: A TEACHABLE MOMENT

"So the Lord said to Cain, "Why are you angry? And why has your countenance fallen? If you do well, will you not be accepted? And if you do not do well, sin lies at the door. And its desire is for you, but you should rule over it." Now Cain talked with Abel his brother; and it came to pass, when they were in the field, that Cain rose up against Abel his brother and killed him. (Genesis 4:6–8)

The Lord's questions here aim at stirring up Cain's heart and pointing him to two realities: the real reason for his anger and a perspective of justice that exists outside his feelings about his brother.

Consider a few possible responses from Cain to God's questions: "I don't know—is there a problem?" "I thought my offering would be accepted, and I'm angry because I don't understand why it wasn't." "I'm angry because I'm jealous of my brother." (Note the increasing honesty of each answer.)

Incredibly, after a direct question and a strong warning, there's no answer—at least no verbal answer. Cain's response to God's question was his dialogue with Abel and its bloody aftermath.

Notice the Lord doesn't stop after the first question, but asks three in a row. As He steers Cain toward honesty with the first question, he "heads him off at the pass" from answering too quickly by asking the other two. This provides a teachable moment where God warns Cain about the power of sin and its dangerous closeness. Cain was in trouble spiritually, and the Lord was giving him a warning.

Perhaps God has put you in that teachable moment. Perhaps His Spirit—directly, through the Word, or through a friend—has touched an issue, and now the Lord is working to teach you, warn you, or encourage you. If so, ask, knock, and seek what else He has to say in addition to what you've heard. May we take warnings when they're given and receive any teachings or perspectives that come our way.

Father, help me to be open when You question me. Help me to hear and be honestly responsive. Then help me continue to hear what You say. Forbid it, Lord, that my head should take over at that point. I pray I will keep listening with an open heart.

SEPTEMBER 13
AN OPEN AND SHUT CASE

"A fool takes no pleasure in understanding, but only in expressing his opinion. A fool's lips walk into a fight, and his mouth invites a beating." (Proverbs 18:2, 6 ESV); "He who guards his mouth preserves his life, but he who opens wide his lips shall have destruction." (Proverbs 13:3)

In their coolly expressive wisdom, the observations we find in Proverbs are invariably true, often funny, and full of sage advice for those willing to receive it.

The fool and the wise person are the two opposites presented in wisdom literature, and we learn much by their juxtaposition. Perhaps no age in history has been in more need of the wisdom of Proverbs than our own, where continual (and public) expression is encouraged to a damaging degree.

While we're encouraged in today's culture to express/share/talk, the Scriptures caution against an excess of expression. The warning is clear: loose talk can cause great personal damage. Perhaps Proverbs 18:2 presents the reason for much of the damage: our heart's inclination.

If our goal is simply to express ourselves, with no real interest in hearing others (otherwise known as learning), we're bound to get into trouble. The overly expressive heart is a proud heart, and pride comes before a fall. A person who delights in understanding, who listens, who has an open heart to learn is humble—and humility comes before honor.

Most of us need to embrace the call to less self-expression. Whether quiet or talkative, we all need to heed the call to guard our mouth and to be someone who delights more in understanding than in expressing our own hearts.

Father, remove any strain of verbal foolishness within me and replace it with the wise and edifying use of my lips. Touch my heart to be more inclined to listen and learn than to express myself.

SEPTEMBER 14

PREPARING TO PLANT

"Give ear and hear my voice, listen and hear my speech. Does the plowman keep plowing all day to sow? Does he keep turning his soil and breaking the clods? When he has leveled its surface, does he not sow the black cummin and scatter the cummin, plant the wheat in rows, the barley in the appointed place, and the spelt in its place? For He instructs him in right judgment, His God teaches him." (Isaiah 28:23-26)

God knows exactly what He's doing with the trials and tests He sends our way. It may sometimes seem that they're are all the same and unceasing, but God doesn't "keep plowing all day." He doesn't "keep turning his soil and breaking the clods." Like the farmer, He's only preparing the soil for planting.

Notice the different actions here: plowing, breaking up the clods, leveling the surface, sowing and scattering seed, and planting other seeds in rows that have to first be created. The following verses (27-29) describe the different instruments used for the different seeds. One size doesn't fit all when it comes to how the ground and seed must be prepared, cared for, and harvested. It all depends on what's being planted.

God has purpose, from beginning to end, in all that He does in our lives. He is moving forward, even if we can't see it. There is fruit at the end, and He has a complete and wise design behind every action taken toward the planting and harvesting of that fruit.

We may believe His hand is doing the same thing throughout our lives. Perhaps we first recognized His hand as He broke up the clods of our heart. We might make the mistake of thinking that every subsequent touch of His hand was to do the same thing, when perhaps he was creating rows for planting or even watering and feeding the plants. God has a purpose and a direction in His planting and harvesting. He will not always plow.

Father, help me remember there's a purpose and direction even when I don't see it. I receive the word of this passage that there are seasons and reasons behind all You do. Help me to work with You in every stage of the planting You do in me.

MARK DUPRÉ

SEPTEMBER 15

WHAT GOD'S WISDOM LOOKS LIKE

"Who is wise and understanding among you? Let him show by good conduct that his works are done in the meekness of wisdom. But if you have bitter envy and self-seeking in your hearts, do not boast and lie against the truth. This wisdom does not descend from above, but is earthly, sensual, demonic. For where envy and self-seeking exist, confusion and every evil thing are there. But the wisdom that is from above is first pure, then peaceable, gentle, willing to yield, full of mercy and good fruits, without partiality and without hypocrisy. (James 3:13-17)

"Lord, how do I know what Your will is? What's Your wisdom here?" It's a question we ask of the Lord on a regular basis. If we're asking about adultery, murder, or thieving, we have some well-known commandments that make His will clear. But what about all the other choices we're presented with? The house we want to buy, the career direction we're considering, the person who may be our future spouse? There aren't specific commandments about those kinds of choices, but God has given us a great deal of direction in these few verses in James.

If it's not the wisdom of God, it's the wisdom of this world, which is sensual, even demonic. Check your heart and look for the fruit of how you're wrestling with the issue at hand. If there's any "evil thing" we're constantly wrestling with in the process, perhaps we're insisting on our own agenda and not God's.

If you're moving in God's wisdom, however, there's a whole different spiritual landscape. There's purity and peace, and we don't have be defensive about our efforts. God's wisdom is willing to yield (especially to the input of others), and is distinguished by His mercy and the good fruits of His Spirit.

The process may take a while and will likely involve some dying to self. But we can thank God that He's given us a description of the final product so we know when we're "there."

> *Father, thank You that You've given us a description of what Your wisdom is like. Convict me of envy and self-seeking as I walk through this life. Help me recognize bad fruit when it's in my seeking process, and lead me to the fullness of Your wisdom.*

SEPTEMBER 16

MEETING US WHERE WE ARE

"Then all the children of Israel, that is, all the people, went up and came to the house of God and wept. They sat there before the Lord and fasted that day until evening; and they offered burnt offerings and peace offerings before the Lord." (Judges 20:26)

Some men from the tribe of Benjamin com-mitted a horrific crime (Judges 19). For the first time in a long time, the rest of Israel was united—in revenge. They inquired of God how to wage war against their brother tribe. God told them the battle (which they initiated, not God) should be led by the tribe of Judah.

Israel's first attempt ended in defeat, as did their second. The third time, they went before the Lord in both desperation and dependence (Judges 20:26–28). This time, for the first time, the Lord promised victory.

God can even use even depravity and self-willed efforts to draw His people to Himself. But since Israel "gave Him an inch," God took a mile. He met them in the middle of their self-initiated, revenge-driven activities and worked with them where they were. They continued seeking the Lord (as He continued drawing them) until they got the result they were seeking.

God got the results He was seeking too. Israel learned to press into God, moving from prayer for a quick answer to fasting, worship, and spending real time with the Lord.

Our God is a God of covenant. He uses whatever He chooses to draw us to Himself. He made a covenant with Israel and was faithful to it. He's made a similar covenant with us. We need to keep turning to Him in the middle of our struggles and questions and let Him direct us from there. No matter what our goals might be, His always include drawing us closer.

Father, thank You for meeting me even when I'm being selfish and self-centered. Thank You for taking me from faith to faith and glory to glory when I turn to You.

MARK DUPRÉ

SEPTEMBER 17

OBEDIENCE IS VICTORY

[Phinehas asked],"Shall I yet again go out to battle against the children of my brother Benjamin, or shall I cease?" And the Lord said, "Go up, for tomorrow I will deliver them into your hand." (Judges 20:28)

Yesterday, we noted how God used Israel's dire circumstances to draw them closer to Himself. Yet a question arises from this story: If God directs, does that mean victory every time?

Clearly, the answer is no, at least not in terms of victory as we define it. It's true Israel should have asked the Lord if they should go into battle in the first place; asking how to conduct the battle was second best at most. God in His grace met them where they were and gave them direction. Yet they were defeated not once, but twice—each time after asking the Lord for direction. It was only following the third, most sincere seeking of His face that God promised the victory they were looking for.

There are two lessons here. One is that obedience is victory. In following the Lord's directives, Israel was victorious each time it obeyed. Military victory eventually came, but spiritual victory came the moment Israel listened and obeyed.

The second is more sobering. Just because the Lord directs us to do something doesn't guarantee we'll be "successful." Sometimes, if there are many "tries" involved, we err by assuming we "missed the Lord" if things don't work out as planned. Sometimes, He's working to draw us closer. Sometimes, He's working perseverance into us. Sometimes, our very tries are witnesses to others. Sometimes, we're just walking in obedience and it's up to Him how He chooses to use that obedience. The point isn't our version of success; the point is obedience and trust that He knows what He's doing.

Father, help me to hear and obey and then trust You for the results. I want to be satisfied in obeying, not just in getting what I hope for. Help me to focus on that and to trust the rest to You.

SEPTEMBER 18

WE'RE ALL IN CHILDREN'S MINISTRY

"Josiah was eight years old when he became king, and he reigned thirty-one years in Jerusalem. And he did what was right in the sight of the Lord, and walked in the ways of his father David; he did not turn aside to the right hand or to the left." (2 Chronicles 34:1–2)

Never underestimate what God is doing in a young person or even in a child. King Josiah was only eight when he ascended the throne. At sixteen, he began one of the greatest reform movements Israel had ever seen. His actions were as brave as anything done by David in battle; tearing down idolatrous altars and images was asking for trouble. That kind of courage is the product of years of walking with the Lord.

If you're a Christian, you're in children's ministry. We're all called to build up the next generation. That involves connecting with children—and not just your own. We're all examples. The young are watching, learning, and absorbing. There may be a "Junior Church" in your church, but there's no "Junior Holy Spirit." God can do deep work in a young heart.

Perhaps younger children don't have our vocabulary or the life experience to contextualize all they hear and learn. But they're capable of understanding deeper things of the Spirit than we tend to give them credit for. We can encourage them by not watering down the gospel or God's principles. The burden is often not on them to try to understand as it is on us to hear from the Lord how best to relate and impart.

The next time you find yourself with a young person who has an open heart and a desire to learn, it may not be their lack of faith that prevents them from understanding spiritual truths. It might be ours!

> Father, help me to "suffer the little children to come to" us, as they did to You. Help me to see them with Your eyes, and to be used by You to model Christ and speak His word. Thank You that there's only one Holy Spirit and He can work in anyone's heart.

MARK DUPRÉ

SEPTEMBER 19

THE RULE IS MORE GOLDEN THAN WE THOUGHT

"Love your enemies, do good to those who hate you, bless those who curse you, and pray for those who spitefully use you. To him who strikes you on the one cheek, offer the other also. ... And from him who takes away your goods do not ask them back. And just as you want men to do to you, you also do to them likewise." (Luke 6:27–31)

Jesus places what we know as the Golden Rule right in the middle of a sermon about those who don't love us, which includes our enemies. (Read Luke 6:27-36 for the whole picture.) The least weighty situation He describes is lending to those we know can't repay. Other circumstances are things we'd rather not encounter—people who hate us, curse us, and spitefully use us. Then the scenarios escalate to personal violence and theft.

It's in that setting, with those violations and offenses against us, that He tells us to do something positive. Under those circumstances, it would be challenging enough to refrain from doing some-thing negative. Most of us would rightly consider that a major spiritual victory in that situation.

Reminding us that God is "kind to the unthankful and evil" (Luke 6:35) Jesus tells us the Golden Rule involves loving our enemies (referring to moral love, as seen in action, not as evidenced in personal affection), doing good (a positive action), and giving (which is what lending with no thought of return really is). Luke 6:36 brings final definition to what Jesus is saying here: "Be merciful, just as your Father also is merciful."

The Golden Rule isn't sweet; it's defiant against every fleshly tendency we have to retaliate when hurt. It's powerful in its call to "not be overcome by evil, but [to] overcome evil with good" (Romans 12:21). Let's keep it strong by remembering how Jesus presented it.

Father, I receive the force and power of this obligation of love. Help me understand its power and its call and receive it deeply into my heart and spirit. I pray You'd help me to obey its call the next time I find myself in one of the situations Jesus describes.

SEPTEMBER 20
GREATER AND LESSER DEBTS

"Therefore the kingdom of heaven is like a certain king who wanted to settle accounts with his servants. And when he had begun to settle accounts, one was brought to him who owed him ten thousand talents. But [he] was not able to pay." (Matthew 18:23–25)

The parable of the unforgiving servant presents us with one of the great contrasts in the Scriptures. The servant owed a nearly uncountable amount—10,000 talents. According to one source, one talent was worth six thousand denarii. Ten thousand times that amount is a sum no one could repay, certainly not a servant.

Once that debt was forgiven, the servant who owed so much demanded payment of a hundred denarii—the approximate equivalent of one hundred days' pay. Of course, the obvious lesson is that we should forgive the relatively small offenses we've received from others in the light of the great forgiveness granted by God.

Let's look at the larger amount, setting the small amount aside for a while. This 10,000-debt breaks the outer limits of our comprehension. But that's God's perspective on our sin, the state we're in before His grace and forgiveness came to us.

Perhaps we didn't realize our dire state and our depth of sinfulness at the time we came to Him, but we do now. Remember Romans 8:1—"There is therefore now no condemnation to those who are in Christ Jesus." Before the debt was erased, there was a huge price to be paid. We'll never comprehend the extent of our lost state on this side of the grave. Yet we can agree with this parable that the debt was huge, and His grace is amazing.

Father, I agree with You in Your Word here that my debt was practically incalculable. Thank You for mercy and forgiveness that is also incalculable. May the reality of Your grace help me to keep those one-hundred-denarii offenses in proper perspective.

MARK DUPRÉ

SEPTEMBER 21

WE'RE NOT ANIMALS

"For You have made [man] a little lower than the angels, and You have crowned him with glory and honor. You have made him to have dominion over the works of Your hands; You have put all things under his feet." (Psalm 8:4–6)

We're created in God's image. Yes, we've fallen into sin as a race and have twisted and perverted that image, but it remains. We're made from on high, not from beneath. According to His Word, He used the dust of the earth to create our physical bodies. But we were heaven's idea, and we're a heavenly creation.

Some rant and rave about how we're equal to other animals. What dangers lie there! We're not to look down to animals to see how we ought to relate, think, and live. We're to look heavenward, to God, and to those things He's given us—His Spirit, His Word, His church. These are the things that give us context and direction, not other species. We've been made a little lower than the angels, not a little higher than the animals.

Our models can never be other creatures with which we share body types, air, food, and space. Our model is God Himself, given human form in Jesus Christ. He's the One we look to, knowing full well that we fall far short, and being ever grateful for His forgiveness, mercy, and restoring grace.

We're called to treat our animals well (Proverbs 12:10) and to properly steward that over which we hold dominion. But even failing those things, we're still set above all creation, made in His image, looking upward. We can enjoy, rescue, and eat animals. But we look to God for how we're to act and even think of ourselves.

Father, help me stay near to what You say in Your Word about me as a human being. Thank You for making us a little lower than the angels and above all other creation. May I be a good steward of all that I'm called to care for, and may I be grateful for being in Your image, living above creation and under You.

SEPTEMBER 22

"BUT IT'S NOT FAIR!"

"Truly God is good to Israel, to such as are pure in heart. But as for me, my feet had almost stumbled; my steps had nearly slipped. For I was envious of the boastful, when I saw the prosperity of the wicked. For there are no pangs in their death, but their strength is firm. They are not in trouble as other men, nor are they plagued like other men." (Psalm 73:1–5)

Everyone—especially any parent—has heard the words "It's not fair!" You may have heard them come out of your own mouth. Scripture honestly recognizes and addresses the struggle. Asaph, the author of Psalm 73, saw apparent inequity everywhere he looked.

God is not "fair". But He is just. He loves justice and righteousness and promises that vengeance will occur—in His way and time. While working for justice here on earth, we must settle it in our hearts that God knows what He's doing, that He loves justice more than we do, and that if we had a glimpse into the next life, we would never complain about the issue of fairness again.

Yet even in this life, it's a blessing that God is not fair. If God were "fair," we'd have to pay for our own sins. If God were "fair," Jesus wouldn't have had to pay for them. We were the sinners, yet we inherit eternal life and a relationship with God when we turn to Christ. Jesus lived a perfect life and received the opposite of what was fair: the King of Kings was mocked, grossly misunderstood, beaten, and killed—all for sinful people. That's not fair. But it's merciful.

One last thought. When I heard "it's not fair" from my young children, I responded that the only meaning of "fair" in the Bible was "good looking." It may not have sunk in deeply, but it worked to derail their erroneous thought process, and it gave them something to think about!

Father, thank You that You operate out of love and mercy, not out of our limited sense of what's fair or not. I agree with Your Word that You love justice and reward it. Change my heart to reflect a more eternal view of justice and fairness, and soften it to see that the greatest injustice of all was that done to Jesus for me.

MARK DUPRÉ

SEPTEMBER 23

THE "SECRET" TO KNOWING GOD'S WILL

"Jesus went up into the temple and taught. And the Jews marveled, saying, "How does this Man know letters, having never studied?" Jesus answered them and said, "My doctrine is not Mine, but His who sent Me. If anyone wills to do His will, he shall know concerning the doctrine, whether it is from God or whether I speak on My own authority." (John 7:14-17)

Jesus was in Jerusalem for the annual Feast of Booths. He began teaching in the temple and, as usual, was equal parts impressive and confusing. Some questioned how Jesus could possibly have this level of understanding when He hadn't been taught by any well-known rabbi. Jesus told His listeners if they set their will to do God's will, they'd receive the revelation that He was speaking the words of God.

Jesus' answer echoes down the centuries in its application. The key to understanding the will of God isn't found in the mind, but in the heart and will. The "secret"—which is only a secret to those who don't read God's Word—is that the key to finding God's will is to be willing to do it.

It's a waste of time to fool ourselves into praying, reading, and even fasting to discover God's will if we never have any intention of doing it. Those are wonderful avenues of pursuing God's will when we simultaneously fear Him and desire to act on what He says. There's no condemnation if we initially discover we're not completely inclined to do His will. If that's the case, that's where we put our prayers and spiritual focus.

The Lord can show us direction in a split second; it often takes much longer to get our hearts rightly positioned to receive that direction. If that's where the work has to begin, rejoice that He's pointed it out, and that He'll hear our prayers to soften and reposition our hearts.

Lord, continue to soften my heart to do Your will as I walk with You. Show me by Your Spirit when I'm not being honest with myself. Thank You that You can change a heart. I am willing to be made willing to do Your will.

SEPTEMBER 24
THE GREAT SHIFT

"Truly God is good to Israel, to such as are pure in heart. But as for me, my feet had almost stumbled; my steps had nearly slipped. For I was envious of the boastful, when I saw the prosperity of the wicked. For there are no pangs in their death, but their strength is firm. They are not in trouble as other men, nor are they plagued like other men." (Psalm 73:1–5)

There are many great shifts in tone and focus in the Scriptures. Perhaps the two most famous are found in Isaiah, from chapter 39 to 40, and in Romans, from chapter 11 to 12.

In Paul's shift in Romans, we see a pattern we often find in Paul's other books: teaching followed by application. In Romans, Paul is summing up all he's taught the readers in his previous eleven chapters: powerful words that have revolutionized people and nations. He then hits the subtotal button, metaphorically speaking. In essence, he says, "Okay, we've learned a lot about God and truth—how does that translate into action?"

Paul spends the rest of the book telling us how the marvelous truths he expounded earlier help us to live. These truths translate into godly action in the areas of Christian relationships, love, service, human government, and our relationship with the Lord. What we learn is supposed to be translated into action. In fact, it's really only "learned" when it's absorbed enough to work its way out again in some kind of expression.

Our challenge is twofold. We're to absorb truth as deeply as we can, to meditate, pray about what we're learning, and allow God's Spirit to move away any and all obstacles to fully receiving God's truth. Then we're to allow God to take information and make it revelation, transformation, and finally, godly action. What we learn needs to find an outward expression—a great shift in our own lives.

> Lord, thank You for what You teach me in church, Your Word, small groups, and personal relationships. Help me to fully receive what You show me. May everything You show me end up being expressed outwardly in loving, obedient action.

MARK DUPRÉ

SEPTEMBER 25

YOU BELONG

"Now, therefore, you are no longer strangers and foreigners, but fellow citizens with the saints and members of the household of God." (Ephesians 2:19)

There are forces working in society, culture, and business that tend to isolate us. We're told far too often to view ourselves as independent and separate. This can lead to feeling alone, disconnected, and detached.

But we're not alone. If we know Jesus, we're members of the most extraordinary group of people ever created—the family of God. How astonishing this group is—comprised of every kind of personality from every corner of the earth, bursting with all different manner of gifts, and united by the most powerful force on earth—the Spirit of God.

There are few things more spiritually exciting than running into another serious believer in an unexpected place or context. If ever we wondered about the spiritual unity we have with other believers, it's moments like this that remind us how powerful and joyful that connection can be. Some people feel that New Testament references to the church being like a family are metaphor. Not true. We're not "like" a family—we *are* a family! We're part of one another, and we belong together. The only difference is that Dad is perfect and He's invisible! In fact, if we've truly been chosen by God since before the foundation of the earth (Ephesians 1:4), then the idea of the church being a family preceded the creation of the first natural family!

Don't believe the lies of the enemy. You're part of something great; you're part of the family of God. You belong—today, tomorrow, and forever.

Father, thank You for not just calling us to be a group of individuals, but to be a family. Help me to see it and to receive it in the deepest part of my heart. Open my eyes to see spiritual connections I've missed before, and help me enjoy the unity You've created.

SEPTEMBER 26

IS GOD WAITING FOR US TO DO SOMETHING?

"For as we have many members in one body, but all the members do not have the same function, so we, being many, are one body in Christ, and individually members of one another." (Romans 12:4–5)

Yesterday, we revisited the marvelous reality that we belong, specifically to the family of God. As members of a family, we have family responsibilities. We don't all have the same function, but we're all equipped (Romans 12:3, 6).

Remember, the body of Christ, the church, is not like a family; it *is* a family. In the same way, the body of Christ is not like a body, it *is* a body. Paul didn't just notice an interesting metaphor that helped explain some spiritual truths. He saw a spiritual reality. As with the idea of family, the idea of a body being created to express the Lord Jesus Christ was hatched in eternity, long before Adam had a physical body.

So if we're the body, Jesus wants to use His body to move, to build, to heal, to wage warfare, to create, to love—all the things a body does. And as anybody does, we get direction from the Head. Imagine how you'd feel if your mind directed your arms, legs, or mouth to do something and they didn't respond.

How different so many things would be in this world if the church began to really act as the body of Christ, doing everything the Head leads us to do. Instead of always waiting for God to move (a real spiritual exercise we need to do at times), perhaps we should position ourselves to listen and obey. We may be surprised and blessed by what we hear.

Lord, I don't want to mess things up by getting involved where I don't belong. But I don't want to be waiting for You to do something when You're waiting for me to do something. Help me be a cooperative member of Your body.

MARK DUPRÉ

SEPTEMBER 27

FEELINGS, NOTHING MORE THAN FEELINGS

"For we do not have a High Priest who cannot sympathize with our weaknesses, but was in all points tempted as we are, yet without sin." (Hebrews 4:15)

What to do with our feelings is one of the great struggles of the Christian life. Feelings are personal, complicated responses to internal and external stimuli that can bring us joy, sadness, fear, or confusion. Even the most cursory reading of the Old Testament demonstrates that the Lord Himself is a God of sometimes intense feeling.

The ancient Hebrews were an emotional people; one of the few drawbacks of the King James Version of the Scriptures is how it elevated to heights of literary majesty a written language that was much more intense, colorful, and rough-and-tumble in the original. The story of God's connections with man is laden with intense emotion.

While the Lord doesn't want us to be slaves to our feelings, being tossed to and fro by every wind of emotion, He also doesn't want us to suppress them. That's simply another form of emotional slavery. He wants us to rule over our feelings in the power of the Holy Spirit, embracing the healthy ones with all the joy they bring and equipped to do spiritual battle against those that seek to wrongly influence our actions.

Emotions can be helpful to us, even the negative ones. More on that tomorrow. But for now, let's rejoice that our Savior understands, as He was tempted in every way we are. Yet He didn't sin, which means He not only has the plan and power to overcome the temptations of negative emotions, but He's already conquered them. Camp a bit around that thought today.

Father, help me have a healthy connection with my feelings. I want to feel all the emotions you want me to, but I don't ever want feelings to lead me. Please put them in their proper place in my heart and my life, and help me see Jesus' victory in this area.

SEPTEMBER 28

WHO'S THE BOSS?

"Peace I leave with you, My peace I give to you; not as the world gives do I give to you. Let not your heart be troubled, neither let it be afraid." (John 14:27)

As we walk in faith, it's healthy to be aware of how we feel. Our feelings can point us to areas that may need healing and deliverance. If we consistently feel something negative about a circumstance or person, or are constantly resisting something, it may be that like a physical pain, our emotions are calling attention to an area that needs help and ministry.

The issue for us as believers is not whether to have emotions or not. They're inevitable. The question is who is boss. We're called to live by faith, not feelings. God's Word is our true guide. The great news is that we don't have to be led around by how we feel; we're free in Christ to obey Him, even if that means we must deny our feelings to do so.

God doesn't want us to ignore or suppress our feelings as much as allow Him to redeem and transform them. We may have to deny some feelings at times to show them who's boss—that we're going to obey the Lord no matter how we feel. But this denial of feelings is only temporary. It's actually a step toward replacing our negative feelings with His peace.

It's often said that faith is the engine on the train and feelings are the caboose. Where the engine goes, the caboose inevitably follows. God doesn't want you to deny your feelings—He wants to free you from them, put them under your feet in His name, and ultimately redeem and transform them!

Father, open my eyes and my heart to see how You want me to cooperate with Your Holy Spirit in doing battle against the enemy's emotional attacks. Help me know the victory I have in You and teach me to stand in the power of Your Word and Your name.

MARK DUPRÉ

SEPTEMBER 29

FILL THAT GAP WITH FAITH!

"[The devil] was a murderer from the beginning, and does not stand in the truth, because there is no truth in him. When he speaks a lie, he speaks from his own resources, for he is a liar and the father of it". (John 8:44): "Your word is truth." (John 17:17)

Learning how to do spiritual battle in the area of our emotions can be difficult at times. When we're hit by strong negative emotions, our first instinct is to withstand them (a normal survival move). As we step back to try to make sense of what happened, a gap forms between us and our emotions. It's in that space where the battle takes place.

As we regain our equilibrium, the enemy tries filling that gap with lies he attempts to pass off as our own thinking. His intent is to have us judge others, ourselves, or worse, come to a judgment against the Lord Himself. If he can make us believe these lies are our own thoughts, he's won the battle. If we fill the gap with enough lies enough times, we form a series of related thoughts that we return to regularly when we're struggling emotionally. It's good to resist them, but it's even better to replace them.

This is why we need to be soaked in God's Word, walking close enough to Jesus to hear His voice. Instead of accepting the enemy's thoughts (remember, he's the father of lies), we can fill the gap with faith and God's truth. That makes us godly masters of our feelings, not slaves.

As we replace the enemy's lies with God's truth, His peace and joy replace the pain of our former emotions, and we grow stronger in His grace. This is more than walking in faith; it's leaping in faith.

Lord, teach me how to replace the familiar lies the enemy has embedded in my heart and mind through emotional attacks. Help me replace them with Your Word, which is truth. Thank You for the grace and strength to do that.

SEPTEMBER 30
LORD, YOU KNOW

"For if our heart condemns us, God is greater than our heart, and knows all things." (1 John 3:20)

John is encouraging us that even when our own hearts condemn us, God—with all He has done and promised us—is bigger than all those thoughts and accusations. In fact, He knows all things. We can rest in the fact that no matter what we're struggling with, He's aware of it all, including what He has purchased for us and His promises toward us (e.g., Romans 8:1). Who knows better than God about those things we struggle with and about all the things He's done for us in Christ?

Releasing ourselves to the God who knows all things is one of the great surrenders we can make. Sometimes we try to figure out what's going on spiritually, struggle to "feel" forgiven, or wrestle to position ourselves rightly before God. There may well be issues God wants us to face or work through, and we should be faithful to follow His Spirit's lead.

But we must realize when we have come to the end of the line of what we can understand or take genuine responsibility for. It's then we must say, "Lord, You know." This is a powerful acknowledgement and a great leap of faith. It brings with it a temporary sense of panic followed by His peace. Next time you hit that wall, let go and release it all to Him in the light of His omniscience and goodness.

Father, help me to be faithful to follow You when You're working within. Help me know when we reach the end of what I need to do. Make it clear that the next step of obedience is to let go and trust You. I agree with John: You know all things.

MARK DUPRÉ

OCTOBER 1

WHERE WAS GOD?

"Jehoiakim was twenty-five years old when he became king ... And he did evil in the sight of the Lord, according to all that his fathers had done." (2 Kings 23:36-37); "Jehoiachin was eighteen years old when he became king ... And he did evil in the sight of the Lord, according to all that his father had done." (2 Kings 24:8-9); "Zedekiah was twenty-one years old when he became king ... He also did evil in the sight of the Lord." (2 Kings 24:18-19)

The story of the last three kings of Judah appears as one discouraging parade of failure. All three "did evil in the sight of the Lord." The end result of their reigns was complete conquest and the Babylonian exile. When we read this account of sin and transgression, it's easy to wonder where God was in all of this. Had he stopped speaking? Had He abandoned His people?

Quite the opposite. We need to look to another book to see the loving, warning voice of God during this time: Jeremiah. Though not alone, Jeremiah was the main prophet God raised up to speak the word of the Lord to these kings.

The question wasn't whether or not God was speaking; it was whether or not people were hearing. Jehoiakim heard Jeremiah's words as they were read to him on a scroll, and promptly cut up the scroll and threw the pieces into the fire. Zedekiah asked Jeremiah to pray for him and even asked him what the Lord was saying. When Jeremiah told him, the king threw him into prison.

Thank God the depravity and disobedience we see in 2 Kings 24 and 2 Chronicles 36 wasn't the whole story. Even in our dark age, God is speaking through His Word, His Spirit, and His anointed leaders. Many may ignore or even actively reject God's Word; others may toy with His Word, never really submitting to it. But for those who seek His Word with the intent of obeying it, we are never without His voice.

Father, help me to not be distracted or discouraged by evil and failure. Thank You that even in the midst of it, You are speaking.

OCTOBER 2
STRUGGLE TOWARD TRUTH

"Whom have I in heaven but You? And there is none upon earth that I desire besides You. My flesh and my heart fail; but God is the strength of my heart and my portion forever." (Psalm 73:25-26)

Psalm 73 is the famous psalm of struggle over the apparent unfairness of how the wicked prosper with seeming impunity—and the negative effect that line of thinking can produce in the soul. (Read the entire psalm for context.) Those inaccurate thoughts on the wicked lead to the great lie the devil uses to tempt the psalmist: "All in vain have I kept my heart clean and washed my hands in innocence" (v. 13).

What a defeat this would have been if Asaph (the psalm's author) had not wrestled with this diabolical lie and won this battle! His first victory was realizing that sharing his doubts would have caused his fellow believers to stumble. His next victory was recognizing how his heart attitude affected his view of God.

Asaph says he was "foolish and ignorant" (literally "stupid and not discerning"), like "a beast" before God (vv. 21-22). Why? Because of a bitter heart. How quickly bitterness can lead to devilish assumptions about God, His heart, and His ways. The change from one bad thought to an even more destructive one is evident from verse to verse in this psalm. And it all stemmed from a hardening heart.

Asaph found his answer when he encountered God's presence in the temple (vv. 16-17). We can keep our hearts from bitterness by spending time with Him, reading His Word (adding our faith to what we read), and by not forsaking assembling together with fellow believers (Hebrews 10:25). Nothing new here. But staying close to God often requires the diligence and humility of Asaph.

Father, strengthen me to be diligent to keep my heart in Your truth. Point out bitterness before it grows into doubt and faithlessness. I want to keep my heart clean to keep my spiritual vision clear. Amen.

MARK DUPRÉ

OCTOBER 3

LOVE YOUR NEIGHBOR AS YOURSELF?

"And the second [commandment], like it, is this: 'You shall love your neighbor as yourself.' There is no other commandment greater than these." (Mark 12:31)

Oh, what the devil has done with this beloved commandment! The heart of God is that we treat our neighbors with the same actions we show ourselves in everyday life. We feed ourselves, protect ourselves, build ourselves up, and in general, make sure we're taken care of. Jesus was speaking with the understanding He knew all his listeners possessed: that we innately love ourselves and show it in normal actions every day.

What modern psychology has done to twist this Scripture is try and remove that built-in awareness. It works to pretend that real, healthy self-love isn't a part of every human being and must be created over a period of years before we arrive at some anemic semblance of self-acceptance. This is a tragic perspective, as it radiates an entire spectrum of lies.

Sin has distorted God's gift of healthy self-perception but certainly hasn't destroyed it. In fact, it could be argued that hating oneself, or having a negative self-image, is self-love taken to a sinful extreme. We have no right to hate anyone, including ourselves. Hatred of self doesn't need to be worked on; it needs to be repented of.

The issue is not whether we can connect to this love of self emotionally or not. The issue is whether we're in Christ or not. If we're not in Christ, we cannot love our neighbors as we love ourselves. But rest assured that in Christ, with His grace and power, we can.

> *Lord, thank You that I can love others freely and that it's based on Your love for me, not on how I feel about myself. Help me see that You've given me an inborn, healthy love for myself. Lead me to repent of any self-hatred I begin to walk in, and teach me to love with Your unending supply.*

OCTOBER 4

RIGHT WHERE YOU ARE

"Seek the peace of the city where I have caused you to be carried away captive, and pray to the Lord for it; for in its peace you will have peace." (Jeremiah 29:7)

The children of Israel were about to fall under the harshest judgment God had given His people: they were to be exiled to Babylon, far from Jerusalem, the temple, and their homeland. They'd be ruled by the despised heathen and would have to be in contact with the Gentiles, something most of them considered anathema.

Before that event, however, the prophet Jeremiah had a word for them. Contrary to the thinking of most of God's people, God was the one behind their 70-year exile. Some found it unthinkable that God would allow, much less ordain, that they live among unbelievers, under complete foreign rule.

Without Jeremiah's prophetic word, it would have been easy to think of escape—and escape as early as possible—as the only intelligent or godly response to the situation. But God wanted them to stay in their situation, build their lives, and pray for their city—yes, even a city ruled by and filled with the ungodly.

There are times when we're called to move out of an ungodly or unhealthy situation. But there are other times when we're called to stay in an uncomfortable, unavoidable situation. Perhaps God's plan is that we use the power of our prayers to bring God's power to bear upon our circumstances.

Freedom was indeed part of God's plan for His captive people. But 70 years of exile was ordained first. So in the meantime, they were to be praying and seeking right where they were.

Father, help me know when I should escape a situation or when I need to exert Your authority in prayer instead. Use me in whatever place I find myself to bring in Your kingdom.

MARK DUPRÉ

OCTOBER 5

NOTHING CAN STOP US FROM SERVING HIM

"Thus says the Lord of hosts, the God of Israel, to all who were carried away captive, whom I have caused to be carried away from Jerusalem to Babylon: Build houses and dwell in them; plant gardens and eat their fruit. Take wives and beget sons and daughters; and take wives for your sons and give your daughters to husbands, so that they may bear sons and daughters— that you may be increased there, and not diminished." (Jeremiah 29:4–6)

These verses precede yesterday's verse from Jeremiah. God has more to say than to encourage us to "pray for the peace" of whatever "city" we find ourselves in.

Most of those exiled thought worship would come to an end. The best they could do was mark time in Babylon. God knew better. God's people could no longer offer sacrifices in Jerusalem, study in the temple (which had been destroyed), or go to annual feasts. But Jeremiah's words assured them God wasn't putting them on hold. He had things for them to do, to serve Him even there. Their worship was their obedience—building houses, raising children, planting gardens, and praying for their new home.

Sometimes we find ourselves in "foreign" situations, where our normal expressions of worship, praise, and service aren't possible. We may lose the opportunity to serve in a particular ministry, some activity "dries up," or our external circum- stances take a drastic turn (prison, divorce, a physical move). We may think that in our current condition or circumstances we cannot serve the Lord.

Jeremiah's words encourage us that nothing— no person, no circumstance, no physical limitation, no seeming barrier—can stop us from serving the Lord. Nothing. We may no longer be able to serve Him the way we used to. But like the exiles, we have direction available from the Lord.

God always wants us to move forward, even when being chastised. We're to move from faith to faith, from glory to glory. As long as we have breath, nothing can stop us from serving Him.

Lord, thank You that I can always serve You. Help me see new ways to serve You in my present circumstances, and help me to discover new ways to serve You if and when those circumstances change.

OCTOBER 6

GOD WILL ANSWER HIS WAY

"[Naaman] went away in a rage. And his servants came near and spoke to him, and said, "My father, if the prophet had told you to do something great, would you not have done it? How much more then, when he says to you, 'Wash, and be clean'?" So he went down and dipped seven times in the Jordan, according to the saying of the man of God; and his flesh was restored like the flesh of a little child, and he was clean." (2 Kings 5:12–14)

Naaman's story in 2 Kings 5:1-15 is almost funny except that his error is so common. Being a "great man," Naaman was expecting a certain degree of deference to be given him. He also had his own prideful ideas about how his healing would come. The living God really had no place in his thinking, much less his heart.

The real heroes of the story are Naaman's servants, who used simple common sense and logic to get past their master's pride. Fortunately for Naaman, he listened. As he humbled himself before the Lord, Elisha, and his servants, he was healed.

Naaman wanted healing. God wanted to heal him but was up to more. He wanted Naaman to know who He was. Revelation attended obedience, and Naaman came to understand.

When he returned to Elisha, he said, "Indeed, now I know that there is no God in all the earth, except in Israel." (v. 15). His body was healed, and his mind and spirit came alive.

How often we have preconceptions about how God is going to do something! Like Naaman, we take a step of faith. But sometimes our pride and our own thinking take over. We may have to humble ourselves greatly to receive what God wants to give us. We may need to listen to people we don't pay much attention to, saying things that are easy to dismiss or that seem ridiculous at first glance. But perhaps, as with Naaman, God has something greater than our request in mind—more than we could imagine.

Father, help me see and hear Your answers when they come to me. Forgive me for the times I've dismissed Your words because they didn't meet my expectations or make sense to me. Thank You for the grace to humble myself enough to receive all You have to give me.

MARK DUPRÉ

OCTOBER 7

DON'T ROB YOUR FUTURE: SEX

"For I know the thoughts that I think toward you, says the Lord, thoughts of peace and not of evil, to give you a future and a hope." (Jeremiah 29:11)

While many folks take this verse as a personal, individual promise, it's really a reflection of God's heart to bless His people in the proper season. In context, it was God promising that He still had good plans for His people, even while putting them through 70 years of exile for their disobedience. It's an assurance that God has our future in His hands and good things planned, either in this life or the next.

When we try to pull the blessings of the future into our present, they're wrenched outside of their proper time. In other words, we rob our own futures. There are many blessings we can attempt to steal from our tomorrows, but perhaps the most common is the sexual and emotional intimacy of the marital relationship.

God is for sex in marriage, and He also knows how damaging it is outside of marriage. In fact, God considers the sexual relationship so important that He forbids sexual abstinence for married people except in rare circumstances (1 Corinthians 7:5).

Some Christian couples, in their godly attempt to avoid fornication, fall into a trap of instead becoming *emotionally* intimate to an unhealthy degree. They depend on one another to the point of codependence, usually pulling away from others in the process. This kind of emotional and spiritual connection is supposed to be part of the "becoming one" process God ordained for marriage. Again, those connections that work for good for the married couple can have a negative effect on the unmarried. Certainly the blessing and presence of God in all our relationships makes a big difference!

> Lord, forgive me if I robbed my future by stealing aspects of the marriage relationship that should have waited until I was married. I confess that as sin and ask for forgiveness. Help me to help others wait for the right time to receive Your blessings.

OCTOBER 8

DON'T ROB YOUR FUTURE: MONEY

"A faithful man will abound with blessings, but he who hastens to be rich will not go unpunished. A man with an evil eye hastens after riches, and does not consider that poverty will come upon him." (Proverbs 28:20, 22)

Financial advisors tell us to never take out money early from retirement accounts, as there are significant financial penalties. We compromise our fiscal futures by using now what should be left alone to enjoy in the future.

Likewise, we can rob our futures by striving to bring forth the financial blessings of God. Some folks accrue wealth rather easily. God bless them for that. The issue isn't wealth itself. It's hastening and diligence. When we hasten, we tend to rush, ignoring things that need our attention. We can push past and even hurt people and things when we hasten. It isn't a healthy approach to anything, either physically or psychologically.

God calls us to faithfulness and diligence. If riches become ours as we remain faithful to His call, diligently doing what He's given us to do, it's the "blessing of the Lord [that] makes one rich, and He adds no sorrow with it" (Proverbs 10:22).

God knows we have needs, and He may have financial blessing in our futures. But if there's any "hastening" in the process of earning (or making) money, if we don't treasure the concepts of faithfulness and diligence, then we're likely to suffer from those sins. In that case, our futures may be as compromised as those who drain their accounts ahead of time.

Let's be faithful to what God is showing us to do and do it diligently. Then if his financial blessings come, there will be no sorrow with it.

Father, if I'm hastening to be rich in any way, please show me. Help me focus instead on faithfulness and diligence. May all my blessings be given to me in Your time and Your way.

MARK DUPRÉ

OCTOBER 9

DON'T ROB YOUR FUTURE: REST

"I must work the works of Him who sent Me while it is day; the night is coming when no one can work. As long as I am in the world, I am the light of the world." (John 9:4-5)

A subtle way to rob our future is to attempt to wrest our heavenly rest, and even our eternal rewards, from God's hand ahead of His timing. How could we possibly do that? By structuring our retirement years so that they're spent pursuing pleasure and rest above all else.

There's nothing wrong with retiring from a particular employment. But we can swallow the lie that this is the season where we're to inherit our rest and rewards, where we're supposed to take what we've earned and "spend it on [our] pleasures" (James 4:3).

God's indeed promised us rest, in this life and the next. Yet, as the light of the world, we're to let our lights shine, continue our good works, and keep on glorifying God. Many people carry this godly vision into retirement, finding new and vibrant places to serve in the kingdom. Young women need older mentors, church nurseries love grandmothers, and all that wisdom and experience needs to be passed on to the next generation.

Some Christians categorize serving God as part of their employment history. Yes, we may be more tired and perhaps more limited physically than before. But those hitting retirement age have gifts and callings crucial to building up the body of Christ.

How we serve Him is going to change over the years, and God knows retirement is a major time of transition. But He never stops having plans for us. These are years when He desires to make good on all the investments He's made in us over the years.

Father, I pray for those I know who are retiring soon who know You. May they seek You until they find You and move into the plan You have for them at this time of their lives. May I not try to find heaven's rewards in this life, but continue to "press on, that I may lay hold of that for which Christ Jesus has also laid hold of me" (Philippians 3:12).

OCTOBER 10

QUESTIONS WITH STRANGE ANSWERS: GENESIS 4

"Then the Lord said to Cain, "Where is Abel your brother?" He said, "I do not know. Am I my brother's keeper?" And He said, "What have you done? The voice of your brother's blood cries out to Me from the ground." (Genesis 4:9-10)

God again asks a question He already has the answer to. He's not asking for information but is working to reconnect Cain with his murdered brother, Abel. He's offering Cain a chance to accept responsibility before He gets more direct.

Of course, Cain doesn't accept God's offer of engagement. In fact, He compounds his sin by 1) lying and 2) working the flip against God Himself. Cain knows, of course, where Abel is: presumably right where Cain buried him. What a ludicrous thing to do—to lie to an omniscient God! But it shows the power of sin to lead us into more sin.

Since Cain wasn't willing to accept blame, and there was no other human around to blame, we witness a breathtaking attempt to both dodge the guilt bullet and simultaneously aim it at God.

Guilt, once created by sin, seeks a home. It fits best on the shoulders of the sinner, but if we're not willing to accept our own guilt, we try and get rid of it somehow—usually by trying to place it on others, on outward circumstances, or on God Himself. That merely compounds the problem by hurting others and deceiving ourselves. Accepting our guilt is the first step in connecting with God, whether it's the first time we come to Him for salvation, or the umpteenth time we bow our head in shame, seeking forgiveness for a particular sin.

Father, forgive me for all my attempts to transfer the guilt that belongs on my shoulders. I know Jesus died for my guilt and shame, but I sometimes fail to give it to Jesus because I haven't first taken ownership of it. Thank You that my guilt has been paid for along with my sin.

MARK DUPRÉ

OCTOBER 11

HE TOOK OUR SHAME

"Instead of your shame you shall have double honor, and instead of confusion they shall rejoice in their portion." (Isaiah 61:7); "Surely He has borne our griefs and carried our sorrows; yet we esteemed Him stricken, smitten by God, and afflicted." (Isaiah 53:4)

We know Jesus paid for our sins. He took our judgment on Himself and by His stripes we are healed. Yet what about shame? What about that feeling of guilt, humiliation, or embarrassment that accompanied our sin? And what about the sins of others that might have spilled shame onto us—such as family failure or scandal we didn't cause, but which may cling to us in the form of shame?

Yes, He died to take that away too. We can see in Isaiah 61 that God wants to replace, not just take away. When it comes to shame, His promises of restoration for His people include replacing shame with honor, even double honor.

Yet shame is in the realm of the soul—the mind and emotions. That may make it seem out of reach of His forgiveness. We can feel shame long after we've agreed with God that He's forgiven the sin. This can be especially true if the shame originated from someone else's sin.

Shame is one of our "griefs" and "sorrows" Jesus has "borne" and "carried [away]." It's part of the reach of the atonement. We may need to stand in that truth awhile to feel it, but it's our portion as forgiven children.

If our shame results from someone else's sin, we need to forgive. As we do, our own forgiveness dissolves the shame. No matter where the shame originated, Jesus died to take it away. Let's make sure that Christ's death isn't going to be in vain for us in any aspect!

Father, I hand You all the shame I feel, for my own sins and because of the sins of others. I release the shame of my sin to You because You already paid for it. And for those who sinned and left me with shame, I forgive them, both for the sin and for the shame that came with it.

OCTOBER 12

SOMETIMES GOD DOES IT ONE WAY, SOMETIMES ANOTHER

"And it shall come to pass, as soon as the soles of the feet of the priests who bear the ark of the Lord, the Lord of all the earth, shall rest in the waters of the Jordan, that the waters of the Jordan shall be cut off, the waters that come down from upstream, and they shall stand as a heap." (Joshua 3:13)

We all love the Exodus story. It's full of drama, retribution on the wicked, wondrous miracles, and blessed freedom. It also contains the dynamic image of Moses stretching out his hand and inviting dry land to spread out before a people more than happy to flee to safety.

There's a similar story of another river crossing not long after the Exodus. It involves Joshua, Moses' successor, taking the Israelites across the Jordan to begin the conquest of the Promised Land. But here, instead of a leader making a clear, miraculous way to cross, God instructs the priests to walk straight into the river *before* the waters part.

Most of us prefer the first scenario. We're happy when God opens a clear path for us. We're less comfortable with starting to walk down an impossible, impassible walkway, with the promise that things will open up as we move in faith. Yet this is clearly another method of God's getting us from A to B.

In both scenarios, God's people had His clear instruction to move. Sometimes we're told to walk down a path with no evidence of what will happen when we do. Even if the path isn't clear, we aren't to stop looking for a way to walk forward in faith. Perhaps our "soles in the water" are our prayers, our waiting on God (not *for*, but *on*), or simply standing in faith over time. Let's stay as close to the water's edge as possible while waiting for that word to come.

Father, I admit I prefer the clear and evident pathway over the promised one. But please show me how to walk in faith toward the rivers You want me to cross. Help me to be actively walking in faith so that I am moving forward in the Spirit even when I'm not sure exactly where I'm going.

MARK DUPRÉ

OCTOBER 13

DELIGHTING IN HIS WORD

"I will delight in Your statutes; I will not forget Your word. Open my eyes so that I may contemplate wonderful things from Your instruction. Your decrees are my delight and my counselors." (Psalm 119:16, 18, 24, HCSB)

What do you delight in? A great friendship, God's creation, a good book, a hot bath, a great cup of coffee? Your list might encompass more spiritual delights, such as being in a great worship service, hearing God's Word preached with power and passion, or seeing someone you know brought to Christ.

How about God's Word, the Bible? Certainly we're delighted when something comes alive to us, or as we often put it, "jumps off the page." We know that's the Holy Spirit using God's Word to speak something specific to us.

But what about the other times, when those "Holy Spirit moments," those *rhemas*, are few and far between? Check your heart. Do you approach the reading of His Word with a dutiful heart? With fear? With anticipation? Curiosity? Joy? The author of Psalm 119 delighted in God's Word. Delight is obviously more than simply a favorable feeling. Delight goes deep and brings a profound and often moving sense of joy.

We might see a gap between where the psalmist is and where we are in relation to God's Word—and we might get discouraged. Let's not do that. Instead, let's see that delighting in His Word is a real possibility. If the psalmist can find that delight, so can we.

God knows His Word and also knows us. He knows what it will take to move us to that position of delight. Let's begin with a desire and prayer, and allow Him the freedom to bring us to that delight.

Father, I want to be like the psalmist; I want to delight in Your Word. Please do Your part and help me to do mine. Direct, add, subtract—do whatever it takes. But lead me to see and receive the delights of Your Word.

OCTOBER 14
HOW DO YOU THINK ABOUT HEAVEN?

"Nevertheless we, according to His promise, look for new heavens and a new earth in which righteousness dwells. Therefore, beloved, looking forward to these things, be diligent to be found by Him in peace, without spot and blameless." (2 Peter 3:13-14)

What role does heaven play in your thoughts, your heart, and your life as a whole? Some Christians barely give it a thought while others seem to live only for it.

Perhaps some believers are focused on doing God's will right here, right now. They know Scripture isn't that specific about heaven, so they leave it in the realm of the mysterious, unknowable future. Others may suffer so greatly in this life that they derive the strength to go on from the hope heaven brings—an end to pain. Still others are so heavenly minded that they're no earthly good, anticipating the future so avidly that they lose some sense of God's calling on them now.

As trials come and go and we near the end of our lives, heaven will take an ever-changing place in our thoughts and hearts. But in general, we're to joyfully anticipate heaven while living obediently in the present. Heaven is not our mental place of escape in challenging circumstances; the Lord is our refuge. He wants us to know Him that way in this life.

Scripture makes clear that since we're awaiting a new heaven and new earth, that anticipation should impact our lives today. Heaven, or the new age, will mean the age of grace, the time of the gospel, will be over. We can rejoice in that sure future while digging deep to share the good news with others, being obedient to all we know, and following God as closely as we can.

Father, I admit I prefer the clear and evident pathway over the promised one. But please show me how to walk in faith toward the rivers You want me to cross. Help me to be actively walking in faith Father, help me to have a right attitude toward heaven. Help me to anticipate it rightly and to let that hope empower and encourage me here. May that living hope affect my thoughts and actions in just the way You'd like.exactly where I'm going.

MARK DUPRÉ

OCTOBER 15

FROM STRENGTH TO STRENGTH

"And let us not grow weary while doing good, for in due season we shall reap if we do not lose heart." (Galatians 6:9)

Spiritually, we're either progressing or regressing, growing or stagnating. Living things are supposed to grow. Many times we grow unhindered. But in that process of growth, we're occasionally going to hit barriers.

Some hurdles arise because we're finally ready to go over them. We're finally strong enough to resist the devil so he will flee. Perhaps one or more of Satan's mental/emotional constructs has finally been broken, and we can hear God in places we couldn't before.

Perhaps Romans 8:28 (that all things work together for good to those who love God, to those who are the called according to His purpose) has finally caught fire in our hearts and we're looking at things differently. Perhaps we finally have the support we've needed to break through, or we've finally forgiven someone, so we can see the power of forgiveness in a way we never did before. Maybe we finally got some healing and are able to push through barriers that would have held us back yesterday. We may have hit a growth barrier not because of something wrong, but because of many right things—because it's finally God's time!

God is a wonderful trainer, a great general, and a wise strategist. Describing the man whose heart is set on pilgrimage, David writes in Psalm 84:7 that he goes "from strength to strength." That's God's plan. You may not be feeling it at the moment, but God's planning the next breakthrough for you right now. The bigger victories just take more time, more strength, and more arrangement, that's all. Hang in there, keep walking by faith, and let Him continue to prepare you for the next breakthrough.

Father, thank You for the promise of victory. Thank You that You always know what You're doing and Your Word is always true. Do what You need to do in me to bring me from strength to strength.

OCTOBER 16

SPIRITUAL DISCIPLINES: CONNECTING WITH GOD

"So then neither he who plants is anything, nor he who waters, but God who gives the increase." (1 Corinthians 3:7)

We tend to think of spiritual disciplines as the rather dry habits spiritually "mature" people practice because they're the right thing to do: praying, reading God's Word, going to church, etc. But a true spiritual discipline repeatedly brings us back in connection with God. These disciplines can't save us or make us holy, but they can heighten our desire, awareness, and love of God.

The heart of spiritual disciplines is the person of Jesus Christ. Connecting with Him is our goal. Without the presence of God's Spirit, they can be dry. But their true purpose is to place us in a position to receive His life-changing grace.

In nature, God causes a seed to grow, but first the farmer needs to plant the seed. No one expects the farmer to cause growth or expects God to plant the seeds. Both actions are needed—to God be the glory!

Spiritual disciplines are the seeds we plant, believing God to cause those seeds to grow. As we grow in godly habits, we cultivate our daily lives into fertile ground in which God can bring growth and change.

In nature, it's a cooperative relationship between the farmer and God. In the spiritual realm, it's a cooperative relationship between us and the renewing Spirit of God. The farmer plants in faith, knowing that no matter how small the seed may look, he can joyfully anticipate the crop those seeds will become. Daily, we can plant seeds in faith and rejoice in knowing they'll become the source of a godly spiritual crop over time.

Father, help me to be faithful to place myself before You, planting spiritual seeds in my life on a routine basis. I trust that as You cause natural seeds to grow, You also cause spiritual seeds to grow. Help me rejoice in that growth even when I don't necessarily feel it happening.

MARK DUPRÉ

OCTOBER 17

SPIRITUAL DISCIPLINES: RIDING THE RIDGE

"For we do not have a High Priest who cannot sympathize with our weaknesses, but was in all points tempted as we are, yet without sin. Let us therefore come boldly to the throne of grace, that we may obtain mercy and find grace to help in time of need." (Hebrews 4:15-16)

Spiritual disciplines—prayer, meditation, fasting, attending church, reading the Scriptures—help us keep our relationship with God in good working order. Of course, no discipline can create a relationship with God; He's already done that in Chris. Since grace has done away with any need to earn our salvation, there are no brownie points to earn. Spiritual disciplines are simply tools that are a part of cooperating with God's Spirit to help remake us into who God wants us to be.

There's a tension we need to maintain in being consistent with any spiritual discipline. Keeping up with them has been compared to standing on a narrow ridge with a sheer drop-off on either side. There's the abyss of trust in works on one side and the abyss of faith without deeds on the other. On the ridge is a path, representing the disciplines of the spiritual life. The path doesn't produce change, but it places us where change can occur. We have to be careful not to slide down either side of error.

We live in such a feelings-oriented age that we're in danger of missing our connection with God at times. This can happen when we believe the enemy's lie that we shouldn't come before Him unless we can thoroughly, emotionally connect to the experience. This is actually falling down the abyss of works. In Hebrews, God tells us to come boldly before His throne. We already have the invitation, and it doesn't contain qualifiers.

He wants us to come. Let's always accept His invitation.

Father, thank You that I can come before You always. No matter how I feel, or how much or how little I feel it, You're always calling me to Yourself. Forgive me for not fully believing that You've made me worthy to come into Your presence. Sensitize me to those lies, and strengthen my heart to more deeply believe in what You've already done for me.

OCTOBER 18
SPIRITUAL DISCIPLINES: THE GOOD NEWS

"So I said: "Woe is me, for I am undone! Because I am a man of unclean lips, and I dwell in the midst of a people of unclean lips; for my eyes have seen the King, the Lord of hosts." (Isaiah 6:5)

One of the great joys of keeping up with spiritual disciplines is that they help us stay on course with God when our moods swing. Feelings may come and go, ebb and flow. Yet we know Jesus is the same yesterday, today, and forever. He never changes, so our emotional ups and downs have no effect on His desire for us to come into His presence.

Once we put our sense of unworthiness aside, the enemy has one more trick to pull on us—something that occurs when we start to come into His presence or begin a spiritual discipline. The Lord is holy, and beginning to connect with Him can shed light on our unholiness. This can result in our shrinking back and pulling away from the Lord, like Isaiah was tempted to do above.

The reality and the good news are as follows: We can never do anything with a completely pure heart. Our heads will be distracted. Our theology may never be perfect.

But the great news is that Jesus is our sufficiency (2 Corinthians 3:5). We know we're not complete in ourselves, but Colossians 2:10 reminds us we're "complete in Him." How freeing that is! What a wonderful reason to relax about spiritual disciplines and just keep on presenting ourselves to Him—in prayer, in reading, in assembling together with the other saints.

When the enemy tells you that you're incomplete, just agree that in yourself, alone, he's right. But in Christ, we're complete. Then stand on that truth!

Father, forgive me for all the times I've let the enemy convince me of an unworthiness that You've already taken care of. I believe that I am complete in You and that You always want me to come to You. Thank You that Your invitation always remains open.

MARK DUPRÉ

OCTOBER 19

SPIRITUAL DISCIPLINES: PRAYER

"Likewise the Spirit also helps in our weaknesses. For we do not know what we should pray for as we ought, but the Spirit Himself makes intercession for us with groanings which cannot be uttered." (Romans 8:26)

We pray, first and foremost, because Jesus told us to. On top of that, we're told to "pray without ceasing" (I Thessalonians 5:17). This can seem overwhelming if we don't realize what prayer really is. But first, some things prayer is not ...

Prayer is not thinking. We often feel we've prayed about something when it's never actually left our minds and ascended to the throne. Prayer has a direction! It is our heart, mind, and lips directed toward God!

Prayer is not telling God what to do! We sometimes pray not for what our hearts are genuinely crying out for, but for the specific plan we have in our heads. We need to hear the Lord asking us, "What is it you really want?" instead of praying for a suggested course of action, which is our "wisdom" trumping His! Prayer is not about what we want; "Your will be done" is part of how Jesus taught us to pray. This means seeking God's purposes instead of our own desires.

Prayer is back-and-forth communication, which is how we can pray without ceasing. That includes listening, practically a lost art in our culture, and a rare aspect of the modern Christian's prayer life. Just come into His presence as you are. There's no preparation necessary.

Prayer is like any other activity; the more you do it, the "better" it gets. Start with what is real and heartfelt. Open your heart to Him and watch things grow from there.

Lord, thank You for simply receiving me as I am. I also thank You that You are going to change me and my prayer life over time. Lead me to pray according to Your will and teach me how to listen to You as I pray.

OCTOBER 20
SPIRITUAL DISCIPLINES: THE SCRIPTURES

"Be diligent to present yourself approved to God, a worker who does not need to be ashamed, rightly dividing the word of truth." (2 Timothy 2:15): "Your word I have hidden in my heart, that I might not sin against You." (Psalm 119:11)

There are so many reasons to read God's Word. Of course we want to live according to God's truth by storing up His Word in our hearts. But Bible study also connects us with all of salvation history. That's a grand panorama we need to acquire so we have a backdrop against which to study and appreciate individual Scriptures.

There are several approaches to taking in God's Word. We can study it with commentaries, concordances, and study guides. Every serious believer should have those times of study. But we can also allow the Holy Spirit to dig in us, by reading it devotionally. We can sit with both the Word and its author, allowing the Holy Spirit to sift through our thoughts and meditations as we read.

This isn't the same as grabbing our Bibles and trying to find an encouraging verse or a quick answer to a problem. It's submitting to God and letting His Word sink in, enlightening and challenging us. Private, quiet Bible reading is sometimes so close to prayer that it's nearly indistinguishable from it.

What we call "quiet time" is a deliberate, intentional rejection of the pace and demands of modern life, with the goal of leaving ourselves open to the Lord and His working. No, sitting with Jesus and His Word is not the same as serious biblical study. But serious biblical study isn't the same as opening our hearts in His presence. Both are required, and one feeds right into the other.

Father, help me have an increasing appreciation of Your Word and its many facets and benefits. Help me to approach Your Word both studiously and devotionally. Grant me the strength and wisdom to create and protect my time with You and Your Word that I may continue to be transformed.

MARK DUPRÉ

OCTOBER 21

WHAT LOVE LOOKS LIKE

"But God demonstrates His own love toward us, in that while we were still sinners, Christ died for us. (Romans 5:8); "Greater love has no one than this, than to lay down one's life for his friends." (John 15:13)

We're bombarded with images of love. Billboards, TV, films, advertisements, novels, magazines—these major in presenting visual and written versions of love that pretend to accurately reflect it. Images range from a charming baby to parents holding said baby to cuddly animals. (Actually, many of these are images of innocence, not love.)

Images of love also include children playing together, parents with children, and finally, what's considered the apex of love—love between a man and woman. Yet even the most thoughtful image of a loving couple isn't the clearest picture of love we have. The central image of love is described in Romans 5:8. Jesus, arms outstretched, beaten, broken, and nailed to a cross. That's love.

Love is sacrificial. Love loves in action even when the object of that love doesn't receive or understand it. Christ's love wasn't shared at first. It was simply given.

Of course, that was the Son of God. How are *we* called to express love? John 15:13 says we're called to imitate Christ and His sacrifice. The highest expression of love, says Jesus in John, is laying down our lives for those dearest and closest to us. It's not a feeling; it's not attraction; it's not romance. It's sacrifice.

Sacrifice is expressed in any number of ways. It can be seen in small acts of thoughtfulness, a word spoken, or a word not spoken. In all cases, it's putting someone else first and saying no to something we want. The essence of real love is sacrifice; the image of such a love is Christ crucified.

Father, please keep reminding me of what real love is. Help me stay centered on the image You give us in Your Word, of Your Son giving His life when we were against You. May that love in turn, by Your grace, find many expressions in my life.

OCTOBER 22
RECEIVING CORRECTION

"All Scripture is given by inspiration of God, and is profitable for doctrine, for reproof, for correction, for instruction in righteousness, that the man of God may be complete, thoroughly equipped for every good work." (2 Timothy 3:16–17)

Correction is part of the normal Christian life. Few people like it, because few people really understand it. Correction can be painful and when it is, the pain associated with it can cloud its benefits. If we accept the lie of our enemy, we'll learn to run from correction because we've associated it solely with pain.

But correction is simply getting us back on the right track, moving toward health and wholeness. It has a purpose. It's not rebuke, antagonism, or reaction. Genuine correction assumes we're heading down the right path but need the occasional adjustment to make sure we stay on the right path.

In the book of Acts, Apollos had just appeared on the scene. According to Acts 18:26, he'd been instructed in the way of the Lord, but "when Aquila and Priscilla heard him, they took him aside and explained to him the way of God more accurately." This was correction. Apollos knew a lot, but he needed to know more.

We need to learn the difference between the Lord telling us to stop something, rebuking us, chastising us, and correcting us. It's true that some of God's stronger chastisements can cut deeply, but the only true damage from correction is to our pride. Pride is our enemy. Correction, while painful to our pride, is beneficial and therefore our friend.

Remember the next time God corrects you that the sting of correction isn't the point. It's simply to help you down the highway of God and prevent you from sliding off to the right or left.

Father, thank You for loving us enough to correct us. Help me to learn to receive correction. Right now, I humble myself before You and ask You to correct me whenever I get off the right path. Help me see correction for the blessing it is.

MARK DUPRÉ

OCTOBER 23

THE POWER OF SELF-CONTROL

"Whoever has no rule over his own spirit is like a city broken down, without walls." (Proverbs 25:28); "So then, my beloved brethren, let every man be swift to hear, slow to speak, slow to wrath; for the wrath of man does not produce the righteousness of God." (James 1:19-20)

Keeping our cool is not just a benefit because of what it avoids, but also for what it produces. Keeping our tempers prevents disagreements and even arguments and outright fights; it also prevents spiritual invasion from the enemy (Proverbs 25:28). But more than that, Scripture says it makes us better than the mighty, gives us power and authority, rewards us with great understanding, protects us, and helps produce the righteousness of God.

We can infer from James 1 that resisting anger positions us to receive the grace that produces the righteousness of God. Anger is an outwardly-directed negative expression that prevents us from taking in and applying the positive values of grace, which is offered by God and received as an inwardly-directed gift. It's easy to see how anger and wrath can prevent us from receiving His grace.

Gaining self-control is imperative for every believer. It may be more work for some to "rule over his own spirit," but it's clearly important to God and His purposes that we learn to be swift to hear, slow to speak, and slow to wrath. We can't use our personality styles or our national backgrounds as excuses for not having self-control. Yes, some of us are more expressive than others. But being expressive doesn't mean we have a pass on losing control.

Our tendency to express must come under the lordship of Christ, especially when emotions are high. But the number of Scriptures dealing with the subject tells us how important this issue is to God.

> Lord, help me learn self-control, not just for my benefit, but for Your glory. Teach me to overlook transgressions and not take them personally. Help me to rule my spirit (Proverbs 16:32).

OCTOBER 24

WHERE SIN BEGINS

"But each one is tempted when he is drawn away by his own desires and enticed. Then, when desire has conceived, it gives birth to sin; and sin, when it is full-grown, brings forth death." (James 1:14-15)

We all know what the wages of sin is: death (Romans 6:23). We see it played out all around us in murder, addiction, adultery—each an outward manifestation of sin.

These horrible ends all had a similar origin—they began in the heart and mind. They started with a thought that came from within or without, but which somehow "caught" inside. Our mistake is to "regard" iniquity (Psalm 66:18)—or in other translations, "entertain" or "cherish" it. Instead of rejecting it, we hide it inside and treasure it quietly, pulling it out and spending time with it when we're frustrated or unhappy.

Following James's conception-to-birth picture, conception of any destructive, life-changing sin is a quiet thought accepted. Like human conception, it's invisible to the naked eye, and it happens quietly. But it grows.

Through a conceived egg, given time and nourishment, a fully formed human is brought forth. "Bringing forth" sin and death is what the enemy's trying to do with the thoughts we receive and "regard." That's why it's important to guard our hearts and master our thoughts. We can't prevent every evil thought from entering our brain. It's what we do with it next that matters.

When these thoughts come, we look to James 4:7: "Therefore submit to God. Resist the devil and he will flee from you." It's never easier to submit or resist than when the stakes are small. Let's bring to fruition peace, joy, love, and righteousness—and destroy the beginnings of sin before it even gets a chance to grow.

Father, help me recognize evil thoughts when they come. Forgive me for entertaining and cherishing them. Help me submit to You quickly and resist the devil right away. Thank You that You've already won the victory.

MARK DUPRÉ

OCTOBER 25

WHERE SIN GROWS

"And this is the condemnation, that the light has come into the world, and men loved darkness rather than light, because their deeds were evil. For everyone practicing evil hates the light and does not come to the light, lest his deeds should be exposed." (John 3:19-20)

Terrible things can happen in the dark. Many a novel, film, and television show plays on our fears of what we can't see. In biblical language, sin is equated with spiritual darkness, and terrible things can happen there too.

One of the dangers to a believer is what can happen in the dark—the slow growth of sin we don't pay attention to. Whether or not we consciously feed our sin, left unattended it will still grow from bad seed to full-blown sin, which leads to some kind of death and judgment.

Many "spiritual tragedies" begin years before there's any outward manifestation. Somewhere in the quiet, dark place of the heart, a decision was made: to get out of a marriage, to leave one's ministry, to follow a sinful desire of some kind. Over time, when that quiet decision isn't brought to the light and dealt with, a spirit of self-deception begins to take hold.

Our only hope is to stay close to the Lord, asking, "Search me, O God, and know my heart; try me, and know my anxieties; and see if there is any wicked way in me" (Psalm 139:23-24). God is full of grace and rescues us from more than we'll ever know. "If we walk in the light as He is in the light, we have fellowship with one another, and the blood of Jesus Christ His Son cleanses us from all sin" (1 John 1:7). Let's work to stay in that light.

Father, thank You for Jesus' constant intercession and for Your constant deliverance. Please expose any small deception and help me to learn to walk in Your light every day.

OCTOBER 26
KEEP WALKING

"But the path of the just is like the shining sun, that shines ever brighter unto the perfect day." (Proverbs 4:18); "Your word is a lamp to my feet and a light to my path." (Psalm 119:105)

The world tells us to build our life. Get your education or training, find a mate, get the house, raise the family, work, retire, and then if you have the money and energy, enjoy life. In this "milestone" way of thinking, there are certain resting places and plateaus built in. For example, a couple who reaches the "empty nest" stage rests and readjusts to having it be just the two of them again.

These are normal life phases, to be sure. But while we experience them as steps with beginnings, middles, and ends, the Lord looks at our lives differently. His heart for us is to keep on growing spiritually through it all, to keep walking forward as He shines His light on our paths.

Proverbs 4:18 indicates a continual forward movement, one made possible by light that shows the way. It also suggests that the act of moving forward spiritually supplies even more light for the next step. Likewise, imagining the famous visual of Psalm 119:105 as someone standing still with a light in his hands is ludicrous—the light is to enable the person to keep moving forward.

We're never to let down our lights. No matter what stage of life we're in, no matter what natural stops and starts make up our lives, we're to continue to move forward in Him. There's always more light available and a bright path to be discovered. Let's keep pressing on to know the Lord (Hosea 6:3).

> Father, be the glory and lifter of my head here. When I feel stuck in my life, show me the path to keep on moving in You. Thank You for Your Word that illuminates my heart and the path before me.

MARK DUPRÉ

OCTOBER 27

A CURIOUS ORDER

"If we say that we have fellowship with Him, and walk in darkness, we lie and do not practice the truth. But if we walk in the light as He is in the light, we have fellowship with one another, and the blood of Jesus Christ His Son cleanses us from all sin." (1 John 1:6-7)

The beginning of 1 John describes the Light that had come into the world, Jesus Christ. John then contrasts light and dark, encouraging God's people to walk in the light. After that, John makes a statement with a curious order: "But if we walk in the light as He is in the light, we have fellowship with one another, and the blood of Jesus Christ His Son cleanses us from all sin."

One might assume the middle portion of that sentence was almost unnecessary. Shouldn't the statement be more like, "If we walk in the light ... the blood of Jesus Christ His Son cleanses us from all sin"?

What does being cleansed from sin as we walk in God's light have to do with "fellowship with one another"? As it turns out, our genuine love and connection with one another greatly depends on our walking in the light, being close to God, and obeying His Word. We sometimes think of fellowship as the cherry on top of the sundae or an option we can take or leave. If we're to believe what's said about Jesus so that we can fellowship, if we're told to walk in the light so that we can fellowship, then it must be important to God. It's all one interrelated expression to Him: being forgiven, loving, and being in right fellowship with one another.

If you want more of God, look at how your fellowship is going. If you decide that fellowship isn't a big deal after all, you may want to look at your relationship with God.

Lord, I see the importance of fellowship in Your Word here. Help me see the connection between walking in the light and fellowshipping and help me to embrace fellowship with Your heart.

OCTOBER 28
OUR PATTERN

"Imitate me [Paul], just as I also imitate Christ." (1 Corinthians 11:1)

God has given us some marvelous human examples of faith, love, and grace. We often say, "I want to be like so-and-so when I grow up," even up to old age. There's something accessible about another human being that makes it easy to look at them and learn from them.

Of course, we're supposed to be examples to one another. The youth are called to be examples in speech, love, faith, and purity (1 Timothy 4:12). Peter calls elders to be examples to the flock (1 Peter 5:3). Hebrews encourages us to remember our leaders, consider their way of life, and imitate their faith (Hebrews 13:7).

Behind these encouragements is the reality of the pull of the Holy Spirit. The Lord's Spirit is at constant work to transform us into the image of Christ—not just into the image of a leader we respect or someone we wish to be like. Paul expresses the limits on learning from others' examples: "just as I also imitate Christ."

We learn from others so that we become more like Christ, not more like them. As no one is perfect, there will always be a limit to the anointing on a comparison with someone else. No matter how godly a human example can be, all imitation must be made in the context of our transformation into the image of Jesus Christ. We will appreciate people, and the Lord, even more as we get a right understanding of how He uses others to teach and encourage us.

> *Father, may I be more open than ever to learning from others as You give them to me as an example. May I learn what You want me to, and prevent me from being distracted from You by their strengths or even their weaknesses. It's You I want to be like.*

MARK DUPRÉ

OCTOBER 29

GOD DISTINGUISHES, AND SO SHOULD WE

"Her priests have violated My law and profaned My holy things; they have not distinguished between the holy and unholy, nor have they made known the difference between the unclean and the clean." (Ezekiel 22:26)

One responsibility of Israel's leaders was to help God's people understand the differences between the holy and the unholy, the clean and the unclean. It's still up to God's leaders to do that for His people.

God makes many distinctions: male and female, married and not, sacred and profane, wisdom and folly, righteous and wicked. One of the enemy's latest moves is trying to tear down God's kingdom by breaking down distinctions that God created. We rightly rejoice when ungodly distinctions disappear, such as racial prejudice and the subjugation of women.

But as priests in God's kingdom, we must all do our best to maintain distinctions where He does. Genesis 1:27 says when God created humankind, "male and female He created them." Many try to live somewhere in between and ask us to honor that; we can love, but we cannot honor that. Sexual relations are reserved for the married, which is in turn reserved for a man and woman. We do no one any good to be guilty of the sin of the priests rebuked in Ezekiel 22:26 by equivocating or waffling on difference where God has clearly placed it.

To honor the Lord, we must be faithful priests. We must first settle these issues in our own hearts and understanding. Then we must work in our churches and culture to keep alive God's distinctions, especially where they're under attack.

The French have it right in the area of gender: "Vive la différence!" Let's join them in celebrating every other godly difference.

Father, show me where I might be failing to make distinctions where You make them. Forgive me my pride in thinking that my thoughts could be more advanced than Yours. Give me wisdom to be the godly priest You want me to be.

OCTOBER 30
THE CHALLENGE OF THE FAMILIAR

"The Jews then complained about Him, because He said, "I am the bread which came down from heaven." And they said, "Is not this Jesus, the son of Joseph, whose father and mother we know? How is it then that He says, 'I have come down from heaven'?" (John 6:41–42)

John 6 is a chapter of great unbelief. Jesus' brothers didn't see who He really was, and many of Jesus' own countrymen were divided over the same issue. Admittedly, Jesus was saying some challenging things ("I am the bread of life"), but always in the background was the familiarity of Jesus' listeners. Many of His listeners knew Him "in the flesh" and were unable, or unwilling, to receive what He was saying.

We often do the same thing. The Lord tries to speak with us, or even comes to us in answer to our prayer, and we reject Him. We reject Him because of how (or through whom) He chooses to speak to us. The vessel God chooses is up to Him. If we're open to Him, it shouldn't matter how He comes to us or who He uses.

Sometimes, the problem is the person is someone we know very well. We know their family, or their past, or their struggles. We may feel we know them inside out, as Jesus' listeners felt about this man who came from an area they knew, born from parents they were familiar with.

Our challenge can extend to parents, spouses, friends, pastors, teachers, and other church leaders. We may know them so well "after the flesh" that we miss what God's saying when He's using them. The one who's open to whatever God is saying, through whatever vessel He wants, is the one who will hear God. This is faith; this is walking in the Spirit. And it releases both God and the vessel.

Father, forgive me for how quickly I dismiss people that You may be trying to use to bless me. Help me to see people with Your eyes, in the Spirit, and not after the flesh. Tune me into Your Spirit more than I'm tuned into my own thoughts.

MARK DUPRÉ

OCTOBER 31

POOR SUBSTITUTES

"It happened in the fifth year of King Rehoboam that Shishak king of Egypt came up against Jerusalem. And he took away the treasures of the house of the Lord and the treasures of the king's house; he took away everything. He also took away all the gold shields which Solomon had made. Then King Rehoboam made bronze shields in their place, and committed them to the hands of the captains of the guard, who guarded the doorway of the king's house. And whenever the king entered the house of the Lord, the guards carried them, then brought them back into the guardroom." (1 Kings 14:25-28)

Such a sad tale, full of prophetic irony! Rehoboam, King Solomon's son, "did evil in the sight of the Lord," extending idolatry throughout Judah. Rehoboam plundered the temple and his own royal house, paying off the Egyptian invader. The tribute Rehoboam paid included the gold shields his father had made. Rehoboam replaced them with shields of brass (or bronze, depending on your translation). After all, brass "sort of " looks like gold, and having the guards bring them out was "sort of" like when the king had gold shields to walk past.

Our enemy desires the precious things that connect us with God—our own gold and silver. He tempts us toward compromise: replacing what's real with things that look almost as good—to ourselves and to others.

We can be slipping in our walk with Christ and still be reading our Bibles. We can be backsliding in our hearts and still attend church with a smile and a good word. We can be going backward in any number of ways and still keep up appearances, like Rehoboam. But brass isn't gold and never will be.

Is there any brass in your life you've substituted for the gold of a strong, real connection with the Lord? Are we coasting along with, and perhaps even seeming to get away with, a life that only looks like gold? It's bound to happen from time to time. But when we find brass, we need to look to God to help us reverse the swap and replace it with His gold.

Lord, have I traded any of Your gold for brass? Show me if and where I have. Help me to be real with You and grant me the grace and strength to repent and go back to gaining the treasures You died to give me.

NOVEMBER 1
EQUAL YOKES

"Do not be unequally yoked together with unbelievers. For what fellowship has righteousness with lawlessness? And what communion has light with darkness? ... And what agreement has the temple of God with idols? For you are the temple of the living God. As God has said: 'I will dwell in them and walk among them. I will be their God, and they shall be My people.'" (2 Corinthians 6:14-16)

This Scripture has been used (rightly) to keep Christians from marrying unbelievers and to prevent ungodly alliances in the business world. For instance, a Christian and an unbeliever can't "walk together [spiritually], unless they are agreed" (Amos 3:3). While such a marriage can "work" in a shallow sense depending on the people involved, it can never have the spiritual unity and power it would have if both people were believers.

For business partnerships, the message is that it's dangerous for Christians to hand over control to people who don't belong to Christ. This is Paul's New Testament interpretation of being "unequally yoked," harkening back to agriculture, plowing, and oxen. It can put the believer in an untenable position when it comes to the moral side of future business decisions, leading to personal hardship and business stress, if not outright failure.

But the deepest reason for not being "unequally yoked" has everything to do with God, not us. The real issue is that we're temples of the Holy Spirit. God's desire is to "dwell in [us] and walk among [us]." He's purposed to be deeply involved in the lives, thoughts, and actions of His people. If we partner with someone who is not the temple of God, this is an affront to God and an obstacle to His dwelling and walking with us.

Yes, it's smart and right and good of us to obey God. Obedience to God is rewarded many times over. But the ultimate reason stated here is for His benefit, glory, and pleasure, not ours.

Father, thank You that You give us warnings to protect and bless us. Give me eyes to see, though, when the primary reason Your Word states something is for Your benefit and glory. May I make the kind of decisions that allow You to dwell in me and walk with me freely.

MARK DUPRÉ

NOVEMBER 2

APPROACHING GOD

"Make a joyful shout to the Lord, all you lands! Serve the Lord with gladness; come before His presence with singing. Know that the Lord, He is God; It is He who has made us, and not we ourselves; we are His people and the sheep of His pasture. Enter into His gates with thanksgiving, and into His courts with praise. Be thankful to Him, and bless His name." (Psalm 100:1-4)

Psalm 100 is all about coming into God's presence in a way that honors Him and puts our hearts in the right place. While each line fairly bursts with joy and can be meditated on individually, the psalm as a whole is a call to worship.

As we begin to gather, the psalm provides inspiration and direction. Coming before His presence with singing is more than an outward action; it's a heart that's already blessing the Lord. To enter His gates with thanksgiving begins before we enter church. A thankful heart is a sign of connection with our Lord; it's a heart poised to receive from God.

In Old Testament language, coming into His courts means we're getting closer to the temple's inner room where God's presence dwelt. In our New Testament experience, we already have access to God because Jesus' death removed the veil separating us from His presence (Matthew 27:51). Now we press in closer to God, giving Him the praise He deserves—both for who He is and what He's done.

There's no "formula" for entering God's presence. But Psalm 100 inspires us to prepare our hearts and minds as we prepare our bodies and clothes. It reminds us that we're not just "going to church" or praying; we're coming into the presence of a loving, giving God to whom we owe the deepest gratitude and worship. Let's hear this call to worship as clearly as they did thousands of years ago and press into Him with thanksgiving, praise, and blessing.

Father, forgive me for the cavalier attitude I have sometimes when I come into Your presence individually or corporately. Remind me of this psalm and help me to allow You to draw me, step by spiritual step if needed, into a precious closeness to You.

NOVEMBER 3
CAN YOU HEAR ME NOW?

"Many are called, but few are chosen." (Matthew 22:14); Then one of the seraphim flew to me, having in his hand a live coal which he had taken with the tongs from the altar. And he touched my mouth with it, and said: "Behold, this has touched your lips; your iniquity is taken away, and your sin purged." Also I heard the voice of the Lord, saying: "Whom shall I send, and who will go for Us?" (Isaiah 6:6-8)

Two questions: How can we hear the call of God? And, if many are called but few chosen, does that leave us with hope that we can be among the chosen?

There's a way of thinking, popular among many of God's people, that's simply wrong. Any version of "Whatever God wants is what ends up happening" is unbiblical and misguided. In Matthew 22:14, the context is a wedding feast to which many were called but few ended up attending. They heard the invitation with their ears, but their hearts were unresponsive.

God's words and invitation are going out every moment, but can we hear them? Isaiah's experience seems to carry the key to really hearing. After a live coal touched Isaiah's lips and his sin was purged, Isaiah shared a profound occurrence, which carries a profound lesson for us—he heard the voice of the Lord. The phrasing implies God was already speaking but that Isaiah couldn't hear him until he'd been cleansed. It wasn't that "God spoke and said"; it was that Isaiah could hear him now.

Isaiah was convicted of his sinfulness because he'd received a clear view of the Lord. As we keep God clear before us, by praying, reading His Word, loving our brothers and sisters in Christ, and obeying what we know to obey, we're pressing in. As we allow conviction of sin and receive His forgiveness, our spiritual ears open and, like Isaiah, we can begin to hear what He's been saying to us.

Father, I want to live with fresh words from Your Spirit to my soul. I want to be close enough to You to see my constant need of You, and receive all You have for me in Christ. I believe that as I press into You, I am pressing forward.

MARK DUPRÉ

NOVEMBER 4

KNOWN COMPLETELY

"For now we see in a mirror, dimly, but then face to face. Now I know in part, but then I shall know just as I also am known." (1 Corinthians 13:12)

Isn't it a joy when you get to know someone who genuinely "gets" you? Someone who tracks with your thinking, your sense of humor, your interests, and even your quirks? These are blessings from the Lord, partly because they give us a picture of His own heart and actions toward us.

Psalm 139 is generally considered the go-to psalm for this thought. But 1 Corinthians 13:12 also makes a heavenly promise with a powerful implication. After explaining that the gifts of the Spirit will only last until Jesus returns, Paul gives us a glimpse of heaven. Then, he implies that we're deeply and completely known by God now. As we live, breathe, act, and even sleep, the Lord knows us completely. He "gets" us. As our Creator and our Savior, He understands us inside and out.

Know that you are known, and even with that knowledge, loved. Even when others don't understand you, He does. Even when your behavior is confusing to your friends, or even to yourself, He completely understands you. You're not a mystery to Him. He understands your prayers before you pray them and comprehends your thoughts "afar off" (Psalm 139:2).

If the Lord sends you friends who "get" you, be thankful and rejoice for the gift. But even if friends betray, leave, move away, or occasionally get confused by the things you do, He still completely, thoroughly, deeply, and fully understands you. What peace that brings!

> *Father, thank You that You fully know me. I stand with David that such knowledge is too wonderful for me, but I nevertheless want to receive that truth as deeply as I can. May I grow more appreciative of it every day.*

NOVEMBER 5
HOW HE GIVES WHAT WE NEED

"And do not seek what you should eat or what you should drink, nor have an anxious mind. For all these things the nations of the world seek after, and your Father knows that you need these things. But seek the kingdom of God, and all these things shall be added to you. Do not fear, little flock, for it is your Father's good pleasure to give you the kingdom." (Luke 12:29-32)

A good deal of the twelfth chapter of Luke deals with the foolishness of pursuing riches before all else and is an encouragement to us that God knows what we need and will supply. We all need to get it down deep in our hearts that "your Father knows that you need these things."

Yet there's a different perspective we're to take to those things that we need. The Lord doesn't say, "Seek after these things and I will make sure they shall be added to you." The Word says, "But seek the kingdom of God, and all these things shall be added to you." That's a whole different emphasis. Phrased differently, God promises to meet our needs as we put Him first. That's the order: Him first, then our needs are met.

What's often lost in our fear of letting go and seeking His kingdom first is the promise of verse 32. Unlike in the world, where we often have to swim upstream, fighting the "sharks" and burning the midnight oil to get ahead, God shows us His heart: He's not only willing to give us the kingdom, it's His pleasure to do so.

We will always face spiritual warfare as we seek to put His kingdom first. But before, during, and after any struggle, it's always His good pleasure to give us the kingdom. As we keep putting His kingdom first, we come to see how much He wants to give it to us.

Father, help me see this principle of Your kingdom more clearly than I ever have. Help me to make the spiritual leap to putting Your kingdom first and trusting You for the rest. Give me eyes to see how You give me Your kingdom.

NOVEMBER 6

QUESTIONS WITH STRANGE ANSWERS: HAGGAI

"Now therefore, thus says the Lord of hosts: "Consider your ways! You have sown much, and bring in little; you eat, but do not have enough ... You looked for much, but indeed it came to little; and when you brought it home, I blew it away. Why?" says the Lord of hosts. "Because of My house that is in ruins, while every one of you runs to his own house. Therefore the heavens above you withhold the dew, and the earth withholds its fruit." (Haggai 1:5-10)

"Is it time for you yourselves to dwell in your paneled houses, and this temple to lie in ruins?" (Haggai 1:4). Now here's a question phrased to provoke a quick answer! When someone posits a question with such an ironic tension, the answer is a slightly appalled, "Of course not!" God cuts to the heart of the matter emotionally to set the stage for a teaching rebuke. The question is a heart-opener, not a mind-opener. (Read Haggai 1:1-10 for the big picture.)

The Lord quickly adds truth to the reader's newly acquired perspective: they've been out of order in their hearts and behavior. "Bad fruit" has been part of their lives for a while—just unrecognized. They've sown, eaten, clothed themselves, and worked—all to little avail. And there was a reason for that.

God wasn't after a quick agreement to a rhetorical trick. He used the question to lay the groundwork for an increased understanding of His ways and to press the point that His people hadn't stayed true to His ways. If they agreed with His main point about their houses being built before His, they should more readily agree with Him about the reasons for the reaping that was unequal to the sowing.

God will often grab our attention not for our first reaction, but to reposition us to begin to hear a whole new conversation. If God works so dramatically to get our attention, we should spend some serious time opening our hearts to all He has to say.

Father, grant me the grace to "stay with You" and hear You when You catch my attention. Help me to slow down, listen, and let You speak Your whole heart to me in those moments. Thank You for loving me enough to stop me occasionally for a deeper conversation.

NOVEMBER 7
JOSIAH: HIS LIFE PLAN

"Josiah was eight years old when he became king ... In the eighth year of his reign, while he was still young, he began to seek the God of his father David; and in the twelfth year he began to purge Judah and Jerusalem of the high places, the wooden images, the carved images, and the molded images." (2 Chronicles 34:1, 3)

Josiah, Judah's last good king, became the last reformer before the Babylonian exile. He "began to seek the God of His father David" when he was sixteen. Thus began a series of unanticipated, nation-changing events. He destroyed idols, cleansed the land of ungodly practices, and ordered the temple repaired. But there was more.

When Josiah began seeking the Lord, he didn't know what would happen next. He couldn't have anticipated his reforms would turn toward the temple and that the Book of the Law would be found during the cleanup. Or that the reading of it would shake him like nothing ever had, leading to a renewed covenant between God and His people. He certainly couldn't have foreseen that his reforms would reach all the way into Assyrian-occupied Israel.

But all these things happened because Josiah had one plan: seek the Lord, do His will, and leave the rest to God. Seeking God's will for Josiah was like following divine breadcrumbs, eventually leading him to complete a reformation he never could have planned himself.

What's our plan? Is seeking God and doing His will our first and highest plan, with everything else a subset? Or do our plans just include prayer, Bible reading, church attendance, etc.? Planning is necessary for many projects in our lives. But our overall life plan should be simple: seek the Lord first, follow His will, see where it goes, and hold everything else loosely.

Seek, obey, repeat. There will be lots of smaller plans in our lives. But those three simple words are the best life plan imaginable.

> Father, help me repent of creating any plan in my life other than seeking You and doing Your will. Like Josiah, I have no idea where this will lead, and I get fearful about that at times. But I see glory in Josiah's life and I want to follow his example.

MARK DUPRÉ

NOVEMBER 8

JOSIAH: THE RIGHT RESPONSE

"Now the king sent them to gather all the elders of Judah and Jerusalem to him. The king went up to the house of the Lord with all the men of Judah, and with him all the inhabitants of Jerusalem—the priests and the prophets and all the people, both small and great. And he read in their hearing all the words of the Book of the Covenant which had been found in the house of the Lord." (2 Kings 23:1-2)

Josiah's response to the reading of the book of the law found in the temple is exemplary on several levels. First, his response was deep and immediate. Upon hearing the words, he tore his clothes in the classic expression of grief. He responded directly to what the Word said, with a teachable, open heart.

Next, he asked for spiritual guidance. Josiah immediately sent for the prophetess Huldah (the "go-to" prophetic figure of the day) to ask for advice and direction. She confirmed the seriousness of the words—judgment was indeed coming on the nation. But she assured him that because of his tender heart and humble attitude toward God's Word, he wouldn't see it.

Most of us would've breathed a sigh of relief at this point and thanked God. But Josiah took one extra step that set him apart. He used his godly influence to have God's Word read to the people and drew them into a corporate covenant.

What authority do you have to effect godly change? Probably a lot more than you imagine. Even if you're the only Christian in your workplace, you can do wonders through prayer and spiritual warfare. If you're a parent or a leader, you have great authority over your family or group, for good. The next time the Word of God strikes you hard, stay open to the Lord showing you how you should respond not only for yourself, but also how to use all the authority He's given you to bring about godly change.

Father, help me respond well to the reading and hearing of Your Word. May I be open and humble like Josiah. Show me the fullness of my "spiritual territory," and lead me to use my authority to bring Your presence and power to bear upon it.

NOVEMBER 9

JOSIAH: NO TURNING BACK

"And [Josiah] brought out the wooden image from the house of the Lord ... burned it ... and threw its ashes on the graves of the common people. And he brought all the priests from the cities of Judah, and defiled the high places where the priests had burned incense ... Then the king defiled " the high places that were east of Jerusalem ... And he broke in pieces the sacred pillars and cut down the wooden images, and filled their places with the bones of men." (2 Kings 23:6, 8, 13, 14)

These are only a few of the actions Josiah took once the Word of God captured his heart. But these actions included a defiling of the unholy places so definitive that it made it impossible for God's people to slip back into idolatry without great effort. Josiah didn't just destroy the false altars and high places; he ruined them for future use. He may not have been able to change people's hearts—only God can do that. But he made it nearly impossible for the Judeans to easily slip back into ungodly patterns of worship.

Elisha's response to God's call is similar. When Elijah threw his cloak over Elisha's shoulders, passing his prophetic call and anointing to the younger man, Elisha made sure he couldn't go back to his old life. As a former farmer, Elisha had a hefty investment in the tools of his trade. So what did he do? "He took the yoke of oxen and sacrificed them and boiled their flesh with the yokes of the oxen" (1 Kings 19:21). That single act meant the end of Elisha's tools and animals. He was now only fit to follow the call of God.

Are there doors back to an ungodly past left open in your life? Is it possible, or even easy, for you to go back? Have you held onto relationships, habits, or ways of thinking that pull you back? Josiah and Elisha are examples of those that made sure slipping back was next to impossible. Can we say the same for ourselves and those we're closest to?

> Lord, thank You for these examples of such acts of faith and devotion to You. Please identify any open doors to former ungodliness in my life. I want to close them for good.

MARK DUPRÉ

NOVEMBER 10

DISCIPLESHIP: MOVING BEYOND MERE BELIEF

"And whoever does not bear his cross and come after Me cannot be My disciple. So likewise, whoever of you does not forsake all that he has cannot be My disciple." (Luke 14:27, 33)

When Jesus sent out his closest followers, it wasn't simply to get other people saved. It was to make disciples. Disciples are not just believers. James says even the demons believe—and tremble (2:19). We're called to more than believing.

Disciples have masters (in our case, Jesus Christ). Disciples are always in the process of training, always learning, always seeking to grow. They don't have their own agendas but seek the Lord's agenda for them. They stay away from self-serving, self-promotion, and self-ambition.

Far too many of us "believers" do little more than that—believe. There's a twofold problem with that. One, Jesus said to go and make disciples, not simply get people to believe. Two, that means the Holy Spirit is constantly leading us into a state of discipleship. If we resist that leading and simply "kick back," we end up resisting God. All of God's promises and gifts are in the context of His leading us down the discipleship path. Those promises and gifts don't make sense if they aren't seen and received from that perspective.

Your salvation experience was your entrance into the kingdom. It was a starting point, not a stopping one. Yes, you have to die to yourself, but He promises that "whoever desires to save his life will lose it, but whoever loses his life for My sake and the gospel's will save it" (Mark 8:35). Find your real life by reckoning yourself a disciple, and you'll find yourself tracking with His Spirit and moving in His power.

Father, take me from where I am and help me to become more of a disciple. I recognize this is my true identity as a Christian. I confess my fears and my selfishness. Forgive me and lead me on.

NOVEMBER 11
DISCIPLESHIP: DON'T STOP BELIEVING

"And he brought them out and said, "Sirs, what must I do to be saved?" So they said, "Believe on the Lord Jesus Christ, and you will be saved." (Acts 16:30-31)

Disciples enter the kingdom of God by believing—believing in their inherent sinfulness and then believing that Christ's death on the cross was a sufficient sacrifice for that sin. That's the first believing we do. After that, we're challenged with believing more—one step of believing leading to (and supporting) the next.

Just look at a few of the things we're called to believe: 1 John 4:16 (God's love for us), Matthew 21:21-22 (when we ask in prayer, believing, we receive), James 1:5-6 (God will give us wisdom when we ask without doubting), Romans 8:28 (God works everything together for our good because of His love for us), 1 Corinthians 10:13 (God always provides us with an escape from temptation), Hebrews 13:5 (God will never leave or forsake us).

These are only a few points of belief for growing Christians. What's God asking you to believe right now? It might be something deeply personal; it might be finally, fully believing something in His Word. Like the Israelites, we can hear and read God's Word all we want, but what changes things is when we mix what we hear with faith (Hebrews 4:2).

Jesus said it was work to believe. He was right. Sometimes it's fairly easy work; sometimes it's the hardest thing to do. But it's the way we walk as disciples. As we're challenged to believe again and again, we can say with the father in Mark 9:24: "Lord, I believe; Help my unbelief!"

Father, help me to be honest with myself about what I believe and what I really don't yet. As I walk the walk of a disciple, please remove every obstacle to believing that's still in my heart. Thank You that it's Your will that we go from faith to faith.

MARK DUPRÉ

NOVEMBER 12

DISCIPLESHIP: LIVING IN COMMUNITY

"If I then, your Lord and Teacher, have washed your feet, you also ought to wash one another's feet." (John 13:14); "Therefore let us pursue the things which make for peace and the things by which one may edify another." (Romans 14:19)

The experience of discipleship involves the deepest and most intimate of issues. We need to take personal responsibility for the things that only we can do. Only we can read His Word for ourselves; only we can obey His commands to us; only we can pray those prayers that have been put on our hearts to pray; only we can receive the conviction and corrections that He sends us.

Yet there are things that we can only do together. We can only worship corporately with others. We can only hear (and receive) the preached Word together in a group—a whole different dynamic than hearing it individually. We can only learn to love others in a way that shows the world that we're His disciples (John 13:35) when other people are around to love. We can only learn to minister to others when there are others present to minister to (1 Corinthians 12–14).

Being a disciple of Christ means getting in there in the lives of others—serving them, ministering to them, experiencing life with them, experiencing God with them, and yes, loving them when they make it difficult. Withdrawal from others is one of the enemy's biggest tactics to the growing disciple. It's tempting, it can feel spiritual, and it can seem to makes life simpler. It's also a significant defeat from which it can be difficult to recover. Stay connected. It's part of growing in Christ.

Father, help me to live properly in community. Help me to develop my relationship with You personally as I live out my faith in the context of others. Thank You for the grace to minister to Your body and to receive from Your body as well.

NOVEMBER 13
DISCIPLESHIP: YOU CAN DO IT TOO

"You therefore, my son, be strong in the grace that is in Christ Jesus. And the things that you have heard from me among many witnesses, commit these to faithful men who will be able to teach others also." (2 Timothy 2:1-2)

There's a dynamic of continuous training in discipleship. We're discipled so that we may in turn disciple others who are to disciple others. Chances are, if you're a serious Christian you're in some kind of discipleship relationship already, even if you've never thought about it in those terms.

Intense training relationships such as Jesus' training of the twelve apostles—in particular, Peter, James, and John—involve discipleship plus leadership training. So was Paul's training of Timothy and Titus. Not all Christian discipleship is leadership development. But Paul made it clear there was to be ongoing discipleship that didn't stop with the person being discipled.

You may not think of yourself as a discipler of others. Yet you are, and it's likely you're already functioning that way. If you've ever explained something you've learned to another Christian, you've discipled. If you've affirmed or encouraged, you've discipled. If you've taught anyone anything, you've discipled.

Most people who back away from discipling others do so out of fear or misunderstanding. Here are a few thoughts you may need to take to heart: 1) The Holy Spirit convicts of sin and illuminates the heart—not us; 2) People grow spiritually at different rates; 3) You don't have to become a counselor and fix people or their problems.

Don't take on more responsibility than you need to, but use your gifts to bless others. If you desire to dominate someone else, pull back and get more discipling yourself. If you long to serve others, start giving them what you've received.

Father, give me direction in serving others in this area. I offer You my heart and willingness. I admit I don't fully know what I have to give. Show me what I can pass along in service to others and help me to take the place of discipling that You have for me.

MARK DUPRÉ

NOVEMBER 14

REMAIN AT YOUR POST

"If the spirit of the ruler rises against you, do not leave your post; for conciliation pacifies great offenses." (Ecclesiastes 10:4); "Let each one remain in the same calling in which he was called. Were you called while a slave? Do not be concerned about it; but if you can be made free, rather use it. Brethren, let each one remain with God in that state in which he was called." (1 Corinthians 7:20-21, 24)

These two Scriptures describe widely different circumstances to make similar points. The first is where someone's acted wrongly in a way that affects you. The second is part of a set of instructions on issues from slavery to marriage. The bottom line for both is the same: stay put unless God calls you elsewhere.

There's an epidemic in the church today of those "leaving their posts." Far too many say, "It's time to move on" because they haven't heard a clear word from God. They haven't waited long enough to receive the wisdom promised in James 3:17. When they "move on" outside of God's will, they tear the fabric of where they came from.

In no instance are we speaking of physical or spiritual abuse or when new employment calls one away. One must leave any situation with the former. As for the latter, all offers must be placed at the feet of Jesus for His direction.

This also doesn't mean God doesn't want change. Paul says if a slave has the chance to become free, he should take it. Yet for slaves with no opportunity for freedom, or for married people, or single people, Paul's message central message is clear: remain as you were when called by God until He directs otherwise.

Yes, it's difficult at times to stay put, let your roots grow, and serve. Yet God's plan for our growth often includes the challenges that can only come with staying put. So unless, and until, God clearly calls us to make a change, He's telling us to stay.

Father, rid me of those things that reflect the weakness of today's society. Help me to see my life as You do. Forgive me when I've left my post out of selfishness. May I only "move on" at Your clear direction, and thank You for the grace that comes with staying put.

NOVEMBER 15

WHEN SILENCE IS GOLDEN

"A fool vents all his feelings, but a wise man holds them back." (Proverbs 29:11); "A fool's wrath is known at once, but a prudent man covers shame." (Proverbs 12:16); "Even a fool is counted wise when he holds his peace; when he shuts his lips, he is considered perceptive." (Proverbs 17:28)

Many Scriptures talk about talk. We're encouraged to use our words to edify others, to bless the Lord, and to proclaim God's wisdom. One strand of thinking, however, stands so directly against prevailing cultural norms that it almost seems like an odd foreign concept.

Its central idea is that sometimes it's best to stay quiet. Consider how our society encourages us to keep talking. Every reality show includes people going on (and on) about what they're worried about, how they feel, and what they think on a myriad of different subjects.

As believers, what we should be thinking about, and expressing, is what the Lord thinks about a given issue. Regarding people, we should be thinking about how we can show them God's love, not how they measure up as a potential audience for us.

Instead of venting all our feelings, let's be wise and hold them back. If we're tempted toward wrath, let's behave in such a way that others don't know what we're feeling. The Scriptures above don't promote stuffing one's feelings and doing internal emotional damage. But not every feeling/thought/emotion needs verbal expression. Many should be brought to God instead—and some should be allowed to die a normal, healthy, unexpressed death.

We must position ourselves against the pattern of continual expression too often found in our society. Try thinking before saying anything today. It may feel awkward at first. But you may discover the joy of not having to express yourself and the peace that accompanies the holding of your peace.

Father, help me speak when I need to and resist the temptation when I don't. Help my thoughts to become focused outwardly on You and others and less on me and my thoughts. I want to be taught the value of being silent.

MARK DUPRÉ

NOVEMBER 16

GOD STILL MANAGES TO HAVE HIS WAY

"But [Rebekah] said to [Jacob], "Let your curse be on me, my son; only obey my voice, and go, get them for me." (Genesis 27:13)

The story of Abraham's quest for a wife for his son Isaac in Genesis 24 is the stuff of romantic legend. Yet as time goes by, Isaac and Rebekah both reveal themselves to be controlling, deceptive, and manipulative, especially in the subject of the paternal blessing.

In the verse above, we might look at Rebekah's conniving and spiritually insensitive comment to Jacob regarding their deception of Esau and wonder how such treachery might have stood in the way of God's plans. It did—and it didn't.

It certainly wasn't God's will that parents wouldn't love their children equally or that Jacob would become a deceiver or that Esau would have such little regard for spiritual things. It most definitely wasn't His will that Rebekah would call a curse down upon herself. But God continued to have His way through these very imperfect people.

God's larger purposes weren't stopped. His promise to Abraham to make a great nation of him continued (Genesis 12:2). Jacob ended up with Leah and Rachel, when that wasn't the plan. He reaped what he'd sown with his deception. His beloved wife Rachel made the boneheaded decision to give him her maid to have children through her. And yet ... Rachel ended up having a couple of children herself, one of whom was Joseph.

Then, in spite of his arrogance and "side trips" to slavery and prison, Joseph was placed by God in the right position at the right time to save his nation. No one could have seen this coming. No one, that is, but God.

Father, thank You that while we can mess up greatly, You're still going to have Your way in the big picture. Help me keep my eyes on Your faithfulness rather than our failures. May You be able to use me and my obedience to further Your plans instead of having to work around me.

NOVEMBER 17
NO OTHER PLACE TO GO

"Therefore many of His disciples, when they heard [His challenging statements about being the Bread of Life], said, "This is a hard saying; who can understand it?" From that time many of His disciples went back and walked with Him no more. Then Jesus said to the twelve, "Do you also want to go away?" But Simon Peter answered Him, "Lord, to whom shall we go? You have the words of eternal life." (John 6:60, 66-68)

There are times when it all seems too hard, when things are just too confusing. People frustrate us, and the body of Christ disappoints us. Christian leaders fall. Trusted Christian friends prove untrustworthy. We know that His ways are higher than our ways, but sometimes knowing that doesn't seem to help.

What do we do then? Do we close down and cut ourselves off from others—or from the Lord? Many have chosen to do one or both. This hurts us, damages the church of God, and grieves the Holy Spirit. Since God will always be unfathomable at times, and people will always give us reason to write them off if we choose, there will always be plenty of "evidence" to justify pulling away.

But, like the disciples, where shall we go? One of the great joys and hard facts about Christianity is that Jesus isn't "a" truth. He said He was "the" truth (John 14:6). Being the ultimate realist, He wants us to work and walk with Him. Any other way isn't the way of truth and only hurts us as we hit our heads against brick walls.

We're never going to understand everything going on in and around us. But as hard as it may seem at times, any action other than turning to Him is digging an empty well (Jeremiah 2:13). Aren't we glad that what we're vitally connected with is an unshakeable eternal reality and not an ever-changing internal preference?

> Lord, You are the Way, the Truth, and the Life. I believe that. There is no other way, truth, or life than You. I confess this may be hard for me at times. But it's also glorious. Thank You for allowing me to see that.

NOVEMBER 18

ABUNDANT LIFE?

"I have come that they may have life, and that they may have it more abundantly." (John 10:10)

A promise we gratefully take to heart is what Jesus says in John 10:10. On the surface, it can be taken to mean that He's come to give us a great and blessed life. That's true. The "rub," to quote Hamlet, is what "abundant life" means.

Some believers stumble over the verse not because of what it says but because of how they interpret it. If we think Jesus is promising a life of temporal blessings, constant good health, and lollipops and rainbows, then we might become sadly disappointed in His "failure" to give us that life. It's more than a matter of defining terms; it's about which reality we're focusing on and our ability to see and understand the greatest one.

Luke 12:15 says, "One's life does not consist in the abundance of the things he possesses." We readily agree, but then where do we focus, and where do we find our joy? We focus on Him (Hebrews 12:2) and on growing "in the grace and knowledge of our Lord and Savior Jesus Christ" (2 Peter 3:18).

To enjoy the abundant life Jesus promised, we must first set our minds on things above. Then we'll begin to take on the heart of Jeremiah: "Let not the wise man glory in his wisdom, let not the mighty man glory in his might, nor let the rich man glory in his riches; but let him who glories glory in this, that he understands and knows Me" (Jeremiah 9:23-24).

Father, forgive me for ever accusing You of denying me any aspect of an abundant life. In You, I have everything I need or ever will. Help me to continually set my mind and heart on things above.

NOVEMBER 19

THAT WE WILL KNOW...

"And the Egyptians shall know that I am the L, when I stretch out My hand on Egypt and bring out the children of Israel from among them." (Exodus 7:5)

God is insistent about making a point of who He is at key moments. He wanted Israel to know it when they began their life as a nation (Exodus 7:5), when He showed them how much He was their personal protector and sustainer (Exodus 16:12), and when He brought them back to the land after exile (Ezekiel 20:42-44). But He also wanted the Egyptians to know this—a foreshadowing of His being the Lord of all the earth (Revelation 22:13), so often alluded to in the Psalms, and in the outreach to the Gentiles in Acts.

These Scriptures are only the tip of the iceberg. But they all end with the same demonstration: He is the Lord. God wants all the world to know He is the Lord. For us as believers, this may seem about evangelism. It is, partly. But there's a bigger truth here. If knowing "I am the Lord" is behind so many actions in the Old Testament, we can begin to see this is the reason and goal behind so many of His actions in our own lives.

We often believe we've "learned the lesson" after a work of God in our hearts, meaning we picked up something about ourselves, God, the Word, or even "life." Yet it appears the lesson behind virtually everything God does in the earth and in our lives is ultimately so that we may know He is Lord. It's been His purpose throughout history; it's been His purpose in Your life.

Father, help me see right through everything I go through until I see in my spirit that what I have learned again, more deeply this time, is that You are the Lord. Don't let me stop short with a lesser understanding. I see this in Your Word, and in spite of my limited understanding, I embrace it by faith.

MARK DUPRÉ

NOVEMBER 20

EVANGELISM 411: THEY KNOW

"The heavens declare the glory of God; and the firmament shows His handiwork." (Psalm 19:1); "For the wrath of God is revealed from heaven against all ungodliness and unrighteousness of men, who suppress the truth in unrighteousness, because what may be known of God is manifest in them, for God has shown it to them." (Romans 1:18-19)

God has given us a help in our prayers and actions toward the salvation of others. It's the simple fact that in spite of the fall, people have an innate sense of the reality of God. According to Psalm 19, man can look at nature and hear the message that God is Creator. If the heavens are declaring it, everyone hears it.

Romans 1 shows us why not everyone claims to hear this message. It's not that the message isn't received; it's that it's suppressed. When the Scriptures say, "The fool has said in his heart, 'There is no God'" (Psalm 14:1), we're not speaking of intellectual or behavioral foolishness. Foolishness in the Bible is a moral issue, a failing in the realm of ethics, faith, and thought. It's a purposeful rejection of what God has made patently obvious.

Only God knows what it will take for that suppression of truth to be stopped in someone, and only He can bring the life and power necessary to stop the suppression. But it will do us well to realize that we don't really need to convince anyone of the reality of God. In spite of intellectual constructs, fears, judgments, and general sinfulness, somewhere "in there" is an awareness of God.

May this knowledge sink in deeply. Let it relieve you of an unnatural pressure to bring about an awareness that's already there—and may it cause you to more quickly find the Lord's individual approach for each person He is working to save.

Father, I receive that there is a deep understanding somewhere inside of everyone that there is a God. Help me to share Your Word to others with that in mind and in heart. Lead me to work with Your Holy Spirit as together we bring new people into the kingdom.

NOVEMBER 21
EVANGELISM 411: THE ISSUE OF TRUST

"Do not put your trust in princes, nor in a son of man, in whom there is no help." (Psalm 146:3); "Blessed is that man who makes the Lord his trust." (Psalm 40:4)

All human beings place their trust in something or someone. It's how we are created and how we operate in this world. We all trust in many things we can see. We trust people who have proven themselves trustworthy, and we trust the chair will remain steadfast when we sit down. We also trust in unseen things—like the fact that the sun will rise or that certain kitchen ingredients will react in certain ways when mixed together and heat is added—and we make our plans accordingly. Most would agree that we have to trust in many things—seen and unseen—to just go about our day.

As believers, we've simply gone one step beyond. We've found the one who's completely trustworthy and have put our trust in Him. We believe in what He did, in what He says, and in what He will do. Since we constantly place our trust in things unseen and not understood (e.g., gravity, the presence of germs, the existence of faraway stars), it's not that much of a stretch to extend our trust to the unseen reality of God and the atonement.

Even if they don't yet share our faith, many unbelievers can at least agree with the concept in the preceding paragraph. Those who don't believe in God are not that different from us. We've all built our lives on some kind of trust. Many have built their lives on trust in something related to themselves: their wealth, feelings, perspectives, mental or physical strength, or their self-confidence. We've simply shifted our trust onto Him.

Lord, may my life demonstrate Your trustworthiness. Help me to trust You more and more and encourage others to do the same. May my own life be the greatest argument for the value of trusting in You.

MARK DUPRÉ

NOVEMBER 22

EVANGELISM 411: WORSHIP

"You shall worship the Lord your God, and Him only you shall serve." (Matthew 4:10); "For where your treasure is, there your heart will be also." (Matthew 6:21)

Most people would agree that we put our trust in many things (see yesterday's devotional). It's a concept that's easy to explain. Where unbelievers don't agree as much is in the area of worship. We who have what the unbeliever would call a "religious context" or "perspective" see that everyone worships something.

Few folks in first or second world countries make physical idols of wood or stone anymore. But if worship is defined as an act of respect or deference to a god, especially with others who believe the same thing, it's easy to see that many "unbelievers" in God essentially believe in and "worship" actors, music stars, successful businesspeople, politicians, famous speakers, and even holidays. Some worship a cause of some kind, and sometimes the world is a better place for their dedication. But some false worship, of course, results in death and destruction, all in the name of a false god.

When the Bible tells us to "worship the Lord," it's not suggesting we *start* to worship. It's telling us to *direct* our worship toward the Lord. Worshipping the Lord means taking whatever worship we have going on in our lives and bringing that worship to Him as the only one worthy of it. As with the concept of trust, we're not that different from the unbeliever. We just recognize that we're all worshippers, and we choose to direct our worship to our God and Savior.

Father, I worship You! Please remove all other worship from my life. May I be more than a believer—I want to be a true worshipper, giving You only the praise, attention, time, and energy You deserve.

NOVEMBER 23
AUTHORITY: ITS SOURCE

"Let every soul be subject to the governing authorities. For there is no authority except from God, and the authorities that exist are appointed by God. Therefore whoever resists the authority resists the ordinance of God, and those who resist will bring judgment on themselves." (Romans 13:1-2)

We live in a particularly rebellious age, when even the idea of authority is under attack. The very word *authority* is often expressed and received as if it had the word *abusive* in front of it. But as we can see from Romans 13, the concept of authority is from God Himself. As disciples of Jesus Christ, we must come to terms with what authority is, how it's manifested in this earth, and how we're supposed to deal with it.

The first issue we need to get straight in our hearts is that we're to submit to, or work with, authority where we find it. Since authority is from God, it is to be honored. It is to be adjusted to, perhaps even bowed to in our hearts.

The attack on the idea of authority is, at its foundation, an attack on God, as authority is from Him. The great struggle for many of us is the constant parade of abuses of authority in history and in our own lives. But man's misuse of God's authority doesn't negate its reality. We shouldn't let it blind us to where God's authority can be found in our lives.

While much of the rest of the world is blind to authority, dismissive of it, or even rebellious against it, the Christian should be eager to locate God's authority in every aspect of his or her life. We should be eager to use that authority to bless and just as eager to submit to authority as unto the Lord.

Father, cleanse my heart of the rebellion that comes to the surface when I consider the issue of authority in my life. I repent of using man's misuse of authority as an excuse not to follow You in that area. Help me to see where You've placed authority in my life, and help me to honor You in working with it.

MARK DUPRÉ

NOVEMBER 24

AUTHORITY: TRACKING IT BACK TO GOD

"For rulers are not a terror to good works, but to evil. Do you want to be unafraid of the authority? Do what is good, and you will have praise from the same. For he is God's minister to you for good. But if you do evil, be afraid; for he does not bear the sword in vain; for he is God's minister, an avenger to execute wrath on him who practices evil." (Romans 13:3-4)

Jesus Christ is the Alpha and the Omega (Revelation 22:13), and according to Ephesians 1:23, He fills all in all. One thing He's filled this earth with is His authority. Since all authority comes from Him (Romans 13:1) and He fills all in all, He's the ultimate authority behind every human authority He's appointed.

This means that we're ultimately bowing to God's authority when we submit to authority in the human realm. Teachers, police officers, parents, earthly rulers of every kind—every bit of their authority originates in God. We're not just submitting to human beings; we're submitting to the authority God has placed in them, and therefore submitting to God.

In the realm of the spirit, we're not subjecting ourselves to a person. We're submitting to the anointing God's given to that person. Recognizing this distinction shouldn't be an excuse for disrespect; there are plenty of Scriptures telling us to honor those in authority over us. Rather, it should be an encouragement to grant them great respect, even as we acknowledge that behind our respect for them is our love and respect for God.

We should be able to trace all our submitting to authority right back to God. As the wife who learns that great spiritual lesson that godly (and rightly understood) submission to her husband is really submission to God, we need to have the eyes of our understanding enlightened (Ephesians 1:18) to see the same principle at work all around us.

Father, help me see Your authority in all the relationships I have with family, Christian leaders, bosses, and every kind of civil and governmental authority. Give me eyes to see the straight line of authority right back to You, even when it's working in people that are failing to use it rightly.

NOVEMBER 25

AUTHORITY: GOD'S SOVEREIGN AUTHORITY

"Therefore God also has highly exalted Him and given Him the name which is above every name, that at the name of Jesus every knee should bow, of those in heaven, and of those on earth, and of those under the earth." (Philippians 2:9-10)

Today's devotional is simple. As King of Kings and Lord of Lords, our Creator and our Savior, God is our Sovereign Authority, as well.

In terms of authority, He is it. Like the historic axiom "all roads lead to Rome," all concepts and issues of authority lead to God. The downside is that this is too much for us to get our heads around. The upside is that a true understanding of this reality makes life easier. How? Well, if God is our authority—all knowing, all powerful—then all we need to know is if something is God's will or not. If God convicts and directs by His Holy Spirit, then we only need to know what He wants us to do, including how and when. If His Word says something, that provides our direction.

We don't have to figure out the entire situation first, "fix the problem," or get anyone else to do anything. We merely have to seek His will and do it. That's our portion and our responsibility. Far too much of our mental and emotional energy is spent trying to understand, as if our understanding releases wisdom and power. What does release His wisdom and power is our obedience.

Let's all take a big breath and back away from the drive to understand everything that's going on before we act. Once we know His will, we've reached our true goal. We can go ahead and act in obedience, fully trusting in the wisdom and love of our Sovereign Lord.

Father, change my thinking and my habits so that I seek Your will before I work to seek an understanding that's beyond my limited capacities in the first place. Your will is my one desire—finding it and doing it. Help me to sharpen that focus.

NOVEMBER 26

AUTHORITY: TRUTH

"Jesus said to him, "I am the way, the truth, and the life." (John 14:6)

Part of submitting to God's authority is submitting to truth. If Jesus is the truth (as well as the way and the life), we need to seek, respect, and submit to truth as much as we would the Lord Himself. In any given situation we need to have a heart poised to align with truth; any other agenda is sin.

If we've come to a conclusion on something, then discover a new piece of information, we need to allow that new piece of truth to change what we think and feel about that situation. If we push away even a kernel of truth, we're pushing away the Lord. Though it's humbling to be proven wrong about something, we should rejoice more in learning more of the truth than in being disappointed that we are wrong.

We should always submit to the truth of God's Word. It's not a suggestion or a guide or a higher thought on a given subject. God's Word is truth. As truth, we should submit to it as we would submit to the Lord. God's Word contains power as well—power to transform our hearts and minds as we submit to Him and receive the truth of His Word.

Jesus promises His disciples that the truth would set us free. Our enemy hates this freedom and is working to distort and destroy the very idea of truth. As we stand fast about where we find truth (Jesus and His Word), we'll discover a clear, brave, and bracing way of living that will continually set us free.

Lord, help me to value truth as much as You do. Help me to welcome it in my life when I discover it. May I see Your Word as the truth that it is and may I continue to grow in obedience to it.

NOVEMBER 27

AUTHORITY: THE CONSCIENCE

"Therefore concerning the eating of things offered to idols, we know that an idol is nothing in the world, and that there is no other God but one. However, there is not in everyone that knowledge; for some, with consciousness of the idol, until now eat it as a thing offered to an idol; and their conscience, being weak, is defiled." (1 Corinthians 8:4, 7)

God's sovereignty includes an authority we cannot hope to fully understand. Yet, since we're created in His image, we're allowed to have some of this authority in the deepest parts of ourselves. This is the authority of conscience.

First Corinthians 8:4-7 makes clear there are strong and weak believers, those who understand the freedom we have in Christ and those who do not. We're encouraged to be a good example of our Christian freedom. But we're forbidden to judge or force people to do anything against the authority of their conscience, even if we have no issue with the action ourselves.

If we can do a certain action in good conscience, good for us. But if someone believes that action to be against his or her conscience, it's sin for him or her (Romans 14:23). This may seem silly, sad, or even laughable to us. But our call from God is to leave it alone and not force the issue or the action. God promises to take care of it in His way and in His time.

Only the Holy Spirit can truly convince anyone of anything. We can persuade and we can model what we believe to be mature Christian behavior. But it's God and God alone who can reach into a heart and settle an issue, especially one that means moving away from a bondage to a truth. So, for the free and mature believer, our challenge is to honor God by honoring the authority of His creation's conscience—and leaving transformation up to Him.

Help me to grow in sensitivity to issues of conscience that others are dealing with. I want to know all the freedom You've purchased for me in Christ, but help me to honor the authority of the consciences of others that feel differently than I do, trusting in You to do the convincing.

MARK DUPRÉ

NOVEMBER 28

AUTHORITY: HIS DELEGATED AUTHORITIES

"Obey those who rule over you, and be submissive, for they watch out for your souls, as those who must give account. Let them do so with joy and not with grief, for that would be unprofitable for you." (Hebrews 13:17)

It doesn't require a great deal of humility to be obedient to God's direct authority or to the authority of His Word. But it requires humility and an understanding of how God works to easily submit to His delegated authorities. It's easy to provide our own reasons for why anything coming through people can be taken with a grain of salt, received as an opinion, or simply ignored. People aren't perfect, and they never will be this side of the grave. So, the heart that's not inclined to obey God will always have a good reason not to receive from people.

But it's His sovereign plan to grant people His authority, and to use that authority (and therefore, those people) in our lives. As the sovereign God, He gets to choose how He's going to use people to guide, help, and encourage us. If we're open to His Spirit, we won't care about the vessel He uses; we'll just be grateful that He's chosen to speak to us.

If we have "eyes to see," we'll see that no person has inherent authority in himself or herself anyway. But if we're willing, we'll be able to trace the authority chain from that person all the way to our loving Lord. In recognizing that the authority we're being asked to submit to is actually from God, and in submitting to that authority, we're honoring God. In response, He will honor us in our obedience.

Father, I confess that I sometimes don't want You to use certain people or certain kinds of people to bring Your Word to me. I sometimes have problems being directed by people. Help me to see that this is Your plan and that I'm blessing You by submitting to Your authority in others.

NOVEMBER 29
AUTHORITY: OUR WORDS

"But let your 'Yes' be 'Yes,' and your 'No,' 'No.' For whatever is more than these is from the evil one." (Matthew 5:37); "Lord, who may abide in Your tabernacle? Who may dwell in Your holy hill? He who swears to his own hurt and does not change." (Psalm 15:1, 4)

Once upon a time, a person's word meant something in society. Contracts used to be agreed on verbally. We no longer live in that kind of culture. Yet Matthew 5:37 is clear: we should simply say what we mean and mean what we say. Anything more is not from God.

Our words carry weight before Him. We see throughout Scripture, especially in Proverbs, that our words have an impact on people. What we say and how we say it can either build people up or tear them down. In that light, it means something spiritually when we verbally commit to doing something. We should determine to make our own speech clear and precise, and we should be dedicated to the fulfillment of everything that's been promised. Our words have authority, and that authority should be honored.

Because our words have authority, we also need to be sure to never break a promise if it's in our power, no matter how inconvenient or painful it might be. That's what "swear[ing] to our own hurt" means. The authority of what comes out of our mouths trumps any difficulty we might encounter in backing up our words with action. We need to remember to think before we speak, let our words be few, and not make a promise if we can't back up our words with action.

If we embrace the fact that God has put authority in our words, we'll be less likely to speak unthinkingly and more likely to speak words that we will honor.

Father, help me recognize that my words have authority. While I may have to take others' words lightly, I pray that others will never have to take mine lightly. Help me to say what I mean and mean what I say and to back up what I promise to do with action, even if it hurts.

NOVEMBER 30

AUTHORITY: CUSTOM

"Paul wanted to have [Timothy] go on with him. And he took him and circumcised him because of the Jews who were in that region, for they all knew that his father was Greek." (Acts 16:3)

God is eternal and unchangeable and lives in heaven. We aren't and don't. According to His wisdom, He's placed us in times and cultures that have a great deal of influence on us. Some of the conventions of all cultures need to be overcome or replaced by gospel truths. Others are simply a matter of custom. Those customs need to be respected—especially if the gospel is at stake. Stripped of sin and idolatry, every culture is a reflection of the creativity and imagination of our God and should be honored as such.

It's a historical cliché that many a missionary attempt has failed because of insensitivity to the customs of the group they were trying to reach. British missionary work has the historical reputation of trying to impose culture alongside the gospel in a way that confuses both.

Some cultural customs are not moral issues. They're simply a reflection of a culture's history, weather, and/or geography. Christians need to be flexible in such matters so as not to give offense or confuse the message of the gospel (see Paul's actions in Acts, above). Respecting others' customs, and culture, can be a powerful witness of God's love to those we're trying to reach. Paul put aside his strong opinions on faith in Christ alone and had Timothy circumcised because of custom. We need that same understanding and ability to stay focused.

"Lord, give me spiritual eyes and a heart to honor the customs of the people I minister to. Help me see the real issue at stake that goes deeper than some tradition or convention. Help me to "become all things to all men, that I might by all means save some" (1 Corinthians 9:22).

DECEMBER 1
AUTHORITY: FUNCTIONAL AUTHORITY

"There are diversities of gifts, but the same Spirit. But one and the same Spirit works all these things, distributing to each one individually as He wills." (1 Corinthians 12:4, 11)

God has graciously given the body of Christ many talents, gifts, and skills. While we may individually one or more of these gifts, corporately we're rich with talent. As we submit to the authority of the gifts given to others by God, we reap the benefits that authority brings with it.

We submit to this authority of gifts and talents (sometimes called functional authority) when we visit the doctor, get our car repaired, or call a plumber. Most of us would prefer to submit to the skills of a non-Christian surgeon than to submit to the unskilled workings of the best-intentioned Christian with no medical background. These gifts have an authority from God.

The principle of authority is even more pronounced when we speak of spiritual gifts. God gives gifts to the body of Christ as He chooses, to build up the church. The Corinthians had a problem receiving and using them properly, emphasizing some gifts over others. We may find ourselves jealous of someone's gifts or resistant to receiving something of God through another person. But if we recognize God's authority at work, we'll see submitting ourselves to the gift as submitting to our loving God. It's never about the vessel. It's about God.

We're rich when we realize the gifts and talents of others become ours as we receive them as from the Lord. We can give what we're strong in to others and gratefully receive the strengths of others in the areas where we lack.

Father, thank You that You've given me gifts and talents. Thank You that You've given others those things, too. I repent of jealousy and thank You that as I submit to Your authority in others' gifts, I obtain the blessings that come with receiving what You've given them.

MARK DUPRÉ

DECEMBER 2

A PROPER THANK YOU

"What shall I render to the Lord for all His benefits toward me? I will take up the cup of salvation, and call upon the name of the Lord." (Psalm 116:12-13)

This passage begins with a simple question: What can I give to God for all He's done for me? What answers come to mind? I can work harder for Him. Witness to more people. Do this or that work of service. Focus more on my sanctification, allowing Him to dig deeper into my soul and my habits. "Clean up my act" more. Stop doing this and start doing that.

But what this psalm presents as the appropriate response isn't doing anything for anyone or giving anything back. The action the psalmist takes is *receiving*: "taking up the cup of salvation." The most common reference to a cup in the Old Testament was the cup of God's wrath. The contrast between that common expression and this one would not have been lost on the original audience. This isn't God's wrath we're drinking of, but His salvation.

We know, of course, that we "receive" salvation; we can't earn it. But we need to keep receiving after first believing. Receiving is the correct and appropriate response of a grateful heart.

Salvation is more than just a one-time, "fire insurance" moment in the life of a Christian. It's broad enough to include every good gift that comes with being transferred to the kingdom of God. The word "receive" is also used for correction, that sometimes-painful process of letting God redirect us and replace our old ways of acting and thinking with His new and vastly improved ones. We also "receive" wisdom, of which we are all in constant need.

What can we do for God to show our gratitude? Keep receiving from Him.

Father, I'm so grateful to You for all You've done for me. Help me show my gratitude by staying open to all You have for me. May I keep on receiving all You are offering to me.

DECEMBER 3

QUESTIONS WITH STRANGE ANSWERS: EXODUS 4

"Then Moses answered and said, "But suppose they will not believe me or listen to my voice; suppose they say, 'The Lord has not appeared to you.'" So the Lord said to him, "What is that in your hand?" He said, "A rod." And He said, "Cast it on the ground." So he cast it on the ground, and it became a serpent; and Moses fled from it." (Exodus 4:1-3)

Moses' insecurity and how God changed Him has been an inspiration to millions. Moses was stubborn, resistant, fearful, and full of challenging questions—just like us. When He told Moses to go speak with Pharaoh, God promised him his nation would listen to him and that He'd do wondrous things against Egypt and for them (Exodus 3:20–21). But Moses was looking for more assurance.

The Lord responded to Moses' concerns by asking him what was in his hand, thereby calling attention to it. Then He told Moses to cast that rod on the ground. It became a serpent, scaring Moses (and perhaps many around him). Next, the Lord told Moses to pick up that slithering serpent, a seemingly dangerous proposition.

But he obeyed, and the snake became a rod again.

Though the Lord never expressed it directly, He was giving Moses two answers. One was directional: "Obey Me and don't be concerned about anything else. If you obey Me, anything is possible, and coming to me for direction is always the answer to questions that begin with 'What about ...' or 'Suppose that ...'."

The second was that God Himself was concerned with making His identity known. He was going to make sure that more people than Moses knew who was behind him, supplying the miracle power and the plan. The bottom line for Moses: "I will provide everything needed, and I will make sure people get the message they need to get."

> Lord, help me to pay more attention to what You've already spoken to me. I confess that I often quickly forget and go right to my fears. Help me remember that when You're behind something, all I need to do is listen and obey.

MARK DUPRÉ

DECEMBER 4

HE WHO HAS EARS TO HEAR, LET HIM USE THEM

"He who answers a matter before he hears it, it is folly and shame to him." (Proverbs 18:13)

Scripture speaks in many places about loving and receiving others. One of the best ways we can do both is by listening—really listening. For some of us, listening is little more than not talking while someone else is, biding our time until it's our turn to speak. The Scripture above calls this foolishness—a moral failing—as well as shameful.

Of course it's rude to speak before we really hear what's being said; it's disrespectful and unloving. But it's also counterproductive. We may think we already know the best response to what's being said and are just waiting as patiently as we can to deliver our thoughts. But we truly don't know what to answer until we've heard everything the other person has to say. Until they're done, we don't have all the information we need to give an intelligent response.

Really listening to what a person is saying goes beyond just not speaking over them. It involves putting our thoughts aside for the moment and "leaning in" to take in words, body language, and intonation. That's receiving and respecting someone. It's also the only real way of understanding what's being said, a prerequisite to a good response.

Listening has become something of a lost art in our culture, which overvalues self-expression. As believers, we're called to love. That includes opening our hearts and receiving others, preferring them to ourselves. In our listening, let's be examples of the kind of love that in lowliness of mind esteems others better than ourselves (Philippians 2:3).

Father, help me really listen to others, giving them the time and attention love demands. Forgive me for the times I've run roughshod over what others were trying to say to me. Transform my communications that I may put my desire for expression aside to instead honor and prefer the one I'm speaking with.

DECEMBER 5
SEEING WONDROUS THINGS

"Open my eyes, that I may see wondrous things from Your law. Make me understand the way of Your precepts; so shall I meditate on Your wonderful works." (Psalm 119:18, 27)

God is many things to us and wants to be even more. God wants to bring us salvation, sanctification, and deliverance—and more. But God also wants to dazzle us.

In the middle of Psalm 119—the longest in the Psalter—stand some verses that break out of the focus on respecting and obeying His commandments. Verse 18 speaks of seeing "wondrous things" from God's law. Not logical things, not even understandable things, but wondrous things.

Apparently, those wondrous things are already there, waiting to be discovered. Yes, the writer wants to obey the Lord, give Him glory, and know more of God's statutes and precepts. But he also wants to be lost in things about our God that astonish and amaze, things that transcend mere understanding.

The New Testament takes these sentiments into hyperdrive. In Ephesians 3:14-19, Paul prays the Ephesians—and by extension, all believers— might comprehend the incomprehensible: the full extent of God's love in Christ and all that love has accomplished. Paul didn't pray for increased understanding of the head or even of the heart. The "end goal" was that they might be filled with all the fullness of God.

No amount of meditation or study could accomplish this. Here Scripture points us to the ineffable, encouraging us to find treasures we haven't discovered before and to be stretched to the breaking point and beyond by His love.

Can you still be dazzled? Will you allow yourself? Can you receive these Scriptures as your own?

Father, I want You to have complete freedom in me. I don't want to be limited in my relationship to You by my understanding or even by what my heart can contain. You are astounding. Astound me by Your Word and Your presence.

MARK DUPRÉ

DECEMBER 6

TO JUDGE OR NOT TO JUDGE: UNRIGHTEOUS JUDGING

"Do not speak evil of one another, brethren. He who speaks evil of a brother and judges his brother, speaks evil of the law and judges the law. But if you judge the law, you are not a doer of the law but a judge. There is one Lawgiver, who is able to save and to destroy. Who are you to judge another?" (James 4:11-12)

Oh, what our society has done with the word *judge* and the very concept of "judging." Sometimes the only Scripture some seem to know is the beginning of Matthew 7. This is taken to mean that any expression of disapproval is wrong, and God wouldn't want that (hence the quoting of the Bible, sans any understanding of where the verse might be or what the context might include).

James 4 shows us it's the attitude of negativity and criticism that's condemned. Two chapters earlier, James speaks of the position of the heart that breaks the law of loving one another (2:8). "Speaking evil of one another" is what's objected to, not the making of a valid judgment call. James was dealing with divisions among the saints in this chapter, and the admonition against judging has to be seen in this context.

We'll address righteous judgment in tomorrow's devotional. But let's obey the proper rules for biblical interpretation and make sure we see Scripture in its proper context. There's a kind of judging that is sin: having a judgmental spirit, looking out for weaknesses, looking down on our brothers and sisters, and laying a judgment upon them that traps them under our pride and lack of love. Thankfully, that kind of sinfulness can be broken by repentance and adherence to what James says in 4:10: "Humble yourselves in the sight of the Lord, and He will lift you up."

> Father, help me see when I am operating out of this kind of judgmental spirit. I don't want to bring division or contention to Your body. Forgive me for times I've done that. I turn to You and ask for forgiveness and grace to be humble and loving.

DECEMBER 7

TO JUDGE OR NOT TO JUDGE: RIGHTEOUS JUDGING

"Dare any of you, having a matter against another, go to law before the unrighteous, and not before the saints? Do you not know that the saints will judge the world? And if the world will be judged by you, are you unworthy to judge the smallest matters? Do you not know that we shall judge angels?" (1 Corinthians 6:1–3)

We're never called to judge with condemnation in our hearts; we leave that kind of judging to God, who alone is able to judge the heart of another. We're not to be unkind, negative, or critical toward our Christian brothers; that is sin.

But Matthew 7:1-5 (about the plank in our eye and the speck in our brother's) indicates that we're to be involved in making judgment calls with some of our brothers and sisters. The main idea is not to stop making evaluations of another's sin, but to realize our own sinfulness and get some perspective via repentance and humility. Then we're able to help remove the speck from another's eye.

First Corinthians 6:1-3 (and 5:12-13) goes even further in describing situations where we're actually called to judge. In situations where a brother or sister is opposed to another in the church, proper judgment of the situation is assigned to the church. To do that righteously involves making judgment calls. Nothing here implies a negative or critical attitude, but rather a clear-headed approach that honors God, His Word, and the people involved.

Since the Lord is the ultimate judge, we might ask why He would entrust us with matters of judgment here on earth. One is clearly the stewarding of His authority in the context of properly pastoring (and protecting) local churches. The other is more cosmic: we're going to be judging angels. If that's the case, it's good to get proper and godly practice on this side of the grave.

Father, help me make proper value judgments and judgment calls in situations where I have the authority and Your call to do so. May I have Your heart and the mind of Christ when I do this. Please take out anything in me that would compromise that process and help me to be led by Your love and Your Spirit.

MARK DUPRÉ

DECEMBER 8
IF THE LORD WILLS

"Come now, you who say, "Today or tomorrow we will go to such and such a city, spend a year there, buy and sell, and make a profit"; whereas you do not know what will happen tomorrow. For what is your life? It is even a vapor that appears for a little time and then vanishes away. Instead you ought to say, "If the Lord wills, we shall live and do this or that." But now you boast in your arrogance. All such boasting is evil." (James 4:13–16)

A century ago, it wasn't uncommon to see the letters "DV" at the end of correspondence written in English. The two letters meant *Deo Volente*, Latin for "God willing." While not directly quoting James 4, it was a clear reference to its main idea. Letters with "DV" at the end often contained plans or hopes that were to be ultimately considered in the light of God and His plans.

There are several heart issues attached to this perspective. One is trust in the Lord. If we trust in Him and His goodness, believing He works everything together for good for us, then it's easier to submit our plans to Him. If we tend to be control freaks—both fearful and controlling—then it's hard to let go, as we've placed our trust in the plan itself and/or our own ability to make things happen. When DV is in our hearts, we can trust in Him when our plans change. If it's not, then we lock down on our plans under pressure, and God help those that get in the way.

Another issue is simple humility. We can't assume that just because we've planned something that it's the best-case scenario for us. God may well have something better or be protecting us from things unseen.

Let's remember to hold our plans loosely. Our thoughts and plans can be developed, but then they must be held onto lightly, with us neither carelessly dropping them nor grasping them tightly. All our plans must be an offering.

Father, help me to have the right heart attitude toward my plans. Help me grow in trust so I can hold plans loosely and my heart can rest fully on You, not on what I plan or foresee. Thank You that You always know best.

DECEMBER 9

HE HEARS AND ANSWERS: HE REALLY HEARS

"For there is not a word on my tongue, but behold, O Lord, You know it altogether." (Psalm 139:4); "Now this is the confidence that we have in Him, that if we ask anything according to His will, He hears us. And if we know that He hears us, whatever we ask, we know that we have the petitions that we have asked of Him." (1 John 5:14-15)

Let's look at one aspect of prayer we sometimes struggle with: God hears us right away. We don't have to shout to be heard or say the prayer ten times for it to make it up to heaven. While we're encouraged to never stop praying, God says He hears us right away. We need to settle it in our hearts that God's heard us and He's on it—He is answering. This truth can change how we view our communication with God.

We face two challenges in this area. The first is whether we're praying in His will. Romans 8:26 assures us the Holy Spirit is with us, leading us in our prayers and making intercession for us. The more we read His Word, grow in grace and truth, and live in His light, the more we'll come to understand His will and become more assured that we know how to "ask anything" according to it.

The other challenge is to let God answer the way He thinks best. We sometimes base our faith in God's hearing us on how circumstances and people around us change and get closer to the vision of what we believe God's answer might be. We can't rest our faith on those kinds of shifting sands. Either we believe He's heard us because He says He does, or we don't. Though every other expectation of our heart may have to change, and our ideas be brought to the cross as an offering, we believe He hears us because He's told us so.

Father, help me put faith before my understanding in the area of prayer. I believe You hear me when I pray. I bring my expectations of how You're going to answer to the cross, leave them, and turn around and walk away.

MARK DUPRÉ

DECEMBER 10
HE HEARS AND ANSWERS: KEEP PRAYING

"Pray without ceasing." (1 Thessalonians 5:17); "Then He spoke a parable to them, that men always ought to pray and not lose heart." (Luke 18:1)

Prayer, especially continued prayer, changes us. Prayer over time can produce every kind of fruit. We can grow in patience, die to ourselves, become less selfish, and gain a greater spiritual perspective. For example, as we pray over time we get a greater understanding of His will so we can pray according to it. How many times have we waited a long time for an answer to prayer, only to see it come about in a way we could've never imagined?

God also works through time. If Romans 8:28 tells us God works everything together for good, we need to recognize that "everything" is quite a lot. It will likely include many things of which we're not aware. Our prayer may be joined with the prayers of many others to do something so big, so wonderful, that we couldn't pray for the whole thing because we couldn't imagine it.

In that light, we must keep praying. Our prayers may well be part of something that will take God decades or more to bring about. Perhaps God wants to do something so much bigger than just answer our one prayer. Later—in this life or the next—we'll understand.

In the meantime, let's believe He hears us right away and that He also encourages us to continue praying. We really have no idea what the big picture is that God is working on, but we can rest assured that our prayers have great impact and eternal value and will help bring about His will.

Father, I want to help bring about Your will in this earth through my prayers. Help me when I falter with discouragement. Remind my soul that as I continue in faithful prayer, I'm walking in Your will.

DECEMBER 11

WHO'S YOUR (REAL) PASTOR?: A MATTER OF THE HEART

"Obey those who rule over you, and be submissive, for they watch out for your souls, as those who must give account. Let them do so with joy and not with grief, for that would be unprofitable for you." (Hebrews 13:17)

Rightly relating to our spiritual authorities is a matter of the heart. We may belong to a certain church with a certain pastor or group of elders, but being submissive to them as spiritual authorities isn't a given. It's up to us to make sure that happens.

Some of us simply don't like the concept of someone being "over us." If we really understood spiritual authority, we'd realize pastors are accountable directly to God (not always an enviable position). A good pastor is a servant-leader, not someone who "lords over those entrusted to [him]" (1 Peter 5:3).

There are different kinds of relating to the pastor. Some will be relationally close, some directly mentored. For others, the only contact they have may be hearing the pastor preach or seeing the pastor at a distance. There's also a great deal of teaching from good writers and preachers available to everyone. But no matter how much we may receive from other leaders or teachers, we still have to rightly relate to the pastor God's given us.

If God's called you to a place, submit in your heart to that pastor and leadership team. Recognize their spiritual authority as a covering and protection over you. Believe God will use them to help you grow as you listen in faith. Continue reading and learning from videos and podcasts to your heart's content. Just place yourself under your pastors' and leaders' authority and care.

If you can't, perhaps you're too stubborn, too independent and rebellious, or in the wrong church.

Lord, I recognize that You've established churches and ordained leadership in those churches. Help me to have a proper, prayerful attitude toward the pastor and leadership team in my church. No matter what contact I may have, or how much other ministry I receive from others, help me to be rightly related in my heart to the ones You've put over my church.

MARK DUPRÉ

DECEMBER 12

Who's Your (Real) Pastor?: Rightly Relating

"And we urge you, brethren, to recognize those who labor among you, and are over you in the Lord and admonish you, and to esteem them very highly in love for their work's sake." (1 Thessalonians 5:12-13)

If you attend a church, you have a pastor. Submit your heart to that pastor, pray for him or her and the leadership team, and believe God will speak through them to build you up.

You don't have to put that pastor on a pedestal and limit your input to that pastor alone. In fact, you may regularly take advantage of all the good teaching available from the many esteemed writers and speakers we have in the body of Christ.

But as encouraging as these writers and speakers may be, they aren't your pastor. So, don't put their teaching in the place of the real-life person the Lord has put in your life. Learn from them, but don't submit your heart to them.

Another pretender to the position of pastor is the influencer. Influencers are people with obvious leadership qualities who have the ability to draw people to themselves and away from the church. If someone listens to them more than their church leadership, that influencer is their de facto pastor. Don't be that influencer—start submitting your leadership gifts to your church leadership! And don't be that follower.

The bottom line is: Whoever you really listen to—that's your pastor. We can relate to lots of different kinds of friends. We can learn a great deal from books, videos, and podcasts. But there's room for only one pastor in your heart. Give that place to the pastor or leadership team in your church.

Father, help me to position myself rightly to my pastor. Help me not to place too much on my pastor's shoulders, but to receive everything that You want me to through the leadership of my church. If I'm putting the wrong person in my pastor's place in reality, please show me.

DECEMBER 13

Questions with Strange Answers: John 5

"Now a certain man was there who had an infirmity thirty-eight years. When Jesus saw him lying there, and knew that he already had been in that condition a long time, He said to him, "Do you want to be made well?" The sick man answered Him, "Sir, I have no man to put me into the pool when the water is stirred up; but while I am coming, another steps down before me." (John 5:5-7)

This story is a heart breaker. On the surface, of course, it's the wrong answer to a simple yes-or-no question. Instead of answering Jesus directly, the man *reacts* first and then *responds*. Apparently, he was so deep in despair that instead of an obvious yes, his feelings of disappointment led him to describe what hadn't happened and his understanding of why it hadn't. He *experienced* the question rather than hearing it.

This is a great lesson about the power our speech has to draw forth unexpected responses. We often have no idea how even words filled with love and good intentions can prick a heart or stir up a painful memory. Sometimes we're just looking for an answer to a question, but the person we're asking is experiencing something different—something so individual or personal that both the speaker and hearer are taken aback by the response.

Jesus' goal in asking this question was to heal the man (John 5:8-9). Perhaps it was also to stir up the man's faith or express God's love. But what we can learn at first glance is the power words have to effect a deep response in others.

Jesus responded to this man's answer with healing—love in action. What do we do when someone responds (or reacts) passionately, painfully, or even inappropriately? Can we proceed in love without being derailed by the response? It takes wisdom to know how best to reply when we encounter an unintended response like this. God's promised to provide that wisdom when we ask (James 1:5).

Father, help me understand that my words or intentions may occasionally stir up surprising, unexpected feelings or responses in others. Help me to do Your will in my response. Help me to hear Your voice and sense Your Spirit guiding me in those moments.

MARK DUPRÉ

DECEMBER 14
FORGIVING GOD?

"When a man's folly brings his way to ruin, his heart rages against the Lord." (Proverbs 19:3 ESV)

A popular thought in some Christian circles is the concept of "forgiving God." Its goal is to free believers from attitudes they hold against the Lord for difficult struggles they've experienced. The aim is to release feelings of resentment and anger and come to a place of peace.

There's only one thing wrong: while it sounds vaguely spiritual, it's based on a falsehood. It can never accomplish the goal of true internal peace for one simple reason: our God doesn't do wrong things; He has no need for forgiveness.

Of course there are painful and confusing times in our lives. Many of us have been treated outrageously, lied about, abused, and attacked. What we may feel is a "need" to forgive God is really a need to do the hard work of forgiving those who've been hard to forgive.

The hard reality is that sometimes our own bad decisions may have led to our current state of affairs (see Proverbs 19:3). Yet even if we've been blameless in the painful situation, God doesn't need to be forgiven. We may be so offended intellectually by what's happened that our inability to understand our situation leads us to arrogantly accuse God. This places us over Him rather than being submitted to Him.

"Forgiving God" is a kind of fool's gold, looking like a breakthrough emotional event (one that tempts our pride by seeming spiritually mature), but actually a worthless counterfeit. There isn't just one road to go down when faced with anger and pain, but this one should say "Road Closed."

Father, help me avoid this trap in my life. It may be easy for me to grasp onto, but I see that it's an appeal to my pride and my flesh. When hard times come, help me continue to turn to You for grace.

DECEMBER 15

GOD OUR FATHER

"He shall cry to Me, "You are my Father, My God, and the rock of my salvation." (Psalm 89:26); "In this manner, therefore, pray: Our Father in heaven, hallowed be Your name." (Matthew 6:9)

The term *Father* in reference to the Lord is found throughout the Old Testament, but it isn't as common as we might think. With the Incarnation, however, came a virtual explosion of the term. In the first three Gospels, Jesus used the term 65 times. In John, Jesus referred to God as Father more than 100 times. The rest of the New Testament continues the term, with Paul using it more than 40 times in his letters to the church.

But today this term is under attack. It's true that God is a Spirit, neither male nor female. This might be one reason why someone might want to back away from the term, particularly in light of the current attack on the very concept of patriarchy. Then there are those who've struggled with the concept of a good God equating Himself, at least in name, with a human father who is less than a good representative of the Father heart of God.

The final word in the discussion, however, is that Jesus told his disciples—and by extension, us—to call God our Father. That should settle it. For someone with father issues, Jesus points the way toward healing by calling God Almighty Father. For those who haven't wanted anyone telling them what to do, calling God Father is a positive step in acknowledging His authority over them. For most Christians, however, it's a sign of love and intimacy that resonates deeply.

Yes, God transcends all human definitions as a spiritual being. But He's told us to call Him Father. Let's obey, submit, and yes, rejoice to call Him Father.

Lord, thank You for telling us to call You Father. I pray for those who find it difficult, that You would bring healing or whatever they need to be able to do that with a free heart. Help me discover the blessings that come with the Abba relationship.

MARK DUPRÉ

DECEMBER 16

THE M/OTHER SIDE OF GOD

"For thus says the Lord: "Behold, I will extend peace to her like a river ... Then you shall feed; on her sides shall you be carried, and be dandled on her knees. As one whom his mother comforts, so I will comfort you." (Isaiah 66:12-13)

While the Lord's clearly told us to call Him Father (see yesterday's devotional), He's also exhibited characteristics we usually associate with mothers. Scripture, including Isaiah, doesn't shy away from telling us how tender our Father's heart is toward us by using classic maternal images such as bouncing a child on her knee.

No, God isn't male or female. But as disciples, we must be open to receiving everything God tells us about Himself, including the human examples He provides as springboards for understanding Him more. For example, moms tend to be more merciful than fathers. God is merciful. We're told in Hebrews 4:16 to come boldly to the throne of grace to find mercy. Generally, moms comfort far better than fathers do. God calls Himself a comforter. John 15:26 even calls the Holy Spirit the Comforter (KJV), and 2 Corinthians 1:3 calls God "the Father of mercies and God of all comfort." That's quite a definition of tenderness and consolation.

Moms are also generally on our side, with fathers often taking a counter position to teach us things. If you're a believer, God's on your side. Romans 8:31 definitively states, "If God is for us, who can be against us?" That's a position closer to what we might experience with mothers rather than fathers.

The bottom line? God's bigger than whoever we think He is right now. Let's let His Word stretch our understanding of who He is by including the maternal aspects He tells us He has.

Father, I accept everything You say about Yourself, including your mercy, Your desire to comfort, and Your kindhearted tenderness to us. Open my eyes to see these things about You, and thank You for telling us more about Yourself in Your Word.

DECEMBER 17

TWO IMPORTANT FAMILIES

"And it happened, as He spoke these things, that a certain woman from the crowd raised her voice and said to Him, "Blessed is the womb that bore You, and the breasts which nursed You!" But He said, "More than that, blessed are those who hear the word of God and keep it!" (Luke 11:27-28)

In this passage, Jesus demonstrated the perfect balance of love for natural family and love for our spiritual brothers and sisters. This Jesus, who at twelve knew He was to be about his Father's business and went home to be subject to His parents (Luke 2:51), also made sure—while on the cross!—to guarantee protection for his mother by pointing her to John and John to her. He was a good, obedient son.

As important as His natural family was to Him, Jesus knew there was something more. He called His disciples His mother and His brothers! Then He extended that family relationship to anyone who does the will of God (Matthew 12:46-50).

It can be easy to get sentimental about the Lord. After all, He is love. We may be tempted to bring the sweetness of children and families into our understanding of what Jesus was like with His family—especially with Mary. That seems to have been the case with the "woman from the crowd" in the passage above. Jesus wasn't rude to her. He was simply elevating her thinking. He called her to a higher understanding of what was blessed and important in His eyes.

God bless those of us who have loving, supportive natural families. Families are obviously important to God. But there's a family dearer to our Lord than His own natural family—the family of God. Let's follow His example of honoring our own family yet finding that place in our heart to treasure our spiritual family even more.

Father, help me to love Your called ones, Your bride, Your body, even more than my own natural family. May I never fall short in loving my own family, and may I also see with Your eyes the loveliness of the spiritual brothers and sisters You've given me. Help me to never be slack in loving and appreciating them.

MARK DUPRÉ

DECEMBER 18

QUESTIONS WITH STRANGE ANSWERS: MARK 12

"Then one of the scribes came, and ... asked Him, "Which is the first commandment of all?" Jesus answered him, "The first of all the commandments is: 'Hear, O Israel, the Lord our God, the Lord is one. And you shall love the Lord your God with all your heart, with all your soul, with all your mind, and with all your strength.' This is the first commandment. And the second, like it, is this: 'You shall love your neighbor as yourself.' There is no other commandment greater than these." (Mark 12:28-31)

The Sadducees had just asked Jesus what they hoped would be a "gotcha" question, one that would trip Him up and show the absurdity of the idea of resurrection. But Jesus put them in their place: "Is this not the reason you are wrong, because you know neither the Scriptures nor the power of God?" (Mark 12:24 ESV). These are strong words of rebuke. We should take them as our own challenge to make sure we submit ourselves to the continuous study and proper understanding of his Word.

Then a scribe asked a timeless question: "Which is the greatest commandment of all?" How surprised he must have been when Jesus answered with two commandments, not one. Jesus first pointed to loving the Lord with everything we have. But Jesus then immediately lists the second—loving your neighbor as yourself—calling it "like" the first. Clearly Jesus considers the two inextricably linked.

What God has joined together here, the enemy loves to put asunder. How many times have you heard, "I love God; it's His people I can't stand" or a version of the same? You can't really do the first unless you're also loving His people.

We can make a division in our minds, but we must, must ask ourselves: If Jesus doesn't make this division, how can I? If the one great commandment is a two-parter, then our real love for God is manifested in how much we love Him and how much we love our neighbors as ourselves.

Father, my mind sometimes divides these two commandments that Jesus called one. Help me see all the connections here that I've been missing. I bow to what You say is one and ask for eyes to see.

DECEMBER 19
SALVATION AND BROTHERLY LOVE

"We know that we have passed from death to life, because we love the brethren. He who does not love his brother abides in death." (1 John 3:14)

What wondrous revelations and observations we find in 1 John. In this verse, we get another "proof of salvation" that helps us know we've found life in God. St. Augustine says it clearly: "Let each go to his own heart; if he find there love to the brethren, let him feel assured that he has passed from death unto life."

First John 4:20-21 presents the flip side of that issue. We can't say we love God while hating our brother. Some of us harbor feelings of animosity and unforgiveness for some we'll spend eternity with. Yet God calls those "honest" enough to say they hate their Christian brothers and sisters—liars.

What's the lie? Not that we don't love others. It's that we aren't honest about the other half of the equation: we really don't love God as much as we think.

John hits this logically: How can anyone love God, whom he's not seen, and not love his brother, whom he has? Since we don't see God, it's easy to keep falling into the trap of trying to re-create the Creator, making Him after our own image. If we live in a state where we're not convicted of our sin of hating our brother or sister, then we've re-created the God of the universe into a god who doesn't think that loving God and loving others are inseparable commandments.

So, if you believe you love God but you hate your Christian brother or sister, hear well God's Word: "He who loves God must love his brother also."

> *Lord, show me by Your Spirit where I harbor any level of hatred toward my Christian brothers and sisters. I may have reasons for having been hurt, but Your commandment tells me to love them if I love you.*

MARK DUPRÉ

DECEMBER 20

WORK OUT YOUR OWN SALVATION

"Therefore, my beloved, as you have always obeyed, not as in my presence only, but now much more in my absence, work out your own salvation with fear and trembling; for it is God who works in you both to will and to do for His good pleasure." (Philippians 2:12-13)

A misunderstanding of this Scripture has brought a great deal of confusion to believers over the years. If read out of context, it can seem to imply that being saved isn't simply a gift from God. It rests on our shoulders, at least in part, to "work out" our salvation ourselves. However, in light of all the Scriptures that tell us salvation is a free gift of God, it can't be true that there's anything we can add to that free gift.

In Scripture, salvation can refer to the one-time-only act God works in us, saving us from His wrath and bringing us into His kingdom. It can also refer to the ongoing process of growing in grace, which we call sanctification. And it can refer to the time we enter the next life, when the fullness of salvation comes our way. Here, it's kind of a combination of the first two. We've been saved (once for all), but that salvation doesn't sit still.

We're to take what has been "worked in" to us (saving grace, His power, etc.) and make it manifest by turning it into action. We're gloriously saved, delivered from sin, and set for heaven. But in the meantime, we've been prepared for good works. That involves expressing that salvation by works of obedience (as Jesus did). The great news is that we not only have Jesus' example but also God is working in us to want to do His will, and He works alongside us to give us encouragement, grace, and empowering by His Spirit.

Lord, thank You for the free gift of salvation. Show me the path of obedience so I can demonstrate what You've done for me and in me by what You direct me to do. Thank You for willing and working in me for Your good pleasure.

DECEMBER 21
JUST THE WAY HE WANTED

"My frame was not hidden from You, when I was made in secret, and skillfully wrought in the lowest parts of the earth. Your eyes saw my substance, being yet unformed. And in Your book they all were written, the days fashioned for me, when as yet there were none of them." (Psalm 139:15-16)

One of our most important questions as a person and as a believer is our identity. As Christians, we must finally come to the conclusion that it is not we ourselves but God who gets to tell us who we are. The enemy may call us names, and we may even join in the name-calling at times. But as we continue in His Word and in relationship with God, we eventually must yield the final question of identity to Him. He gets to tell us who we are—forgiven, saints, loved, made worthy, strong in Christ. No matter how we may feel at times, we are who He says we are.

One of the devil's most pressing tactics is having people—made originally in God's image— fight against even the natural identity God's given them. You were born in this age—not in Jesus' time, in the Middle Ages, or even in the 1800s. You were born in a certain place, not somewhere else. You are of a certain ethnicity. That is God's plan. And you are a certain gender. That too is His plan.

Most of us have no real trouble accepting all of this. Certainly compassion for those struggling with it is called for. Yet ultimately, it's not God's will that anyone would finally turn against the natural identity He's given them.

Male, female, black, white, Asian, born yesterday or 100 years ago—we're all fearfully and wonderfully made. God calls us all to honor His wisdom and handiwork.

Father, may I be an example of someone who has completely accepted how You've created me. You have purpose in all of it, and I embrace Your whole plan for me. Use every part of me to advance Your kingdom, including how I am formed.

MARK DUPRÉ

DECEMBER 22

BROKEN AND CONTRITE

"The Lord is near to those who have a broken heart, and saves such as have a contrite spirit." (Psalm 34:18); "The sacrifices of God are a broken spirit, a broken and a contrite heart— these, O God, You will not despise." (Psalm 51:17)

The Lord is compassionate and understanding beyond our imagination. Psalm 138:6 says, "Though the Lord is on high, yet He regards the lowly." We can only look in awe at His heart toward those who've been beaten down by life and circumstances.

Yet the Scriptures above make a small distinction between the broken and the contrite. It's possible to be broken and not be contrite. According to Psalm 34, God is near to the brokenhearted, but He saves those who have a contrite heart. The great psalm of repentance—51—calls for a broken heart combined with a contrite spirit to be acceptable to God. While brokenness is noticed by the Lord, it becomes a sacrifice when it's combined with contrition.

In referring to Himself as the cornerstone in Matthew 21:42, Jesus quotes the prophetic Scripture, Psalm 118:22, then adds: "Whoever falls on this stone will be broken; but on whomever it falls, it will grind him to powder" (Matthew 21:44). We're to fall onto the Lord in humility and repentance, or He'll eventually fall upon us in judgment.

Being broken is not the same as being humble. It certainly isn't the same as being contrite. To gain His redemptive touch on our lives, brokenness must be combined with humility and a contrite heart. Brokenness can often be a precursor to humility and contrition, but only a soft and teachable heart combines with brokenness to produce conditions for receiving His grace.

Lord, please help me to be humble and contrite when I'm broken. Use me in leading the broken and stubborn to humility and contrition.

DECEMBER 23
AFTER WE STOP ASKING WHY

"I will say to God my Rock, "Why have You forgotten me? Why do I go mourning because of the oppression of the enemy?" (Psalm 42:9); "Joseph said to [his brothers], "... as for you, you meant evil against me; but God meant it for good, in order to bring it about as it is this day, to save many people alive." (Genesis 50:19-20)

"Why?" is possibly the most popular question we ask God. It's also the most frustrating because there's rarely an answer.

Joseph had clearly worked out that question by the time he came face-to-face with his brothers, years after they'd sold him into slavery. There's no way he could have understood what was going on at the time—that his brothers' sinful actions, coupled with unjust imprisonment (for doing the right thing!), would lead to saving his family and untold millions of his countrymen. Somehow the urge to cry "Why?" had played itself out in Joseph. And yet, God did show him the why. For us, we need to be honest about crying out to God. But then we must let the need for the why play itself out in us too. God desires to make sense of things to us, but in His time and His way and for His glory. Pounding on His chest only hurts us, not Him.

The better question to ask when the fires of asking "Why?" begin to die down is simple: "What do you want me to do now, Lord?" That question is always appropriate and is the way out of the tail-chasing pursuit of why. Asking what to do and then doing it keeps us moving along the path of faith. It's also the way to eventually understanding the why. By the time we get "there," though, our drive to know why may well be dissolved in our faith in a trustworthy God.

Lord, help me get past the drive to know why the next time I find myself in a circumstance I don't understand. Deliver me quickly to just wanting to know and do Your will for me. Use me in helping others get to this point too.

MARK DUPRÉ

DECEMBER 24

BORN TO DIE

"He is despised and rejected by men, a Man of sorrows and acquainted with grief. And we hid, as it were, our faces from Him; He was despised, and we did not esteem Him. Surely He has borne our griefs and carried our sorrows; yet we esteemed Him stricken, smitten by God, and afflicted. But He was wounded for our transgressions, He was bruised for our iniquities; the chastisement for our peace was upon Him, and by His stripes we are healed." (Isaiah 53:3-5)

The passages above are usually reserved for the week before Easter. It's not generally thought of around our celebration of the birth of Jesus. It should be. This is why He came in the first place. He was born to die.

Even the most "Christmasy" of Scriptures around Jesus' birth have this dark shadow around them. In Matthew 1:21, for example, an angel spoke to Joseph in a dream: "And she will bring forth a Son, and you shall call His name, for He will save His people from their sins." The history of Israel made it clear that there was no salvation from sin and its judgments apart from the shedding of blood. This child was born to be *the* sacrifice for sins, the one that so many prophecies, and the entire sacrificial system, had been pointing to all these years.

Three times in Mark (chapters 8, 9, and 10), Jesus tried to get His disciples to understand that He'd be rejected by the religious leaders, suffer many things, and be killed. Yet it still came as a shock to most of them. In thinking about His birth, we need to rejoice over not only *that* He came but *why* He came. He came to die. For us. To meet our greatest need—forgiveness. Because He loved us.

The usual images of Christmas are the animals, shepherds, and angelic announcements. As we look in the background of these idyllic scenes, however, those with spiritual eyes will see something else—the cross.

Father, help me to rejoice fully in the birth of Jesus. As I enjoy family, friends, and fellowship, let me find my deepest joy in the knowledge that Your love and Your desire to knock down the barrier of sin in us was the reason You sent Your Son. Thank You for His coming and for His whole life, death, and resurrection.

DECEMBER 25

LOVE IS BORN

"And the Word became flesh and dwelt among us, and we beheld His glory, the glory as of the only begotten of the Father, full of grace and truth." (John 1:14)

The phrase "Love is born tonight" is the name of a song and included in many other songs about the birth of our Lord. It's a tender thought. Depending on how you look at it, it's either sentimental and unreal or profound and breathtaking.

To read it as love being born, as in *created*, is, of course, an error. As lovely as the image of a newborn surrounded by cute animals, otherworldly lighting, and heavenly choirs might be, love had been around a long time before Jesus' birth. It was found all throughout the Old Testament—in the creation, God's covering of Adam and Eve's sin, the promise of a Messiah, the rescue of Israel in the Exodus, the story of Ruth, and God's continual preservation of the messianic line. Then there are the two great commandments, both of which feature love: love of our Lord and of our neighbor as ourselves.

Love isn't a concept or an idea or a feeling. It's a person: Jesus Christ. Love came to earth, put on fleshly clothing (John 1:14), lived among people for a season, and then took on the sins of us all so that we could be forgiven and have fellowship with the Father.

Love being born isn't a sweet sentiment or an ethereal spiritual mystery. God is love. He took on flesh, coming as a baby. Then He showed us what love looked like in action.

Let's treasure the thought: two millennia ago, in a despised outpost of a conquered land, in the least comfortable of circumstances, love was born. Hallelujah!

Thank You! I welcome You again in my life and heart!

MARK DUPRÉ

DECEMBER 26

HE MEANT THE WHOLE PSALM

"For the kingdom is the Lord's, and He rules over the nations. All the prosperous of the earth shall eat and worship; all those who go down to the dust shall bow before Him, even he who cannot keep himself alive. A posterity shall serve Him. It will be recounted of the Lord to the next generation, they will come and declare His righteousness to a people who will be born, that He has done this." (Psalm 22:28-31)

Some of us are quite familiar with the first verse of Psalm 22: "My God, My God, why have You forsaken Me?" These are the words Jesus spoke on the cross. When we hear them, our thoughts go right to His suffering and His agony at the removal of God's presence when He was bearing the weight of our sin.

With these words Jesus was pointing to the entire psalm. As we read through the rest of it, we see there's a great deal more and we discover how astoundingly prophetic this entire psalm is. It describes what happened with Jesus (the piercing of His hands and feet, v. 16; the casting of lots for His garments, v. 18), as well as how He felt (vv. 2 and 19).

Yes, Jesus was expressing Himself and His anguish with these first words. But He was also declaring He was the predicted Messiah. He was declaring He was the fulfillment of this prophetic psalm and many other passages. And He was declaring victory! Praise would arise from what He was doing. God would rule over the nations. Every knee would bow. Every generation would hear of it and learn that everything in this psalm was being accomplished (v. 31). What was once known as David's expression would forever become Jesus' testimony.

Lord, help me know Your Word well enough that I would know the context of the Scriptures I hear as these listeners would have. Help me, too, to never go by the first thing I hear (as with this first line of the psalm), but wait until You've spoken everything You have to say about a situation before I think I understand what You're saying or doing.

DECEMBER 27
WHOSE VOICE IS IT ANYWAY?: A FEW TIPS

"Behold, the Lord passed by, and a great and strong wind tore into the mountains and broke the rocks in pieces before the Lord, but the Lord was not in the wind; and after the wind an earthquake, but the Lord was not in the earthquake; and after the earthquake a fire, but the Lord was not in the fire; and after the fire a still small voice. So it was, when Elijah heard it, that he wrapped his face in his mantle and went out and stood in the entrance of the cave. Suddenly a voice came to him, and said, "What are you doing here, Elijah?" (1 Kings 19:11-13)

Identifying the Lord's voice is a struggle for many, as there are many voices in our heads. It will always be a kind of tension: Are those my own thoughts or is that from God? There's no quick and easy "one size fits all" approach to learning His voice. God wants us to lean into Him to learn the way we're to hear from Him, not discover a "method."

But there are a few things we can do that can position us to better hear His voice. Soaking ourselves in God's Word is a sure way to know His mind and heart. That helps us identify His voice when we hear it. We also can't expect to hear His voice clearly without putting a lot of His thoughts into our heads first. We need something against which we can measure what we think we're hearing.

Obedience is another way to open us up to hearing His voice. If we haven't been obedient to the things He's already shown us, why should He continue speaking when we're not listening with an intent to obey? If we're having problems hearing what He's saying now, we might be wise to go back to the last thing we're sure we heard and ask ourselves (and/or Him) if we've responded fully to that communication. We're to walk by faith. God has His reasons for speaking things to us in His order.

God wants us to hear His voice even more than we want to hear it. Today's suggestions—and tomorrow's—may help open our ears.

> Lord, lead me to put more of Your written Word in my head, that I may be able to receive more of what Your Spirit wants to impart. Also, please show me if there is anything undone that needs to be done, so I can "clear the way" for all the rest of the things You have for me to hear.

MARK DUPRÉ

DECEMBER 28

LETTING GO OF THE ENEMY'S THOUGHTS

"For the weapons of our warfare are not carnal but mighty in God for pulling down strongholds, casting down arguments and every high thing that exalts itself against the knowledge of God, bringing every thought into captivity to the obedience of Christ." (2 Corinthians 10:4-5)

Today's focus is on how we think about others. Take a look at your less-than-gracious thoughts about others. If there's an accusation against anyone that just sits there unchanged and unchallenged by you, it's from the enemy, "the accuser of our brethren" (Revelation 12:10). It's not your original thought, though it might feel that way in the midst of pain or anger.

If there's judgment and condemnation, it's not from God. Ask yourself, "Would Jesus speak this way to me about so-and-so?" Or "Is this how Jesus looks at him/her?" Jesus isn't naïve. He sees situations and human hearts more clearly than any of us. But He brings His grace, mercy, and love to all situations.

If there's any other kind of thought you've borrowed from the enemy about another person, you need to repent of holding onto it. Release it to the Lord, who paid for it on the cross. Remember, if it's not a thought of grace, mercy, or love, and you feel that it's your thought, it's not. You just temporarily borrowed it from the accuser. Return it. Then replace it with the kind of thoughts God has for others.

It's not our inheritance to have the enemy's thoughts in our brains. We don't have to put up with his lies and accusations. As we bring them to the light, let's begin the process of disassociation— untangling our feelings and thoughts about others to only include God's gracious thoughts.

Father, I confess I have a hard time telling which thoughts are mine and which are from the enemy. I don't want to have his thoughts in my mind. Help me discern the difference and give me wisdom on how best to take these thoughts captive.

DECEMBER 29

THE GRAND REPLACEMENT

"But with me it is a very small thing that I should be judged by you or by a human court. In fact, I do not even judge myself. For I know of nothing against myself, yet I am not justified by this; but He who judges me is the Lord. Therefore judge nothing before the time, until the Lord comes, who will both bring to light the hidden things of darkness and reveal the counsels of the hearts. Then each one's praise will come from God." (1 Corinthians 4:3-5)

Many of us struggle with self-condemnation. We think being hard on ourselves is normal and natural. It's difficult to untangle thoughts we have against someone else, but it's even more challenging to get a hold of our own "self-talk," which can be as sinful as what we might think about others. We've been tricked into believing those condemning, harsh thoughts are our own thoughts.

These thoughts don't originate from us. They belong to the accuser. Since we tend to guard what we think is ours, we hold on to this "stinkin' thinkin'" as part of our identities, and it becomes harder to pry it away from our minds.

This is a demonic victory against us. We may think we deserve such self-flagellation, but we know better. Jesus paid it all, which means there's now no condemnation (Romans 8:1). Not the slightest bit. Not even for you! God doesn't speak such things to us—conviction of sin is clean, not muddy and harsh. Jesus died to free us from such condemnation, even mental or verbal forms of it.

As disciples, we must reject the accuser's thoughts—even toward ourselves—and replace them with God's thoughts. This takes work, but we have no right to bear toward ourselves the kinds of negative, enemy-inspired thoughts we don't want to have toward others. We must face our enemy in the name of Jesus, submit ourselves to God, and resist these foreign thoughts. God's thoughts toward us are peace, giving us a future and a hope. Let's aim to do a grand replacement.

Father, forgive me for harboring negative thoughts about myself. I want to be genuinely humble, but I don't want to agree with the accuser and adopt his negative and condemning thoughts. I want Yours instead. Teach me how to replace all his thoughts with Yours.

MARK DUPRÉ

DECEMBER 30

WHERE WE REALLY LIVE

"For our citizenship is in heaven, from which we also eagerly wait for the Savior, the Lord Jesus Christ. (Philippians 3:20); "Then the King will say to those on His right hand, 'Come, you blessed of My Father, inherit the kingdom prepared for you from the foundation of the world.'" (Matthew 25:34)

We don't really live here. We're physically in this world, but our life cannot be found here. We're citizens of heaven and are not "of" (even while being "in") this world. That reality bursts with meaning for our lives here.

For one, we can't find our identity in this world. According to Colossians 3:2-4, our life is hidden with Christ in God—which directs us to heaven. What God does in us, to us, and through us will only make complete sense once we're there (though He's gracious enough to supply occasional understanding to us here). We're certainly to be used here (walking in the "good works" of Ephesians 2:10). But we're also being prepared for the place Jesus said He's prepared for us (John 14:2). Sooner than we think, we'll experience the truth of Matthew 25:34 for ourselves.

Home. What a powerful word. It resonates about as deeply as any word in a person's language. Our home isn't here. It's awaiting us in heaven. It's where we'll feel, well, at home. We'll fit. We'll make sense. We'll have a healthy family around us. We'll know more than ever that we belong. God is right now preparing you for that life.

So "reckon it to yourself" that you don't ultimately belong here. We can build a career, a family, even a reputation, and it can all be done in God. But all of it has the word *temporary* stamped all over it. We're citizens of heaven. Our identity and heart investments should be found there.

Father, I get so distracted by who I think I am and what I think my role is here on earth. Help me live in the light of heaven, being faithful to You as I live the life You've given me here. Thank You that I'm an eternal being who has a home with You in eternity.

DECEMBER 31
LOOKING TO JESUS

"Let us lay aside every weight, and the sin which so easily ensnares us, and let us run with endurance the race that is set before us, looking unto Jesus, the author and finisher of our faith." (Hebrews 12:1-2)

Christianity, salvation, walking in grace and love, bringing delight and glory to God through our obedience, living in community with other believers—these are all marvelous things. But Jesus is more marvelous. He's the reason all these other things are so wonderful. He's the source of them all, the person around which they revolve.

The one thing we must never lose focus on is Jesus. We can read the Word every waking minute but get lost in doctrine and interpretation, losing the connection with Jesus that God's Spirit is always working to make as we read. We can be a stellar, deeply involved member of our church, serving everyone around us, and yet forget that all we do is really unto Him.

We can pursue our callings, discover and strengthen our gifts, and even find a successful ministry path, but we can let our relationship slide with the One who started it all and who keeps it going by His power. We can forget the real reason we're doing what we're doing.

If the enemy can't keep us from going to hell, he'll work to make sure we're not "looking to Him." There's so much to learn, so much work to be done, so much service to render, so many treasures to find in His Word, that we can get distracted by good things, things that may keep our eyes from viewing the best thing.

We can, and we must, place and keep our eyes on Him. And may He grow ever clearer to us through the years.

Father, I want to be like those who came to Philip (John 12) and said, "Sir, we wish to see Jesus." Lord, as a disciple, I want to see Him more and more clearly, and I set myself to look to Him and press into Him in all circumstances until I see Him who is at the center of everything.

MARK DUPRÉ

MARK DUPRÉ is a pastor, former film professor, and author living in Western New York. This book represents 40+ years of Mark's preaching, teachings, and seminars. Mark is also the author of *The Christian's Guide to Adulting* and the co-screenwriter and assistant director of *I Am Rochester*, a documentary on the spiritual and social history of Rochester, NY. He's also written a musical theatrical version of *Pilgrim's Progress*. Mark has a film website (www.film-prof.com), a grammar website (www.dedicatedtogrammar.com), and a site for his Christian writings (www.markdupre.com). Mark and his wife Diane have three children and a growing number of grandchildren.

www.ingramcontent.com/pod-product-compliance
Lightning Source LLC
Chambersburg PA
CBHW071259110426
42743CB00042B/1106